Trust Practitioner's Handbook

Related titles by Law Society Publishing

Execution of Documents: A Practical Guide
1 85328 980 9
Mark Anderson and Victor Warner

Elderly Client Handbook (3rd Edition)
1 85328 872 1
General Editors: Caroline Bielanska and Martin Terrell
Consultant Editor: Gordon R. Ashton

Practice Management Handbook
1 85328 915 9
Peter Scott

Probate Practitioner's Handbook (4th Edition)
1 85328 831 4
General Editor: Lesley King

Solicitors and Money Laundering: A Compliance Handbook
1 85328 920 5
Peter Camp

Will Draftsman's Handbook (8th Edition)
1 85328 826 8
Robin Riddett

Titles from Law Society Publishing can be ordered from all good legal bookshops or direct from our distributors, Marston Book Services (tel. 01235 465656 or e-mail **law.society@marston.co.uk**). For further information or a catalogue, e-mail our editorial and marketing office at **publishing@lawsociety.org.uk**.

TRUST PRACTITIONER'S HANDBOOK

Gill Steel
with contributions by Robert Mowbray and Charles Christian

To Mum
with love always
Gin x

The Law Society

ISBN 10: 1–85328–945–0
ISBN 13: 978–1–85328–945–3

Published in 2005 by the Law Society
113 Chancery Lane, London WC2A 1PL

Typeset by J&L Composition, Filey, North Yorkshire
Printed by TJ International, Padstow, Cornwall

Contents

PART THREE
TAXATION OF TRUSTS

About the authors

Gill Steel is a solicitor and a member of the Law Society's Wills and Equity Committee. She is a member of the Society of Trust and Estate Practitioners (STEP) and on the STEP UK Probate and Estates Committee. Her other qualifications include ATT (Association of Tax Technicians) and AIMC and she has an MBA in Legal Practice Management.

Charles Christian is a former practising barrister turned independent writer and commentator who has been following developments in legal technology and online legal services since the late 1970s. He is the publisher of the industry newsletter *Legal Technology Insider* and, the regular IT columnist for the Law Society *Gazette* and an independent adviser to the Law Society on its annual *Software Solutions Guide*.

Chapter 16 was specially written for us by Charles Christian and we are most grateful to him for doing so.

Robert Mowbray is a partner in the 48 partner chartered accountancy firm of MacIntyre Hudson. Over the last 14 years he has devoted an increasing proportion of his time to the development of financial and management consultancy and training courses for solicitors. He has acted for over 300 law firms and worked with many of the largest firms in the City and across the UK as well as working abroad with some of the larger international firms. He has written a book entitled *Maximising the Profitability of Law Firms* and is an Industrial Fellow of the Business School of Kingston University. In July 2001 Robert was awarded the 'Trainer of the Year' award by the Legal Education and Training Group.

Chapter 15 was written for us by Robert Mowbray and we are most grateful to him for doing so.

Acknowledgements

I wonder when we start on the adventure which is our career whether we can ever anticipate the many wonderful and important people, places and experiences which will influence what we become. Perhaps not, but these are the people I want to acknowledge for their help and support along my road to date.

- My parents whose love and guidance were inspirational.
- Sheffield University, where I developed a taste for Revenue Law under the tutelage of Charles Machin (among others) who I believe still practices at the Manchester Bar.
- Tony Craven, David Dickson, John Lord and Derrick Forrest at Napthens (then Houghton, Craven and Dicksons) where I was the first female articled clerk and received a cracking training.
- Chris Hall, Chris Gwyn-Evans and Godfrey Knowles for some amazing opportunities in trust administration when I came to Winchester.
- All my then staff at White & Bowker but in particular my right hand person Janet Randall and an enthusiastic trust administrator, Frances Room, whose willingness to help develop practical systems was a boon.
- My first rate personal assistant Sue Hoath, without whom I am lost, the marvellous librarian Ken Woods, who can always find that reference, and Caroline Biggs who has recently joined my team.
- Janet Noble, Ben Mullane, Marie Gill and the staff at Law Society Publishing for steering me through the publishing process.
- Robert Mowbray and Charles Christian for bravely agreeing to contribute to this book.
- The authors and editors over the years of the hugely important leading texts on trusts: *Lewin on Trusts* and Underhill and Hayton *Law Relating to Trusts and Trustees* where one always turns for the answer to those technical problems.
- My colleagues on the lecturing circuit who act as my mentors, even if they don't know it – in particular Chris Whitehouse, Lesley King, Geoffrey Shindler, and Helen Clarke.
- All my clients and customers to date who have given me the opportunity to explore a fascinating subject.

- On the domestic front I would not be able to do what I do without the tireless efforts of Lilian Bruce and Jeff Lawson, so my thanks to them for keeping me going.

Special thanks goes to Alison Romeril for her help in preparing the Case Study to this book and generally in her work with me on a number of projects in recent years.

Finally, to my long suffering husband John, my thanks for your patience and endless support.

Gill Steel
August 2005

Abbreviations

A&M trust	accumulation and maintenance trust
APR	agricultural property relief
ATP	authorised third party
BPR	business property relief
CGT	capital gains tax
CTO	Captial Taxes Office
CTT	capital transfer tax
DPB	Designated Professional Body
EPA	enduring power of attorney
FSA	Financial Services Authority
FSMA 2000	Financial Services and Markets Act 2000
GROB	gift with reservation of benefit
HMRC	Her Majesty's Revenue and Customs [the department responsible for the business of the former Inland Revenue and HM Customs and Excise from April 2005]
IFPDA 1975	Inheritance (Provision for Family and Dependants) Act 1975
IHT	inheritance tax
IHTA 1984	Inheritance Tax Act 1984
IT	information technology
ITTOIA 2005	Income Tax (Trading and Other Income) Act 2005
MLRO	Money Laundering Reporting Officer
NCIS	National Criminal Intelligence Service
NRB trust	nil rate band discretionary trust
NRB	nil rate band
PET	potentially exempt transfer
POCA 2002	Proceeds of Crime Act 2002
PPR	principal private residence
PR	personal representative
RAO	Financial Services and Markets Act 2000 (Regulated Activities) Order 2001, SI 2001/544
RDS	relevant discounted security
ROI	return on investment

SDLT	stamp duty land tax
STEP	Society of Trust and Estate Practitioners
TCGA 1992	Taxation of Chargeable Gains Act 1992
TDA 1999	Trustee Delegation Act 1999
the Scope Rules	Solicitors' Financial Services (Scope) Rules 2001
TLATA 1996	Trusts of Land and Appointment of Trustees Act 1996
WIP	work in progress

Table of cases

Table of statutes

Table of statutory instruments

PART ONE

Setting up a trust

CHAPTER 1

Why have a trust?

1.1 MOTIVES

Introduction

A trust may be created expressly during the settlor's lifetime or may be included in a will, or it may arise by operation of law (implied) or as a result of the courts assessing the behaviour of a person towards some or all of their property or that of another person (resulting or constructive trusts). There are special cases such as protective trusts, trusts created for disabled persons, trusts directed by court order as a result of personal injury claims, pension trusts, charitable trusts – indeed, trusts of all sorts exist.

If, however, you were to ask clients if they might want to create a trust, the answers given might vary from 'I've heard it is a good way to save tax' to 'No thank you – I've read Dickens's *Bleak House* and see that the only real beneficiaries of trusts are the lawyers who draft and administer them'.

Although the reasons why trusts are created are many and varied, for the private client (as opposed to the charitable or pension trust), the suggestion of creating a trust often comes from the advisers as a means to address the client's chosen objectives rather than being the initial object in itself. Many clients would in fact be confused if you began your initial meeting by asking them if they wanted to set up a trust. Instead, if you discover the client's objectives first and then offer a particular type of trust as a means of achieving those goals, the client may be more receptive to the idea of creating a trust.

Why then would a practitioner suggest that a trust might provide a solution to the client's needs?

To protect the assets

A client or his family may have worked for generations to create a business, a farming enterprise or to manage a landed estate and desire to protect these assets from any future unfortunate liaisons, poor business decisions, spendthrifts and playboys in the family!

At the other end of the spectrum, even if there are no substantial assets involved, just a reasonable nest egg for the family, a parent may very well wish to ensure that these assets are preserved as such because otherwise the parent fears that they will be dissipated sooner rather than later. (For example, they may have a son or daughter with an addiction which impairs their ability to make sensible use of the assets.)

In many ways the protection or preservation of the assets will be necessary if the funds are to provide assistance to more than one group of beneficiaries. The obvious dilemma for many people is how to ensure that funds that are needed by a surviving partner or spouse will be preserved for their children once that surviving partner or spouse has formed a new relationship or subsequently passed away.

There are many examples of why clients need to be advised of the dangers of 'just trusting' their surviving partner or spouse but a case that illustrates perfectly the need for the practitioner to raise what are not easy issues is the case of *Birch* v. *Curtis* [2002] EWHC 1158 (Ch). The facts of this case were that Philip and Penny married in 1982. Both had been married before and had children from those earlier marriages: four in Penny's case, two in Philip's. Both spouses contributed to the purchase of Fullers Hill, the matrimonial home.

Penny was found to be terminally ill in January 1986. On 14 February 1986 she made a will in which she left the house and its contents to her husband Philip, if he survived her, and her entire residuary estate in favour of her four children in equal shares. Ten days later Philip made a will in which he left his estate, apart from certain chattels, to his two children and Penny's four children in equal shares. Penny died in May 1986 and her husband received £150,000 from her estate.

In 1990 Philip married again. He persuaded his new wife, Jacqueline to give up her job in 1992 when he retired and they sold Fullers Hill and moved to Mill Farm, Norfolk. Most of the proceeds of sale of Fullers Hill were used in the purchase of the new property. In 1995 Philip made a new will in which he left his entire estate to Jacqueline, apart from some small gifts to his own two daughters. He died four years later and Penny's children brought a claim against his estate arguing that the 1986 wills were mutual wills and that Philip's estate should be distributed in accordance with the 1986 will and not his last 1995 will.

The court found that there was no express or implied agreement on the part of the testator that the wills made in 1986 were to be irrevocable. Rimmer J accepted that:

> it was common for husbands and wives to make Wills in reciprocal terms, and that such Wills are invariably the fruit of some agreement or arrangement between them. It did not follow though that they intended to be irrevocably bound by that arrangement for all time.

The court found that Jacqueline would not have given up her career or agreed to move if she had known that the six children might have a claim to her husband's estate.

This case illustrates well the danger of 'just trusting' each other and why practitioners need to discourage clients from making arrangements which may well produce an unintended outcome.

It may be that if Philip and Penny had discussed what they would have ultimately wished to happen to their respective estates if one of them died and the survivor married again, the answer could quite easily have been 'I would like my contribution to the family assets to be inherited by my children'. Reliance on equitable remedies such as mutual wills, as in the present case, will often produce unwelcome results for one of the parties affected.

To answer clients' concerns about protection of the assets for their chosen beneficiaries the practitioner needs to be able to explain the opportunity afforded by an appropriate express trust over the seemingly attractive 'simple' approach of relying on everyone to act as the client would have done if they were alive – which runs the inherent risk that this is not what happens.

To protect the beneficiaries

Some clients believe that their offspring will never know best and would love to protect their hard-earned savings from wastrel children. There are many examples of the first generation of a family creating wealth through an original idea or simple hard graft, who can then offer their offspring a different childhood experience from their own. The children then inherit the assets but it may be that only one of them has the necessary drive and ambition to build on the nest egg. The inheritance may be devalued by division or through lack of the same opportunities that were available to the parent and perhaps lack of need, thus by the time the third generation comes along little of the original fortune remains to be passed on.

Trusts cannot prevent beneficiaries making poor choices of life partner or remove the risk of failing performance of investments in difficult markets but they can provide, in the form of trustees, a reasonable hand on the tiller to act as a guide or a disciplinarian in the acquiescence or otherwise to requests by beneficiaries for money or other resources.

Some parents may have children with learning disabilities who will never be able to manage their own resources and worry what can be done, at a time when both parents have died, to protect their children from unfortunate 'friends' and 'carers' who may not be all they appear to be. Indeed, in the current climate of public funding for care, discretionary trusts have a role to play in preserving some or all of a family's estate to be used to enable positive benefits for the disabled child without making the loss of means-tested benefits a certainty. In other words, the chosen trustees can act as a benign parent would have hoped to have done if the parent had lived and provide special resources to make the beneficiary's life more enjoyable without losing the underlying basic care provided by public funding.

Some parents have perfectly able-bodied children who have sadly become addicted to drugs or alcohol to such an extent that providing a large sum of money to them as an outright gift would endanger their lives. Instead, the parents might prefer their assets to be managed by someone to provide a roof over their son or daughter's head, which that child could not sell, so at least the child was safe, in the hope that the addiction problems might be overcome and their child survive to enjoy a healthy and happy later life. The role of trustee in this scenario can be difficult. The office may need to provide small regular distributions in cash to meet everyday necessities and manage a property purchased in order to ensure there is a roof over the beneficiary's head.

Express trusts afford clients who feel the need to protect their beneficiaries with a suitable tool to protect the chosen beneficiaries from, effectively, themselves!

To retain control over assets and beneficiaries by setting out the terms of use in the trust deed

The ability to transfer assets out of personal ownership but to still effectively dictate their use is attractive to some clients. It may be that a gift is made during lifetime rather than on death to a trust where the donor is one of the trustees so in that way, as one of the trustees, the donor controls the trust fund, although of course he must act entirely in accordance with the trust deed and in the best interests of the beneficiaries. Nevertheless, it is not the same as handing complete control of the assets directly to the beneficiaries.

Alternatively, the gift may well be to a trust created under a will so that control beyond the grave is achieved in as much as the people given the job of managing the fund are those chosen by the testator. The chosen trustees are also directed by the testator's will to manage the assets required by the testator and the circumstances in which a beneficiary becomes entitled, if at all, to receive income and or capital can also be predetermined by the testator.

In the case of a family company inherited or created by the client it may be that the client does not wish to see the company broken up by a piecemeal division of the shares between beneficiaries. Rather he may prefer to see the company retained intact and sold as one entity. The client may want all his chosen beneficiaries to enjoy the success of the company either in the form of dividends or ultimately by sharing in the capital value on its sale but meanwhile the client may not wish any one beneficiary to have control over the day-to-day business of the company. A trust is a popular mechanism for holding shares in a family business to achieve these objectives.

To treat income and capital of a gift in different ways

A client will often have two main categories of people he wishes to benefit – his surviving partner and his children. The partner may be financially dependent on the client and would need access to the client's resources if he died to maintain a reasonable standard of living. If capital were given outright to the surviving partner this would leave the surviving partner free to use it as they saw fit. Whilst this may be entirely satisfactory for some clients, others may have either more complex lives or less faith in the ability of their surviving partner to be able to manage those resources appropriately. By using an interest in possession trust the income can be paid to the surviving partner whilst preserving the capital for the children.

A client who has been married before and has children from that relationship would expect to be able to preserve some or all of his estate for his children to benefit from, but if he gives it directly and absolutely to his new partner there is no guarantee that his previous children would ever benefit.

A client who has always managed the family's finances and who has left the spouse to care for the welfare of the children, and not carve out a paid career, may feel that the surviving spouse would find suddenly having the responsibility of managing money difficult. Such a client may prefer to ensure that there is sound management of the money by trustees, who would provide a suitable stream of income for the surviving spouse.

In other cases an elderly relative may need help with the payment of outgoings and need income to do this, but have no need of the capital to generate this income, which can be directed elsewhere on the death of that relative to other beneficiaries of the settlor's choosing.

Providing income for beneficiaries whilst they are too young to handle large amounts of capital is a popular use of trusts for children and grandchildren, thus providing funds for school fees, day-to-day maintenance and other benefits whilst they are under a specified age. However, once the client feels that the children have reached an age when they will be responsible enough to have control of their own funds, the capital will usually pass to them on attaining that specified age.

To save tax

Trusts are often a way of helping a client and spouse save capital taxes. For the couple who want to minimise inheritance tax (IHT) on their joint estates, the tax adviser would encourage making use of both their individual nil rate bands worth of asset value. This could be done with lifetime giving to make use of the potentially exempt transfers (PETs) which may drop out of charge to IHT if the donor survives seven years from the gift; or may be used in each spouse's will to ensure that on the first death the value of the nil rate band is used in such a way that on the death of the second spouse it will not be aggregated with the second spouse's estate and be taxed as part of that (see further **Chapter 14**).

Whilst in any of these scenarios an outright gift to others rather than to each other could achieve the same tax savings, trusts are often suggested and used. In the case of lifetime gifts, this may typically be because the chosen beneficiaries are too young to enjoy the amount of cash outright and the donors would rather see it managed for them until they reach a specified age. Another common situation is where the donor does not have spare cash to give away but rather only has chargeable assets which if he gave them away would generate a chargeable gain on which he would have to pay capital gains tax (CGT) at his marginal rates, which could be as much as 40 per cent. If the chargeable assets were gifted to a discretionary trust, for example, the donor could utilise a CGT relief (s.260, Taxation of Chargeable Gains Act 1992 (TCGA 1992)) and thus avoid an unwelcome tax bill.

In the case of gifts in wills, the nil rate band of the first spouse to die is often transferred to a discretionary trust rather than outright to the children in order to include the surviving spouse as a potential beneficiary of the funds. The trust can therefore be used to benefit the surviving spouse during her lifetime without those funds being aggregated with the surviving spouse's own assets on her death. This simple use of the discretionary trust will save the married couple substantial IHT on their joint estates (for 2005/06, £110,000).

Not only will the trust mechanism generate a saving of tax because of how the assets are held but also it may help to preserve entitlement to either business property relief (BPR) or agricultural property relief (APR) where in each case entitlement to relief includes ownership criteria which involve minimum periods of ownership. If outright gifts were made it might make it difficult in certain circumstances for the recipient to achieve that ownership period, while if the trustees retain ownership of the assets for the trust period the entitlement to relief is preserved.

To avoid the need to obtain a grant of probate

When an individual dies domiciled in England and Wales, the legal title to the deceased's assets vest in his personal representatives (PRs). In the case of a client who leaves a will, the PRs will be his executors, and in the case of the intestate, the PRs will be administrators identified by the Non-Contentious Probate Rules 1987 (as amended). To be able to provide evidence of the legal ownership a grant of probate has to be issued to the PRs.

Whilst in many estates this is straightforward, once the estate is taxable accurate valuations are necessary and the PRs will have to undertake a reasonable amount of work to identify and value all the assets, liabilities and beneficiaries in the estate. All this takes time, and during this period assets cannot be easily changed or managed without a grant.

Although there are procedures which will enable an expeditious grant to be obtained, even this is nevertheless not instantaneous and could temporarily leave the beneficiaries without access to financial support. The advantage of the trust is that the deceased is not the owner of the assets managed by the trustees. The trustees own the legal title to the assets in the trust fund and so are able to continue managing them following the client's death. This means that the trust's beneficiaries continue to have access to the support that they enjoyed before the donor's death, and more particularly the trustees have authority to switch investments as and when required, allowing them to react to the rises and falls of the markets.

Practice point

A trust practitioner should strive to find what it is that is motivating the client and what objectives he wants to achieve. This will help to determine whether or not a trust solution should be proffered and ultimately which type of trust might be the most suitable or appropriate for the client's situation:

- Identify the clients' goals.
  If you are dealing with two spouses/partners make sure that you are aware of *both* people's views.
- Extract the *facts* about your clients' resources and dependants.
- Examine with the clients the external environment outside the family: tax, work, political change, etc.
  It is useful to understand the financial landscape surrounding the clients and how changes to, say, interest rates or tax rates, might affect their thinking.
- Analyse the internal environment within the family – needs, problems, resources, etc.
  It is essential if assets are to be moved from personal ownership to trust ownership to understand what are the risks to those structures in the event of a family disaster, such as an untimely death or divorce. What problems might an untimely death or divorce generate, and what resources might the family need in such circumstances?
- Assess the clients' attitudes to risk.
  Some clients, for example, are willing to take part in highly contentious tax-saving schemes which are likely to be challenged by Her Majesty's Revenue and Customs (HMRC) (the new department responsible for the business of the former Inland Revenue and HM Customs and Excise), whereas other clients may be unwilling to face an investigation of that sort or to undertake litigation.
- Design approach, taking into account these factors.

1.2   OVERVIEW OF THE DIFFERENT TYPES OF TRUST

Although there are many types of trust, this book considers the practical administrative techniques for the three main types of trust found in practice:

1.   interest in possession;
2.   discretionary; or
3.   accumulation and maintenance (A&M).

It is worth pointing out that although a trust starts out in life as a particular type of trust, it can subsequently change its nature by the operation of the powers given to the trustees by law or by the trust instrument. Clients when deciding on what to do with their estates both during life and on death often need a simple explanation of the distinction between the three types of trust in order to decide whether to use a trust at all, or which type of trust might be the most suitable for their particular situation.

Interest in possession

In this type of trust a beneficiary is entitled to the *immediate* enjoyment of a right in or over trust property. The basic structure of such a trust is for the payment or entitlement to payment of income from the trust as it arises to one (or more) individuals during a specified period, usually that person's lifetime. Where the income is paid during the individual's lifetime, the individual is referred to as the 'life tenant'. Once the interest in possession ends it is followed by a gift of the capital to other individuals (known as 'the remaindermen'). In this way there is a separate treatment of the income and capital of the trust fund.

Although there is a key statutory default provision permitting trustees to advance some of the trust fund in certain circumstances (s.32, Trustee Act 1925, see Appendix 3.3) the trustees may be given wide powers by the terms of the settlement deed to override or revoke some of the provisions of the trust, with a view to achieving what the settlor had hoped when the trust was drafted. At the time of drafting no one could second guess what might happen in the future, but overriding powers provide flexibility for the trustees to attend to any unforseen events that may occur.

There are three main categories of overriding powers:

1.   *Powers of appointment*: which permit the trustees to create new trusts for the beneficiaries.
2.   *Powers of resettlement*: which allow the trustees to transfer funds to a new settlement for the beneficiaries.
3.   *Powers of advancement*: which give the trustees the power to apply capital for the benefit of a beneficiary.

Although these powers are dispositive (that is, they permit permanent change to the destination of the original trust fund) provided that they are drafted properly they will not undermine the treatment of the trust which contains them as an interest in possession trust. It will be treated as such until the point at which the powers are used.

It is possible that the powers will never be exercised, so until that time the beneficiary with the interest in possession continues to be entitled to the trust income as it arises. But, with overriding powers vested in reliable trustees, there is scope for ending the surviving spouse's life interest or altering the trusts in reversion to meet changing needs, e.g. nursing home problems or newly acquired stepchildren.

The use of these flexible life interest trusts with sufficient powers to make them defeasible has grown in popularity since 1984 and the introduction of the potentially exempt transfer (PET) for IHT purposes. This is because creating such a trust during the settlor's lifetime is a PET and exercising the overriding powers will in many cases be treated as a PET by the life tenant.

If the trust continues until the death of the life tenant he is treated as owning the capital of the trust fund (s.49, Inheritance Tax Act 1984 (IHTA 1984)) with the result that it is cumulated with his own estate on his death and IHT is charged on the total, after the application of the deceased's nil rate band. A worked example of this treatment can be found in **Chapter 9**.

Income tax is charged on the trust income at the basic rate (i.e. 22 per cent for 2005/06) or at the relevant rate applicable to the income paid net of tax, such as bank interest paid net of savings rate.

CGT is charged at a flat rate of 40 per cent on chargeable gains made by the trustees above an annual exemption, which is half that available to an individual.

Discretionary trusts

A discretionary trust exists where the trustees have discretion over the distribution or accumulation of income and/or the appointment of capital. An essential feature is that whilst the power of accumulation of income exists or the power to appoint capital exists no beneficiary has any right to require the trustees to exercise their discretion in the beneficiary's favour. This means that a class of beneficiaries exists from which any may be chosen for benefit, but no particular beneficiary within the class has any right to enjoy income or capital at a particular time.

There is complete flexibility for the trustees to exercise their discretion according to the needs of the beneficiaries. The settlor may give the trustees guidance as to how he would like the discretion to be exercised by way of a letter of wishes.

A discretionary trust is therefore in complete contrast to the interest in possession trust because no beneficiary has an interest in possession in the fund. This means that the death of a beneficiary is not an occasion when IHT is payable, whereas it is a chargeable event in interest in possession cases. Instead, there are two occasions when a charge to IHT arises in discretionary trusts:

1. *Every 10 years from the inception of the trust* which is calculated as though a transfer of value is made of the property in the settlement on the tenth anniversary of its creation, together with any related property and by a settlor who had a cumulative total for IHT equal to the value of the chargeable transfers made by the settlor in the seven years prior to the creation of the trust plus the amounts upon which IHT has been charged on any distributions from the settlement in the previous 10 years. The rate of tax charged can, currently, never be more than 6 per cent.

2. *When assets leave the trust* an exit or proportionate charge is levied on distributions from the settlement. These are charged at a proportionate rate of tax – one-fortieth (for each complete quarter which has elapsed since the inception of the trust or since the last 10-yearly anniversary) of the effective rate (if the trust has passed its first 10-year anniversary) or the rate fixed on inception (if the distribution is within the first 10 years) (s.69, IHTA 1984).

For a worked example of the tax treatment, see Chapter 9.

Income tax is charged at a special rate known as 'the rate applicable to trusts' which is 40 per cent on all income apart from dividends, on which the dividend trust rate of 32.5 per cent applies. The Finance Act 2005 has introduced, with effect from 6 April 2005, a new basic rate band on all trusts without an interest in possession. The first £500 of income will therefore not be taxed at the rate applicable to trusts nor at the dividend trust rate.

A flat rate of 40 per cent CGT is charged on the trustees, just as with interest in possession trusts, but with the ability to utilise a CGT holdover relief under TCGA 1992, s.260 on disposals by way of gift – something which is not available to interest in possession trustees.

Accumulation and maintenance trusts

The accumulation and maintenance trust (A&M trust) is a special form of discretionary trust and is specifically a trust which meets the criteria contained within IHTA 1984, s.71 (see **Appendix 3.1**). This is largely for a class of beneficiaries who are all children of a common grandparent or their substitutes or if not, then the trust must last only in this form for 25 years. The beneficiaries all have to achieve a vested interest by a specified age, not greater than 25. It is this requirement for vesting by a specified age which distinguishes it from a discretionary trust. The wording of trust documents can look similar, and sometimes it is hard to determine whether a trust is discretionary or A&M. If the trust practitioner can establish whether or not there is automatic vesting, then this will be the determining factor.

This can be summarised as follows:

1. automatic vesting = A&M;
2. discretion over vesting = discretionary trust.

An A&M trust, therefore, is something of a hybrid, as whilst the class of beneficiaries is described and the members are under the specified age they will not be entitled to the income or the capital of the trust fund (subject to ss.31 and 32 of the Trustee Act 1925), which is similar to the pure discretionary trust, but when the specified age is attained then a particular beneficiary achieves a vested interest and so the beneficiary's interest becomes one in possession, like the life tenant of the interest in possession trust.

The A&M trust is a popular way of parents and grandparents providing for children by tying up the capital and income rather than making over to them large sums of money when they may be too young to be able to manage it. The income might be paid at, say, the age of 18 but capital might not be payable unless and until they reach 25. Although this difference in age will give rise to some difficult CGT issues it is a popular distinction.

Since the income is accumulated until the specified age for income has been reached income tax is charged at the rate applicable to trusts, which is 40 per cent, until the beneficiary attains a vested interest in income, at which point that part of the fund in which there is an interest in possession is taxed at the basic rate (i.e. 22 per cent for 2005/06).

Just like the other types of trust, CGT is charged at the flat rate of 40 per cent on chargeable gains made by the trustees. If the conditions in s.71(4) of the IHTA 1984 apply at the time when a beneficiary becomes absolutely entitled to his share of the fund or to an interest in possession in it, any CGT due may be held over by virtue of a special provision, i.e. s.260(2)(d) of the TCGA 1992.

The creation of an A&M trust during the lifetime of the settlor is a PET so no IHT is payable at that time. If the settlor survives the following seven-year period there will be no IHT payable either then or when the capital is ultimately paid to the beneficiaries.

However, if the settlor dies within the seven-year period following the gift, the trustees could find themselves liable to IHT on his death as the PET becomes chargeable. It is common practice for a settlor to take out insurance against this possibility.

The creation of an A&M trust in a client's will will only give rise to a charge to IHT if on the client's death his estate exceeds the nil rate band. Otherwise, there will be no charge to IHT on the trust fund until the A&M regime no longer applies. Capital payments to beneficiaries whilst the trust is within the A&M regime are IHT free. Where the beneficiaries are *not* all children of a common grandparent then the trust will only have this favoured IHT treatment for

25 years from its inception and thereafter will be subject to IHT charges, as if it was a discretionary trust. (See the *Inland Revenue Tax Bulletin*, December 2000, for an explanation of how IHT will apply in these circumstances.)

1.3 USING TRUSTS

Apart from the issue of negligence, clients and their families will not thank the adviser for choosing an inappropriate trust. For some people the idea of using a trust is attractive. There have been many articles published advocating the use of trusts in tax planning and clients often arrive clutching an article that they have seen in the press. Since house prices rose by 130 per cent in the period between 1997 and 2004 (according to a report by Friends Provident in August 2004) and the nil rate band increased only by 22 per cent in that time period, many people have looked to the use of trusts to help mitigate IHT. Nevertheless, given the amount of money or asset value available, a trust might not be an appropriate vehicle for a particular client. A trust can be a costly mechanism to operate and may therefore generate resentment if it is not run efficiently.

1.4 RELEVANT FACTORS TO CONSIDER

Value of the estate

The smaller the estate, the less likely it is that practical lifetime planning can be done without adversely affecting the security of the donor or his spouse for the future. In estates where the total value of the estate of the donor and spouse amounts to no more than £500,000, the likelihood is that the bulk of the value is in the family home.

Since 1986 and the introduction of the anti-avoidance provision of gifts with reservation of benefit, there have been a number of tax-saving schemes in recent years which try to reduce the overall impact of IHT on the family home, and some of these schemes involve the use of trusts. For a detailed discussion of tax-saving schemes, see McKie and Anstey, *Tolley's Estate Planning 2004–05* (LexisNexis, 2004).

Such was the extent of the Government's concern over the loss of revenue as a result of the use of these schemes, a new charge to income tax was introduced with effect from 6 April 2005. This is a charge to income tax on what are defined as 'pre-owned assets'. This charge effectively taxes a certain value each year to income tax in respect of land, chattels and intangibles transactions which are caught by the detailed rules set out in s.84 of, and Sch.15 to, the Finance Act 2004 and the subsequent Charge to Income Tax by Reference to Enjoyment of Property Previously Owned Regulations 2005, SI

2005/724, and the *Pre-Owned Assets – Technical Guidance* issued by HMRC and updated on 1 April 2005.

This charge to income tax effectively discourages the use of all the popular lifetime giving schemes involving the family home apart from those covered by specific exemption or exclusion. As a result, most major gifts of interests in the family home will be included in the client's will.

The pre-owned assets charging arrangements are complex, and for a detailed review of the new regime see Chamberlain & Whitehouse with McCuthcheon, *Pre-owned Assets – Capital Tax Planning in the New Era* (Sweet & Maxwell, 2004). Note, however, that it was written before HMRC published the Regulations and Guidelines.

For the smaller estate, both during the parties' lifetimes and on death, it is likely that outright gifts to the other spouse will be used to protect the financial position of the other spouse, or that the will of the first spouse to die will create an interest in possession trust in favour of the surviving spouse for life with remainder to any children.

Where the total estates exceed two times the current nil rate band for IHT purposes, each partner needs to own at least the nil rate band's worth of assets. During lifetime or by deed of variation after the death of the first spouse the ownership of assets needs to be separate so that the couple own either independently or as tenants in common sufficient assets to use up their respective nil rate bands. Each spouse will usually only consider using their own nil rate band as part of their gifts in their respective wills.

In this situation the discretionary trust is often used, so that the surviving spouse can be included as a beneficiary of the trust and therefore have access to the assets of the trust fund whilst alive, but the trust fund will not be treated as being part of that spouse's estate on death for IHT purposes. A popular tool used in many married couples' wills over the past 10 years or so is the nil rate band debt scheme. For a summary of how this arrangement is used and how it affects trust administration, see **Chapter 14**.

It is the larger estates which can make most use of lifetime planning (albeit in a more restrictive way since 6 April 2005). The adviser will identify which of the lifetime tax reliefs can be utilised in passing on assets now, perhaps protecting any gifts by taking out a suitable life assurance policy which is written into trust for the beneficiaries who would bear any IHT in the event of an untimely death within the seven-year period.

The larger the estate, the more likely it is that trusts will be created during lifetime and possibly also be used on death. It is unlikely that a settlor and the settlor's spouse or civil partner can enjoy immediate and continuing benefits from a trust that the settlor creates without it being treated as a gift with reservation of benefit for IHT and without the income and gains arising in the trust being taxed on the settlor. (Note that same sex couples who enter into a registered civil partnership post 5 December 2005 are likely to be treated as if they were spouses for tax purposes, but at the time of writing legislation to effect this has not been laid.) So for a trust to be effective for tax purposes and create the potential for some tax savings, settlors who create a trust during their own lifetime must be able to afford to live without access to the resources being placed into the trust. A widow or widower can benefit from a trust created by their spouse without these difficulties but not a living spouse who was the settlor's spouse at the time when the trust was created.

Choice of available assets

The types of assets in the estate that benefit most from estate planning are those that are likely to grow in value, e.g. business assets, real property. Maximising the use of business property relief and agricultural property relief for IHT at the highest rates should be a priority. (For an explanation of these reliefs, see **Chapter 9**.) Sometimes it is difficult to do this without falling outside the criteria for the reliefs or causing the gifts with reservation rules to apply. This is where the use of trusts can often help by providing some control over assets by trustees but passing the value out of the donor's estate.

For a settlor to make a transfer into an *inter vivos* settlement the two critical issues to consider initially will be:

1. Does the settlor and the settlor's spouse or any civil partner in any way depend on the proposed assets to produce income on which they live?
2. Will transferring the assets to the trust fund create a liability to tax?

The choice of assets to transfer into the trust fund will to a large extent depend on the answers to the above questions and also some of the issues below concerning the pros and cons of putting certain types of asset into a trust.

Post-gift income requirements

No gifts can be contemplated if they are likely to leave the prospective donor and the donor's spouse or partner with insufficient income on which to live. In the current climate pension policies may be insufficient and some capital assets may need to be retained to generate income to live on. Where the client is self-employed proper pension provision should be the first priority for any surplus funds so that the income levels in retirement are realistic. Only when the parties are satisfied that their likely income levels are sufficient to meet their standard of living both now and on the first death should income-producing assets be divested away from them.

Family circumstances

A single person with no dependants may have a desire to save tax but have no fixed ideas as to who from a group of relatives, friends and charities should benefit. The use of trusts again may be appropriate if there are assets that are suitable for transfer, e.g. cash into an A&M trust for the benefit of all the donors' nephews and nieces. This trust could, for example, be created when only one nephew or niece had been born and subsequently grow to accommodate all nephews and nieces born within a specified period. Such a trust could equally well be created during the lifetime of the settlor or in the settlor's will. Tax savings will only really be generated with a lifetime gift that is made more than seven years prior to the death of the settlor, otherwise any such gift in the will simply uses some or all of the deceased's nil rate band on death.

A married couple with children can make use of the inter-spouse exemptions to pass moneys between them in order to both make use of gifts to their children, again perhaps into discretionary trust, so as to maximise the use of their respective nil rate bands for IHT.

Where the parties are not married there is currently no inter-partner exemption for transactions between *unmarried* people and therefore any gifts made between them will start to use up the nil rate band. See the case of *Holland* v. *CIR* [2003] WTLR 207 for a failed argument to extend the spouse exemption under s.18, IHTA 1984 to cohabitants. For same sex couples, the Civil Partnerships Act 2004 comes into force on 5 December 2005 providing those couples who register as civil partners with similar treatment under the law to married couples.

Gifts during lifetime between unmarried couples and same sex couples who are not registered as civil partners will be subject to both CGT and IHT. To the extent that the nil rate band is available for IHT, no tax will be payable at the time. If tax saving is the driving force, then the sooner the process starts the more likely it is that the donor will live long enough (i.e. at least seven years) to ensure that any gifts are outside the donor's estate on death.

More use could be made of the discretionary trust for the unmarried or unregistered partner and any children on the first partner's death if security is the issue; as there is no IHT saving apart from the unused nil rate band, it does not really matter which type of gift is made once the value exceeds the nil rate band as 40 per cent IHT will be levied on the excess. It makes sense to take into account flexibility and protection, and a discretionary trust provides that.

Distinction between income and capital

If the beneficiary is not in need of capital but does require income, for example an elderly parent, then the interest in possession trust enables the donor to transfer assets to trustees who will manage the assets to generate income for the elderly life tenant but with the capital reserved for the settlor's children. Such a trust is a PET when made during the donor's lifetime, and even exempt if made for dependent relatives, so such trusts can be useful if life tenants have little capital of their own. If the life tenant has capital which together with the trust fund is likely to exceed the current nil rate band, there will be no tax saving as there will be a charge to IHT on the life tenant's death unless there is a reverter to the settlor (s.54, IHTA 1984).

Table 1.1 Pros and cons of putting assets into a trust

Asset	Pros	Cons
Buildings	• Tangible. • Provides an opportunity for income (rent) and capital growth. • Could provide a beneficiary with accommodation.	• Difficult to convert into cash for division between beneficiaries or to pay tax. • Immovable. • Requires maintenance fund. • Requires insurance. • May have to make decision as to which beneficiary can reside in the property and if they have the right to do so what compensation might have to be paid to other similar beneficiaries who are not in occupation.
Sole trader's goodwill		• Often the goodwill of the sole trader dies with him so of no real value to the trust. • Virtually impossible to divide between different beneficiaries in this form. • Likely to be unable to provide enough income (rent or interest) for the trust whilst providing enough income (profit) for the person running the business for the trustees. • Generates huge personal liability problems.
Private company shares	• Prevents the potential break up of the company holding which could occur with individual gifts of shares to different beneficiaries. • Permits ongoing control of the company to remain in the hands of the trustees not the individual beneficiaries.	• No ready market for sale. • May be no regular income if dividends are not normally declared. • Trustees will need to act as relevant shareholders, holding directors to account by exercising the trust's voting rights.

Table 1.1 Pros and cons of putting assets into a trust – cont.

Asset	Pros	Cons
	• May preserve entitlement to certain tax reliefs which might be lost to the beneficiaries. • It is possible to transfer the shares to the beneficiaries easily if required. • Will often be entitled to CGT holdover relief under s.165, TCGA 1992 on gifts out of the trust.	• Conflicts of interest can arise in making decisions between trustee beneficiaries employed in the business and those beneficiaries who are not trustees and not involved in the business. • May potentially incur CGT on disposals.
Quoted equities	• Provide opportunity for income by way of dividends and capital growth. • Easy to sell to realise funds for distribution and costs and to switch between holdings.	• Require good management to avoid losses. • Discretionary management of the investments must comply with Trustee Act 2000 requirements. • Non-refundable tax credits cannot be added to the 'tax pool' used in the administration of non-interest in possession trusts. • Will potentially incur CGT on disposals.
Agricultural property	• Enables all beneficiaries to share in the value of the land and possibly the farming enterprise even though they are not the farmer. • Prevents the break up of the estate. • May preserve eligibility for tax reliefs not available to the beneficiaries individually.	• Immovable. • Security of tenure issues and succession to tenancy problems. • Conflicts potentially between farming beneficiary and non-farming beneficiaries. • Will potentially incur CGT on disposals.
Cash	• Readily available for distributions and costs. • Requires minimal management. • No CGT on distributions as sterling is not a chargeable asset for CGT.	• If not invested, capital value eroded over time by inflation.

Halting the growth in the value of an estate

Transferring assets into a trust effectively freezes the value of the gift as far as the settlor is concerned so that any subsequent growth in value of those transferred assets does not accrue to the settlor but rather develops outside the settlor's estate. This is true whether the gift is a PET or a chargeable transfer. It is only if the settlor dies within seven years of making the gift into trust that the gift's value at the date it was made, rather than what it is worth at the time of death, is taken into account in assessing the value of the deceased's estate on death.

1.5 WHICH TRUST TO CHOOSE?

A settlement needs to be flexible to enable the trustees to take action to reflect changes in circumstances both amongst the beneficiaries and in the tax system throughout the life of the trust.

A simple interest in possession trust is somewhat inflexible in as much as only the beneficiary enjoying the vested interest is entitled to receive any return and that is limited to the income of the fund. Without any express powers to enable them to do so, the trustees cannot advance capital automatically to the life tenant. Even the implied power to advance capital to the remaindermen waiting for the capital on the termination of the interest in possession under s.32, Trustee Act 1925 (see **Appendix 3.3**) can only be exercised in favour of the remaindermen with the consent of the person enjoying the interest in possession and only then automatically up to a total of one-half of the remainder beneficiary's presumptive or contingent interest.

To make the interest in possession trust more flexible, any such trust should be drafted to include overriding powers of appointment to enable the trustees to effectively rewrite the trusts of the settlement as it seems appropriate in the light of any changes to beneficiaries' circumstances or to tax law.

Unless the exercise of these powers was expressed to be revocable the exercise would be a once and for all event, being used only once to bring the trust to an end or change its nature.

By contrast the discretionary trust is very flexible as it gives the trustees the opportunity to decide whether or not to accumulate income as it arises rather than having to pay it out to a particular beneficiary. This enables choices to be made between beneficiaries at any time and from time to time, which can be based on need, reward or any reasonable factor. It allows for the fluctuating needs of all eligible beneficiaries to be taken into account and enables new beneficiaries who join the class to be considered.

Also, capital payments can be made to any beneficiary in the class again at any time in exercise of a power of appointment, with provision for what would happen at the end of the trust period if no exercise of the trustees' discretion is made.

An A&M trust is something of a hybrid. Whilst the beneficiaries are under the specified age for entitlement to the income, the trustees decide whether to pay out the income to or for the beneficiaries or whether to accumulate it. However, once the beneficiary has a vested interest in income the trustees no longer have discretion.

The IHT and CGT treatment of each trust is often one of the main factors in selecting the right trust. For example, if the settlor wishes to reduce his estate for IHT purposes on death he may choose to make a trust and hope to live at least seven years so that the gift will drop out of the charge to tax on death. If the settlor wanted to provide for more than just his children and issue, a discretionary trust should be considered, with the resultant 10-yearly and exit charges for IHT. The act of transferring assets to a discretionary trust is an immediately chargeable transfer so any gift of chargeable assets worth more than the nil rate band available will be subject to a 20 per cent IHT charge at the time of the transfer into trust on the excess value over the nil rate band. If the settlor's choice of beneficiaries is limited to just his legitimate children or grandchildren an A&M trust looks more attractive, as there are no IHT charges on creation or periodically or upon the beneficiaries attaining a vested interest.

However, if all the settlor has to transfer to the trust are chargeable assets, rather than cash, then making a PET to an A&M trust may well be too expensive in terms of the CGT charge on the settlor in disposing of those assets. If the settlor is eligible for relief (perhaps because the assets qualify for business asset taper relief and s.165, TCGA 1992 holdover) or the settlor has significant losses to cover the gains, then a PET to the A&M trust may still be suitable.

If the settlor does not have the luxury of business assets reliefs but does not want to face a large CGT bill, then again the only solution would be to make an immediately chargeable transfer to a discretionary trust so that the CGT could be held over under s.260, TCGA 1992.

Therefore, the choice of trust to be used will always be a balancing act between flexibility and taxability; between protection of the beneficiaries and protection of the assets; and between the type of assets owned and the particular needs of the beneficiaries.

1.6 PRACTICE POINT

Considering the correct form of trust to meet the needs of the client's situation and the relevant tax breaks is the key to choosing the appropriate option (see the checklist in **Appendix 2.2**). Practitioners are advised to use a questionnaire when taking instructions to help in the selection of an appropriate trust. A suitable questionnaire is provided at **Appendix 2.3**.

CHAPTER 2

Creating a trust

2.1 THE FORMAL REQUIREMENTS – WHAT CONSTITUTES A TRUST?

The three certainties

The trust practitioner is often asked to explain to clients what is the essential nature of a trust. It is also necessary to be able to determine whether a particular gift or document has in fact created a trust or not. For clients, a simple way of describing a trust is to say it is a 'gift with strings attached', but in law for a trust to exist the three certainties must be present, as described by Romer J in *Green* v. *Russell* [1959] 2 QB 226: A trust is a clear obligation (certainty of words) imposed by its creator (the testator) upon a person or persons (the trustees) to manage property under their control (trust property – certainty of subject matter) for the benefit of persons (the beneficiaries – certainty of objects) whose interests are protected by the courts.

It is clear from this definition that the trustees are not personally the owners of the trust property. They are simply the custodians of that property appointed by the settlor to manage it for the benefit of the settlor's chosen beneficiaries.

To the outside world, and in fact, the trustees are the legal owners of the assets held in trust. However, they do not own the equitable interest in the property. Indeed, there are equitable rules which are enforceable against the trustees in the courts to protect the beneficiaries' interests and which are enforceable by the beneficiaries.

Certainty of words

With many modern precedents available it may seem strange to suggest that there could be uncertainty as to the wording of a trust document. However, precedents are a guide to drafting and when creating a trust they may prove to be merely a starting point. The danger is that the tailoring of the precedent to meet the clients' requirements may involve the draftsman in making adjustments, particularly to definitions, but because the alterations are not followed through consistently the document produced is not coherent. Many court decisions are concerned with the interpretation of wording both to individual clauses and to the document as a whole. So often it is the small connecting words like 'and' and 'or' which cause the problems. For example, which beneficiaries are included in the following class?

> The children or remoter issue of the settlor and Mrs Jean Jones namely Felix Jones, Ethan Jones, Clare Jones and Susan Jones.

Do these words imply that only the children of both the settlor and Mrs Jean Jones are covered by the provision? What if Felix and Ethan were children of the settlor by his previous wife, would they be excluded from this class? It is likely that a court would find that only the children of both the settlor *and* Mrs Jean Jones would be covered. If it was intended that all four children should be covered then changing the wording from being the children of the settlor *and* Mrs Jean Jones to the children or remoter issue of the settlor *or* Mrs Jean Jones would overcome this difficulty.

What about the fact that the clause in its original form lists the four children? Does this create uncertainty as to whether or not the beneficial class is limited to the four named children and their issue and therefore excludes any future children of Mrs Jean Jones and the settlor and any remoter issue?

It may also seem pedantic to say that for there to be a clear obligation imposed by the settlor on the trustees somewhere in the document there needs to be clear direction from the settlor that the trustees are to hold the trust fund upon the terms set out in the trust deed. This also means that there has to be an effective transfer of the property in the trust fund to the trustees following the correct legal procedures and factually handing them over to the trustees. Otherwise, the gift will be ineffective.

There is a key distinction to be made between making a trust (where the obligations imposed are mandatory) and giving the trustees merely powers (which simply leave exercise of the powers to the trustees' discretion).

If there is a failure to use imperative words such as 'to my trustees on trust for (A)' or 'I transfer Whiteacre to (T) and direct him to hold it for (A)' then a court will have to determine whether what was intended was to grant a trust or a power.

A court may be asked to consider whether a document has created a trust or whether it should be construed as a power of appointment. If the court decides it is a trust the beneficiaries, in particular the default beneficiaries, would be entitled to the trust assets if the trustees failed to make a selection between them. However, if the document is construed as a power of appointment and the trustees fail to make a selection between the beneficiaries, the money would revert back to the settlor or, if the settlor had died, to the settlor's estate.

For tax purposes, the consequences of this for an *inter vivos* trust could be fatal in so far as the settlor will be taxed on the income and capital gains of the settlement from its inception.

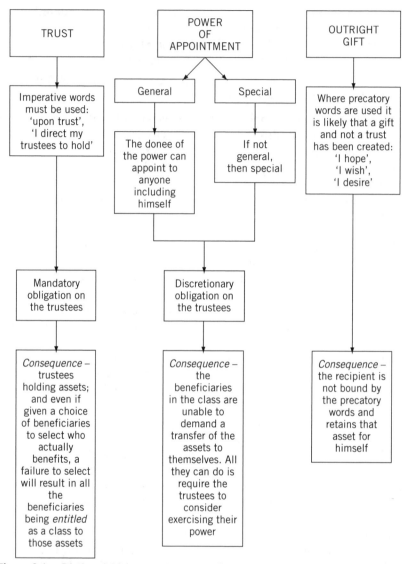

Figure 2.1 Distinguishing a trust, power of appointment, and an outright gift

Certainty of subject matter

Although this is probably the least likely certainty to fail, it is necessary to remember there are two aspects to it.

1. *Trust property* – the identification of the trust property itself must be clear so where vague words like 'the bulk of my estate' or only 'blue chip

shares from my portfolio' are left to trustees there is a danger that a court may not always interpret these words as the settlor intended. For example, they may regard 'the bulk of the settlor's estate' to mean the majority of it (i.e. 51 per cent) as opposed to almost all of it (i.e. 99 per cent).

2. *The definition of the beneficial interests* – where more than one beneficiary is to benefit it has to be possible to ascertain the interest to be taken by those beneficiaries. It is of course acceptable for trustees to be given the assets under a discretionary trust so that they determine what interest each beneficiary is to receive. However, it would not be acceptable and a trust would fail if the trustees were holding assets in such way that the beneficiaries were given an order of priority in choosing an asset from the fund and the beneficiary with the prime choice failed to choose. This would leave uncertainty as to the interests of the secondary beneficiaries and therefore the trust would fail.

Certainty of objects

In the straightforward case where only named beneficiaries are to benefit then the objects are certain. However, if a description label is used rather than named individuals then there is always the danger that the requirements are not met and so there are no individuals who can benefit from the trust.

In the case of charitable trusts the objects are not individuals but the purposes for which the trust is created.

In deciding whether there is certainty of objects a distinction has been made in the courts between trusts where the interests are fixed (i.e. where a beneficiary has an interest in possession in an ascertainable part of the net income of the trust); or discretionary (i.e. where a beneficiary has no absolute current right to direct the trustees to pay him an ascertainable part of the net income of the trust).

The first essential, to avoid a failure of a fixed trust, is to be able to ascertain precisely who is included in the definitions and who is excluded from the definitions. In other words there has to be *conceptual* certainty. For example, a trust to divide the income between the settlor's children is conceptually certain because the law defines who may be included in the definition of 'children'. It is then a factual task to produce a list of who are the relevant children. By contrast, if a settlor was to ask the trustees to divide the income amongst 'my friends' this would be void as it is impossible to distinguish between current friends, old friends, deceased friends, etc.

It is important to note that even where there is conceptual certainty it is still necessary to be able to draw up a list of those who are entitled under the definition of beneficiary. If it is not possible to draw up such a list because the evidence needed to establish the list is incomplete, the trust will still fail for uncertainty.

Since the landmark decision of *McPhail* v. *Doulton* [1970] 2 All ER 228 the test for certainty of objects in a discretionary trust is less stringent than that for fixed trusts in so far as it is not necessary at the outset to be able to produce a list of beneficiaries who are included in the trusts and those who are excluded, but rather it is possible to wait and see whether a particular person is included or not at a time when that person claims an interest.

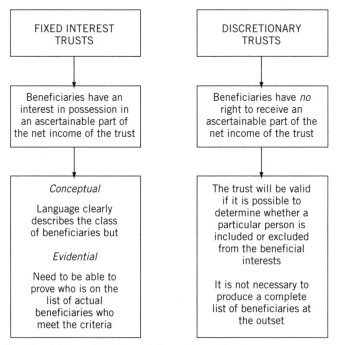

Figure 2.2   Fixed interest trusts and discretionary trusts

Duty of care

It is the duty of the adviser to ensure that the client understands the nature of the client's objective and whether the advice given is appropriate. If the client's objective has various possible solutions each with differing tax consequences, the adviser should carefully point these out. Any limitation on the adviser's retainer will not be successful if the client does not understand the implications of agreeing to the restriction. This is illustrated by the case of *Estill* v. *Cowling Swift & Kitchin* (2000) Lawtel, 26 January, Ch D.

The claimants, the executors of Mrs Estill, who died on 12 May 1994, and the trustees of a discretionary settlement made by her on 22 July 1988, brought actions against the defendants, a firm of solicitors and a Chancery barrister, seeking damages for professional negligence arising out of advice given to Mrs Estill in connection with the setting up of the settlement. She had sought advice about how to deal with her shareholding in a private company such that she would be relieved of day-to-day decisions, but she emphasised that she did not wish to pay *any* tax as a result of any suggested solution to her problem.

The settlement recommended by the solicitor was a discretionary trust which on the facts of the case had resulted in adverse tax consequences. It was not claimed, however, that Mrs Estill would have been better off if the settlement had not been executed, rather that she had suffered loss because the gift of shares was not into an interest in possession trust or a reorganisation of the rights attached to the shares but was an immediately chargeable transfer for IHT.

It was agreed that if the claimants proved their case on liability and causation, namely, that but for the breach of duty by the defendants Mrs Estill would on the balance of probabilities have entered into a PET of one of the types alleged by the claimants, the quantum of the claimants' claim inclusive of interest up to December 1999 was £170,000.

The solicitors sought to claim that their retainer was restricted as they had not professed to be trust specialists and had called on the services of a barrister to prepare the document and advise. They failed to explain the remit of their purported restriction on the retainer and failed to explain to the barrister that the client did not want to pay any IHT on the creation of the trust. The firm simply instructed counsel to prepare a discretionary trust. This was done but counsel failed to explain the taxation consequences of the drafting and how discretionary trusts operated for tax purposes. The law firm did not seek to address this omission in reporting to the client. The court decided that in applying established principles to the facts the defendants and counsel were negligent in the advice they gave to Mrs Estill and the trustees with respect to the settlement, and that if they had not been negligent Mrs Estill would have set up an interest in possession trust, rather than a discretionary settlement and would have saved IHT accordingly.

2.2 HOW IS A TRUST PROPERLY CREATED?

A trust can be constituted by one of two methods.

1. By declaration of trust by the settlor in which he declares that he now holds his assets on trust for somebody else. Here, the settlor is the trustee.
2. The settlor transfers assets to trustees and declares that they hold the property upon trust for his chosen beneficiaries.

In either case the declaration must be irrevocable and completely constituted. In the case of the declaration of trust by the settlor it must be an unequivocal declaration, and in order to avoid it being regarded as a sham it is wise for the settlor to communicate his declaration to the beneficiaries concerned. Otherwise, to the outside world, it would appear as though nothing had changed since with a declaration of trust the settlor is both settlor and trustee of the asset.

In the case of a transfer of assets to trustees to hold upon trust, the settlor must have done all that is necessary to effect the transfer of the property to the trustees or else the trust will be incompletely constituted, with the result that the gift will fail.

If completion of the transfer of the assets was left to a third party and that third party failed to complete it (for example, a transfer of property to the trust was referred to in the trust deed but the solicitors never transferred the legal title to the property from the settlor to the trustees) then the settlor is deemed to hold the asset on trust for the beneficiaries until the trust is completely constituted.

Gifts made into trust during the settlor's lifetime must be completed according to the type of property which is involved in the gift. For example, in the case of registered land, the trustees would need to be registered on the land register as proprietors of the land. This would happen on the day when the appropriate documents were delivered to the Land Registry. If registration is not deemed to have yet taken place but the settlor has done all that is necessary for him to do, such as signing the transfer form and delivering it to the trustees (together with the land certificate, if not already de-materialised), the settlor will be treated exceptionally as holding the property on trust for the beneficiaries.

In the case of a trust gift under a will, then as long as the will is valid and any debts and expenses or other liabilities do not cause the gift to be exhausted the PRs of the deceased settlor must again vest the assets in the names of the trustees to be held for the benefit of the beneficiaries. Note that until the subject matter of the trust has been ascertained beneficiaries simply have a chose in action as against the PRs and not an equitable interest under the trust.

Any type of asset may be included in a trust gift unless it is illegal to transfer assets of that type under the law or the asset concerned is foreign land and the trusts would undermine the law of the jurisdiction in which the land is situated, e.g. that country's forced heirship rules.

It therefore follows that a trust will be void if it is created for an illegal purpose, for example, it would breach the perpetuities or accumulation of income rules or was attempting to oust the jurisdiction of the courts under say the divorce rules or Inheritance (Provision for Family and Dependants) Act 1975 (IPFDA 1975) claims.

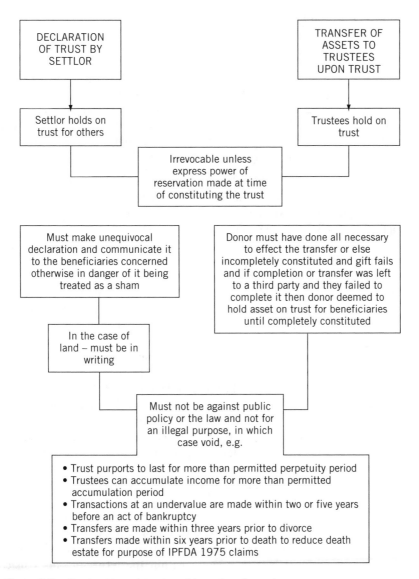

Figure 2.3 Declaration of trust and transfer of assets

2.3 TRUSTEES' POWERS

Implied powers

Given that trusts can arise by operation of law, e.g. under the intestacy rules, just as much as they can arise by way of express trusts, then the law has to provide certain default powers of an administrative nature to enable the trustees to carry out their task. The trustees' implied powers, particularly delegation and investment powers, were substantially improved by the Trustee Act 2000 and currently include the following.

1. *Advancements* (s.32, Trustee Act 1925). Trustees may at their sole discretion advance capital up to one-half of the beneficiary's presumptive share to be applied for his advancement or benefit. Where a surviving spouse has a life interest in the fund in question the consent of that spouse is required in writing to any such advancements of capital. When the beneficiary becomes absolutely entitled to his share any such advancement has to be taken into account in distributing the final capital sums.

2. *Delegation.* In certain circumstances trustees can employ and pay an agent to transact business done in the execution of the trust, for example, organising insurance or collecting money (s.23, Trustee Act 1925). It is also possible for a trustee to delegate his powers by way of power of attorney for a period not exceeding 12 months (s.25(1), Trustee Act 1925). Since the introduction of the Trusts of Land and Appointment of Trustees Act 1996 (TLATA 1996) on 1 January 1997 there is a further ability to delegate to a beneficiary who has an interest in possession certain trust powers under s.9 of that Act. Sections 11–23 of the Trustee Act 2000 (with effect from 1 February 2001) have extensively improved the ability of the trustees to delegate part of their management function to agents, nominees and custodians upon certain conditions.

3. *Insurance.* Section 19 of the Trustee Act 1925 permits trustees to insure against loss or damage by fire of any building or other insured property. The Trustee Act 2000 extends the original provisions to allow for 100 per cent cover and the premiums may be paid from capital or income.

4. *Investment.* Prior to the Trustee Act 2000, in the absence of express powers the trustees had to operate within the terms of the Trustee Investment Act 1961. This was unduly restrictive and it was therefore common practice in an express trust to widen the powers to permit trustees to invest in any suitable type of investment as if they were an absolute owner. This is now the case for all investments other than land by virtue of s.3 of the Trustee Act 2000. The TLATA 1996 provides a more limited default power to invest in land.

5. *Maintenance.* Section 31 of the Trustee Act 1925 authorises the trustees to apply the whole of the income of a trust fund for the maintenance, education or benefit of the beneficiary. Any income that is arising in the

trust, which is not used for the maintenance and advancement of minor children, must be accumulated. Section 31 applies where the beneficiary will be entitled to the income (i.e. the beneficiary has a vested interest in the income). In the case of a contingent interest (i.e. some limitation has to be satisfied before a vested interest is gained), s.31(3) states that it will only apply if the limitation or trust carries with it the 'intermediate' income in respect of the property.

6. *Infants.* Trustees generally are not entitled to transfer assets to infants because they cannot give a valid receipt for capital monies. However, under s.31 of the Trustee Act 1925 trustees are authorised to apply income for the maintenance of an infant beneficiary and such payments may be made to the parent or guardian of the child. Section 32 also authorises trustees to advance capital up to a maximum one-half of the fund.

7. *Land.* Trustees have extensive powers to sell trust property. The functions of trustees in relation to land in the trust are implied in s.6 of the TLATA 1996. Section 10 of that Act provides that if the consent of more than two people is required in exercise of any of their functions relating to land, a purchaser from trustees needs only to satisfy himself that the consent of any two of the people giving consent has actually been obtained. There are also some implied duties under the Act imposed on trustees to consult with beneficiaries who are of full age and beneficially entitled to an interest in possession in the land, so far as practicable. This duty can be expressly excluded.

Express powers

In creating express trusts it is common practice to amend the implied powers and to add to them. For example, if the settlor is transferring business assets to the trust the trustees will need to have some powers to carry on the business. Most precedent books for wills and trusts contain examples of suitable administrative provisions.

The Society of Trust and Estate Practitioners (STEP) was founded in 1991 and has grown rapidly into an international professional body. It commissioned James Kessler QC to produce some standard administrative clauses which could be incorporated into settlements and wills, by reference, so as to enable these documents to be shortened and simplified. These provisions were published in 1995 and have become widely used. They are known as the Society of Trust and Estate Practitioners Standard Provisions (first edition). They can be incorporated by reference into any will or trust document by use of the clause: 'The Standard Provisions of the Society of Trust and Estate Practitioners (first edition) shall apply.'

However, the Standard Provisions *do* need to be amended in the following respects.

1. If the intended settlor or testator wishes to include an interest in posses-
    sion trust and provide for the trustees to have power to appoint capital
    to the life tenant, it will be necessary to add this clause since the STEP
    provisions do not include it. It has not been included in the Standard
    Provisions because it is such an important dispositive power that whether
    or not it is needed in any particular case should be discussed with the
    settlor.
2. The first edition was produced prior to the coming into force of the
    TLATA 1996 and therefore the following is suggested as standard in the
    light of that Act: 'The Standard Provisions of the Society of Trust and
    Estate Practitioners (first edition) shall apply with the deletion of para-
    graph 5. Section 11 of the Trusts of Land and Appointment of Trustees
    Act 1996 (consultation with beneficiaries) shall not apply.'

It is important when using the Standard Provisions to draw to the client's
attention the fact that they include a power for the professional executors and
trustees to charge for the work done.

The trustees of a trust are not individuals but a continuing body of people
who were entrusted either by the settlor personally or deemed to be appointed
by a court or through operation of law to hold the legal estate of the trust
property on trust for the benefit of the beneficiaries. In order to enable them
to carry out their task effectively the trustees need to be empowered to
manage the trust property effectively.

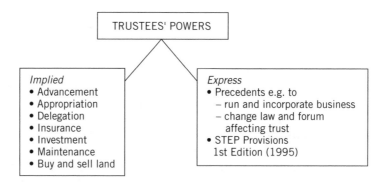

Figure 2.4   Trustees' powers

Powers retained by the settlor

It is common practice in offshore jurisdictions and it is also becoming
increasingly the case in the UK that *inter vivos* trusts will reserve some of the
powers which might have traditionally been given to the trustees in favour of
the settlor.

Where professional trustees or a trust corporation are appointed to the role of trustee then there is the danger that no one who actually knows the beneficiaries and their families will actually be involved in the day-to-day management of the trusts. For these reasons the settlor, who has given up any rights and interests in his assets to the trustees, may feel that he wishes to be consulted personally over certain major decisions while he is alive. Care must be taken not to reserve too many powers to the settlor since the more powers he retains the more likely it is that it will look as though the trust is a sham. In an extreme case, all that may have been done is to change the name of the owners to the trustees, but effectively all decision-making powers have been left to the settlor. In this extreme example, the trustees will be little more than nominees.

A common power that has been used in tax planning recently is the power to revoke the trust. This was done in the case of *Melville & Others* v. *IRC* [2001] EWCA Civ 1247.

The settlor made a discretionary settlement on 3 December 1993 with a transfer of £10 into trust. The settlement included the settlor as a potential beneficiary and conferred on him, after 90 days had elapsed, a power to direct the trustees to exercise any one of their discretionary powers of appointment, including the power to transfer all or any part of the trust fund to the settlor absolutely.

On 22 and 23 February 1994 the settlor transferred cash (£6,000) and securities (923,077 Development Securities plc ordinary shares and £11.1m unsecured loan notes 2000) to the trustees to be held on the terms of the trust. The transfers were chargeable transfers for IHT purposes. The question to be decided was what was the amount of the transfer of value by the settlor: was it the full value of the assets leaving his ownership to go into the trust; or the 90 days' use of these assets, given that the power to direct all the fund to the settlor was power which he could exercise over the whole fund after 90 days had expired.

The Inland Revenue (as it was still known) argued that the statutory context for the treatment of settled property did not permit general powers of appointment over settled property to be treated as 'property' but required them to be ignored for IHT purposes. The Court of Appeal decided that the IHT scheme charges tax on chargeable transfers by individuals. They also identified the holder of a general power of appointment as having an unquestionably valuable right, the value of which must be taken into account in assessing the amount of any chargeable transfer.

Clearly, the use of this tool was to achieve CGT holdover relief on the transfer of the securities into the discretionary trust whilst minimising the impact of IHT. The fact that there was a reservation of a right in favour of the settlor would have meant that at this stage there would have been a gift with reservation of benefit (GROB) for IHT purposes but doubtless it was part of the plan to then give away the right either outright or to another trust which would have been a PET by the settlor.

The Inland Revenue reversed this decision in the Finance Act 2002, advising that if it did not take this step then unfortunately there would be the need to charge IHT on the estates of people who enjoyed a power of appointment over trust assets – which at the time the Inland Revenue did not assess to IHT.

Other common powers which are sometimes reserved to the settlor include the following.

1. The power to appoint or remove trustees.
2. The power to add and remove beneficiaries from the class.
3. The power to alter administrative provisions.
4. A power to restrict the exercise of the trustees' discretions.

In recent years there has been debate about whether an arrangement can be a true trust where the person or persons holding the trustees to account in the exercise of their powers is a person other than a member of the class of beneficiaries. It has been a feature of English trust law that the relationship between the trustees and beneficiaries rests on the ability of the beneficiaries to apply to the courts to have their beneficial interests enforced against the trustees. If the person who is vested with the power to enforce is not a member of the beneficial class, the question has been raised as to whether or not it can be a true trust. Professor David Hayton in his article 'The irreducible core content of trusteeship' (in A.J. Oakley (ed.), *Trends in Contemporary Trust Law* (OUP, 1996) p.47) concluded:

> The essential ingredient of trusteeship is the duty to account which affords the beneficiaries a correlative right to have the court enforce the trustees fundamental obligation to account.

More recently Professor Hayton has been criticised for suggesting that it is possible to provide a third party such as a trust protector with the right to call the trustees to account. (See Paul Matthews, 'From obligation to property and back again?' in D.J. Hayton (ed.), *Extending the Boundaries of Trusts and Similar Ring-Fenced Funds* (Kluwer Law International, 2002).)

Until there is case law defining the extent to which powers can be reserved to the settlor without undermining the very essence of a real trust it would be wise to take care in the drafting of trusts to ensure that the extent of reserved powers is not so extensive as to create a sham.

2.4 DRAFTING POINTS

Taking instructions – settlor's goals

It is vital to ascertain what it is that the settlor is trying to achieve. The case of *Estill* v. *Cowling Swift & Kitchin* mentioned earlier at p.26 illustrates well that a failure to do this can result in the draftsman being held to have been negligent.

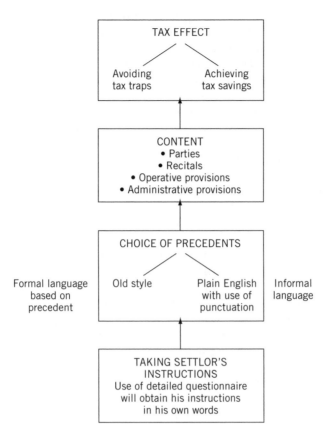

Figure 2.5   Drafting points

Given that once a trust is set up the negligence may not be spotted for some time to come, another consequence will be the problem of dealing with unhappy beneficiaries, particularly where there is little or no flexibility to make changes to improve the situation.

For these reasons it makes sense to use a detailed questionnaire (see the Trust Instruction Sheet in **Appendix 2.3**) to obtain the settlor's specific instructions in his own words.

Flexibility

A settlement needs to be flexible to enable the trustees to reflect changes both amongst the beneficiaries and in the tax system. This is particularly important as the Chancellor announced on 10 December 2003 a consultation regarding the tax treatment of trusts which has only been partially enacted in 2005 and may yet produce further changes in 2006.

Sufficient flexibility may be achieved through the judicious use of over-riding powers of appointment. A simple interest in possession trust can be made more interesting and useful if overriding powers enable the trustees to rewrite the trusts of the settlement as appropriate in the light of changes to the beneficiaries' circumstances or changes in the tax law. It is generally regarded as cheaper to administer an interest in possession trust because on the whole it is a simpler mechanism, but often it will not be possible for the settlor to choose this trust if an *inter vivos* settlement is required, as it can be an expensive trust to create from a CGT point of view, as transferring chargeable assets into the trust will be a chargeable disposal for CGT purposes as far as the settlor is concerned. An immediate chargeable gain will arise on the gift to the trustees unless the settlor has unused losses to set against the gain, or the assets are business assets when any gain would be covered by a combination of business asset taper relief and business asset holdover relief.

From an IHT point of view, if the chosen beneficiaries are such that the three conditions contained within s.71 of the IHTA 1984 can be met, an A&M trust would have advantages over a discretionary trust. However the discretionary trust is more flexible. With a discretionary trust it is possible to have, for example, a much wider category of beneficiaries and this has the advantage from a CGT point of view of being an immediately chargeable transfer when created during the lifetime of the settlor, whereas the A&M trust is a potentially exempt transfer. Again, the effect of this is that assets transferred to a discretionary trust may have the advantage of s.260, TCGA 1992 holdover relief whereas transferring similar chargeable assets to an A&M trust would not carry with it the same relief and could therefore create a charge to IHT.

Nevertheless, for some clients the A&M trust may be attractive, particu-larly if they are transferring cash to the trust, as this would remove the need for the complicated IHT charging structure to which discretionary trusts are subject. Generally speaking, the greater the flexibility afforded, the greater the likelihood of higher administrative costs and potentially higher tax costs. Clients should be made aware of this so that they can assess just how much flexibility would be sufficient.

Revocable or irrevocable?

The danger of not expressing a trust to be irrevocable is that when a trust is created during the lifetime of the settlor, the act of revoking the trust would be to return the assets contained in the trust to the settlor. Whilst the settlor might welcome the opportunity to call back the assets, the tax consequences will generally be unacceptable. It would be unusual to find a modern English *inter vivos* trust that was expressed to be revocable although a power of revocation might be used for tax planning purposes.

For the avoidance of doubt the draftsman will usually express the creation of the trust to be irrevocable and may reserve a power of revocation to the settlor if this is thought necessary.

Punctuation

Until quite recently it was usual to find no punctuation in any legal documents, least of all trusts. However, the more modern trust precedents do include punctuation, which definitely makes it easier for a layman to follow a trust document. However, punctuation can change meaning and a mistake in typing a word is perhaps more likely to be noticed than a mistaken piece of punctuation.

If a court has to construe the document, it may be that it construes it completely differently from what was intended because of the inclusion of punctuation. On balance, the use of punctuation should be considered but kept to a minimum and used only to aid comprehension.

Administrative provisions

All the major precedent books include a set of administrative provisions. Indeed most of them include two versions, a short version and a longer one. Whilst the administrative provisions will often add many pages to a trust document, it certainly makes the life of the trust administrator easier if all the provisions are set out in the trust deed.

The Society of Trust and Estate Practitioners Standard Provisions which were mentioned earlier at p.31 are often incorporated by reference, particularly in wills. This shortens the length of the will and makes the use of these provisions attractive. Although legal shorthand is sometimes to be welcomed it does mean that the trust administrator must have to hand whatever version of these provisions has been incorporated by reference into the deed. For these reasons the preferred approach is either to set out all the provisions within the document or to keep a copy of the incorporated provisions with the trust deed.

Apart from simple estates it is usually best to use the longer version of administrative provisions in the precedent books, so that the trustees will have sufficient powers to cover most eventualities in administering the trust fund. It is, of course, hard to envisage all the uses to which the fund and its assets may be put in the future, particularly if the trust lasts for 80 years. However a popular administrative provision to include is the ability for the trustees to amend the administrative provisions so that the trustees can vary the trust without the need to make a court application.

Excluding or modifying the duty of care

Trustees have a duty to act with care and skill in the administration of a trust. If the trustees fail to do this and loss is caused to the trust fund then a beneficiary may have a right to apply to the courts for a breach of this duty. Historically the duty was imposed by the common law but the Trustee Act 2000 introduced a statutory duty of care for the first time. Section 1 of and Sched.1 to the 2000 Act introduced the statutory duty of care that applies to the exercise of powers and the performance of duties imposed by the 2000 Act. This statutory duty of care is not of general application so the common law duty applies still to those areas outside the Trustee Act 2000 provisions.

The duties of trustees are examined in Chapter 3 but as far as drafting is concerned there have been several recent cases addressing the validity of exemption clauses and much has been written and commented upon as to whether or not a professional trustee can validly exclude liability for gross negligence or worse by use of such an exemption or an exoneration clause.

Section 30 of the Trustee Act 1925 exempts a trustee from liability for certain types of breach of trust except in the case of wilful default. To be guilty of 'wilful default' the trustee must 'be conscious that, in doing the act complained of or in omitting to do the act which it is said he ought to have done, he is committing a breach of his duty, or is recklessly careless whether it is a breach of his duty or not' (per Maughan J in *Re Vickery* [1931] 1 CL 572.)

There are two different kinds of clause which are used in the precedents.

1. A clause which excludes the liability of the trustee for having committed a breach of trust, for example 'no trustee shall be liable for any loss or damage (to the capital or income of the trust fund) at any time or from any cause whatsoever unless such loss or damage shall be caused by his own actual fraud' – taken from clause 15 in the settlement the subject of *Armitage* v. *Nurse* [1997] 2 All ER 705.
2. A clause which does not exclude the liability but excludes or reduces the duty, so there cannot be a liability, e.g. 'the trustee shall have no responsibility or duty with respect to the property until the death of the survivor of the testator's very elderly brother and sister' – *Hayim* v. *Citibank* [1987] AC 730.

The Law Commission was asked to investigate trustee exemption clauses following the coming into effect of the Trustee Act 2000. A consultation document was issued on 2 December 2002 with comments invited by 1 May 2003. Although final recommendations are awaited, the provisional proposals indicated that the Law Commission felt that the current law was too deferential to trustees, particularly professional trustees. The

Commission went on to propose that a distinction should be drawn between the professional trustee and the lay trustee. The Commission's view is that professionals should not be able to rely on clauses which exclude their liability for breach of trust arising from negligence. Nor would they in those circumstances be able to claim indemnity from the trust fund.

Since one type of trustee exoneration clause is to remove the duty from trustees, the Law Commission advises that the courts should have the power to disapply duty exclusion clauses where reliance on such clauses would be inconsistent with the overall purposes of the trust and it would be unreasonable for the trustee in the circumstances to be exempted from liability.

Given the current uncertainty the following points should be noted.

1. Exemption clauses should only be used in special circumstances.
2. A typical special case would be where there were only unpaid trustees. However, arguably s.61 of the Trustee Act 1925 would relieve any unpaid trustee where the trustee acted 'honestly and reasonably'.
3. A draftsman acting for trustees rather than a settlor would be right to include a wide exclusion clause to protect his client but the effect of the clause would need to be explained to and approved by the settlor, preferably in writing.
4. Paid trustees *can*, for the moment at least, absolve themselves from liability resulting from breaches of their duties of skill, care, prudence and diligence provided that the clause is drawn to the attention of the settlor who understands its effect and approves it.
5. If there are any doubts or conflicts in the wording and application of any exclusion clauses the courts will decide against the protection offered to the trustees.
6. The STEP Standard Provisions restrict liability to unpaid trustees for acts of negligence only. Clause 12(1) states 'a capital trustee (other than a Professional Trustee) shall not be liable for loss to the Trust Fund unless that loss was caused by his own fraud or negligence'. It does not protect professional trustees nor does it protect any trustee affected by strict liability offences.

2.5   LIFETIME CREATION OR 'ON DEATH'

The significant differences between creating a trust during lifetime and on death will be the tax opportunities and traps.

If a trust is created on death, the settlor, by definition, has died so the tax anti-avoidance traps do not apply. If a trust is created during the settlor's lifetime there are CGT considerations as well as IHT considerations but there is the possibility that if the settlor lives another seven years, the opportunity to use a new nil rate band for IHT purposes will be gained.

Anti-avoidance traps which affect lifetime creation

1. If the settlor or the settlor's spouse (and possibly in the future civil part-
    ners) retains an interest in the trust fund, income and gains will be
    assessed on the settlor (s.625, Income Tax (Trading and Other Income)
    Act 2005 (ITTOIA 2005) and ss.77–79, TCGA 1992). Retaining a benefit
    is widely defined so if property or any derived property is, or will, or may
    become, payable to or applicable for the benefit of the settlor or spouse
    in any circumstances whatsoever, the settlor is treated as retaining a
    benefit. There is an exception to this in s.625(2) where a settlor may
    become entitled to settled property as a result of a disposition by or the
    bankruptcy or death of a beneficiary in certain circumstances. The recent
    case of *Unmarried Settlor* v. *IRC* [2003] WTLR 915 illustrated that even
    where the settlor was a homosexual and was in a stable long-term same-
    sex relationship at the time of the creation of the settlement the court
    was entitled to assume that since the spouse of the settlor was not
    excluded from benefit the settlor's circumstances were not such that he
    would *never* marry. As a result, since it was possible for the spouse of the
    settlor to benefit under the terms of the settlement, the settlor had an
    interest in it and therefore the trust gains could be both attributed to and
    taxed on him.
2. If the settlement is created for the benefit of the settlor's children, any
    income paid out to infant, unmarried children will be assessed as the
    settlor's (but not income that is accumulated). Payments of capital will also
    be treated as income of the settlor to the extent that they can be matched
    against undistributed income (s.631(1), (2) and (3), ITTOIA 2005).
3. If the settlor is not excluded from benefit the reservation of benefit rules
    will apply for IHT purposes. The property will be treated for IHT as part
    of the settlor's estate on death. This is disastrous as it will be included at
    its death value so there is no 'asset freezing' advantage to making the
    transfer. Moreover, the asset is included only for IHT purposes, so for
    CGT purposes it does not form part of the estate and will not benefit
    from the tax-free uplift on the settlor's death. The same rule applies if the
    settlor's spouse (as spouse rather than as widow) is included in any
    discretionary trust class of beneficiaries.

So as not to fall foul of these provisions, a settlement made during the
settlor's lifetime will normally contain at least two references to the exclusion
of the settlor and the settlor's spouse. These will be found in the following
places.

1. In the power to add beneficiaries – stating that the power will not be used
    to add the settlor or the settlor's spouse.
2. In the exercise of the trustees' powers contained in the administrative
    provisions.

In addition, to ensure that an *inter vivos* discretionary trust is not void for perpetuity and there is no prospect of the trust fund reverting to the settlor (because at the end of the trust period there may still be some assets left for distribution) it is essential to make sure that there is an effective ultimate default clause; that is, the beneficiary chosen to receive any undistributed assets at the end of the perpetuity period must be living at the date of the creation of the trust and be given a vested interest in the trust fund, e.g. 'to X absolutely'. In this way if the chosen beneficiary is no longer living at the end of the perpetuity period the gift falls into the deceased beneficiary's estate and does not revert to the settlor's own estate.

Suggested procedural steps when creating a trust during lifetime

1. Obtain a copy of the settlor's passport and recent utility bill (less than one month old) to confirm the identity of the client and confirm the source of funds to be transferred to the trust in compliance with the Money Laundering Regulations 2003 and the Proceeds of Crime Act 2002.
2. Provide the client with an estimate of costs, and if you are a solicitor, comply with Rule 15 procedures.
3. Take clear instructions and ascertain which assets are to be transferred to the trust. A valuation will usually be required.
4. If a chargeable transfer is made, for IHT purposes complete IHT100 and send it to HMRC Capital Taxes by the later of:

    (a) twelve months after the end of the month in which the transfer took place; and
    (b) three months after the date on which the person delivering the account became liable to IHT.

5. IHT is due on chargeable transfers made between 6 April and 30 September in any year by 30 April in the next year. On transfers made between 1 October and 5 April it is due by the sixth month after the end of the month in which the chargeable transfer is made. Tax paid late is subject to interest and that interest is not deductible for income tax purposes, so it can be expensive to delay payment.
6. Compute the amount of CGT, if any, arising as a result of giving a chargeable asset into a trust and agree the calculation with the settlor's tax office as soon as possible after the creation of the trust by completion of form CGT34. If the gain is to be held over rather than the tax paid at the time, submit the last two pages of helpsheet IR295 which contain the holdover computation form. This should be submitted to the settlor's own tax office before CGT is due, which will be on 31 January following the end of the tax year in which the disposal to the trust was made.

41

7. Notify the trust tax office (i.e. *not* HMRC Capital Taxes) of the creation of the trust by sending in Form 41G with Form 64-8 if you are acting as the trustees' agent for income tax and CGT purposes. See further **Chapter 8** and **Appendix 1.5**.

8. Deal with any transfers of assets to the trust from the settlor to the trustees and register the title of real property in their names.

9. A stamp duty stock transfer form with suitable exclusion will be relevant to transfers for stocks and shares, but note that stamp duty no longer applies from 1 December 2003 to transactions in land. Only if there is a transfer of land (for money or money's worth) will Stamp Duty Land Tax apply to the transfer. There is still a £5 fixed stamp duty fee on the actual trust deed itself where stocks and shares are transferred to the trustees.

10. Issue your invoice.

11. Ensure that the trust administrator has all the information required to set up the administration procedures – see **Chapter 4**.

12. Close your file when your invoice has been paid.

CHAPTER 3

Trustees

3.1 APPOINTMENT AND RETIREMENT OF TRUSTEES

In express trusts the starting point for the appointment of trustees is Part III of the Trustee Act 1925. In it we are advised that trustees of land must not number more than four (s.34) and usually shall not be less than two in number unless a trust corporation (s.37(1)(c)). Given that often the beneficial class will contain minor beneficiaries the settlor will usually wish to appoint at least two trustees to manage the trust fund who can provide a valid receipt for capital monies should any assets in the fund be sold while those minor children are under 18.

In wills, the testator will frequently appoint the same people to be both the executors and the trustees of any ongoing trusts. It should be remembered that this may not always be appropriate, because:

1. The task of administering the testator's estate might well be over within a few years whereas the management of the trust has the potential to last up to 80 years (depending on the terms of the trust and its specified perpetuity period). It might therefore be viewed differently by those appointed, and someone who would be willing to be responsible for the administration of the estate might feel the longer commitment for the trusteeship would be too great a burden.
2. The nature of the powers and directions given to the executors and trustees is such that they need to enter into contractual relations with each other which may be inherently in conflict, or the desire to have a binding contract necessitates that the contracting parties should differ (s.82, Law of Property Act 1925). This is of particular relevance when implementing the nil rate band discretionary trust debt scheme: see **Chapter 14**.

The settlor in an *inter vivos* trust will transfer the trust property to the named trustees and in so doing appoint them as trustees of the fund, putting them in charge of the management of those assets for the benefit of the settlor's chosen beneficiaries.

Once the trustees are appointed, either by will or lifetime trust instrument they act as a body which can be added to, changed or reduced save that in principle they must be between two and four in number, and they must be adult and competent. The power of appointing new or additional trustees is often specified in the trust deed. Sometimes with lifetime trusts there is a power for the settlor to choose new trustees and even nominate who might in future make the choice after the settlor's death.

Given that statutory trusts arise where there are no trust documents in which to include an express provision, for example in the case of intestacy, there has to be a default position. This is set out in s.36 of the Trustee Act 1925, which states that where a trustee:

(a) is dead;
(b) remains out of the UK for more than 12 months;
(c) wishes to be discharged;
(d) refuses to act;
(e) is unfit to act;
(f) is incapable of acting; or
(g) is an infant

then, if there is no person nominated by the trust instrument to be responsible for appointing new trustees or if that person is not able and willing to act, the surviving or continuing trustees or trustee for the time being or the PRs of the last surviving or continuing trustee will appoint the new trustee.

Any appointment of a new trustee should be in writing and there are any number of precedents available to meet the common situations. See, for example *Practical Trust Precedents* (Sweet & Maxwell, looseleaf).

Under s.40 of the Trustee Act 1925 certain types of property vest automatically in the new trustees as a result of their appointment, e.g. freehold land and bank accounts. Unfortunately, this automatic vesting does not apply to stocks and shares, and thus when a new trustee is appointed it will be necessary to ensure that the trust assets are properly vested in the current body of trustees. With the use of nominee companies to hold trust share portfolios to aid discretionary management of the investments this is made easier since there can be a single notification to the nominee company rather than notifying the company registrar of every holding held by the trust. Clearly, where the assets are not held by a nominee company, stock transfer forms will be required to be completed for each holding.

There may be other circumstances where the new trustees have to give notice of the new trusteeship. For example, where the trustees lease land the landlord will usually require not only that his permission is sought to the change but also that he is informed when the change has taken place. Also, there may be grant-making bodies involved, such as government departments, which may have placed conditions on earlier agreements between themselves and the trustees. It may be necessary to give notice to such bodies of the change, in order to release the retiring trustees from any such conditions and to substitute the new trustees.

Under s.41 of the Trustee Act 1925 a court may 'whenever it is expedient to appoint a new trustee or new trustees, and it is found inexpedient difficult or impracticable to do so without the assistance of the court' make an order appointing a new trustee or new trustees either in substitution for or in addition to any existing trustees, or where there is no existing trustee.

Section 41(1) specifically envisages making an order where a trustee has become incapable by reason of mental disorder within the meaning of the Mental Health Act 1983 of exercising his functions as trustee, or is bankrupt, or is a corporation which is in liquidation or has been dissolved.

Since 1 January 1997, when the Trusts of Land and Appointment of Trustees Act 1996 (TLATA 1996) came into force, additional means for appointing new trustees arose. By s.19(2) of the TLATA 1996 the benefici-aries of a trust may give a direction to the trustees for the time being or the PRs of the last trustee if there are currently none, appointing the person(s) specified in the direction.

Beneficiaries can only so direct if:

1. there is no person nominated for the purpose of appointing new trustees by the instrument, if any, creating the trust, *and*
2. the beneficiaries under the trust are of full age and capacity and (taken together) are absolutely entitled to the property the subject of the trust.

Where there is no person who is both entitled and willing and able to appoint a trustee under s.36 of the Trustee Act 1925, the same beneficiaries can, again by written direction, require the appointment of a substitute trustee if a trustee is incapable by reason of mental disorder of exercising his functions as a trustee.

In this situation the beneficiaries' written direction needs to be given to the trustee's:

1. receiver; or
2. attorney who is registered under s.6 of the Enduring Powers of Attorney Act 1985; or
3. person authorised for the purpose by the authority having jurisdiction under Part VII of the Mental Health Act 1983.

When it comes to the appointment of a new trustee the trust administrator will therefore need to:

1. check the trust instrument to see if anyone is nominated to choose who should be a trustee or if any statutory provisions are excluded, such as s.19 of the TLATA 1996; or
2. see if s.36 of the Trustee Act 1925 provides the options; or
3. see if ss.19 or 21 TLATA 1996 applies; or

4. decide whether an application to court is required under s.41 of the Trustee Act 1925.

Unless the appointment of a new trustee has occurred as a result of the death of a trustee, a common situation where an appointment will be needed is because a trustee wishes to retire from office. Obviously, as long as at least two trustees remain in office (or there is a trust corporation) there is no requirement to appoint a replacement.

One of the areas of contention when a trustee seeks to retire is the question of whether he should be discharged from his duties under the trust and indemnified against any breaches of trust. Paragraph 1 of the Trust Law Committee consultation paper of December 1999 summarised it this way:

> Because trusts are not legal entities that can sue or be sued it is the trustees who are personally liable for contractual, tortious or tax liabilities incurred by the trustees acting as trustees (except to the extent that a contracting party may relieve the trustees of personal liability if recourse to the trust fund is inadequate). Thus if T1 ceases to be a trustee and T2 becomes trustee, T1 remains personally liable in respect of events occurring while it was trustee, T2 only becoming liable for events occurring after taking over from T1. Personal liability attaches to the person who was trustee rather than representative liability attaching to whoever holds the office of trustee from time to time. While T1 is trustee, T1 can directly discharge properly incurred liabilities out of the trust fund or discharge the liability itself and reimburse itself out of the trust fund.

It is therefore a concern to a retiring trustee that he is adequately protected against matters such as tax liabilities, the due dates for payment of which may well be after the proposed retirement date. If the trustee's retirement is voluntary, then presumably he will be advised not to retire until his interests have been properly protected. In this regard the trustee should seek independent advice. However, given that a trustee could be replaced or removed by order of the court under s.41 of the Trustee Act 1925, or removed at the direction of certain beneficiaries under s.19 of the TLATA 1996 it is not always possible for the trustee to control what happens on his retirement.

Section 19(3)(b) of the TLATA 1996 does permit a trustee to remain in office until 'reasonable arrangements' have been made for his protection. Otherwise, the court might have to give directions as to what might represent adequate or reasonable protection as part of its order. For example:

1. the retiring trustee might be well advised to retain control over sufficient assets in the trust to cover the likely risks; or
2. the trust assets might be transferred to the replacement trustees with an express indemnity covenant from the new trustee to the retiring trustee; or
3. the retiring trustee could take a legal or equitable charge over specific trust assets.

A trust administrator is recommended to consider the following before dealing with the retirement of a trustee:

1. Check the trust records for any potential liabilities which will affect the retiring trustee's position.
2. Check the trust instrument to see what, if any, exoneration clauses are present which would protect the retiring trustee and would provide a reason for resisting any request by the retiring trustee for a new indemnity from a replacement trustee.
3. Consider what advice the continuing trustees and any new trustee will need to respond to requests for instructions upon the wording of any indemnity requested by the retiring trustee. The retiring trustee may seek a wide and non-specific indemnity such as covering all liabilities that he is forced to discharge, whereas the continuing trustees and the replacement trustee should try and limit the retiring trustee's protection to no more than the trust assets at the time when any claim is made by the retiring trustee.

3.2 DUTIES OF TRUSTEES

Duties and obligations imposed on trustees

Upon the creation of a trust, the trustees become the legal owners of the trust property. Legal title is separate from the ownership of the beneficial interests. Those beneficial interests will be identified in the trust deed (formal settlement deed or will) and may be affected by statute or, in the case of property, by the wording of the conveyance transferring the property to the trustees. It is central to our understanding of what a trust constitutes that given this division between legal and equitable ownership a trustee must honour certain duties and obligations imposed by law in the management of the trust assets, which may be modified by the terms of the trust instrument.

Unfortunately for the individual, if a trustee fails to carry out these duties to the correct standard, personal liability will follow.

1. Information gathering

On being appointed, a trustee should enquire as to the nature of the property, the nature of the trusts affecting it and the whereabouts of the trust documents. He must satisfy himself that the affairs of the trust are in order and that no breach of trust has occurred; if a breach has taken place, steps must be taken to remedy the breach as soon as possible and recoup any loss. For example, on taking office a trustee discovers that a Grade I listed building owned by the trust is in disrepair, in breach of the listing arrangements, and so the trustee must investigate ways in which the property can be restored or sold in order to minimise the risk of enforcement orders being made against the trust.

2. Follow the trust deed

A trustee should clarify the terms of the trust deed and must carry out its terms unless a different course of action is authorised by the courts. For example, on taking office a trustee discovers that income has been accumulated beyond the trust's specified age for vesting because the original trustees were trying to accommodate the concerns of the settlor's spouse about the behaviour of a beneficiary. The new trustee must arrange for the mis-direction to be corrected or, if still possible, investigate the possibility of varying the terms of the trust.

3. Act impartially

A trustee must not show preference between beneficiaries. Conflicts of interest can occur where some of the beneficiaries are trustees and some are not. For example, the landlords of a business property are trustees of a trust, one of them is a beneficiary who is interested in the capital value of the property and the return it is likely to generate, whereas the other beneficiary is running a business from the premises and is paying the rent. It is far more important for the second beneficiary to generate a profit from the business than to receive rental income. For him a low rent is what is required. The trustees should seek the best price possible unless the trust deed directs otherwise. This may bring the trustee beneficiary into conflict with the non-trustee beneficiary.

4. Dispose of wasting and reversionary property, other than land

A trust is managed for the benefit of the beneficiaries and trustees are charged with making a return on the investments to this end. If the trust fund contains assets of negligible value or benefit or which can only go down in value, then in the absence of any direction to the contrary in the trust instrument a prudent trustee will ensure that these assets are disposed of promptly.

5. Balance the interests of a life tenant against those interested in remainder

This important concept has recently been the subject of review by the Law Commission (*Capital and Income in Trusts: Classification and Apportionment* Consultation Paper No.175; see **www.lawcom.gov.uk/files/cp175.pdf**) which said:

The duty to keep what Wilberforce J refers to as 'an equitable balance' is variously known as 'the duty of even-handedness', 'the duty of impartiality' or 'the duty to keep a fair balance'. The duty broadly requires trustees of trusts in succession, when exercising any of their powers under the trust, to strike a balance, so far as is possible, between the competing interests of the income and capital beneficiaries. In other words, trustees must 'be even-handed and not seek to promote the interests of one class over the other'.

6. Payment of outgoings

The general principles until the Trustee Act 2000 were that the income of the trust must bear current expenses including the interest payable on loans. If current income is insufficient, arrears of interest on capital charges must be paid out of subsequent income. Repairs to freehold properties to save them from destruction come out of capital, as do the costs incidental to the administration and protection of the trust property, including the taking of legal proceedings. The above Law Commission report has also made some recommendations as to the treatment of expenses.

Section 31 of the Trustee Act 2000 provides that a trustee is entitled to be reimbursed from the trust funds, or may pay out of trust funds, expenses properly incurred by him when acting on behalf of the trust. There is a school of thought that says that this has produced a change in the law as it makes no distinction between income and capital expenditure, simply suggesting that any expense may be deducted from any part of the trust income or capital. Whitehouse and Hassell in *Trusts of Land, Trustee Delegation and the Trustee Act 2000*, 2nd Edn (Butterworths, 2001) say at page 282:

> Such a conclusion does not seem warranted by the terms of the section: indeed it is thought that the wording is little different from that in the Trustee Act 1925, s.30(2) which it has replaced. It is therefore suggested that all the section does is to give trustees the power to discharge expenses or to reimburse themselves out of either the income or capital of the trust fund but does not address the question of whether the burden of that expense should then rest with the income or with the capital. The trustees may, as an illustration, resort to income to discharge a CGT liability but should then make an appropriate adjustment so that the income deficiency is made good out of capital as soon as circumstances permit.

This conclusion appears more in line with the thinking behind the Law Commission's Consultation Paper No.175 and the need to have balance between income and capital in a trust so that the relevant beneficiaries are not adversely affected. In practical terms, it makes for good beneficiary relations if it cannot be said that the trustees have acted to the detriment of one group to the benefit of the other.

7. Reasonable care in relation to the management of trust assets

This duty is at the heart of proper trust administration and is now enshrined in s.1 of the Trustee Act 2000, albeit that this statutory duty of care can be modified or excluded by the trust instrument. The trustee must not act carelessly or foolishly but to a high standard with a view to maintaining or enhancing the value of the trust fund. A trustee must exercise such care and skill as is reasonable in the circumstances having regard to any special knowledge or experience that he has or holds himself out as having and if he acts as trustee in the course of a business or profession, to any special knowledge or experience that it is reasonable to expect of a person acting in the course of that kind of business or profession (s.1(1), Trustee Act 2000).

8. Investment of trust funds

Trustees must invest trust funds in accordance with the trust instrument or as directed by Parliament. If the trust instrument does not contain an investment clause then ss.3 and 8 of the Trustee Act 2000 would apply. In exercising any power of investment the trustees must take such care as an ordinary prudent person would take if he were minded to make an investment for the benefit of other people for whom he felt morally bound to provide (*Re Whiteley* (1886) Ch D 347).

As Megarry VC said in *Cowan v. Scargill* [1985] Ch 270:

> It is the duty of trustees to exercise their powers in the best interests of the present and future beneficiaries of the trust, holding the scales impartially between the different classes of beneficiaries ... When the purpose of the trust is to provide financial benefit to the beneficiaries, as is usually the case, the best interests of the beneficiaries are normally their best financial interests. The power must be exercised so as to yield the best return for the beneficiaries, judged in relation to the risks of the investments in question; and the prospects for the yield of income and capital appreciation both have to be considered in judging the return for the investment.

9. Payment of trust monies

It is the trustee's duty to ensure the payment of any trust money is made to the right people: e.g. are you accounting for the payment of mineral royalties in the correct way, balancing the income and capital apportionment rules under s.47 of the Settled Land Act 1925 if they apply to your trust?

10. Trustees must not delegate their duties or powers

The duty of the trustees in the day-to-day running of the trust is to manage the property so as to preserve the value of the capital and produce an income for the beneficiaries. Collectively the trustees make dispositive decisions and exercise dispositive powers. Sections 11–23 of the Trustee Act 2000 provide for collective delegation by the trustees of any of their management functions but not of their dispositive powers. A trustee may delegate to an attorney for a limited period or in some cases to a beneficiary upon certain conditions (Trustee Delegation Act 1999) but the body of trustees cannot collectively delegate their decision making.

11. Unanimous decision making

A body of trustees must act in unison unless majority decision making is expressly provided for within the trust instrument.

12. Trustees must not contest the rights of beneficiaries

If the trust instrument gives rights to certain beneficiaries then the fact that an outside party challenges that right does not mean the trustees should support the challenge unless authorised to do so by a court.

13. A trustee must not receive a reward for acting as a trustee

However, a professional or corporate trustee is entitled to reasonable remuneration under s.29 of the Trustee Act 2000. A suitable remuneration clause which may assist a lay trustee or extend the statutory default provision will be included in most professionally drafted trust instruments.

14. A trustee cannot profit from trust property

Where any profits are made by a trustee he will have to show that there was no causal connection between his position as trustee and the personal profits if they are to be retained by him, otherwise he is required to account for those profits.

15. The trustees must be able to produce accounts

Trustees must provide clear and accurate accounts of all monies handled and all assets held in the trust fund when called upon to do so. In addition, a trustee must at all reasonable times produce evidence and allow inspection by or on behalf of a beneficiary who wishes to check the documentary evidence which supports the accounts.

Breaches of trust

Generally speaking, any failure to comply with the above duties and any others identified in the trust instrument will constitute a breach of trust. So making the wrong decisions in the management of the trust fund (e.g. allowing a tenancy of farmland to be granted to a company thereby dramatically reducing the value of the freehold reversion) or applying the wrong accounting or tax treatment (e.g. the different treatment for trust and tax purposes of mineral royalties) can give rise to personal liability for the trustees.

The basis of a trustee's liability is compensation to the beneficiaries for whatever loss may have resulted from the breach, or if an unauthorised profit has been made, the restoration to the beneficiaries of property rightfully belonging to the trust. See **para.3.4**.

Prior to the coming into force of the Trustee Act 2000 the common law standard of care was objective (i.e. measured against the level of competence of a notional reasonable man). Since the Act the trustee who has special knowledge or experience is, in the case of a professional, deemed to have the level of skill of the reasonable trust administrator.

Liability can attach to a trustee who lacks the knowledge or skills to avoid the breach and is doing his incompetent best, if that best is not up to the standard of the reasonable trust administrator. In *Nestle* v. *National Westminster Bank plc* [1994] 1 All ER 118 although the bank had clearly failed in its duty to appreciate the scope of its powers of investment and had not reviewed the investments regularly that was not sufficient to provide a remedy for the plaintiff beneficiary, she had to show that her fund would have been worth more if the bank had diversified, which on the evidence she failed to do.

The trust instrument may vary the extent of any possible liability. For example in *Armitage* v. *Nurse* [1997] 2 All ER 705 clause 15 of the settlement deed said: 'No trustee shall be liable for any loss or damage [to the capital or income of the trust fund] at any time or from any cause whatsoever *unless such loss or damage shall be caused by his own actual fraud*' (emphasis added). The Court of Appeal held that this wording absolved the trustees from liability to the beneficiary who was alleging mismanagement of the investments of the trust fund, because there was no allegation of dishonesty. It was sufficient that the trustees were bound to perform the trusts honestly and in good faith.

3.3 CONFLICTS OF INTEREST

It is clear that given the fiduciary nature of the role of trustee it is not permissible for a trustee to be in a position where his self-interest is in conflict with his fiduciary duties. However, in many cases the settlor will have appointed a family member who may also be a beneficiary to act as a trustee, sometimes with other similar trustees or alongside a professional trustee. The risk of conflicts of interest arising is great and it can be quite hard for a trust administrator to persuade a trustee of the need to act for the benefit of the whole of the beneficial interests and not for his own self-interest. There is a risk that a professional trustee may be seen as acting in conflict when the trust is not economical and should be wound up, but it is continued and the perception of the beneficiaries is that it is only being continued to provide a source of fee income.

As was examined in **para.3.2**, no trustee is entitled to profit from his trusteeship, so the trust instrument will usually provide for remuneration for the trustee who is in business. The professional trustee is entitled to reasonable remuneration by s.29 of the Trustee Act 2000 but a lay trustee who is a family member and beneficiary may not be entitled to any remuneration even though he may have to give up his work time to carry out his duties. This could generate a potential conflict situation where the trust fund comprises shares in the family company in which the beneficiary trustee is a company director who is paid for his services to the company. Sometimes, the trust instrument will provide authority for the trustee director to retain his director's fees, but otherwise he will be in a potential conflict position if the trustees' shareholding is used to vote for higher director's fees. Often this sort of conflict can be resolved by a proper employment contract being put in place for the directors before the shares are put into trust.

Where there is a doubt as to whether there is appropriate authorisation for the trustee director to retain his remuneration it might be wise to apply to the court for directions. Otherwise, the director's fees should really be paid to the trust fund.

It is also common for the trust instrument to permit a trustee to breach the rule against self-dealing where there is a beneficiary trustee whom the settlor would not wish to prevent from benefiting under the trust in the same way as the other beneficiaries. If no such permission is expressly provided for in the trust instrument then a trustee beneficiary cannot purchase trust property nor derive any benefit from it.

3.4 BREACH OF TRUST BY TRUSTEES

Fundamentally, a trustee should not act in breach of his duties imposed by the trust instrument, by statute, or by equitable principles identified in case law. However, where the trust administration is not being carried out correctly, the beneficiaries can take steps to ensure that proper administration takes place in order to preserve their interests under the trust.

An unhappy beneficiary may initially complain to the trustees about the quality of the trust administration and in the absence of any corrective action by the trustees may consider bringing court proceedings against the trustees and their agents for either restitution to the trust or compensation for breach of trust.

It is not easy to bring successful actions against trustees given that a breach of trust action will be statute barred if proceedings are brought more than six years after the date on which the right of action *arose* (s.21(3), Limitation Act 1980). The right of action runs from when the breach is *committed* and not from when the loss arises.

So before embarking upon expensive litigation a beneficiary should consider:

1. Whether there is any evidence of an actual breach of trust or breach of fiduciary duty.
2. Whether the breach has actually brought about the loss complained of which can actually be quantified.
3. If the limitation period applies and has expired.
4. Whether the trustees are insured or if not, whether they have sufficient assets personally to make it worth suing them.
5. Whether an exoneration clause which protects the trustees against liability exists.
6. Whether the trustees' action might not result in personal liability because a court would relieve them under s.61 of the Trustee Act 1925. This section permits exoneration for a trustee who can satisfy the court that he acted 'honestly and reasonably' and ought fairly to be excused. Whilst this may help a lay trustee escape blame it is not common for a professional trustee to successfully call it in aid.
7. Whether it is possible for the trustees to show that the beneficiary knew of the purported breach and either consented to it or acquiesced.

A breach of trust can occur in a number of different ways, so a trust administrator should ensure that the terms of the trust are made known to all the trustees on taking office along with their duties under the law.

For example, a breach can occur in the following circumstances.

1. Trustees may agree with a beneficiary to waive interest on a loan made to the beneficiary when they have no express power to do so – this would be an example of acting beyond the remit of their powers.
2. Trustees as major shareholders in a company may fail to take a close enough interest in the performance of the directors in running the private company whose shares form the largest part of the trust fund. As a result of their omission to act based on the size of the trust's shareholding, if the share price falls and the value of the trust fund plummets, this would be an example of failing to act to prevent loss to the fund.
3. The trustees may fail to keep adequate records detailing the current beneficial interests in the trust such that they distribute incorrect amounts to the wrong beneficiaries and even people who are not beneficiaries. This would be an example of acting in breach of the standard duty of care in s.1 of the Trustee Act 2000 and generally acting improperly.

Sadly, sometimes a breach of trust by a trustee occurs because the trustee has used trust funds for his own benefit rather than for the benefit of the beneficiaries as a whole. In such circumstances the beneficiaries may either require that the trust assets be returned (restored) together with commercial interest, or they may claim the profit made by the trustee's use of the trust's funds.

The litigation procedures for pursuit and defence of trust-related disputes are beyond the scope of this book, but for a brief summary see Section H, 'Action by Disgruntled Beneficiaries' in *Tolley's Administration of Trusts* (Looseleaf). For the work of the Association of Contentious Trust and Probate Specialists (ACTAPS), see their website at **www.actaps.com** where a copy of the draft protocol the organisation has prepared for use in trust and estate disputes can be downloaded.

A trust practitioner should also be aware of the use of independent third parties to perhaps mediate between the warring factions in a dispute to reach a solution, or to provide an expert opinion on the likelihood that the arguments would succeed in a court, or to act as an arbitrator imposing a binding solution on the aggrieved parties. These solutions may result in a more cost effective and private outcome rather than the very public option of a court trial of the issues.

3.5   REMOVING TRUSTEES

If the spirit of trust and confidence between the beneficiaries and trustees evaporates, perhaps as a result of an alleged breach of trust, then coupled with a claim for breach of trust the beneficiaries may seek the removal of a trustee or the whole body of trustees.

The statutory provisions facilitating the removal of trustees are contained in the following.

1. Section 19 of TLATA 1996 provides the beneficiaries with a right of de-selection in certain circumstances. It is unfortunately not possible to rely on this section if it was excluded from applying by express clause in the trust instrument.

2. Section 36(1) of the Trustee Act 1925 provides the person with power to appoint new trustees with the power to remove a trustee if he is satisfied that the trustee is refusing to act or unfit to act. Section 36(1) sets out a list of other possibilities for removal. If the trust instrument gives the settlor, for example, the power to appoint new trustees, then s.36 gives the settlor the power to replace a trustee if the trustee refuses to act or is unfit to act.

3. Section 41 of the Trustee Act 1925 also provides a court with the power to replace existing trustees, envisaging the possibility of removal coupled with a replacement or substitution.

It is not very common in the UK for a power to remove a trustee to be included in the trust instrument, and it is perhaps more likely to be seen in offshore trusts. A professional trustee would be unlikely to want to take office in managing such a trust in the UK as it would surely be seen as a 'threat' by whoever had the power to unseat the trustee if in properly exercising his duty he was seen as 'uncooperative' and threatened with removal. It would clearly act to undermine the trustee's independence where this power was retained by the settlor, for example, and encourage the view that the trust was really a sham, the settlor still being in actual control of the trust fund.

PART TWO

Administering the trust

CHAPTER 4

Getting started

4.1 STRUCTURE AND SYSTEMS

Roles to be performed

Within the trust administration department, however small, various roles will need to be performed.

1. *Manager or department head.* The manager or head of department will often be a partner in the firm as well as a fee earner themselves. The role will generally involve generating ideas for and developing and implementing the department's operating plans in order to meet the targets set by the firm; monitoring progress against the plans; providing coherent leadership to, supervision of, training and development for departmental staff and marketing the department's services.
2. *Administrators or fee earners* responsible for handling a client case load. The fee earners will be responsible for the delivery of prompt, effective and accurate advice and services to clients using the firm's IT operating systems and procedures as well as being responsible for maintaining and developing their own skills and technical legal knowledge.
3. *Secretarial support and data entry.* These roles are essential to accurate maintenance of records as well as good client relations. Typical duties will include filing, data input, photocopying, answering routine enquiries and taking messages, providing wordprocessing, and maintaining the central diary and the fee earners' diaries and appointments.
4. *Accounts.* Within the firm, and in some cases the team, the accounting function will deal with the receipt and payment of money, maintain accurate client records and ensure that the Solicitors' Accounts Rules are being complied with, in particular as far as controlled trusts are concerned. The role may extend to the preparation of trust accounts.

The larger the firm or department the more likely it will be that a number of people will fulfil these different roles and the work of the department may well then be structured between them in a variety of ways. For example:

- by individual – each member of staff administering a mixed workload;
- by size of trust;
- by type of trust; or
- by type of work – i.e. management, administration, accounting, taxation, investment management.

Where the department consists of just a fee earner and a secretary, the roles of manager, administrator, secretarial support and accounts must still be performed. Often in small teams insufficient time and energy is given to managerial tasks such as risk assessment issues and improving procedures. When reviewing the structure of the department and its ability to deliver the operational and strategic plans which have been devised (see **Chapter 15**) it is essential to consider the functions which have to be performed, the roles of the team members in conducting each of the functions and the relevant competences of personnel to conduct these functions. Frequently, freeing up some of the manager's time by delegating appropriate tasks to others can improve the overall performance of the department.

The larger the team the greater the need for the department head to be relieved of day-to-day fee earning and to be allowed to concentrate on the management of the team and its performance in line with the business plan. This may be hard for professional people to do as they will usually have been chosen to head up the department because of their seniority or technical legal know-how rather than their ability to manage. Whilst their experience will still be called into use and their knowledge of particular clients will inevitably involve them in client contact, the effective manager will delegate most of the routine administration matters to an appropriate team member to free up time to allow for planning, implementation and monitoring.

Gaining commitment from others in the team to take on some of these more routine matters and caseload will only be achieved if any promises to deliver on matters that only a partner or manager can implement are kept. This means setting an exemplary example by managing time and work to beneficial effect. There are only 24 hours in the day and seven days in the week for each and every one of us. The Prime Minister has no more time each day than the head of a department in a law firm. It is not about having more time, it is about how the time available is used. Achievement is about being focused, organised and effective.

There are plenty of courses, books and programmes to help people re-think how they manage themselves but the big hurdle to overcome is to recognise this may be a weakness; arrange to do something about it and keep an open mind as to what you may need to alter in your life to change what are essentially bad habits – remember it is easy to make New Year's resolutions but so much harder to achieve them.

As manager, when you have explored the services you are to offer the clients and the ways in which you are going to deliver those services it will become apparent what legal skills are needed in the team and what support services are required. Map out the roles (the people who are to deliver the services) and processes (the methods of delivery) so that you can be sure what competences are needed in the team to ensure that it functions in the way that the firm and, more importantly, the client wants.

Routines to be undertaken

In every trust department there are routine areas of work. Some form part of daily practice and some are less frequent but are no less routine, such as the preparation of quarterly accounts or the completion of annual tax returns. It is important to recognise the typical routines and explore the ways in which the risk to the firm and its clients can be minimised, by allocating tasks to the correct member of staff, having in place suitable systems for checking accuracy and using the routines to generate useful information that can be easily accessed by and through the systems used.

A typical list of regular routines would include the following.

1. Conducting money laundering enquiries.
2. Reporting to and advising trustees.
3. Preparing for trustees' meetings, attending such meetings and preparing the minutes.
4. Preparing trust accounts.
5. Considering and making distributions to beneficiaries.
6. Safe custody of deeds, documents and other items of monetary value.
7. Maintaining and reconciling trustees' bank accounts and client account.
8. Tax return and tax certificate (R185) preparation.
9. Checking tax statements of account and payments on account; paying tax.
10. Tax review and tax claims.
11. Investment management and record keeping.
12. Reviewing the performance of all agents and taking action as necessary.
13. Filing.
14. Maintaining the central diary.
15. Issuing invoices.

Information which should be recorded

In order for the trust management to be efficient there are a number of pieces of information about a trust which should be recorded and be easily retrievable. The need to record information is fairly obvious, in that trusts created today will rarely be wound up by the same person who set them up so the information about, for example, when a beneficiary will become entitled to his share of the trust capital, should be recorded at the outset and a reminder system put in place in order to ensure that the trust administrator at the relevant time is on notice and the payment date is not overlooked.

A basic list of information which is regularly needed in trust administration would comprise the following.

1. Name and matter number for trust.
2. Who acts – partner, manager, administrator.
3. Accounting requirements – year end; who deals with the preparation; by when must the accounts be finalised?
4. Taxation requirements – who deals? Date for submission and review?
5. Who are the trustees and beneficiaries?
6. What does the trust fund comprise?
7. Terms of the trust – who gets what; when? Powers of the trustees?
8. Key dates:

    (a) income entitlement vests;
    (b) capital entitlement vests;
    (c) income payment;
    (d) accumulation period ends;
    (e) rent review date for trust property;
    (f) insurance premiums due;
    (g) rent payable/collectable;
    (h) power of attorney expires;
    (i) tax payable;
    (j) tax administration dates;
    (k) IHT 10-year anniversary; and
    (l) any other miscellaneous matters.

9. Record of trustees' decisions, minutes of trustees' meetings.
10. Advice given; recommendations made, actions advocated.
11. Results of any periodic review.
12. Correspondence.
13. Working papers – e.g. for tax or accounting.
14. Copy documents with reference to locate originals and schedule.
15. Signed and approved accounts.
16. Permanent tax records – matters which have a future bearing on the future of the trust, e.g. tax elections or share histories.

Systems

To make the office efficient and effective, it makes sense to design systems and procedures which capture the key information as part and parcel of conducting the routines of administration. The success of the department and its ability to attract new trusts to the firm will be determined by the willingness of all to adhere to the systems and whether those systems will be robust enough to withstand the changes of staff members over the years of the administration of the trusts.

Larger departments will use IT and much of their surrounding systems will be to some extent dictated to by the way in which the operating system works. Even if the firm cannot justify investing in a trust case management or accounts systems it should endeavour to have a first-rate manual system which might comprise the elements illustrated in Table 4.1

Table 4.1 Trust administration systems

Checklists	Database
• New client – Trust Information Form • Annual review – Trust Review Form • Property information – Property Information Form	• Standard letters – e.g. letter of engagement • Standard forms – e.g. money laundering • Storage of common information – e.g. FTSE holdings held by trusts
Accounting system • Incoming cheques • Outgoing payments • Types of account – controlled trusts; designated/undesignated • Capital account • Income account • Nominal ledger	**Central diary** • To record the key dates in a perpetual diary
Files – types • Current general correspondence • Special matter correspondence • Accounts working papers • Taxation working papers • Working documents • Permanent taxation records • Signed and approved accounts	**Working documents file – to contain:** • Trustees' names and contact addresses, etc. • Professional contacts details, e.g. stock broker • Summary of trust's beneficial interests, e.g. family tree • List of principal assets held and latest valuation • Tax information – pools, elections, etc. • Notes of principal events in the history of the trust • List and copies of key trust documents

4.2   RISK ASSESSMENT

Introduction

The reputation of your organisation depends on the quality of the service you give – that is, both the quality of the advice and also the risk management and quality assurance systems that you operate. Increasingly, professional indemnity insurance is only secured if a firm can demonstrate risk awareness and that robust risk management procedures are in place. A suggested list of possible risks to a trust administrator at the outset of a new trust, particularly ones made during the settlor's lifetime and some suggested ways the perceived risks can be minimised is shown in Table 4.2.

Money laundering

(a)   Background

We live in an era of internet fraud and money laundering, and professional service firms are soft targets for the criminal fraternity who hope to wash the proceeds of criminal activity clean through client accounts. It is therefore of the utmost importance that trust practitioners carefully vet prospective trust clients and only agree to provide trust services for those clients who meet carefully considered, yet practical, due diligence standards. Check the countries to which your potential client might be linked. If a client is linked to countries with a high level of organised crime, e.g. Russia or Nigeria, or which have offshore banking centres, e.g. Cayman Islands, then you should be extra vigilant and if you have any doubts you may feel that this is not a suitable client for your firm.

Until the advent of the Proceeds of Crime Act 2002 (POCA 2002) and the Second EU Directive on Money Laundering only firms carrying out 'relevant financial business' had to have anti-money laundering procedures in place. The Money Laundering Regulations 2003 (bringing into effect in this country the Second EU Directive on Money Laundering) came into force on 1 March 2004 and as a result the anti-money laundering requirements apply to virtually all firms. At the time of writing the Third EU Directive on Money Laundering is likely to be approved without most of the amendments suggested by various professional bodies. The future requirements for trusts and trustees in respect of identification and verification of new clients are likely to get much tougher.

Money laundering is at the top of the world agenda. The IMF estimates that money laundering accounts for between 2 and 5 per cent of the world's GDP – roughly equivalent to the value of the total output of an economy the size of Spain!

Table 4.2 Risk assessment and preventative steps

Event	Risk	Preventative step
Taking on the new client	Failure to spot proceeds of crime could result in a jail sentence.	Maintain money laundering reporting procedures and train all staff in compliance.
Choice of assets available to go into the trust	Failure to recognise chargeable assets and any appropriate reliefs resulting in an unexpected tax bill for client.	Improve knowledge and take relevant expert advice before taking steps if unsure of tax consequences.
Choice of beneficiaries	Drafting wrongly excludes or includes beneficiaries which settlor wants to include or exclude.	Check understanding of definitions used in drafting and take clear and specific instructions. Employ file supervision techniques.
Obtaining valuation of assets	Incorrect valuation obtained and/or failure to agree with HMRC Capital Taxes.	Open market value required at the date of transfer to the trust. HMRC Capital Taxes will refer to District Valuer or Share Valuation Division as appropriate so understand their roles and techniques by checking HMRC manuals.
Income tax	Failing to identify trusts where settlor will be liable personally for the income tax on trust, e.g. ITTOIA 2005, s.625.	Do not provide for unmarried minor children of settlor during settlor's lifetime unless income is to be accumulated until 18 (or earlier marriage).
	Failure to prevent settlor being taxed on the income of the trust.	Check default clause is drafted so currently living beneficiary receives an absolute interest on expiration of perpetuity period.
	Settlor cannot manage on own income after gift to trust and uses trust income – result: reservation of benefit.	Ensure the settlor appreciates that what is given to the trust belongs to the trustees and cannot be used to assist settlor without there being a reservation of benefit.

Table 4.2 Risk assessment and preventative steps – cont.

Event	Risk	Preventative step
	Failure to notify appropriate trust tax office of creation of the trust.	Use Form 41G in every appropriate new trust and advise the Inland Revenue whether you need to receive an annual SA900 Trust and Estate Tax Return.
IHT	Wrong type of trust is chosen for settlor and unexpected tax charge arises.	Improve knowledge of PETs and chargeable transfers.
	Chargeable transfers not spotted as such and Inland Revenue not notified, incurring penalties.	Improve knowledge of chargeable events and exemptions and reliefs. For trust created during lifetime, send IHT100 to HMRC Capital Taxes with lifetime IHT at 20% on excess over available NRB; trusts created under a will are part of the estate in administration initially and therefore covered by IHT200.
	Tax due is not paid on time to HMRC Capital Taxes incurring penalties.	Observe due dates for paying tax and maintain diary dates.
	Due to poor advice settlor makes inadvertent GROB and therefore fails to save IHT on death.	Improve knowledge of GROB rules and the double tax relief provisions.
CGT	Lifetime settlor not advised of taxability of disposal as top slice of income for tax year of disposal at his marginal rates.	Always consider 'what if' computation before transferring assets to a trust created during the settlor's lifetime. Improve knowledge of CGT computation, exemptions and reliefs.
	Agreement to the chargeable gain not instigated on time leading to tax paid late and resulting in interest and penalties.	Use CGT34 procedure to agree gains when disposals made. Improve knowledge of due dates – 31 January following the tax year in which disposal made.

Table 4.2 Risk assessment and preventative steps – cont.

Event	Risk	Preventative step
	Tax is paid which could have been held over.	Read IR295 helpsheet and use for making holdover claims.
Documenting transfers of assets	All procedures to effect transfer not completed with possible resultant tax problems when settlor dies.	Improve know-how for different transfer requirements for different assets. Ensure file management procedures in place to avoid administrative errors.
Billing	Costs estimate inaccurate causing undercharging or complaints from client for charging more than anticipated.	Follow Rule 15 procedure and maintain good costs controls.
	Writing off chargeable time in large quantities.	Proper supervision of staff and identification of training needs before it becomes a problem.

Historically, tax evasion has been the concern of the offshore trust practitioner, but as UK tax rates appear increasingly favourable and the use of trusts in general looks attractive to clients who wish to avoid the civil code 'forced heirship' rules in European countries, the UK can potentially be targeted by other countries as assisting in tax evasion.

Tax mitigation, or tax avoidance as it is often referred to, is generally acceptable as it uses legally available reliefs and HMRC practices to reduce the tax payable. However, tax *evasion* is generally illegal as it usually involves the non-payment of tax that should otherwise be payable, or the deliberate failure to declare income or assets that should be declared to the appropriate revenue authorities. Tax evasion is becoming a major concern to offshore trust service providers particularly as a number of offshore centres have recently included tax crimes within their definition of money laundering activities.

This is one of the few areas where getting the administration of a trust wrong can land you, the professional, in jail.

(b)   The money laundering process

There are three main stages to the money laundering process.

1. *Placement.* For example where cash is derived from a criminal activity, such as tax evasion, is placed in a bank account.
2. *Layering.* This usually involves a complex system of transactions designed to hide the true identity of the funds.
3. *Integration.* The stage reached when the identity of the funds has been sufficiently disguised that the funds, which are in circulation or held in an account or as an asset, appear to have come from a legitimate source.

Money laundering is any part of the process whereby either the identity of the proceeds (whether direct or indirect) of crime (wherever committed) or the true ownership of such proceeds is changed, concealed or disguised (whether successfully or not).

With trusts, practitioners should watch out for the following suspicious circumstances.

1. Formation of a settlement without any apparent good purpose.
2. Appointment as trustees of persons with little or no existing or potential interest or involvement in the running of the trust.
3. Use of funds from an unexplained or dubious source to establish or increase any trust fund.
4. Use of the proceeds from tax evasion to set up the trust.

The usual object of money laundering is to frustrate or complicate the efforts of the authorities to trace the proceeds of crime, and so the varieties are infinite. It is possible and maybe even inevitable that trust practitioners can become unwittingly involved in this process, particularly as it is usual for them to hold money for clients. Those who wish to frustrate the efforts of the authorities to trace proceeds of crime will use solicitors in the belief that solicitors have an absolute obligation to keep the client's affairs confidential in all circumstances. However, this is not always correct. A solicitor can disclose information relating to the affairs of a client in the following situations.

1. Information may be disclosed to the relevant law enforcement agencies in circumstances where the solicitor or the solicitor's advice and services is being used with a view to furthering any criminal purpose.
2. Information concerning any knowledge or suspicion of money laundering may be disclosed to the relevant law enforcement agencies in circumstances where failure to report the matter would be an offence.
3. Information may be disclosed with the express consent of the client.
4. Information may be disclosed in accordance with a court order.
5. Information may be disclosed as a matter of public record.

(c)   The procedures

The Money Laundering Regulations 2003 and the POCA 2002 require firms to have and to keep in place procedures for the following.

1. Preventing money laundering, e.g. by not accepting cash deposits.
2. Identification of clients. Thus personal identification will be required for the settlor, when acting in the creation of the settlement, and for each trustee, when acting in the administration of the trust.
3. Keeping records in relation to certain aspects of the business and identifying the source of the funds which are being used to create the trust, and keeping a record of that investigation.
4. Internal reporting of money laundering or suspected money laundering. There must be a form for staff to use in order to notify the firm's Money Laundering Reporting Officer (MLRO) of *any* suspicions of money laundering. There must also be a form for the MLRO to record his decision. If the MLRO believes a disclosure is required, the NCIS's own form should be used, and this is available from the NCIS website (**www.ncis.co.uk/disclosure.asp**).
5. Training of all staff. The firm should prepare a compliance manual and ensure that all levels of staff understand what is expected of them *and* should appoint a Money Laundering Reporting Officer (MLRO).

For further information, see the Law Society's Money Laundering Guidance produced by Professional Ethics in January 2004 and updated on the Society's website (**www.lawsociety.org.uk**).

(d)   The money laundering offences

The money laundering offences are shown in Figure 4.1.

Key offences which are applicable to *all* solicitors *and* their staff

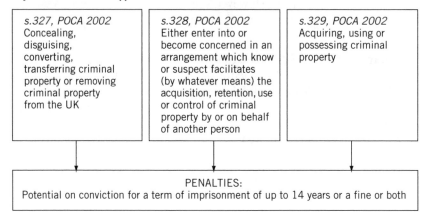

s.327, POCA 2002 Concealing, disguising, converting, transferring criminal property or removing criminal property from the UK	*s.328, POCA 2002* Either enter into or become concerned in an arrangement which know or suspect facilitates (by whatever means) the acquisition, retention, use or control of criminal property by or on behalf of another person	*s.329, POCA 2002* Acquiring, using or possessing criminal property

PENALTIES:
Potential on conviction for a term of imprisonment of up to 14 years or a fine or both

'Tipping off'

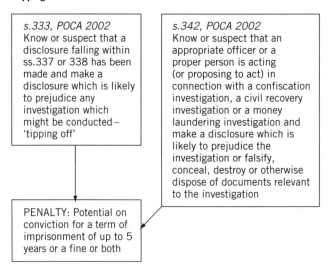

s.333, POCA 2002 Know or suspect that a disclosure falling within ss.337 or 338 has been made and make a disclosure which is likely to prejudice any investigation which might be conducted – 'tipping off'	*s.342, POCA 2002* Know or suspect that an appropriate officer or a proper person is acting (or proposing to act) in connection with a confiscation investigation, a civil recovery investigation or a money laundering investigation and make a disclosure which is likely to prejudice the investigation or falsify, conceal, destroy or otherwise dispose of documents relevant to the investigation

PENALTY: Potential on conviction for a term of imprisonment of up to 5 years or a fine or both

Figure 4.1 Money laundering offences

Offence which relates to *just solicitors* (and those others such as banks, estate agents, accountants and tax advisers in the 'regulated sector'

s.330, POCA 2002

Offence if each of the following conditions is satisfied:

1. Know or suspect or have reasonable grounds for knowing or suspecting that another person is engaged in money laundering
2. The information or other matter on which your knowledge or suspicion is based or which gives reasonable grounds for such knowledge or suspicion came to you in the course of a business in the regulated sector
3. The required disclosure to the authorities was not made as soon as practicable after the information or other matter came to you

↓

PENALTIES:
Potential on conviction for a term of imprisonment of up to 5 years or a fine or both

Offence which applies to *principals and partners* of solicitors' firms and officers of corporate bodies

Reg.3(2), Money Laundering Regulations 2003

A failure to:

(a) Comply with the requirements of regs. 4 (identification procedures), 6 (record keeping procedures) and 7 (internal reporting procedures)

(b) Establish such other procedures of internal control and communication as may be appropriate for the purposes of forestalling and preventing money laundering

(c) Take appropriate measures so that relevant employees are:

(i) made aware of the provisions of these Regulations, Part 7, Proceeds of Crime Act 2002 (money laundering) and ss.18 and 21A, Terrorism Act 2000; and

(ii) given training in how to recognise and deal with transactions which may be related to money laundering

↓

PENALTIES:
Potential on conviction for a term of imprisonment of up to 2 years or a fine or both

Figure 4.1 Money Laundering offences – cont.

Offences which apply *only to MLRO*

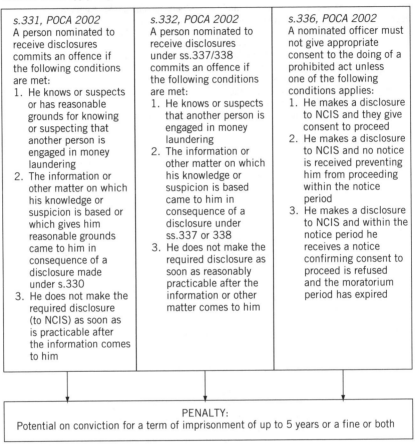

s.331, POCA 2002	*s.332, POCA 2002*	*s.336, POCA 2002*
A person nominated to receive disclosures commits an offence if the following conditions are met: 1. He knows or suspects or has reasonable grounds for knowing or suspecting that another person is engaged in money laundering 2. The information or other matter on which his knowledge or suspicion is based or which gives him reasonable grounds came to him in consequence of a disclosure made under s.330 3. He does not make the required disclosure (to NCIS) as soon as is practicable after the information comes to him	A person nominated to receive disclosures under ss.337/338 commits an offence if the following conditions are met: 1. He knows or suspects that another person is engaged in money laundering 2. The information or other matter on which his knowledge or suspicion is based came to him in consequence of a disclosure under ss.337 or 338 3. He does not make the required disclosure as soon as reasonably practicable after the information or other matter comes to him	A nominated officer must not give appropriate consent to the doing of a prohibited act unless one of the following conditions applies: 1. He makes a disclosure to NCIS and they give consent to proceed 2. He makes a disclosure to NCIS and no notice is received preventing him from proceeding within the notice period 3. He makes a disclosure to NCIS and within the notice period he receives a notice confirming consent to proceed is refused and the moratorium period has expired

PENALTY:
Potential on conviction for a term of imprisonment of up to 5 years or a fine or both

Figure 4.1 Money Laundering offences – cont.

(e)   Important factors

Part 7 of the POCA 2002 came into force on 24 February 2003 and replaced all earlier money laundering statutes (apart from the terrorism legislation). It creates new offences which relate to the proceeds of *all* crime including tax evasion. There is no *de minimis* exception. This legislation covers all offences, no matter how small, down to the last penny.

'Criminal conduct' is defined as any conduct constituting an offence in the UK *or any conduct which would constitute an offence in the UK if it took place in the UK*. In other words, the activity may have been perfectly legal in the country in which it took place but because the client wishes to use the proceeds in instructing a solicitor in the UK, if the activity from which it derived would be criminal conduct in the UK then it will be subject to our money laundering rules.

'Criminal property' is property which is or represents a person's benefit from criminal conduct *and* the purported offender knows or suspects that this is the case. In other words, a client is asking you to act in a transaction using money or assets which that client knows or suspects represent the proceeds of crime.

'Suspicion' has been defined by the courts as not necessarily amounting to belief, but being more than speculation. 'Reasonable grounds to know or suspect' is an *objective test*. You will be guilty of this offence if you should have known or suspected even if you had no actual knowledge or suspicion. Therefore, it is important to make adequate enquiries and apply your mind to assessing the facts rather than 'turning a blind eye' to what presents itself.

Even if you decide not to take on a new client, because from the information obtained you are concerned that you might be committing a money laundering offence if you did so, you will still be subject to the requirement to report suspicious circumstances.

A payment received 'on account of costs' will not generally be viewed as participation in financial transactions so long as your invoice is reasonable for the legal advice involved, and not excessive and so used to facilitate money laundering offences. Care is needed where not all the monies received are used to pay your bill. To the extent that you return the excess to the client you could be committing a money laundering offence and the person who is found to be the legitimate owner of the assets which were the subject of the crime might be able to argue that you were a constructive trustee and should not have parted with those assets, i.e. they may seek restitution from you.

The giving of legal advice, participating in litigation, will writing and publicly funded work are all confirmed by the Treasury as not generally being 'participation in financial transactions'.

Ruth Kelly, in answer to a Commons question, was reported (*Hansard* Parliamentary Question 23 October 2003) as saying:

> The Proceeds of Crime Act requires a person who has knowledge, suspicion or reasonable grounds for knowledge or suspicion, of money laundering as a result of information or other matter that came to him or her in the course of a business in the regulated sector to report this to a nominated person in that organisation, or to the National Criminal Intelligence Service. This obligation to report relates to the proceeds of any crime – regardless of the sum of money involved and will override, in this case, the duty of confidentiality owed to that client.

Solicitors and their employees and barristers are entitled to protect client confidentiality by way of a privilege against disclosure. This legal professional privilege does *not* apply to accountants and not everything that lawyers have a duty to keep confidential is privileged. This area is in need of clarification following the decision in *Bowman* v. *Fels* [2005] EWCA Civ 226.

Privileged communications for these purposes must be either:

1. for the purpose of keeping the solicitor and his client informed so that advice may be sought or given as required. It relates only to communications between the solicitor and his client, and not to correspondence of others involved or notes of meetings which also included other people as well; or

2. confidential communications made after litigation has started or is 'reasonably in prospect' between a lawyer and his client, a lawyer and his client or a lawyer and a third party for the sole or dominant purpose of the litigation.

(f)   Defences

There is a defence if you do not know or suspect that the property constitutes or represents the proceeds of crime. The main defence if you *do* know or suspect, which applies to the three money laundering offences in ss.327,328 and 329, is making an *authorised disclosure*. In the case of a member of staff or partner, a report on the firm's internal reporting form to the MLRO will be an authorised disclosure. In the case of the MLRO, this will be an external disclosure to the National Criminal Intelligence Service (NCIS).

An authorised disclosure can be made either before or after a 'prohibited act' occurs but when done before the prohibited act you must receive appropriate consent (in the case of the staff or partner, from the MLRO; in the case of the MLRO, from NCIS) before completing any transaction which would amount to a prohibited act. When done after the prohibited act, you will need to demonstrate a good reason for failing to report earlier and show that the disclosure was made on your own initiative as soon as practicable.

Employees in the regulated sector have a defence to a failure to report if they have not received the training required under the Money Laundering Regulations 2003 from their employers *and* they have no knowledge or suspicion of money laundering (even though there may have been reasonable grounds for knowledge or suspicion).

The other statutory defence where you know or suspect there has been criminal activity is where you intended to make an authorised disclosure but there was a reasonable excuse for not doing so. No guidance is currently available as to what the courts will determine as being a reasonable excuse.

No offence is committed if you are a professional legal adviser and the information or other matter giving rise to knowledge or suspicion is covered by *legal professional privilege* but note that this defence will not apply if the information is communicated or given to you with the intention of furthering a criminal purpose.

You will not be guilty of 'tipping off' the client if you did not know or suspect that the disclosure was likely to prejudice any investigation or if legal professional privilege applies (except that legal professional privilege will not protect you if the disclosure is made with the intention of furthering a criminal purpose).

(g) Actions required

1. Refer to money laundering rules in your initial terms and conditions of business or client care letter, e.g. 'for the protection of all our clients we operate a money laundering reporting procedure. In certain circumstances, information will be revealed by us to the appropriate authorities in relation to any suspicion of money laundering' and point out, for example, that you will not accept cash in the office.
2. Appoint a Money Laundering Reporting Officer (MLRO).
3. Ensure that all of your colleagues and staff members have received appropriate training. CD Roms, interactive learning, manager's guide and staff compliance booklets can be obtained from Information Transfer, Burleigh House, 15 Newmarket Road, Cambridge, CB5 8EG (Tel: 01223 312227, Fax 01223 310200, e-mail: info@mlro.net).
4. Ensure that you have in place adequate verification of identity procedures for your clients, so that you know with whom you are dealing. You also need a record of the financial aspects of the transaction and why your client wishes to proceed as they do. Use the forms suggested by the Law Society to generate your own internal system.
5. Up-to-date disclosure forms for notification of your MLRO's suspicions to the NCIS can be found on the NCIS website (**http:// ncis.gov.uk/ecb_dguidance.asp**).

What are the potential risks for practitioners?

A practitioner who aids or turns a blind eye to illegal activity risks the possibility that the activity will be uncovered at some stage with the result that criminal action may be taken against you. Do you want your firm faced with a long, expensive and highly publicised court case that you may lose at great financial cost?

As a practitioner, you may become liable as a constructive trustee to pay compensation to the innocent party who has been defrauded by your client, if you:

1. assist the client in perpetrating the fraud; and
2. do so 'knowingly', i.e. knowing that your services are being used as part of a fraudulent scheme or wilfully and recklessly closing your eyes to the obvious, and failing to make enquiries that a reasonable person would make.

Practitioners should also remember the potential damage to their reputation not just in relation to an actual action but also the effect of being subject to an investigation.

Continuing risk management

From time to time your firm will be asked to assume responsibility as advisers to, or become the trustees of, a trust that is already in existence. Although the same due diligence questions above will need to be asked, you should also obtain additional information from the current trustees about the particular trust prior to accepting the business risk. The following will be essential.

1. A copy of the trust deeds.
2. A copy of any letter of wishes.
3. A copy of the trust accounts since inception.
4. The consent of any third party (such as the settlor) as required in accordance with the terms of the trust deed.
5. Confirmation from the trustees that there have been no breaches of trust or other events or actions which the new trustees should be aware of prior to accepting the business. If any potential problems are identified, appropriate indemnities may be needed, or alternatively you may decide not to take over the risk.
6. A draft deed of retirement and appointment of trustees to review.

The process of risk assessment should be ongoing and involves, for example, ensuring that checks are made into the source of any new funds that are added to the trust after it is taken on.

Any changes in the way in which the settlor requests the trust to be administered should be carefully considered, as should any planned changes to the trust structure. A copy of the legal advice or tax advice relating to such a proposal should be obtained.

4.3   TAKING INSTRUCTIONS

Trust information

On receipt of a new trust client, be it from a probate, the application of the intestacy rules or the creation of an *inter vivos* trust, the administrator needs to gather information.

As indicated earlier, this is where the use of a checklist is essential. Whether you operate a manual or an IT system of administration, basic data needs to be collected about the terms of the trust, the details of the beneficiaries and the trust assets, the taxation treatment and relevant advisers. Some of the detail will emerge after the details of any investment strategy have been agreed with the trustees but the Trust Information Form (see **Appendix 2.4**) provides a useful summary of the key data required.

Assets

(a)   Land

Dealing with real property investments also needs care and on the creation of a new trust individual details about each property held within the trust should be collated so that the relevant information for insurance purposes and for use of the property is to hand without having to check the title deeds, which should be kept in safe custody.

The Property Information Form (see **Appendix 2.5**) should include the location of the keys, who is in occupation and what interest they have in the trust, the powers which the trustees have over the property which, for example, may permit occupation by beneficiaries, or the grant of leases or options, or the power to mortgage the property. For insurance purposes it is important to know details of the nature of the freehold or leasehold property's postal district and specific information about its construction and when it was built.

It is not uncommon for properties to be underinsured. Fortunately, s.19 of the Trustee Act 1925 has been extended so that the power to insure is now unrestricted, permitting trust assets to be insured for their full replacement value and for the premiums to be paid either from the income or the capital of the trust fund.

A completed Property Information Form will provide enough information to allow you to review the insurance position and obtain quotes. It may be useful to include in any such Property Information Form details such as the name of the insurance company, the policy number, the amount of cover, the date of renewal of the policy and through which agency the policy has been arranged. Alternatively, this information could be recorded on the Trust Information Form.

If the property is rented, a copy of any tenancy agreement or lease should be kept in the trust document file for ready reference. On the Property Information Form you should record the current rent payable, the date of any rent review and the process for collection. For example, is the firm to act as rent collectors or is there to be a managing agent appointed (in which case details of the managing agent's firm will be required)?

From an accounting point of view a system for collection needs to be set up if the firm is to collect the rent directly but where managing agents are used, payment dates will need to be agreed and the basis of their charges and the payment of these settled.

Special dates, such as the rent review date, the date upon which the tenancy will expire, or the date when any notice has to be served to bring the tenancy to a close, should be recorded in the department's central diary system so that they are not overlooked, as well as on the trust file.

Where the property that is leased is business or agricultural property, the effect of that occupation upon potential business property or agricultural property relief will need to be recorded on the Trust Information Form. In addition, security of tenure arrangements applicable to the type of property will need to be checked and investigated.

Sections 6–9 of TLATA 1996 provide trustees of trusts of land certain powers that are implied by law.

1. All the powers of an absolute owner.
2. Power to purchase a legal estate in any land in the United Kingdom (amended from England and Wales by the Trustee Act 2000), whether for investment, occupation by any beneficiary or for any other reason.
3. Where beneficiaries are of full age and absolutely entitled in undivided shares to the land the subject of the trust, the trustees may partition the land already part of it and provide (by way of mortgage or otherwise) for the payment of any equity money.
4. The trustees may by power of attorney under s.9 of TLATA 1996 delegate to any beneficiary or beneficiaries of full age who are beneficially entitled to an interest in possession in land the subject of the trust, any of their functions as trustees that relate to the land.

These powers and functions of the trustees may be restricted or extended, and the trust deed should be checked to see whether or not these implied powers have been altered.

Since the introduction of TLATA 1996 on 1 January 1997, it is common practice in new wills and trusts to exclude the provisions of s.11 of the Act. This would require the trustees of land to consult, so far as is practicable, with beneficiaries of full age who are beneficially entitled to an interest in possession of the land and, so far as is consistent with the general interest of the trust, give effect to the wishes of those beneficiaries or (in the case of dispute) of the majority of them (according to the value of their combined interest).

If s.11 has not been excluded, trustees will be expected to consult, and to the extent that they do not there will be a breach of trust.

Sections 12 and 13 of TLATA 1996 provide a beneficiary who is beneficially entitled to an interest in possession in the land the subject of the trust with the right to occupy the land provided that:

1. one of the reasons for the creation of the trust was to make land available for his occupation; or
2. the land is held by the trustees so as to be available for his occupation; or
3. the land is not unavailable or unsuitable for his occupation.

Trustees must therefore act reasonably and in accordance with the guidelines set out in s.13 imposing restrictions on the right of occupation. For example, where a beneficiary's entitlement to occupy the land has been excluded or restricted it may be sensible for a trustee to impose on the occupying beneficiary a requirement to pay market rent by way of compensation to the beneficiary whose entitlement has been so excluded or restricted.

Personal chattels

It is sensible to clarify at the outset which assets are included in a trust. If at all possible, household goods and personal items should be kept out of the trust. If such items have been included the trustees should consider if it is possible with the powers afforded to them to appoint them out of the trust, or if it is practical, sell them.

Where chattels are antiques or other valuable (possibly heritage items), an inventory and valuation of the items must be undertaken and insurance must be dealt with in the same way as for real properties. The trustees will need to consider who is responsible for ensuring the security and protection of the items and how frequently spot checks should be done to confirm that all items are in good order and not damaged, destroyed or disposed of.

Where items are subject to a claim for heritage property relief, the requirements of any relevant undertakings to preserve the relief will need to be confirmed and checked.

Business assets

A trust may contain shares in a family company. Unless there are powers contained in the trust deed which can confirm that it is not the duty of the trustees to manage the company, then depending on the size of the shareholding and the rights attached to those shares it may well be implied that the trustees must be active in obtaining information about the activities of the company and making decisions in relation to those activities for the benefit of the trust fund.

In the case of *Bartlett* v. *Barclays Bank Trust Company Ltd* [1980] Ch 515 trustees of a trust fund held 99.8 per cent of the shares in the company. Since they held more than 75 per cent of the shares in the company they had the power to make fundamental changes to the company. The directors of the company owned the remaining 0.2 per cent of the shareholding and decided to embark upon speculative property development.

This took the company into high-risk operations and the trustees of the trust fund did not enquire as to the activities of the company or its change of direction, nor did they request information or make decisions. One of the speculative ventures went badly wrong and the assets of the company were dissipated. Beneficiaries of the trust fund successfully sued the trust company for failing to manage the trust fund.

In the light of s.4 of the Trustee Act 2000 it should be noted particularly that there is a need to decide whether the trustees should diversify the trust's assets. So often, where the main assets of the trust are the shares in a family company, the settlor feels strongly that none of the shares should be disposed of, and that the assets should be retained in the trust so as to keep the company in the family's ownership. Trustees should properly record the review they have undertaken in the light of the fact that s.4 cannot be excluded and therefore operates automatically, affecting all trusts.

Reporting to trustees

At the outset, following receipt of instructions a record-keeping system should be put into place. Once you have reviewed the trust deeds and studied the details of the trust property, you will need to report to the trustees upon the following:

1. the investment strategy;
2. arrangements for the payment of income;
3. banking arrangements (if necessary, obtain cheque signing mandates);
4. taxation arrangements;
5. explain and seek to agree a policy upon the treatment of scrip and enhanced scrip dividends and windfall shares;
6. explain the trustees' duties under the law and, where appropriate, under the trust deed.

Letters of engagement

It is advisable to send to the trustees a letter of engagement setting out your firm's terms of business (including, of course, how you intend to charge for your work), the extent of the retainer (for example, whether or not you are to be responsible for the taxation work) and any significant deadlines for the receipt of responses to investment queries or taxation matters (see **Appendix 1.3**).

Notifying the Inland Revenue

(a)   Relevant trust tax office

When a new trust is created, the relevant Inspector of Taxes must be notified of its creation if income or gains are anticipated. The relevant Inspector of Taxes will be the Inspector responsible for the geographic area in which the trust is to be administered. If your office is to administer the trust, then this will be the trust tax office with which you are used to dealing.

Responsible for all the London Boroughs and the counties of Devon, Cornwall, Somerset, Dorset, Gloucestershire and Wiltshire	HMRC Trusts Truro Lynsnoweth Infirmary Hill Truro TR1 2JD
Responsible for Scotland and Northern Ireland and any trusts under Scottish law or with corporate trustees	HMRC Trusts Edinburgh Meldrum House 15 Drumsheugh Gardens Edinburgh EH3 7UB
Addresses not covered by the above in England and Wales	HMRC Trusts Huntingdon Court 90–94 Mansfield Road Nottingham NG1 3HG

(b)   The forms to be submitted

The method by which the relevant trust tax office is notified is by the submission of Form 41G (for an example see **Appendix 1.4**). This form has four substantial parts:

A – applies to all trusts and needs the basic details of who is involved and whether English law applies to the trust in the normal way and not on some special basis.

B – is for completion where the trust arises on a death by virtue of a will or intestacy or deed of variation.

C – is for completion where the trust is made during the settlor's lifetime.

D – is where you list the assets in the settlement.

It is sensible to advise the Inland Revenue when submitting this form whether or not it is likely that you will need to receive the SA900 Trust and Estate Tax Return. For example, if the only asset in your nil rate band discretionary trust is an IOU, you will *not* require the SA900 until the trustees demand repayment.

Where it is not a controlled trust it is wise also to supply Form 64-8 (for an example see **Appendix 1.5**), which is the trustees' confirmation to the Inland Revenue that it may regard your firm as the taxpayer's agent. This will enable the Revenue to correspond directly with you and ensure that you receive copies of assessments and statements of account.

4.4   SETTING UP THE ADMINISTRATIVE SYSTEMS

Once the firm has decided it is appropriate to accept a new trust client, the systems and procedures decided upon by the department must be implemented to store all the information acquired at the 'taking of instructions' stage.

It should be noted that some trust practitioners now store in electronic format information that was previously held in 'paper' files. The number of organisations that have implemented a system of scanning certain papers and retrieving the data from disk has increased in recent years. As a result, some organisations may not keep hard copies of most trust information. However, it is likely that if this is the case the electronic data will be filed in electronic folders similar to 'paper files'.

Despite the increase in the use of technology to store information, it is unlikely that the offices of trust practitioners will become totally paperless, as some records must remain in hard copy, most notably the original trust deeds. Courts are not yet prepared to accept electronic versions of all trust papers in the event of a trust dispute.

Keeping documents in safe custody

It is advisable for original trust deeds and important trust documentation to be held in a secure place, such as a vault or safe.

Examples of the type of documentation that should be held in safe custody include:

1. the original trust deed;
2. the originals of any supplementary trust deeds, such as deeds of appointment;
3. the original letter or memorandum of wishes;
4. the original paperwork that the settlor completed when requesting the trust services, including such items as the new trust's questionnaire, declarations signed by the settlor (e.g. to confirm solvency) and the due diligence records required by your organisation.

These items are important to the trustees and serious problems could result if any of these were to be lost or destroyed, so they must be stored in a secure place. Some organisations believe that such records are so important that they retain them in safe custody off-site as part of their disaster recovery (business continuation) plan.

Working documents file

Working copies of the papers that are held in safe custody should be held in a file to which the trust administrators have easy access. In particular, a copy of the trust deed (and copies of any supplementary deeds) should be held in this file.

Often it will be useful for the copy trust deed to be marked up with notes designed to summarise the main provisions of the trust and highlight any key issues of which the administrators should be aware. In addition, notes could record the dates of birth or death or marriage and therefore possible changes of name of the various beneficiaries.

In addition to the copy deed or deeds, other items that would usually be held in such a file include the following:

1. a copy of the letter or memorandum of wishes;
2. forms of receipt that beneficiaries have signed to confirm receipt of distributions from the trust;
3. copies of any taxation or legal advice that the settlor obtained either before the trust was created or at any stage thereafter;
4. a copy of money laundering records on the settlor and/or the trustees;
5. any details which have been obtained on the beneficiaries and which the trustees may find useful to assist them in performing their duties or exercising their powers;
6. copies (sometimes originals) of birth, marriage or death certificates relating to the beneficiaries and/or settlor. These can be useful in preparing a family tree; which might be helpful in those trusts where the class of beneficiaries is particularly wide or where it is difficult to determine exactly who could benefit from the trust property.

Correspondence file

A file to hold the day-to-day correspondence relating to the trust is necessary. Often, for ease of future reference a separate folder might be used for each tax year or each calendar year and be labelled as such. The correspondence will usually be filed in ascending date order and contain both incoming mail (such as letters, e-mail, faxes) as well as copies of outgoing mail and internal memoranda.

Minutes of trustees' meetings (to include trustee resolutions)

When trustees hold a meeting or reach a decision on a particular matter, it is generally advisable that a written record should be kept. If a meeting is held, written minutes of the meeting should be taken and filed. However, a decision may sometimes be reached without a meeting being held, perhaps because it was not possible for all of the trustees to meet together at the same time or place. In such situations it would be usual for a written resolution to be prepared, which would be circulated to, and signed by, all the trustees, confirming their agreement to the action that was, or will be, taken.

It is advisable for a file to be created to retain the record of trustee meetings and/or trustee resolutions. A written record of decisions that have been taken is valuable evidence that the trustees have actively managed the trusts and shows their thinking in reaching any decisions.

Investment records

It is common for a trust to hold investments that are quoted on a recognised exchange. Often these investments will be professionally managed, but if the trustees do not have their own investment capabilities, or it was decided not to use the services of an in-house investment manager, the trustees will usually appoint a suitably qualified person or firm to manage the funds.

It is good practice for a separate investment file to be created to contain items such as investment reports and valuations, copies of contract notes and settlement details, as well as any correspondence which takes place between the investment manager and trustees.

Investment portfolios can give rise to a considerable amount of paperwork, especially when you consider that most trustees require a valuation and market report on at least a quarterly basis. It is therefore generally easier and more efficient if the trustees retain investment information at one central point rather than in the trust documents file.

Trust accounts

One of the duties of trustees is to prepare accounts. Trustees usually create a file that contains the trust accounts prepared since inception. Such accounts are generally produced on an annual basis with the accounting date agreed between the settlor and trustees.

Some trust companies file the annual accounts in the trust documents file. However, once the trust has been in existence for a few years (and bearing in mind many trusts have a perpetuity period of 80 years), the documents file may become clogged with accounting records. Locating the accounts for a particular period, or ascertaining the latest balance sheet, could become time consuming.

It is therefore generally felt to be preferable, from an administrative perspective, if a separate accounting file is maintained. This may be one file covering each tax year for the larger and more active trusts, or one file for several years in the smaller and less active trusts.

Tax records

For ease of record keeping, it is useful to have a separate file for each tax year in which you keep your working papers, copy of the signed tax return and supporting records. It might also be wise to have a permanent tax record file to hold correspondence with HMRC regarding such things as holdover claims, or valuations which have been agreed as a base cost for future disposals. These may have arisen as part of a particular tax year's work but they will be relevant to tax calculations in the future and may be hard to locate if stored only in the annual files as someone must then remember in which year, for example, a holdover claim was made.

Record retention

Once a file has been created it should generally be retained for the duration of the trust.

This could mean that a large number of files, particularly correspondence files, will be in place for each of the trusts under administration. This can create considerable storage problems as some trusts will continue for 80 years (perhaps longer depending on the relevant perpetuity period) and the amount of paper generated during this period could be substantial.

The pressure on storage space is another reason why companies are often keen to hold as much paperwork as they can, especially correspondence, in an electronic format. Even after a trust has been terminated, for whatever reason, there is likely to be a requirement that the files are retained for a further period, such as six or even 12 years. Care should therefore be taken before deleting or destroying any trust records.

Setting up the accounting system

Manual accounting systems can be used, which will be account books showing entries for each individual trust. These will doubtless be linked to the firm's own accounts package for running the client and office accounts. Any such system will need to be robust enough to audit the movements of capital and income so that at any one time a balance sheet could be drawn up and to allow annual accounts to be prepared at the end of the tax year to facilitate the preparation of the tax return.

Many firms are starting to use IT for the production of accounts and tax forms at the very least. Software is available to support the administration of trusts (see **Chapter 16**).

Trust accounts

(a) The purpose of trust accounts

The purpose of trust accounts is twofold.

1. To maintain an accurate record of transactions.
2. To provide an explanation of the transactions to the trustees and, where appropriate, the beneficiaries.

(b) Duty of trustees

The trustees must:

1. maintain an accurate record of receipts and payments of trust money; and
2. produce accounts which accurately reflect that trust monies have been applied in conformity with the trust deed.

(c) Form of accounts

There is *no* requirement to follow double entry bookkeeping and in a simple trust, single entry bookkeeping will often be quite sufficient. However, the more complex the trust (and often the larger it is), the greater the need to adopt the double entry system. All the IT packages available will adopt the double entry system.

Given that one of the purposes of the trust accounts is to provide an explanation of the transactions that have occurred to the trustees and beneficiaries, it is necessary to give adequate consideration to how easy the presentation of your chosen method will be to understand.

At present there is no prescribed system for the compilation and layout of trust accounts but STEP has issued guidance notes to help.

(d)   Information collected which will affect your accounts

1. The legal system applicable – it is assumed it is English law, but it is important to check the trust deed as otherwise you may not be competent to deal with it.
2. The type of trust.
3. The trust period.
4. The accumulation period.
5. The beneficiaries' interests in capital and income.
6. Trustees' powers:

    (a) to accumulate income;
    (b) to apply income or capital;
    (c) to appoint capital; and
    (d) of investment – wide, or are there any restrictions imposed?

7. The appropriation of assets to different funds.
8. The allocation of expenses between capital and income.

(e)   What form should your accounts take?

The first item will usually be a synopsis of the trust provisions. A set of accounts should be understandable to the reader without reference to other documents, and introducing the accounts with a basic summary of the trust provisions is essential if the accounts are to be understood. It is important to check the wording each year, since the provisions may have been varied or a beneficiary may have satisfied a contingency or even died since the last set of accounts was prepared.

A report indicating who prepared the accounts and if they are independent of the trustees or not should be provided (a partner may be a trustee and so that should be noted). It is not necessary to have trust accounts audited.

The balance sheet is a snapshot of the trust's assets and liabilities at the date when it is prepared. It is usual for the investments of the trust to be shown in the balance sheet at their original historic cost as this saves explaining wide fluctuations in value where the trust fund comprises quoted investments. However, if one of the trust's assets is a property, part of which has been sold and so it has permanently reduced in value, it would be correct to show this reduction in the balance sheet. Where the figures hide some complex calculations or adjustments, notes to the balance sheet will be necessary to explain how the particular entry has been arrived at. Sometimes it is difficult to value items such as heirlooms or rights that have yet to materialise, such as a right to receive capital on the development of land formerly owned by the trust. In such a case it is best to show these in the balance sheet at a nominal value only.

The capital account will include:

1. additions of capital to the trust fund;
2. distributions out of the capital of the trust fund;
3. profits or losses realised on disposal of trust assets;
4. any revaluation of trust assets;
5. expenses chargeable against the capital of the trust; and
6. tax charged against capital.

The income account states the income and expenditure chargeable to income for the period of the account. Subject to the wording of the trust deed, it is common practice to accrue income due but not yet received and to allow for expenditure incurred but not yet paid, such as administration fees. Be aware that in old trusts it may be necessary to apportion income between beneficiaries and the trust fund at the start and end of an interest, e.g. on the death of a life tenant. Usually in modern trusts this will not be necessary, but always check the trust deed!

In A&M trusts there will invariably be beneficiaries who have attained a vested interest in the income but who have not yet satisfied the age contingency for receipt of capital and those who are under the age for entitlement to income. In this case the funds allocated to the vested interests must be shown separately from those that have no vested interest in the income.

Notes to the accounts are used to explain the accounts where a simple reading of the figures is insufficient to aid understanding of the treatment of the funds. So rather than have a complete list of the investment income where the trust fund comprises a share portfolio, it is common to have a dividend schedule listing the payments. Again, if the trust disposed of an oil painting which was just one of a collection, the balance sheet would show a reduced value in the capital assets of the trust, the capital account would show the disposal and any tax costs, but a note would explain which painting was sold, the sale price and disposal costs.

For an example of a set of accounts prepared for an A&M trust, see **Appendix 1**.

Controlled trusts

The Solicitors' Investment Business Rules apply to these trusts, as do the Solicitors' Accounts Rules 1998 (SAR 1998) which had to be implemented by 1 May 2000.

Money held or received by a solicitor in the course of practice in his capacity as a solicitor, on account of a person or trust for whom the solicitor is acting and the solicitor is the sole trustee or trustee only with one or more partners or employees in the firm is *controlled trust money* and must be paid into a client account.

Some firms maintain a separate undesignated controlled trust account for clients, separate from their other client accounts. If this general controlled trust account is an account on which interest is payable, that interest must be paid over to each relevant trust as and when it arises.

Controlled trust money is treated in substantially the same way as client money – SAR 1998, rr.8 and 15 apply except for the payment of interest (SAR 1998, r.24) since under the general law trustees of a controlled trust must account for *all* relevant interest earned. In practical terms, this means that if separate designated accounts are not used the firm will probably need to have a general client account just for controlled trust money.

In addition, where there is money held in passbook operated separate designated client accounts the firm must at least every 14 weeks:

1. Compare the balance on the client cash account with the balances shown on the statements and passbooks.
2. Prepare a list of all the balances shown by the client ledger accounts of the liabilities to controlled trusts and compare the total with the balance on the client cash account.
3. Prepare a reconciliation.

Under the Rules, a solicitor's office must be able to identify the complete list of all controlled trust accounts managed by the firm at any one time. As trusteeships change it is vital to update any list maintained by the accounts department.

Setting up bank accounts

Any cash which is part of a trust fund, perhaps a client account from a probate matter or investment income or capital from the sale of investments, needs to be transferred into effective banking arrangements.

A trustee bank account must therefore be opened to receive trust income and it is recommended that mandate forms be used to ensure that any dividend or other income is paid directly into the account. It is necessary to control the income. A fixed standing order to benefit any life tenant can be made out of this account for the future rather than having the income paid direct so that the trustees have control and can reconcile payments which should have arisen with the payments passed on to the life tenant or other beneficiary. For this purpose, a review is required of when the income arises and falls due to be received so that the relevant level of standing order payments to the life tenant or other beneficiary can be made.

A trustee deposit account or building society account is needed to receive capital. A small balance of under £5,000 is useful to have available in such an account for emergencies.

When opening trust accounts, it is now a requirement under the Money Laundering Regulations 2003 for identification evidence to be produced to any financial institution for each trustee. The trust administrator should remind trustees of this and of the forms of acceptable identification which trustees will be expected to provide.

CHAPTER 5

Administration implications of the Trustee Act 2000

5.1 INVESTMENT POWERS

As we saw in **Chapter 1**, the creation of a trust provides its beneficiaries with an equitable proprietary interest in the trust property which is being managed for them by the trustees. The beneficiaries are enabled by law to call the trustees to account. It is therefore fundamental to the administration of a trust that the trustees realise that they have a duty to account for and manage the trust's investments in accordance with the powers given to them under the trust document or by statute (unless a court orders otherwise), exercising reasonable care and skill.

For most practical purposes the statutory powers of investment are contained in the Trustee Act 2000. In relation to land, the default powers are contained in the TLATA 1996.

Any prudent trustee would surely wish to consider regularly the suitability of the trust's portfolio and whether there was any need to diversify the holdings. The requirement to do this in s.4(2) of the Trustee Act 2000 is therefore not any more onerous than good practice:

> A trustee must from time to time review the investments of the trust and consider whether, having regard to the standard investment criteria, they should be varied.

Proper advice must be obtained before exercising these powers unless the trustees conclude that it is unnecessary or inappropriate (s.5(1), Trustee Act 2000). Good practice requires that such proper advice be taken or a file note will need to be made setting out the reasons and evidence as to why it was thought unnecessary or inappropriate to obtain such advice.

For those trusts with previously restrictive investment and delegation powers an immediate review was required when the Trustee Act 2000 came into force on 1 February 2001, with a view to developing a wider spread of investments over time, coupled with the use of nominees to speed up the administration of transactions and the appointment of agents to provide these services, usually on a discretionary management basis.

The provisions in Part II of the Trustee Act 2000 provide the general power of investment (s.3(1) states that a trustee may make any kind of investment that he could make if he were absolutely entitled to the assets of the trust) and govern the type of investment that trustees may make in the absence of any express power in the trust instrument or in the event of a narrower power appearing in the trust deed, in certain circumstances. In addition the provisions of Part IV permit the appointment and use of agents, nominees and custodians.

Whilst the duty of care in s.1 of the Trustee Act 2000 can be excluded from application or modified in relation to new trusts created after the Act came into force, it is not possible to modify or exclude the statutory duty of care in s.1 from application to those trusts in existence when the Act came into force. Therefore, it is highly likely that the statutory duty of care will apply to most of the trusts that a practitioner has under management.

This duty of care applies when exercising the power of investment and when reviewing the investments, when buying land, when employing an agent, nominee or custodian and reviewing their performance, and when insuring the trust assets. It therefore applies to these activities even though the practitioner is not relying on the statutory powers but on express powers designed to do similar jobs: see Sched.1 to the Trustee Act 2000.

Even if the duty of care is modified or excluded it does not mean that the requirements of ss.4 and 5, for example, are excluded or indeed can be excluded.

Trustees and those administering the trusts on their behalf must therefore in exercising their power to invest (whether an express power or the statutory powers) take into account the standard investment criteria set out in s.4(3):

(a) the suitability to the trust of investments of the same kind as any particular investment proposed to be made or retained and of that particular investment as an investment of that kind, and

(b) the need for diversification of investments of the trust, in so far as is appropriate to the circumstances of the trust.

What must trustees and their advisers do first of all in considering a portfolio of investments for a new trust? Does s.4(3)(a) prevent the selection of high-risk investments or is it only relevant if the statutory duty of care applies?

There is a theory known as 'modern portfolio theory', which was outlined by Harry Markowitz in 1952, which applied economic theory to the behaviour of the financial markets. It was based on certain assumptions about investors and the markets which in essence identified that investment decisions are made on a balance between *risk* and *return*, in so far as the greater the return the greater the likelihood of risk and vice versa.

This theory was referred to in the leading case on investment performance in this country – i.e. the decision in *Nestle* v. *National Westminster Bank plc*. The first instance decision is reported at [2000] WTLR 795 (note that the case was actually heard in 1988 but has only recently been reported in the Wills & Trusts Law Reports; although it went to the Court of Appeal in 1993 the beneficiary lost). Miss Nestle brought an action for breach of trust against the bank which was the sole executor and trustee of her late grandfather's will. He died on 29 April 1922 and the probate value of the trust fund was about £50,000, worth about £1,000,000 in today's values.

In November 1986 when Miss Nestle's father died, she became absolutely entitled to the trust fund. Its value then was £269,203. She alleged that if the bank had managed the fund's investments on a similar basis to her grandfather's original basis by having a proportion of the fund invested in suitable ordinary shares, with the increase in the index of ordinary shares over the period from 1922 (when it stood at 119.8) to 1986 (when it was at 6,353.2) that part of the portfolio would have been worth £1,800,000. Her argument therefore was that the bank had been negligent because it failed to meet this standard.

The bank disagreed with her argument because they said a trustee exercising investment powers is not under a duty to achieve particular results. The trustee's duty is to exercise reasonable skill and care. In particular, where beneficiaries have conflicting interests (such as in this case where there had been a tenant for life and remainderman) then they had to keep a reasonable balance between those needs.

It was Mr Justice Hoffmann, as he then was, who recited the general principle of prudence from the common law as classically stated by Lindley LJ in *Re Whiteley* (1886) 33 Ch D 347:

> The duty of a trustee is not to take such care only as a prudent man would take if he had only himself to consider; the duty rather is to take such care as an ordinary prudent man would take if he were minded to make an investment for the benefit of other people for whom he felt morally bound to provide.

And then went on himself to say:

> Modern trustees acting within their investment powers are entitled to be judged by the standards of current portfolio theory, which emphasises the risk level of the entire portfolio rather than the risk attaching to each investment taken in isolation.

Although the court heavily criticised the bank in its handling of the trust fund, the fundamental complaint of the beneficiary was not upheld as it was recognised that there was no particular formula which could be applied to guarantee a particular outcome.

It would seem that the modern trustee can therefore manage the portfolio as a whole with no specific isolation of individual investments. Overall, the trustees should look to achieve a balanced portfolio, and depending on the size of the fund this might contain a mix of higher risk investments and more modest holdings – different levels of risk producing different rates of return.

The standard investment criteria of s.4(3) of the Trustee Act 2000 therefore encourage this modern portfolio theory which requires proper management of risk in line with the particular circumstances of the trust in question. Indeed, it has been said that modern portfolio theory underpins the philosophy of the Trustee Act 2000.

It is possible for the investment decisions to be constrained or dictated by the settlor; for example, it is quite popular for a settlor to require the trustees to pursue an ethical investment policy. This would obviously have an impact on what might be a prudent approach but the trustees could not be criticised for following the directions laid down by the settlor.

Thus whilst s.4 cannot be modified or excluded by the trust instrument, the trust deed may well indicate the type of considerations the trustees are to take into account in making investment decisions for that particular trust fund. For example, it is very common to see an express power directing the trustees not to diversify the trust's funds where the trust was actually created as a vehicle to keep together the shares in a family company. Clearly a key object of that trust was the maintenance of the investment in the family company. Against that backdrop it would remain a prudent decision of the trustees to avoid diversification of the trust's assets. However, it would be wise to record all investment review decisions against that key objective and to restate that objective in the minutes of the trustees' meetings or in the written resolutions of the trustees connected with the implementation of the investment strategy.

Trustees must obtain and consider proper advice about the way in which the standard investment criteria should be applied when exercising the power to invest and whether in the light of its application the trust investments should be reviewed. Proper advice is defined as being:

> the advice of a person who is reasonably believed by the trustees to be qualified to give it by his ability in and practical experience of financial and other matters relating to the proposed investment.

Somewhat strangely in s.5(3) trustees are allowed to decide against seeking 'proper advice' if it is *unnecessary or inappropriate*. There is no guidance as to the basis on which these decisions may be taken. What happens if the body of trustees comprises both professional and lay members? Lay trustees may be reluctant to take 'proper advice' if it incurs an expense but professional trustees may wish to ensure the best advice is obtained to deflect potential future complaints from beneficiaries and may be obliged to obtain proper advice from an authorised source under the Financial Services Act 1996.

Trusts in existence at the coming into effect of the Trustee Act 2000 acquired the general power of investment, although there are some exceptions:

1. if the trust already has powers of investment – the wishes of settlors and testators which were expressed against the background of a statutory power of investment under the Trustee Investment Act 1961 are preserved;
2. pension trusts;
3. authorised unit trusts;
4. funds established under schemes made under ss.24 or 25 of the Charities Act 1993.

Fortunately, restrictions contained in pre-3 August 1961 (the coming into force of the Trustee Investment Act 1961) trusts deeds are overridden by the s.3 general power of investment, and any trust deeds giving trustees the powers of investment equivalent to the default powers for the time being authorised by law will have the benefit of the new power.

The explanatory notes issued while the Act was a Bill cited an example of the way ss.6 and 7 would operate:

> Take, for example, an express power of investment in a post 2 August 1961 trust instrument authorising trustees to invest 'only in government bonds'. This power would be taken to exclude the general power of investment (clause 6(1)(b)). On the other hand, an express power in another instrument of the same date to invest 'in shares quoted on the London Stock Exchange, but not in shares of X plc' would take effect as the general power of investment, subject to the restriction on investing in X plc (clause 6(1)). Had the trust instrument pre-dated 3 August 1961, the general power of investment would have applied free of either limitation (clause 7(5)) as would the new statutory powers conferred under the 1961 Act when it came into force (Trustee Investment Act s.1(3)).

The general power of investment contained in s.3(1) does not permit a trustee to make investments in land other than in loans secured on land. Instead, s.8 provides trustees with a default power to:

acquire freehold or leasehold land in the United Kingdom –

(a)   as an investment,
(b)   for occupation by a beneficiary, or
(c)   for any other reason.

Section 8 of the Trustee Act 2000 requires that in exercising the power of investment in the purchase of freehold or leasehold land the standard investment criteria must be considered and the general duty of care will apply. Section 8(2) defines what is meant by the phrase 'freehold or leasehold land' – in England and Wales, this means a *legal* estate, i.e. a fee simple absolute in possession or an estate for a term of years absolute. Section 8(3) then gives the trustees all the powers of an absolute owner in relation to the land, so they can hold land jointly with others, sell, lease or grant mortgages in respect of the land.

Some concern has been expressed as to whether the restriction to legal estates in s.8(2) prevents trustees holding a *beneficial* interest as a joint owner. It is common for trustees to acquire an equitable interest in land, for example as part of the basic IHT strategy of leaving half a house held as tenants in common to children. If those children are under the age of majority at the time of the first co-owner's death, a trust is created to hold their interest – will this be outside the general power?

Section 3 excludes 'land', without defining it, from the general power of investment whereas the s.8 power does define land and restricts it to legal estates. For the avoidance of doubt, those drafting wills and trusts will need to include express powers permitting investment in both legal and equitable interests in land.

The provisions equivalent to ss.3 and 8 contained in a trust deed may be wider than the statutory provisions but in exercising the powers of investment the statutory duty of care set out in s.1 will apply unless the trust has come into existence post 1 February 2001 and specifically excludes the statutory duty. In practice, most professionally drafted trusts will either have some exoneration clauses or the particular professionals will accept that they may be liable for acts of negligence and gross negligence.

However, whether or not the statutory duty of care arises the requirements of ss.4 and 5 apply to *all* trusts and cannot be excluded. So although any prudent trustee would surely wish to consider regularly the suitability of his trust's portfolio and whether there was any need to diversify the holdings, this is now a requirement.

For a detailed review of the workings of Trustee Act 2000, see Whitehouse and Hassall, *Trusts of Land, Trustee Delegation and the Trustee Act 2000*, 2nd Edn (Butterworths, 2001).

5.2   DEVISING THE INVESTMENT STRATEGY

General points

Given that trustees must exercise such care and skill as is reasonable in the circumstances and must seek proper advice regarding changes to investments, it follows that trustees often have to engage advice from qualified providers in the management of the trust's investments.

However, trustees must not leave all investment decisions to agents. Trustees should take account of the following general points and be aware of the role that each investment or decision plays as part of the overall strategy.

(a)   Type of trust

The type of trust will affect the investment strategy to be followed.

In an interest in possession trust there will be a beneficiary entitled to receive the income as of right (the life tenant) and there will also be a person, or class of persons, entitled to receive the capital on the death of the life tenant (the remainderman). For example, a trust created in favour of A for life with remainder to B.

It is therefore important that in an interest in possession trust the interests of both the income and capital beneficiaries (A and B) are considered, as the nature of the investments selected will have an effect on the income being generated and the long-term likely capital value of the portfolio.

This specific issue would not arise in a discretionary trust as no person or persons would have an absolute right to receive funds from the trust, although other considerations will apply.

It would be inappropriate to select investment bonds with 5 per cent capital withdrawals for an interest in possession trust which had no powers to advance capital to the life tenant. However, these may be advantageous to discretionary trusts, given the fact that the withdrawals are capital and not income, so there is no income tax at the rate applicable to trusts to pay on these payments to a beneficiary.

(b)   General economic conditions

Clearly it is much more difficult to achieve a profit for the trust in times of deflation so the approach to investment will be affected by the possible impact of inflation or deflation on the trust fund.

(c)   Amount of cash available for investment

It is not usually advisable for the entire cash fund to be invested, as there may be initial administration costs to be met and it is also possible that funds might be needed to make a proposed trust distribution. The trustees should retain a reasonable cash reserve prior to making the investments.

The amount available to invest will also affect the types of investments that may be selected and indeed the strategy to be followed. For example, if there is a substantial sum of money available, the trustees will be able to diversify the investments and purchase a range of investments, perhaps through different markets and in different currencies. However, if the cash sum is relatively small, the trustees will need to select fewer investment media.

The trustees should carefully consider the need for liquidity and regularity of income, which may be needed to fund school fees, for example, and the preservation or appreciation of capital to avoid any erosion of the underlying value of the fund. This capital may have to work hard for a considerable period, or may be directed to different beneficiaries at the end of the period, who would wish the trustees to bear their needs in mind by keeping a reasonable balance between income needs and capital preservation or growth.

(d)   The expected tax consequences

Trustees may need to weigh in the balance the effect of the 'profit' on the particular investment being taxed to income tax or capital gains tax. Even though the rate applicable to trusts applies a 40 per cent rate for income of A&M trusts and discretionary trusts, which is now the same rate as for CGT, this higher rate of income tax does not apply to interest in possession trusts nor to trusts for vulnerable beneficiaries. Thus in some situations an income return might be preferable to capital profits which are taxed at 40 per cent on the gain in certain trusts.

In recent years it has become very common to add additional powers to the wording of nil rate band discretionary trusts in wills to the effect that the deceased's executors may insist on the discretionary trustees accepting in satisfaction of the settled legacy a form of debt or charge over the debtor's estate or assets originally in the deceased's estate, in place of actual cash or appropriation of assets. To ensure that the trust still achieves a return for its beneficiaries the trustees have to consider what sort of return they need – such as interest, indexation on the capital value of the loan, rolling up interest, or no return. Clearly, a significant factor in choosing the type of return in this case will be how the 'profit' will be taxed when received by the trustees.

The tax status of different beneficiaries will also vary. For example, some beneficiaries may be non-resident and this might have a bearing on whether capital gains are generated in a trust where tax is assessed on the settlor or beneficiary rather than on the trustees.

(e) Other resources of the beneficiaries

The trustees may feel that the trust fund could be invested to complement the risks and rewards which the beneficiaries' own resources are likely to achieve. It might therefore affect the trustees' decision making if the beneficiaries' only investments were in equities. The trustees might consider that gilts, bonds and property investments would provide a better balance between risks and rewards overall than if the trustees only invested in equities.

Trustees must be careful, though, of judicious breaches of trust where trying to maintain the value of trust or beneficiaries' assets by using trust funds inappropriately, e.g. *Walker* v. *Stones* [2000] 4 All ER 412.

Some beneficiaries may be in receipt of means-tested benefits and so they would see little advantage in receiving income as this would merely reduce their entitlement to those benefits. In such a situation a trust fund invested for capital appreciation might enable the trustees to make better use of the resources, perhaps by making small capital advances within permitted capital criteria for assessment to the beneficiary, or by purchasing assets for use by the beneficiary but with ownership retained by the trustees.

(f) Special assets

Some assets may have been transferred to trustees to manage to protect and preserve them for the future and may therefore be a particular trust's equivalent of 'the Crown Jewels'. Whilst trustees may yet have to sell these assets or change their nature in order to do a proper job as trustee, nevertheless the value and importance of those special assets to the trust fund will play a significant role in investment decisions and strategies.

For example, private company shares may have been placed in trust in order to avoid the division of the shareholding between individuals, reducing the risk of the break up of the company or the weakening of control in the running of the company.

(g) Extent of investment provisions in the trust deed

The trustees must act in accordance with the powers and provisions in the trust deed or under statute and it is therefore important that the extent and nature of the investment powers are considered before any decisions are taken.

(h) Investment skills of the trustees

An individual who is selected as a trustee will not necessarily have the knowledge required to manage an investment portfolio or make investment decisions.

Indeed, failure on the part of the trustees to make sure that the investments are managed by someone who is qualified and experienced could be construed as a breach of trust, and the trustees could be liable for any losses incurred or potential profits missed. Section 5 of the Trustee Act 2000 requires that *proper advice* is obtained from a *qualified person* unless it is inappropriate or unnecessary.

Investment strategy

It is the job of the trustees to set the investment strategy. They may delegate their function of day-to-day implementation of that policy to others and, indeed, will seek proper advice on the specific choice of investments to advance that strategy, but they will still set the strategy.

There are really only three key strategic options available.

1. The achievement of maximum capital appreciation.
2. The maximisation of a return on income.
3. Reasonable levels of both capital growth and income return (a balance).

Usually, the trustees of an interest in possession trust would follow option (3) although the trustees of a discretionary trust would usually select option (1) in view of the wide powers often associated with such trusts.

The selection of investments should then be made based on the overall strategy that is to be followed. The strategy would not only affect the types of investments to be selected but also the split between equities, bonds and liquidity.

Many trust instruments contain provisions authorising the trustees to invest the trust funds in whatever way they see fit and allowing them to invest in a speculative manner. Some trustees view this type of clause as a wide-ranging form of indemnity and proceed to invest in a highly speculative way in the belief that they will be protected from blame or claims for breach of trust should the trust make a loss and the beneficiaries complain. However, note the development generally with regard to exoneration clauses: *Armitage* v. *Nurse* [1998] Ch 241; *Bogg* v. *Raper* (1998) *The Times*, 22 April and *Wight* v. *Oslwang* (2000) Lawtel, 7 December, CA.

At present the Law Commission is consulting upon the prospect of a reform of trustee exoneration clauses in the light of these cases (see 'Trustee Exemption Clauses' at **www.lawcom.gov.uk/files/cp171.pdf**). Although it may continue to be reasonable for trusts to include such exoneration provisions, trustees must remain mindful of their general duty to invest trust funds in a prudent and reasonable manner. Professional trustees have a higher duty of care in this regard and as a result, a speculative investment strategy should only be considered if the trustees are comfortable that such a decision could be defended as being reasonable in the circumstances which prevail in that particular trust.

Investment reviews

If the trustees appoint an agent in good faith in accordance with the Trustee Act 2000 requirements, the trustees will not generally be liable for the default of the agent and they would be able to sue the agent for any losses caused by his negligence. However, the trustees still owe a duty of care to the beneficiaries in respect of the investment of trust funds, even if an agent has been appointed on a discretionary basis to manage the funds.

The trustees must continue to take an active interest in the role of the agent and the performance of the investments. Otherwise the trustees could be in breach of trust and potentially liable for losses arising from the poor performance or default of the agents. It is therefore advisable for the trustees to request regular reports and valuations of the portfolio from the investment agent (say, on a quarterly basis) as well as details of any transactions that are made. The trustees will then be able to provide evidence of their interest in the actions of the agents, and demonstrate that they retained ultimate control over the assets of the trust.

Trustees should review the terms of any agreement entered into with the agent on an annual basis. As will be seen in **para.5.3** trustees should have agreed a policy statement with their chosen agent and this will contain the benchmarks against which the trustees must review the performance of the agents. If the agent fails to perform his duties in a reasonable manner, any concerns should be raised with the agent and efforts made to correct the issue or, if necessary, the agent should be removed from office and a replacement appointed. Investment review is part of a trust's overall review, and a reminder is included in the Trust Review Form in **Appendix 2.6**.

5.3   CHOOSING AND SUPERVISING THE AGENT/NOMINEE/CUSTODIAN

Trustees usually appoint an agent to manage or advise on the trust investments. This is necessary if the trustees lack the required level of investment
knowledge or expertise.

The trustees should conduct a thorough *review of the capabilities* of the
proposed agent and ensure that he will be able to act in the manner required.
Only someone with the necessary skills, experience and qualifications should
be appointed to manage the investments. In some cases the settlor may ask
the trustees to appoint a family friend or associate to manage the investments.
The trustees should always consider if such an appointment is reasonable,
regardless of the views of the settlor. This is essential as a result of the default
powers in ss.11–28 of the Trustee Act 2000. The trustees would be well
advised to set a list of objective criteria and examine potential advisers
against such a list. The criteria should be set out as part of the minutes of the
trustee meeting where the choice was made, as there would then be evidence
of the objective selection process used by the trustees. The criteria might
include the following.

1.   The availability of nominee services.
2.   The experience in handling funds of this size.
3.   The ability to transact in the particular market places and segments iden-
     tified in the strategy, e.g. the relevant overseas markets chosen by the
     trustees; the commercial property sector in the UK, etc.
4.   Cost.

The trustees also need to decide the extent of the agent's role. Usually, the
agent is given discretionary powers over the investment portfolio, thereby
enabling the agent to buy and sell assets without recourse to the trustees for
approval, if deemed appropriate. However, in certain circumstances it might
be appropriate for the agent to be given advisory powers, under which any
decisions to buy or sell investments must be approved by the trustees.

Even if an agent is given complete discretion over the investments, the
trustees are still ultimately responsible for those funds, in view of their fiduciary duties and responsibilities. The trustees can delegate any of their
management functions but in doing so they do not abrogate their responsibilities. They must exercise control through the terms of the agreement between
principal and agent and be prepared to use the ultimate control of termination
of the contract in cases of underperformance or unsatisfactory service.

The Trustee Act 2000 requires trustees appointing an agent to do so *in
writing* and not to appoint people or organisations (unless there are reasonable grounds for doing so) who have limited liability or power to use substitutes. In reality, most brokerages will be operated through limited liability
vehicles and it would be difficult, if not impossible, to satisfy this principle of
the legislation.

The appointment of the agent should be discussed, against the objective selection criteria, by the trustees, preferably in a meeting and the decision confirmed in the minutes of that meeting. Alternatively, a written resolution of the trustees may be used to confirm the appointment.

An investment agreement should be executed between the trustees and the agent, formally setting out the terms and conditions of the arrangement between them. The execution of this agreement by the trustees should also be confirmed by a trustee minute or resolution. This agreement is usually in practice proffered on the standard terms of the agent and should be carefully considered by the trustees. In the case of the larger trust fund, it is possible for the investment agreement to be set by the trustees.

For all trusts governed by English law, s.15 of the Trustee Act 2000 requires that in addition to the investment agreement the agent must be given a policy statement setting out (amongst other things):

1. The aim of the investment portfolio as far as addressing the needs of the beneficiaries is concerned.
2. A summary of the trust's investment clause and any 'restrictions' on it suggested by the settlor in any letter of wishes.
3. Minimum yield requirement.
4. The trustees' objective in respect of the return on capital.
5. Acceptable level of risk, spread of investments and the degree of diversification required.
6. Timescales.
7. Timing and extent of likely realisations, e.g. for payment of taxes or distributions.
8. Ethical investment considerations.
9. Compensation and extent of insurance in the event of loss or default.
10. Frequency of investment reviews.
11. Basis of remuneration for any nominee arrangements.

The policy statement will be vital at review time – did the agent live up to the terms of the statement? Did the trustees feel that the reason for any failure to achieve the parameters set was due to the general market conditions or some other factor? Drafting the policy statement with the review in mind is a worthwhile effort. It is much easier to establish satisfaction or dissatisfaction with performance if the policy statement set expected returns and actual returns in accordance with approved benchmarks and identified acceptable levels of risk and appropriate weightings.

It will be apparent that the trustee must not simply rely on the knowledge of the chosen broker, but must get to grips with the basics of the theory employed in investment analysis. For an introduction to the mathematics and formulae behind the 'modern portfolio theory' see Isaac N. Legair, 'Modern portfolio theory: a primer' (2000) *Trust Law International* Vol. 14(2), p.75.

CHAPTER 6

Trustees' decision making

6.1 DECISIONS RELATING TO TRUST DISTRIBUTIONS

Beneficiaries frequently need money. It therefore follows that the trust administrator will regularly make distributions from trusts. This is often seen as a routine task, especially for recurring payment arrangements where all that is required is to change the date on the bank instructions. However, making a distribution from a trust, especially from a discretionary trust, is far from a routine matter and should be approached with care and a degree of caution.

Distribution requests

The trustees of discretionary trusts need to consider if the distribution request is reasonable and whether it should be granted. Remember, it is the trustees who will have the final decision in view of the nature of this type of trust. There may be guidance contained in a confidential letter of wishes provided by the settlor.

In interest in possession trusts, the life tenant will have the right to receive the trust income as it arises and may therefore contact the trustees from time to time to request an income payment. The remainderman on the other hand is not usually entitled to funds as of right until such time as the life tenant dies. However, the trustees usually have the power to advance capital to the remainderman ahead of his entitlement, either under the terms of the deed or under statutory powers, and the trustees may therefore receive requests for a capital advance from time to time. The terms of the trust may also empower the trustees to appoint capital to the life tenant.

Factors to consider prior to making a distribution

Before making a decision concerning a proposed distribution, trustees will need to consider a number of factors.

The automatic response from a trustee to a distribution request should be to refer to the terms of the trust deed. If a working copy is kept in the trust's working documents file it will be easily to hand for review.

1. Is the request being made by a beneficiary who is entitled to benefit in this way? A review of the trust deed will enable the trustees to decide if the person asking for the distribution is a beneficiary who is entitled to benefit in this way. This may sound silly but with trusts for 'children and remoter issue' a family tree may be needed to confirm whether a person meets the definition. In some cases with multiple marriages and children from various liaisons it is possible that the individual may not be included in the wording of the relevant clause of that particular trust.

2. If the person referred to above is not a beneficiary, could he be added to the class of beneficiaries? If so, what action will be required to fulfil this? In modern trusts, trustees are often given the power to add additional beneficiaries, sometimes only with the consent of others. It may be that for whatever reason a particular person is unfortunately excluded from the wording of the class, but could be added. This can arise where, for example, a relative falls on hard times, such as after divorce, and because the other beneficiaries want to help, the trustees are encouraged to add that person to the class.

3. Are consents required prior to making the distribution (e.g. from the settlor or life tenant)? Sometimes, with trusts made during the lifetime of the settlor, the settlor reserves the power to give consent or not to, for example, capital distributions from the trust while the settlor is alive. Equally, in interest in possession trusts, it is not possible without wider powers, to make distributions from the capital of the trust fund to the remainderman without following the terms of s.32 of the Trustee Act 1925. This means that no more than up to one-half of the beneficiary's entitlement can be advanced out of the fund and even then it must have the consent of the life tenant. This is for the obvious reason that a reduction in capital will have a negative effect on the amount of future income arising for the life tenant.

4. Should the distribution be recorded by deed or similar instrument? For small sums a trustees' minute or a written resolution signed by the trustees might be sufficient. In some cases, the trust deed will stipulate that the distribution must be recorded by deed, so a deed of appointment will be needed. (For a comprehensive range of subsidiary documents, see *Practical Trust Precedents* (Sweet & Maxwell, looseleaf).)

Once the deed has been reviewed the trustees should then consider practical matters, such as the following.

1. Whether there is sufficient cash available to make the distribution (assuming it is to be a payment from trust funds as opposed to a payment *in specie*, in which case the existence of the asset to be transferred should be verified).

2. Whether the proposed distribution is to be made from income or capital.

3. If the distribution is to be a capital advance, whether the remainderman's entitlement has already been exceeded (s.32 of the Trustee Act 1925 provides that no more than one-half of a beneficiary's entitlement can be advanced and many trust deeds contain a similar provision).

4. Whether the person intended to receive the distribution can provide a valid receipt for the funds (i.e. are they over the age of 18 years and of sound mind). If not, the trust deed may permit payments to be made to the beneficiary's parent, guardian or other representative.

5. Whether the proposed distribution will give rise to any taxation or reporting issues that might affect the trust or the trustees. It may also be prudent to suggest to the recipient of the funds that he also considers any taxation or reporting issues that might arise as a result of the proposed payment.

In a sense the responsibilities that are placed on the trustees of discretionary trusts are much greater than those that apply to the trustees of an interest in possession trust. This is because in a discretionary trust, the trustees usually have the power to offer, accede to, or reject a distribution request. The trustees decide who can receive a benefit, when they can receive it and the extent of that benefit.

Inevitably in discretionary trusts the trustees may benefit some beneficiaries more than others. There is a general duty upon a trustee to act impartially between beneficiaries, but this does not mean that trustees have to treat beneficiaries equally. It simply means that the trustee must act fairly. Chadwick LJ put it this way in *Edge* v. *Pensions Ombudsman* [2000] Ch 602:

> Properly understood, the so-called duty to act impartially is no more than the ordinary duty which the law imposes on a person who is entrusted with the exercise of a discretionary power: that he exercises the power for the purpose for which it is given, giving proper consideration to the matters which are relevant and excluding from consideration matters which are irrelevant. If trustees do that, they cannot be criticised if they reach a decision which appears to prefer the claim of one interest over others. The preference will be the result of a proper exercise of the discretionary power.

There is therefore room for a range of views as to whether a body of trustees has acted fairly. It will only be a breach of trust if 'their decision can be said to be one that no reasonable body of trustees properly directing themselves could have reached' (as per Scott VC in the *Edge* case).

Under no circumstances should the trustees make distributions at the request of the settlor without thoroughly considering the matters listed above. If the trustees automatically do anything asked for by the settlor without question it will give rise to the suggestion that the trust is a sham. In other words, the trust will be seen as simply the settlor's funds because the trustees are not making their own decisions.

Recording the decision

Once the decision has been taken to make a trust distribution, of either capital or income, the trustees should take steps to record their decision. Usually this will take the form of minutes of the meeting at which the proposed payment was discussed, or a resolution covering the decision to distribute. Under the terms of the trust instrument there may be a requirement for the trustees to execute a deed to make or record the distribution.

Mistake

Can trustees remedy their mistakes? There is a principle which has come to be known as the *Hastings-Bass* principle, which, until recently, could be said to answer this question in the affirmative in so far as the trustees failed to consider that which was material to the exercise of their discretion or to exclude from consideration that which was immaterial to the exercise of their discretion.

The case which lent its name to the principle was *Re Hastings-Bass Deceased* [1975] Ch 25 and the 'rule' was famously rewritten in a positive and abbreviated way by Warner J in *Mettoy Pension Trustees Limited* v. *Evans* [1990] 1 WLR 1587 as:

> Where a trustee acts under a discretion given to him by the terms of the trust, the court will interfere with his action if it is clear that he would not have acted as he did had he not failed to take into account considerations which he ought to have taken into account.

For example, in *Green* v. *Cobham* [2000] WTLR 1101 the rule was successfully used to nullify an appointment on A&M trusts by reference to unforeseen tax consequences of a subsequent event.

It had become a wide rule which reached the point where a disposition could be said to be *void* (as opposed to voidable) solely on the basis of an unexpected tax charge even if it could only be said that the trustees *might* have acted differently in the absence of their mistake or lack of foresight.

There has been criticism of the wide application of this principle as providing an escape route for all mistaken actions by trustees. Calls have come for limits on the rule to be established and in *Re Barr's Settlement Trusts* [2003] WTLR 149, [2003] EWHC 114 it was said that fault is an essential condition for the application of the rule, although it is not clear on what authority the judge imposed this restriction.

Abacus Trust Company (Isle of Man) was the trustee of the settlement created by Andrew Barr on 13 April 1992. Colyb Ltd was the protector appointed under the settlement. The application was made by the trustee and the protector for the determination of the validity of a deed of appointment made on 22 April 1992 in which the trustee and settlor exercised a power of appointment. The settlor wanted the trustee to appoint 40 per cent of the funds on discretionary trusts for his sons Brian and Russell. He instructed Mr Ward-Thompson, his accountant who was the main point of contact between the settlor and the trustee, of this. Unfortunately, Mr Ward-Thompson gave the wrong instructions to the trustee's solicitors, requesting that they appoint 60 per cent of the fund to the settlor's sons.

In August 1992 the settlor discovered the mistake but took no action to correct it. He reconsidered the matter in 1994 but did not take any legal advice. Various other appointments were made, in which the April 1992 appointment was recited. In 2001, the trustee was advised that the appointment could be challenged and the trustee applied for the determination. The Inland Revenue and the Attorney General (there was a charity default beneficiary) declined to be joined as parties.

Mr Justice Lightman decided the appointment was voidable and not void. The rule in *Hastings-Bass* afforded the beneficiaries the protection of the requirement that the trustee must perform its duty in exercising its discretion and a remedy in case of default. In the absence of any such breach of duty, the rule did not afford the right to the trustee or any beneficiary to have a decision declared invalid because the trustee's decision was in some way mistaken or had unforeseen or unpalatable consequences. To establish the breach of duty and the application of the rule, the settlor had to show that the trustee was in breach of duty in acting and relying on what it was told.

In giving instructions to the solicitor for the trustee Mr Ward-Thompson could only have been acting as agent for the trustee. In acting as the trustee's agent he misrepresented the settlor's wishes. The trustee failed to take adequate measures to ensure that it received a correct rather than garbled version of the settlor's wishes and was responsible for the default of Mr Ward-Thompson. It failed in its fiduciary duty to ascertain the true wishes of the settlor and therefore the rule applied and made the appointment voidable as a breach of fiduciary duty.

In *Wolff* v. *Wolff & Others* [2004] LTL, 7 September 2004, Mr and Mrs Wolff decided to use a solicitor, Mr Kingshill, in the preparation of a purported IHT saving scheme similar to the one which he had done for their friend, Ms Comberti.

Mr Wolff was a company director, running a business selling tropical plants. Mrs Wolff rang a flower shop with one of their two daughters. Ms Comberti told them that Mr Kingshill had prepared some documents to save her IHT and she gave the Wolffs a copy of the documents. Mr and Mrs Wolff arranged to see Mr Kingshill on 13 January 1997 after initial discussions on the telephone in which Mr Kingshill said that there was no guarantee that the scheme would work.

At the time of the meeting Mr Wolff was 61 and Mrs Wolff was 60. In Mr Kingshill's attendance note of the meeting he recorded that they owned 19 Randall Crescent, London subject to mortgages in favour of Northern Rock Building Society and Barclays Bank. Mrs Wolff owned the freehold of another building which was leased to herself and her daughter for use as the flower shop. The note went on to record that the Wolffs had seen a copy of Ms Comberti's documents and that they wanted to proceed with the same arrangements.

What was then prepared by Mr Kingshill was a trust deed in favour of their daughters and grandchildren and a lease of 19 Randall Crescent which was to start in 20 years time for a peppercorn rent. The Wolffs said they did not recall much about the meeting with Mr Kingshill and that he did not explain what would happen when the lease came into operation. The lease was in favour of the Wolffs' two daughters. It was dated 4 June 1997 and was for 125 years commencing on 4 June 2017 at the yearly rent of a peppercorn, if demanded.

The trust deed was dated 4 June 1997 and was between the Wolffs as settlors, the Wolffs and Mr David Grace as trustees and the two mortgagees. It recited that the settlors wanted to make a settlement in favour of the daughters and had transferred £1,000 and the lease to the trustees. It gave the income of the trusts to their daughters 'in their lifetime' and the capital and interest to such of their children as attained 18 in such proportions as the trustees might appoint but otherwise in equal shares. Clause 3 was a confusing default provision and there was no power to advance capital to their daughters.

The mortgagees consented to the trust deed but it became apparent in their negotiations that Mr Kingshill did not understand the structure he had created. On three occasions Barclays Bank pointed out there was an error in that the settlors could not have settled the leasehold interest but each time Mr Kingshill failed to see the point.

It was not until the autumn of 2001 when the Wolffs went to Bircham Dyson Bell to review their wills that the confusion over the meaning of the documents which had been prepared by Mr Kingshill came to light.

The Wolffs thought they could stay in their home forever and would not have to pay any rent to their daughters but would gain IHT savings by what they had done. It came as a shock to them to discover that on 4 June 2017 they would have to leave the property or commence paying a full commercial rent to their daughters in order to stay in their home. They would be at that time 80 and 81 and had no plans to move out. Also, the Wolffs thought that by the trust deed they had given their daughters access to the capital of the trusts during their joint lives when in fact it confirmed their interests to just income.

The judge had to decide whether the mistakes which occurred were as to the effect of the transaction itself rather than as to its consequences. In other words, did the Wolffs understand correctly what were the legal effects of the lease and trust deed, or did they just not like the consequences of them? If they were genuinely mistaken as to their effects then the court was able to set them aside under the general equitable doctrine of mistake (per Millett J in *Gibbon* v. *Mitchell* [1990] 1 WLR 1304).

Mr Justice Mann concluded that the Wolffs were mistaken as to the effects of the documents and therefore they were to be set aside.

6.2 LETTERS OF WISHES

Over the years it has become common practice for trust practitioners to suggest to the settlor that he prepare a letter which sets out his wishes on how he would like the trustees to administer the trust or exercise any overriding powers, and in particular how and when he would like the trust funds to be distributed. Although not legally binding, such a letter can be useful for the trustees and create a degree of comfort for the settlor, but the extent to which the contents of such a letter are followed can create numerous potential problems for the trustees.

Usefulness of a letter of wishes

The trustees of a discretionary trust are expected to administer a trust that gives them very wide powers and yet they may lack information that would enable them to exercise their powers in a reasonable manner. For example, the trust instrument will usually identify a class of potential beneficiaries but it will not assist the trustees in knowing which of these persons will be in greatest need of funds, nor will the instrument usually provide any guidance on when it might be considered appropriate to make distributions, or to whom.

The purpose of a letter of wishes is to enable the settlor to provide an insight into these areas. The settlor will often make reference to how he would like the trust to be administered after his death, which is not unreasonable given the trust will have been created using the settlor's assets.

What if the letter conflicts with the trust instrument?

There may be occasions when the settlor provides a letter of wishes that is not consistent with the terms of the trust instrument. For example, the trust instrument might refer only to the settlor, his spouse and their issue as beneficiaries but the letter may refer to a suggested distribution to the settlor's mother. In such situations, the trustees should notify the settlor (if still alive) of the inconsistencies and ask him to agree to a revised letter which is not in conflict with the trust deed.

If the settlor is already dead or unwilling to alter the letter of wishes, the terms of the trust instrument will prevail. Trustees are not under an obligation to follow a letter of wishes and should not do so if the letter either is inconsistent with the terms of the trust deed or if the actions proposed in the letter are considered by the trustees to be unreasonable.

The 'reasonableness' test is central to the administration of trusts. Whether an action is 'reasonable' is subjective as to circumstances and therefore hard to determine. As with the earlier comments on investment and distribution, an action would be considered reasonable if the trustees based their decision on all the available relevant information and took into account the particular circumstances prevailing in the trust at the time. Can the trustees honestly justify the actions they have taken?

If trustees have acted reasonably it is unlikely that their actions would be criticised in the event of a dispute, and it is also most unlikely that a reasonable action would ever constitute a breach of trust.

Sometimes the settlor's letter of wishes will contain suggestions that the trustees consider to be unreasonable. This may not have been the case at the time the letter was written but circumstances may have changed and the wishes not updated. Again, trustees should use their judgement and act reasonably.

Disclosure of trust documents

The question of whether or not a letter of wishes must be disclosed to the beneficiaries has become of considerable importance, not least because it might in fact be the document on which a set of trustees decides to approve or reject a request for funds from a beneficiary.

In *Re Londonderry's Settlement* [1965] Ch 918, the Court of Appeal basically said that a beneficiary has a proprietary right in trust documents but what was difficult to answer was the question of what is and what is not a trust document. The Court said there was not a comprehensive list but the following characteristics would be found:

1. Documents in the possession of the trustees as trustees.
2. Documents containing information about the trust which the beneficiaries are entitled to know.
3. The beneficiaries have a proprietary right or interest in the documents and accordingly are entitled to see them.

Both Danckwerts LJ and Harman LJ agreed that:

> the letters written by individual beneficiaries or other people for that matter to the trustees are not really trust documents at all. But even if they were trust documents it seems to me [that] there must be cases in which documents in the hands of trustees ought not to be disclosed to any of the beneficiaries who desire to see them.

In other words there is a distinction between trust documents which relate to trust property and documents which relate to the exercise by the trustees of their discretion. Trustees have to disclose the trust deed, subsequent appointments and trust accounts but do not need to disclose agendas and minutes of meetings in which the exercise of their discretion is discussed nor the correspondence between themselves or between the trustees and the beneficiaries.

The rights of beneficiaries to discover information from their trustees and the powers and duties of trustees to disclose such information were recently reviewed by the Privy Council in an appeal from the Isle of Man in *Schmidt* v. *Rosewood Trust Ltd* [2003] WTLR 565.

The main point of this case was the issue of whether or not the court has power to order the disclosure of trust documents in situations where the trust gave dispositive powers to the trustees and the beneficiaries are simply the object of these powers without any ownership or rights to any trust property.

On the basis of *Re Londonderry's Settlement* the question had previously been based on 'ownership'. If the documents were trust documents then the beneficiary was simply demanding to see his own documents, as he had a proprietary interest in them. If this is the only basis for disclosure, then in modern discretionary trusts trustees could not be made to account to any of the beneficiaries.

This case decided that the right to seek disclosure of trust documents was an aspect of the court's inherent jurisdiction to supervise and if necessary to intervene in the administration of trusts and did not depend on the right or claim of a beneficiary to a proprietary interest in the trust property.

Rosewood Trust Ltd was an Isle of Man trust company and managed two trusts set up by Mr Schmidt senior: the Angora trust and the Everest trust. They contained over US$105 million. Mr Schmidt senior died intestate in Moscow in 1997. Vadim Schmidt, the son, was entitled to a share of his father's estate and he obtained letters of administration in the Isle of Man and commenced proceedings against Rosewood for breach of trust and breach of fiduciary duty. He obtained an order prohibiting Rosewood from dealing with the trust assets and requiring them to make extensive disclosure.

Subsequently, Vadim commenced further proceedings seeking fuller disclosure of trust accounts and information about the trust assets. He based this action not on the earlier order but by virtue of the discretionary interests he had under the settlements personally and as an administrator of his father's estate. The Officer in the Isle of Man court made elaborate orders for extensive disclosure to accountants and lawyers to be held in confidence. Rosewood appealed, arguing that Vadim and his father never had any interest in the settlements except as the mere objects of a discretionary power of appointment and therefore were not entitled to trust documents or information. The Isle of Man appeal court set aside the original lower court's order and Vadim appealed to the Privy Council.

The Privy Council said there was no reason to draw 'a bright dividing line' between fixed interests and discretionary interests of beneficiaries, or between the rights of beneficiaries under discretionary trusts and the rights of objects under fiduciary powers of appointment. The right to seek disclosure of documents and information in order to make the trustees comply with their fiduciary and equitable obligations was not based on proprietary rights of beneficiaries but was an aspect of the court's inherent fundamental jurisdiction to supervise and, if necessary, to intervene in the administration of trusts.

No beneficiary, least of all a discretionary object, had any entitlement as of right to disclosure of anything which could plausibly be described as a trust document: the court might have to balance the competing interests of different beneficiaries, the trustees themselves and third parties, especially where there were issues as to personal or commercial confidentiality.

There were three areas where the court might have to form a discretionary judgment.

1. Whether a discretionary object or some beneficiary with only a remote or wholly defeasible interest should be granted relief at all.
2. What classes of documents should be disclosed, either completely or in a redacted form.
3. What safeguards should be imposed (whether by undertakings to the court, arrangements for professional inspection or otherwise) to limit the use which might be made of documents or information disclosed under the order of the court.

The case does not alter the fundamental rule that documents concerning the exercise of the trustees' discretion will be exempt from disclosure. Similarly, letters of wishes are treated as confidential expressions of the settlor's wishes and therefore not automatically disclosable. However, some practitioners have started to rely on internal file notes to record the settlor's wishes rather than a letter, so that legal professional privilege would prevent disclosure.

There is another issue to disclosure – to what extent must a trustee of a trust divulge information about the fund and its beneficiaries when the request comes from the family courts? Any of the usual types of settlement could be regarded as a nuptial settlement under s.24 of the Matrimonial Causes Act 1973 if it can be shown that there is a link between the settlement and the marriage itself, e.g. if the settlement was made in contemplation of the marriage or in favour of only the spouse and children.

It is only necessary for a settlement to be a nuptial one at the time of creation for the matrimonial courts to have the ability to make orders in respect of it. It does not have to remain a nuptial settlement by the time that divorce proceedings are brought (*C* v. *C* (*Ancillary Relief: Nuptial Settlements*) [2004] EWHC 742 (Fam)).

Clearly, if it can be shown that the trust was a sham and the settlor continues to behave as the legal and beneficial owner of the assets and that the trustees simply follow the settlor's directions, then the assets would be available to the matrimonial courts for distribution.

The case involving the affairs of a former MP (John Browne) clarified that it was necessary to disclose any trust interest including an interest under a discretionary trust on the 'other financial resources' section of the Form E in divorce proceedings: s.25, Matrimonial Causes Act 1973. Discretionary trusts do afford some protection because a court cannot make an order against the trust assets since no beneficiary has a quantifiable beneficial interest or any legal interest in the trust funds. However, the courts can give 'judicious encouragement' to the trustees in the hope they will benefit the beneficiary such that he will be able to make a fair division of 'his assets'. The effect of this is that the matrimonial court may make an award that is greater than would otherwise be justified on the financial circumstances of the parties in order to put pressure on the trustees to assist the beneficiary in meeting the order made against him personally.

What information must the trustees of a trust caught up in divorce proceedings produce for the court? The trustees need only provide such information as the beneficiary would be entitled to personally. In the case of a discretionary trust, no disclosure need be made of any letters of wishes, minutes and records showing how the trustees have exercised their discretion. However, trustees must confirm whether or not a particular person is within the class of beneficiaries when asked and trustees must prepare accounts and produce those.

In summary, trustees should consider the following.

1. Keeping separate parts to the minutes of trustee meetings so that the decisions about the exercise by the trustees of any discretion can be included in the confidential part of the meeting.
2. Excluding or modifying the beneficiaries' right to seek disclosure. However, any obligation to provide information should not be completely excluded as if this amounted to an exclusion of the duty to account it would surely fail as being inconsistent with a trust.
3. Making voluntary disclosure when asked for information if it is in the best interests of the trust and *all* the beneficiaries.
4. If the request is merely to satisfy curiosity and comes from a remote beneficiary who was never really intended to benefit, the trustees might decide that disclosure is unwarranted.
5. If in doubt, seek directions from the court.

6.3 TRUST PROTECTORS

Trust protectors are not very common in English trusts but are frequently seen in offshore trusts. The usual role of a trust protector is to oversee the actions of the trustees. The extent of the powers granted to the trust protector will vary from case to case but generally they will not be greater than those given to the trustees for management and control reasons. Often, the purpose of appointing a trust protector is to have someone who knows the family helping professional trustees, who may not be fully aware of the needs or problems faced by particular beneficiaries.

In a few English trusts the trustees will not be able to exercise certain powers without the approval of a trust protector. If such restrictions have been imposed under the terms of the trust instrument it is likely that these will extend to the power to distribute trust property. Although obtaining the required approval is not usually a problem for trustees, there can be instances where the consent to distribute may be withheld unreasonably by the trust protector.

If there is a requirement in the trust instrument to seek the consent of the trust protector before making a distribution, the trustees must make sure that this approval is obtained before funds are released to a beneficiary. Failure to obtain this approval would be a breach of trust and the trustees might be required to pay back into the trust any sums that have been released without approval.

If the protector will not provide his consent to distribute the trustees could do the following.

1. Accept the decision (but should not do so if the proposed distribution is reasonable).
2. Ignore the decision and proceed with the distribution in any event – this might be risky as it could result in a breach of trust. It might be better to try item 4 (i.e. ask the trust protector to reconsider) first.
3. Submit a revised proposal in the hope that this will be approved.
4. Argue the decision with the protector and ask him to reconsider.
5. Seek the views of the settlor if he is still alive or the views of the person who is perceived as the 'principal' beneficiary.
6. Attempt to have the protector removed from his role.
7. Seek legal advice on how to proceed.
8. If necessary, seek directions from the court on how to proceed.

6.4 TRUSTEE DELEGATION ACT 1999

The Trustee Delegation Act 1999 (TDA 1999) implements, with minor modifications, the changes to the law recommended by the Law Commission in its report *The Law of Trusts: Delegation by Individual Trustees* (1994, Law Com No.220).

The sections in the TDA 1999 may conveniently be subdivided into five groups.

1. Sections 1–4 create an exception to the general rule that the exercise of trustee functions may not be delegated.
2. Sections 5–6 amend the general statutory conditions on which a trustee may delegate the exercise of his trustee functions and provide for the creation of a statutory form of power of attorney for use by a trustee.

3. Sections 7–9 prevent the rules of law which require capital monies to be paid to at least two trustees from being circumvented by use of a power of attorney, and make provision relating to registered enduring powers of attorney.
4. Section 10 creates a rule of interpretation that an attorney's authority to do an act in relation to land includes authority to do that act in relation to any estate or interest in the land.
5. Sections 11–13 deal with commencement and other supplementary matters.

Background

The primary responsibility of trustees has traditionally been to hold property on behalf of the beneficiaries under the trust. The trustees must safeguard the property and deal with it in the best interests of the beneficiaries. It is a general rule of trust law that trustees, having voluntarily agreed to act as such, cannot delegate the exercise of their powers and duties. The rule is subject to the following exceptions.

1. If the instrument establishing the trust specifically authorises delegation.
2. If delegation is permitted by all the beneficiaries (for this exception to apply, all the beneficiaries must be both mentally capable and at least 18 years old).
3. If delegation is permitted under s.25 of the Trustee Act 1925 or s.3(3) of the Enduring Powers of Attorney Act 1985.

Following criticism of s.3(3) the Law Commission was asked to consider the operation of the present law. It issued a Consultation Paper, *The Law of Trusts: Delegation by Individual Trustees* (CP No.118) in 1991. The response to the paper supported the Commission's provisional conclusion that s.3(3) was inappropriate for delegation by trustees in general, but that special provision should be made for co-owners of land who are trustees. In 1994 the Law Commission published its report *The Law of Trusts: Delegation by Individual Trustees* (Law Com No.220). In the report, the Law Commission concluded that in relation to delegation by individual trustees generally the conditions imposed by s.25 of the Trustee Act 1925 were, subject to certain minor changes, appropriate but that s.3(3) was inappropriate. The Law Commission also concluded that some relaxation of the rules, designed to address the needs of beneficial co-owners of land, was justified.

The TDA 1999

The TDA 1999 has 13 sections and one Schedule that sets out the legislation that the Act repeals. It relates only to England and Wales and came into effect on 1 March 2000.

Sections 1–3 enable a trustee of land to use a general power of attorney under s.10 of the Powers of Attorney Act 1971 if he has a beneficial interest in land. A trustee who does not have a beneficial interest in land cannot so act. An absolute owner can use a general power of attorney, the nature of which is unaffected by the TDA 1999. Thus trustees who do not have a beneficial interest in the land (and PRs are included in this) must use a s.25, Trustee Act 1925 power.

Note that from the commencement date of the TDA 1999 no donee of a new enduring power of attorney (EPA) can exercise trust functions unless the power complies with either s.1 of this Act or s.25 of the Trustee Act 1925. For existing EPAs, this means that the EPA can be used to exercise trustee functions, provided that an application for registration of the power was given within one year of the commencement of the TDA 1999 and then only while the registration is effective.

Section 5 introduces the changes to the s.25, Trustee Act 1925 power to delegate. The effect of the changes is as follows.

1. Section 25 must be used by individual trustees who have no beneficial interest in the land and cannot rely on an express power of delegation.
2. To delegate the exercise of all trust functions, a trustee can use the general trustee power prescribed by s.25(6) or a form to like effect.
3. Alternatively, the trustee could delegate all the trust functions by a power of attorney drafted specifically for the purpose.
4. Where the trustee only wants to delegate some of his powers a specific power of attorney must be used.
5. The period of delegation cannot exceed 12 months from when the delegation takes effect, i.e. when it starts rather than the date of the power.
6. Both a general and a specific power may be created in favour of a sole co-trustee. Where this is done the attorney cannot give a good receipt or overreach equitable interests. They are adequate reasons for not appointing a sole co-trustee under a s.25 power.
7. Both the general and specific powers may be enduring powers.
8. The power of appointment given to an attorney acting under a registered power can be excluded by the donor of the power or the trust instrument.

Section 6 permits delegation under s.25 of the Trustee Act 1925 to be in the form of an EPA but only in respect of new powers created after 1 March 2000. Both the general and specific trustee powers can be enduring but cannot exceed 12 months.

Section 7 requires capital money to be paid to, or dealt with as directed by, at least two trustees or a valid receipt to be given otherwise than by a sole trustee. It similarly provides that at least two trustees are required by deed to overreach the beneficial interests.

CHAPTER 7

Financial services

7.1 FINANCIAL SERVICES AND MARKETS ACT 2000 (FSMA 2000)

The FSMA 2000 came into force on 1 December 2001 and the Financial Services Authority (FSA) became the single regulator for financial services in the UK. From that point the Law Society was no longer able to authorise solicitors in the conduct of investment business.

Under the FSMA 2000, firms carrying on *mainstream investment business* are authorised and regulated by the FSA. Broadly speaking, mainstream investment business is what used to be defined as 'discrete investment business'. However, Part XX of the FSMA 2000 provides for the Law Society to supervise and regulate solicitors who only carry on exempt regulated activities. The Law Society is therefore now known as a 'Designated Professional Body' for these purposes.

The FSMA 2000 defines what are 'regulated activities' (previously these were referred to as 'investment business' under the earlier legislation) but these activities are subject to the exclusions contained in the Financial Services and Markets Act 2000 (Regulated Activities) Order 2001, SI 2001/544 (RAO).

The Government decided to extend the scope of mortgage regulation to include mortgage advice and arranging in addition to mortgage lending and administration from 31 October 2004. Arranging and advising on regulated mortgage contracts is permissible if your firm operates under the Designated Professional Body (DPB) regime, if this is incidental to your trust and estate work, but you cannot recommend a particular mortgage product. To be able to select mortgages for clients and arrange the mortgages requires a firm to be authorised by the FSA.

It was also decided that from 31 October 2004 for long-term care policies and from 14 January 2005 for other types of insurance contracts that the regulatory regime would be extended to *all* types of insurance contracts.

Under the DPB regime solicitors are able to carry on 'insurance mediation activities' where they are incidental to other professional services being provided to clients.

Only approximately 300 solicitors' firms are authorised by the FSA, so by far the majority of law firms continue to be regulated by the Law Society. Such firms should ensure that their notepaper says this: 'Regulated by the Law Society' (and no longer says 'Authorised by the Law Society in the conduct of investment business', which is now incorrect).

7.2 DESIGNATED PROFESSIONAL BODIES (DPB)

Part XX of the FSMA 2000 provides for professional firms which do not carry on mainstream investment business but which may carry on regulated activities in the course of their other work, such as conveyancing, corporate, probate and trust work. Such firms will be treated as 'exempt professional firms' provided that they meet certain conditions and they are allowed to carry on 'exempt regulated activities'.

DPBs are responsible for supervising and regulating firms that carry on exempt regulated activities so that such firms do not need to be regulated by the FSA. For solicitors their DPB is the Law Society.

The Law Society is required to make rules governing the carrying on of regulated activities by its members to ensure that in providing a particular service to a particular client the member carries on only those regulated activities which arise out of or are complementary to the provision by the member of that service to that client.

In accordance with this, the Law Society has replaced the old Solicitors' Investment Business Rules with the new Solicitors' Financial Services (Scope) Rules 2001 and Solicitors' Financial Services (Conduct of Business) Rules 2001. (These rules were updated in October 2004 to reflect the fact that the FSA took over regulation of all types of insurance contracts and mortgage activities. The updated information can be obtained from **www.lawsociety.org.uk**.) The aim of the Law Society has been to try to preserve the old position under the Solicitors' Investment Business Rules, namely that so far as possible where the solicitor is conducting non-mainstream activities they should fall within the DPB regime, and therefore provided that the firm complies with the requirements of the new Scope Rules and the Conduct of Business Rules all will be well. However, if a firm either conducts mainstream investments activities without authorisation from the FSA or strays outside the DPB regime, then the consequences are very serious – indeed the unauthorised firm will be committing a criminal offence. It is therefore vitally important that *all* members of the firm are aware of the rules.

7.3 SOLICITORS' FINANCIAL SERVICES (SCOPE) RULES 2001 (THE SCOPE RULES)

These rules set out the scope of the activities which may be undertaken by firms under the Part XX, FSMA 2000 exemption. They include:

1. A list of prohibited activities.
2. Basic conditions which must be satisfied.
3. Other restrictions relating to particular types of activities/investments.

It should be noted that a new prohibited activity from 31 October 2004 is:

> entering into a regulated mortgage contract as lender or administering a regulated mortgage contract unless this is in the firm's capacity as a trustee or personal representative and the borrower is a beneficiary under the trust, will or intestacy.

The basic conditions of the Scope Rules focus on the fact that the investment activities that the firm are engaged in arise out of or are complementary to the provision of a professional service. In the case of trusts, the examples might be giving legal or tax advice, dealing with trust property, preparing trust accounts and drafting legal documents. It is therefore a similar rule to the old 'incidental exception'.

The exempt regulated activities that are carried on by a firm wanting to rely on the Scope Rules must not form a major part of the practice. The reason for this is that there is a capital adequacy test to which investment firms are subject.

Also, the Scope Rules require the firm to account to the client for any pecuniary reward or other advantage that the firm receives from a third party. This is similar to the Practice Rules. It is possible to obtain the client's *informed consent* to retain any commission and set it against the fees charged for the service. However, there is no *de minimis* provision in the Scope Rules.

A copy of the Scope Rules and other advice on the FSMA 2000 was included in a Professional Ethics Department Information Pack that was sent to all firms in September 2004. Further advice on these rules can be obtained from the Professional Ethics Department on 0870 606 2577.

7.4 FINANCIAL SERVICES AND MARKETS ACT 2000 (REGULATED ACTIVITIES) ORDER 2001 (RAO)

This Order sets out the regulated activities, the conduct of which requires authorisation by the FSA. It is very likely that firms offering conveyancing, corporate, matrimonial, probate and trust services will carry on activities which fall within the definition of regulated activities in this RAO.

The definition of regulated activities under the RAO is generally expressed as being activities relating to particular investments or groups of investments.

It is therefore generally a combination of an activity and a particular investment, as set out in the RAO, which gives rise to a regulated activity. Examples of the most common regulated activities include dealing in shares as principal or agent; advising on and/or arranging the acquisition or disposal of shares; advising on and/or arranging the acquisition or disposal of life policies; advising on and/or arranging the assignment of life polices; safeguarding and administering investments on behalf of clients; managing investments on a discretionary basis as a trustee for example; and entering into a regulated mortgage contract as a trustee.

So if you are conducting an activity capable of being regulated under the RAO and it involves a specified investment (these are listed in articles 74–89 of the RAO) then you will need to be regulated unless:

1. The activity falls within any of the exclusions contained in the RAO (this is the surest way to avoid a problem).
2. The activity is capable of being an exempt regulated activity under Part XX of the FSMA 2000 and the activity falls, in the case of solicitors, within the Scope Rules.

Under r.3 of the Scope Rules certain information must be disclosed in writing to clients before carrying on an exempt regulated activity. For new clients, the wording can be included in the Rule 15 letter. For continuing clients this should be provided in writing before any exempt regulated activity is commenced. If the firm is within the DPB regime, then where the firm is conducting exempt regulated activities it must comply with the Solicitors' Financial Services (Conduct of Business) Rules 2001. These rules regulate the way in which firms carry on these activities.

7.5   AUTHORISED THIRD PARTY (ATP)

Under the old Solicitors' Investment Business Rules most firms doing non-discrete investment business complied with the rules by using a permitted third party who was instructed by the firm to treat the firm's client as its client for the purpose of conducting investment business. The permitted third party had to be skilled and authorised in the conduct of investment business. Firms entered into agreements with suitable organisations.

Under the new arrangements these agreements are no longer required. However, the ATP may be required to confirm in writing the terms of any arrangements between it and the firm. Simply introducing a client to an independent third party, who is authorised by the FSA, with no further contact in relation to the regulated activity, is excluded from the definition of 'arranging' in the RAO. Arranging deals through an ATP is also excluded from the definition of 'arranging' in the RAO where the transaction is entered into and advice given to the client by the ATP.

It is therefore possible to contact an ATP and retain an ongoing role in the activity without being caught by the new rules. A firm may attend meetings, provide information and present the ATP's advice to the client. However, if the ATP gives the firm any commission for the introduction, then this must be accounted for to the client.

If the firm wishes to advise the client *not* to follow the advice of the ATP, this negative advice *will* fall within the definition of regulated activity but it should be covered by the Scope Rules.

Most firms will probably now use the ATP route and should consider whether it will be necessary to keep a central record of any instructions given to an ATP. If the activity is excluded by the RAO, firms will not be required to keep a record. If the activity is an exempt regulated activity firms will be required to keep a record under r.5 of the Conduct of Business Rules.

Rule 5 requires you to keep a record of the:

1. name of the client;
2. terms of the instructions;
3. date when the instructions were given; and
4. name of the person instructed.

This is similar to the information required under the old Solicitors' Investment Business Rules but fortunately it is no longer necessary to keep the information in a central file. Instead, normal file notes or letters kept on file will meet the requirements of the rule.

PART THREE

Taxation of trusts

CHAPTER 8

Introduction to taxation of trusts

Tax and trusts are intertwined and the trust administrator needs to have a sound grip on the way in which tax impinges on the administration of trusts. The trust administrator will need to be able to explain the effects on the settlor, the trustees and the beneficiaries.

8.1   SETTLORS

When a new trust is created, for trusts created during the settlor's lifetime, the taxation issues initially affect the settlor. If the trust was included in the will of a deceased settlor, they will affect his personal representatives (PRs).

If the trust is created during the settlor's lifetime, the settlor makes a lifetime gift of those assets into trust for IHT purposes and at the same time makes a disposal of those assets for CGT purposes. Whether or not he will have to pay two lots of tax in relation to the same transfer will depend on the type of assets involved and the type of trust which is receiving the assets.

If the trust is part of the settlor's will or intestacy there will usually be no CGT in respect of the transfer of the assets to the trustees since there is a tax-free uplift of the value of the assets to the date of death of the deceased settlor (s.62, TCGA 1992). This will form the base cost of the assets for the future in the hands of the trustees. Any IHT due will be calculated on the PRs of the estate and will be payable before the appropriation of assets to the trustees of the new will trust.

8.2   TRUSTEES

Once the trust is up and running, tax will affect both the trustees and the beneficiaries in different ways. Annually, income tax may be due on any income received by the trustees, as the general rule for income tax is that tax is levied on the person who receives the income (although there are some anti-avoidance exceptions to this treatment). There is no separate code for income tax as it applies to trustees. Trustees are not 'individuals' and so cannot be entitled to personal allowances. Neither are they liable to higher rate income tax as such since this is only charged on individuals. Instead, the trustees will pay income tax at the savings, basic and rate applicable to trusts rates, depending on the type of assets and type of trust.

For CGT purposes, trustees can be liable during the annual administration of the trust assets on any changes in the assets in the trust fund, such as sales and gifts of trust assets. Profits or losses can be realised on the disposal of chargeable assets by the trustees and the trustees will be assessed to CGT at 40 per cent on the chargeable gains, after exemptions and reliefs, in just the same way as an individual realising gains. However, a special feature of CGT and trusts is that there are a number of cases which give rise to 'deemed disposals' for CGT, such as a beneficiary becoming absolutely entitled to the assets in the trust. The trustees must remember to calculate the CGT due at these times and reserve sufficient monies or assets to meet the tax liability before making distributions to the beneficiaries.

The liability of trustees is personal yet joint and several so trustees should take care on accepting office to ascertain the current tax status of the trust and obtain confirmation that all taxes due have been paid or are provided for. Otherwise, a poorly advised trustee could be taking on a problem trust with tax charges due which would exhaust the fund and give rise to personal liability for the trustee. One possible reason for this would be the migration of a beneficiary abroad causing the clawback of a previously heldover gain. More simply, it could be that the trust was created during the lifetime of the settlor and that settlor has died causing a PET for IHT to become chargeable on the trust fund.

IHT may become chargeable on the trustees of a trust fund when the trustees themselves make transfers of value. Obviously in a trust situation this will be where capital assets from the trust fund are given by the trustees to the beneficiaries, as a result of which the fund decreases in value. Depending on the type of trust the transfer may be treated as a PET by the life tenant, or a chargeable transfer in a discretionary trust, or a chargeable event in an interest in possession trust because the life tenant has died.

8.3 BENEFICIARIES

Beneficiaries are not personally subject to IHT unless a distribution by the trustees is specifically made from the capital of the trust to them subject to tax. Even then in practice this usually means that any IHT will be deducted before the net capital is distributed. Otherwise, it is usually the trust fund and therefore the trustees which bear the IHT. The exception to this treatment would be where the settlor has caused a reservation of benefit by being included personally or by including his spouse as a beneficiary of the trust fund. In this case, the value of the fund will be taken into account on the settlor's death as part of calculating his IHT bill on death.

With CGT the trustees may involve the beneficiary by using holdover relief in discretionary trusts but otherwise, in general terms, the act of making a capital distribution to a beneficiary will trigger a charge on the trust fund rather than the beneficiary. There are anti-avoidance provisions which enable gains to be assessed on the settlor and even on a beneficiary.

The tax treatment of income will depend on the nature of the beneficiary's entitlement under the trust. The income received by the beneficiary will either be net of basic rate and lower rates of income tax if the trust is an interest in possession trust, or it will be net of the rate applicable to trusts. Either way, the beneficiary is entitled to receive a Statement of Trust Income Form (R185) indicating the amount of tax deducted from his income distribution over the tax year. This certificate is the beneficiary's evidence for use in his own personal tax affairs. If he is a higher rate tax payer he may have to pay some more income tax in respect of the trust income. Conversely, if he is a basic rate or non-taxpayer he may be able to use the tax certificate to claim the tax deducted by the trustees back from HMRC through his own tax office.

8.4 MODERNISATION OF THE SYSTEM OF TRUST TAXATION

The sometimes creative use of trusts has encouraged the view that trusts are mainly used as an abuse of the tax system. Increasingly, the Government has a perception that trusts are *mainly* used for tax avoidance. This negative view is also prevalent in other European countries where trusts are not part of the Civil Code tradition. It would appear that this wariness about how trusts work and the motives for using trusts is now affecting developments in both taxation and also administration, e.g. in the operation and extension of the Money Laundering Directives across the EU.

The current modernisation initiative was started by the Inland Revenue on 18 December 2003 when it presented several consultation papers which contained a package of ideas for the review of the income tax and CGT treatment of trusts. They did not contain any changes to IHT. There is a need for codification and simplification of the tax law relating to trusts, and to some extent this is part of the modernisation discussions as well as trying to design a fairer system for beneficiaries whilst not assisting those who wish to avoid tax.

The first part of the changes was designed to discourage tax avoidance. It came in with effect from 6 April 2004 and changed the rate applicable to trusts for income tax in trusts where there is no interest in possession from 34 per cent to 40 per cent; increased CGT on all trusts to 40 per cent (again a rise from 34 per cent) and increased the dividend trust rate for income tax in trusts without an interest in possession to 32.5 per cent up from 25 per cent.

The second stage of the changes was introduced in the Finance Act 2005 and brought two benefits:

1. A new £500 basic rate income tax band in all trusts without an interest in possession with the admirable aim of removing many small A&M and discretionary trusts from the need to submit annual tax returns and preventing basic rate tax paying beneficiaries from having to go through the red tape of reclaiming excess tax borne on distributions made to them.
2. Removing trusts for vulnerable beneficiaries from the new higher rates of income tax backdated to 6 April 2004 and introducing a different approach, namely, looking through the trust to the tax position of the beneficiary and charging the trust at that rate instead. See further **Chapter 11** on income tax.

The remainder of the original ideas have yet to be finalised into legislation and further changes are expected in the Finance Act 2006.

8.5   DEFINITION OF 'SETTLEMENT'

Currently (although this is one of the anticipated further changes as a result of the modernisation programme), there are different definitions of 'settlement' for each tax.

A settlement is defined for IHT (s.43, IHTA 1984) as any disposition of property that is:

1. Held in trust for persons in succession or for any person subject to a contingency.
2. Held upon trust to accumulate the whole or part of the income of the property. The accumulation of income may be obligatory or only possible by the exercise of a power to accumulate income surplus to that paid out by the trustees for the benefit of any persons.
3. Charged with the payment of an annuity or similar payment for any period.

A lease granted for life or lives or for a period ascertainable only by reference to a death will also be treated as a settlement unless full consideration is paid.

For CGT, settled property is any property held on trust other than property held for any person absolutely entitled as against the trustee or property held for any person who would be so entitled but for being a minor or under a disability (ss.60 and 68, TCGA 1992).

For income tax, ICTA 1988, Part XV distinguishes between settlements under which beneficiaries are entitled to the income from the trust property and those where it may be accumulated. Section 686 of the ICTA 1988 subjects income which may be accumulated or paid out at the discretion of the trustees to the tax rate applicable to trusts (i.e. 40 per cent from 5 April

2004), whereas income arising in trusts where the beneficiaries have a right to receive the income is taxed at 22 per cent. The provisions of ITTOIA 2005 **Chapter 5** may also operate to deem the trustees' income to belong to the settlor and these provisions should be carefully considered when a settlement is created.

HMRC have suggested as part of the modernisation project that the IHT definition should also be adopted for income tax and CGT but with the anti-avoidance provisions for both income tax and CGT retained.

Stamp Duty Land Tax (SDLT) adopts the same approach as CGT (s.105 and Sched.16, Finance Act 2003). However, where trustees acquire a chargeable interest in land they are treated, in trusts other than bare trusts, as purchasers of the whole interest acquired and not just the bare legal title (para.4, Sched.16, Finance Act 2003).

8.6 OVERVIEW

It is apparent that tax affects the creation, the administration and the termination of trusts, their settlors, trustees and beneficiaries. The following chapters in this Part of the book examine each of the taxes in turn and how they affect the three main types of trust. In **Part Four** of the book various practical events are examined and the tasks associated with them are listed together with the tax consequences. **Appendix 1** contains a case study of an A&M trust, with examples of the various tax forms which regularly require completion as part of the administration of trusts.

It is hoped that the combination of **Appendix 1**, **Part Three** and **Part Four** of this book will demonstrate to the trust administrator the effects of taxation on the administration of trusts.

CHAPTER 9

Inheritance tax

9.1 BACKGROUND

Transfers of value

Inheritance tax (IHT) law is contained in the Inheritance Tax Act 1984 and subsequent Finance Acts. It used to be called capital transfer tax. IHT is charged on the amount by which the transferor's estate is diminished in value by the transfer. It may be charged on: certain lifetime gifts, e.g. into a discretionary trust; certain transfers into and out of trusts; and on the value at the date of death of the estate of the deceased.

Husbands and wives are chargeable separately, so each can make full use of individual exemptions and reliefs. This will apply to civil partners from 5 December 2005.

Position on death

On death, the deceased is treated as making a final transfer of the whole of the value of his estate including chargeable lifetime transfers and PETs made within the seven years previous to death. The tax charged depends on the total and the extent to which the threshold is available to set against it.

Note that a deceased's estate includes the value of any interest held as joint tenant or tenant in common (although the interest as joint tenant will pass by survivorship to the other joint tenants) and the capital value of an interest in possession trust fund.

Cumulation period

IHT is a chronological and cumulative tax. A running total of chargeable lifetime transfers needs to be kept. Once the total of lifetime transfers coupled with the value of the estate on death exceeds the tax threshold (£275,000 for 2005/06), tax is chargeable on the excess.

The cumulative total is only relevant for seven years prior to death or seven years prior to a chargeable transfer. Transfers are excluded from the running total outside that period (ss.1–8 and Sched.1, IHTA 1984 and s.93, Finance Act 1997).

Rates of tax

IHT is charged at the rate of 40 per cent (death rate) and 20 per cent (lifetime rate) on the value of the estate transferred above the nil rate band threshold.

Charge to tax

Potentially exempt transfers (PETs) are lifetime transfers upon which no tax is payable at the time that they are made – instead we wait and see whether or not death occurs within seven years. Even so, there will be no tax to pay on them unless the total of all PETs exceeds the relevant tax threshold at the time of death. The PETs do however reduce the amount of this threshold that is then available to set against the value of the estate on death. A PET that becomes chargeable because of death within seven years is brought into account at the value of the gift at the time it was made and the tax is calculated on the basis of the rates in force at the time of death (s.3A, IHTA 1984).

Chargeable lifetime transfers are transfers that are immediately chargeable and therefore could incur tax at the lifetime rate (20 per cent). The main categories of such transfers are transfers to a discretionary trust.

As with PETs, such lifetime transfers are taken into account in assessing the rate of tax on death. If death occurs within seven years of a chargeable lifetime transfer having been made, then tax is recalculated on those chargeable lifetime transfers at the full rate.

The tax on chargeable lifetime transfers is usually paid by the recipient. However if it is paid by the transferor, the amount of tax chargeable is found by grossing up the amount of the gift to allow for the tax which the transferor has had to pay (ss.2, 3 and 5, IHTA 1984).

Lifetime exemptions

When considering the effect of making a gift during lifetime into trust a settlor will take into account the tax reliefs available both to IHT and CGT. The CGT position is considered in **Chapter 10**. Tables 9.2 and 9.3 set out the main exemptions. Table 9.2 lists the exemptions which only apply to lifetime transfers; whilst Table 9.3 applies to both lifetime and on death transfers.

Table 9.1   Charge to inheritance tax

Interest in possession trusts	Accumulation & maintenance trusts	Discretionary trusts
1. If made during the lifetime of the settlor it will be a potentially exempt transfer, i.e. it will avoid tax fully if the settlor survives for seven years.	1. Lifetime transfer is potentially exempt and again avoids tax fully if the settlor survives seven years.	1. This is a chargeable transfer. In the event of a lifetime transfer into discretionary trusts and if the amount transferred is within the nil rate band there will be no IHT to pay but any amount above the nil rate band will be charged to IHT at half the death rate at the time of the transfer.
2. If created on death then it will depend whether the estate of the deceased was taxable or if any exemption or relief applies, for example if the life interest granted is in favour of the surviving spouse then the gift into the trust will be exempt under the surviving spouse exemption – s.18, IHTA 1984.	2. The creation of such a trust on the death of the settlor depends upon whether or not the gift falls within the nil rate band or whether the estate bears IHT.	2. If the trust is created on death, again it will depend upon whether the nil rate band is used, in which case there will be no tax to pay or whether the estate is taxable.

Table 9.2 Exemptions that apply to lifetime transfers

Section no.	Type	Amount
20	Small gifts to the same person	Total of £250 in a tax year to any one person.
22	Gifts in consideration of marriage:	
	By a parent	Up to £5,000
	By a grandparent	Up to £2,500
	By one party to a marriage to the other	Up to £2,500
	By anyone else	Up to £1,000
21	Normal expenditure out of income	Fully exempt if: out of normal income and, taking one year with another occurs regularly, and does not reduce living standard of donor.
14 and 15	Waivers of remuneration and dividends	Exempt provided a waiver of dividends is made within 12 months before any right to the dividend arises.
11 and 51	Capital transfers for family maintenance: Part of a divorce settlement Make reasonable provision for dependent relative	Fully exempt.
19	Annual transfers	£3,000 or less per annum are exempt. Any unused portion may be carried forward for one year only.

Table 9.3 Exemptions applicable to lifetime transfers or on death

Section no.	Type	Amount
18	Transfers between spouses	Fully exempt if both spouses are domiciled in the UK; limited to £55,000 if the transfer is to a foreign domiciled spouse.
23	Gifts to charities	Fully exempt.
24	Gifts to political parties	Fully exempt.
24a, 25 and 26	Gifts of land to registered housing associations, for the national purpose and conditional exemption for heritage property	Exempt, provided undertakings such as for public access are given.
27	Maintenance funds for heritage property	Exempt, if transfers into a settlement established for the maintenance, repair or preservation of heritage property subject to a Treasury direction.

In addition to the reliefs outlined above there are two exceptional reliefs which need special consideration: business property relief and agricultural property relief. In this book only an overview can be provided, but for a specialist text on the subject see Toby Harris, *Tolley's Business and Agricultural Property Relief*, 4th Edn (LexisNexis, 2003).

9.2 BUSINESS PROPERTY RELIEF (BPR)

Basic principles

There are three key conditions which need to be satisfied in order to obtain the relief:

1. Is the business a qualifying business?
2. Is the asset relevant business property?
3. Has the minimum period of ownership been met?

The main difficulties arise where the business is a mixed type of business with some eligible activities and some which are not. The relief either applies to 'the business' as a whole or not at all. Recent cases illustrate where the dividing line lies as to whether the mix of activities produces a qualifying business or not.

Is the business a qualifying business?

'Business' includes a business carried on in the exercise of a profession or vocation but does not include a business carried on otherwise than for gain (s.103(3), IHTA 1984).

A business or interest in a business, or shares or securities of a company, do not qualify if the business (or the business of the company) consists wholly or mainly of dealing in securities, stock or shares, land or buildings or making or holding investments, unless the business is:

1. wholly that of a 'market maker' (before the Stock Exchange reform, a jobber) or that of a discount house and, in either case, is carried on in the UK; or
2. that of a holding company of one or more companies whose business does qualify.

In the case of *Brown's Executors* v. *CIR* [1996] STC SC 277 it was held that the sale of a nightclub, an asset of the proprietor's unquoted UK company Gaslight, resulting in capital being held on deposit interest account pending further investment in a future premises was not a change in the nature of the business carried on by the company. The Inland Revenue had contended that at the time of the proprietor's death the company's business consisted wholly or mainly in the making and holding of investments and therefore excluded the shares from being qualifying business property. However the Special Commissioner found in favour of the taxpayer because the proprietor intended to purchase suitable alternative premises and the deposit account holding the proceeds was of necessity short term to conclude a purchase.

See also *Burkinyoung (Executor of Burkinyoung Deceased)* v. *CIR* [1995] STC (SSCD) 29 for a business of letting furnished flats on assured shorthold tenancies which was wholly one of making and holding investments and so excluded from s.105(3). Also, in the similar case of *Martin and Horsfall (Executors of Moore Deceased)* v. *CIR* [1995] STC (SSCD) 5 the letting of properties as small industrial units was not a business as the units consisted wholly or mainly of the 'making or holding of investments'.

However, the CTO *Advanced Instruction Manual*, para.L99.3 states that furnished holiday lettings will normally be allowed relief where the lettings are short term (e.g. weekly or fortnightly) and the owner (or agent) is substantially involved with the holidaymaker(s) in terms of their activities on and from the premises. In the case of *Hall & Hall (Hall's Executors)* v. *CIR* [1997] STC (SSCD) 126 the letting of caravans on 45-year leases which comprised 84 per cent of the deceased's income in the form of rent and standing charges resulted in the determination that the business had consisted 'mainly of making or holding investments'.

In *A B Farmer (1) C D E Giles (2)* v. *IRC* (1999) SPC 00216 the deceased owned the freehold of a farm at which he had carried on a farming business.

He also let out surplus properties at the farm. The question was whether the business consisted mainly of farming (and therefore eligible for relief) or mainly letting out properties, in which case the relief would be denied.

The farm had a total acreage of 449 acres, of which the rented properties constituted approximately 8 acres. The farm was valued for probate purposes at £3.5 million, of which £1.25 million was attributable to the rented properties. The farming business was managed on a proper basis with two full-time and five part-time employees. The letting business took about one day per week of the son's time. There were 23 tenancies, most of which were residential lettings on shorthold tenancies. The non-rental turnover usually exceeded the lettings turnover but the net profit derived from letting properties usually exceeded the net profit from the farming business.

The Special Commissioner held that: the level of net profits was not the only, or even the principal factor relevant to deciding whether a business consisted 'mainly' of making or holding investments. The following factors were relevant to the decision:

(a) the overall context of the business;
(b) the capital employed;
(c) the time spent by the employees;
(d) the turnover; and
(e) the profit.

Of those factors (a)–(e), the first four supported the conclusion that the deceased's business consisted mainly of farming and was therefore eligible for BPR. Only the last factor supported the opposite view. Taking the whole business in the round and without giving prominence to any one factor, the conclusion was that the business consisted mainly of farming.

More recently BPR was considered by the Court of Appeal in *IRC* v. *George* [2004] WTLR 75; [2003] EWCA Civ 1763, which was an appeal by the taxpayers against the decision in favour of the Inland Revenue in the High Court.

The case concerned the estate of Elsie Fanny Stedman who had held shares in a company that owned land on which it ran a caravan site. The issue raised for the first time in the Court of Appeal was whether or not the business of the company consisting as it did of caravan site, a site for caravan storage and a club for residents as well as other strands, consisted wholly or mainly of making and holding investments for the purpose of s.105(3) of the IHTA 1984. The Special Commissioner found that it did not and found in favour of the taxpayer; Laddie J reversed the decision in the High Court and found in favour of the Inland Revenue. The executors appealed to the Court of Appeal.

The deceased, Elsie Stedman, held 85 per cent of the shares in a company called Dunton Park Caravan Sites Ltd. It owned the land on which it operated and provided services to caravan sites. The deceased's shareholding was relevant business property only if the business that the company carried on was not wholly or mainly making or holding investments. The company carried on eight activities with a total turnover of £633,780.

1. A residential homes park consisting of 167 mobile homes owned by the residents – the company sold the vans and took a commission of 10 per cent on sales of vans on the site.
2. Dunton Park Country Club, which was a function suite with bar – non-investment activity.
3. Caravan storage for touring vans when not in use – agreements were for fixed periods and related to a specific plot. There were 443 vans stored on site at the time of the deceased's death – investment activity (£81,732).
4. The office from which the administration of the business was run.
5. A warehouse and shop which were let out – investment activity (£9,369).
6. Fields let on grazing licences to a farmer – investment activity (included in the £9,369).
7. Insurance agency for caravan owners and residents – non-investment activity.
8. Interest receipts on capital balances – non-investment activity.

At first instance the judge said that:

> what falls within the investment business 'bag' is not only the core holding of land and the receipt of fees and rent in respect of its use but also all those activities which, viewed through the eyes of an average businessman would be regarded as incidental to that core activity.

He went on to say that having separated the investment from the non-investment activities then it is possible to decide whether the business overall consists of wholly or mainly investment activities. That is a qualitative assessment rather than a quantitative one. In this case the only areas of activity that were not investment businesses were the country club receipts and caravan sales. In the light of this analysis the judge held that the holding of investments was the very business of the company and therefore the relief was denied.

The Court of Appeal noted that the business did not include 'dealing in land or buildings' or 'making investments'. It did include 'holding investments' since land was held for the purpose of receiving licence fees for stationing mobile homes and storage; but it was not 'wholly' that of holding investments as it included some other activities carried on for profit such as the sale of caravans and the running of the club.

Lord Justice Carnforth referred to the Special Commissioner's review of the earlier caravan cases and agreed that they did not generally help the question of whether a caravan site type business generally was or was not mainly an investment type businee. The more helpful case was the Special Commissioner case of *Farmer* v. *IRC* [1999] STC 321 as it concerned itself with the need to look at the business 'in the round'.

The treatment of the residential homes park including its utility services was the central issue of this case. Calor gas could be purchased from the company; electricity was supplied by the company through its own powerhouse on the site for which the company paid a single charge to Eastern Electricity and then invoiced the van owners separately based on metered usage. Water supplies were not metered and subject to a fixed charge included in the site fee. These services were supplied at a substantial profit. The removal of refuse was organised weekly by the company but was not charged for separately.

One of the directors explained how many staff worked for the company and how their hours applied to the different activities of the company. The company's accountant produced a breakdown of the turnover, gross and net profit from the different elements of the business and the provision of utility services.

The Inland Revenue's case before the Commissioner was that investment activity included not only the holding of land but also any activities of maintenance and management which are required by the lease or are incidental to the letting. Activities which arise from compliance with the landlord's covenants will not alter the nature of the business from one of holding investments.

On this basis, all the activities surrounding the running of the residential caravan park were investment activities apart from the sales of the caravans and the sale of Calor gas (as this could be bought elsewhere if desired).

The Commissioner took the view that 72 per cent of the site fees goes towards the upkeep of the common parts and the services provided. The service element predominates and the business of the company was the provision of those services rather than the holding of investments; or in the case of the sale of gas, electricity and water, from the purchase and resale of these items at a profit.

He looked at the total turnover of the business (£633,780) and saw that the pure investment activity represented just 14.37 per cent of the turnover. The Court of Appeal did not necessarily agree with the compartmentalised approach nor with the idea that all the receipts from the residential park were non-investment income, but nevertheless did agree with his finding that taken 'in the round' it was a non-investment business.

In fact, Lord Carnforth ends his judgment by saying:

> I find it difficult to see any reason why an active family business of this kind should be excluded from business property relief, merely because a necessary component of its profit-making activity is the use of land.

The issue in *Marquess of Hertford & Others* v. *IRC* SpC 444 [2005] WTLR 85 was whether or not the freehold of a building was an asset used in the business and whether its value was an ingredient in the 'net value of the business' within s.110(b) of the IHTA 1984.

Within seven years of his death, the Eighth Marquess transferred by way of gift to his son the business of opening to the public Ragley Hall, an historic house, together with its contents and surrounding land. The executors of the Eighth Marquess sought business property relief on the whole of the family's mansion house. The whole of the exterior of the house was open to the public but only 78 per cent of the interior was accessible to the public, the remaining 22 per cent being occupied by staff and the family under a lease granted by the Ninth Marquess to his father at a rent of £10,000 per annum.

The Inland Revenue determined that so far as the value transferred by the gift made within seven years of the Eighth Marquess' death was concerned, 78 per cent of the value of Ragley Hall was eligible for business property relief under s.104 of the IHTA 1984 but the remaining 22 per cent of the freehold value was not.

The taxpayer argued that where an asset is used mainly (though not wholly) for the purposes of a business, its value should be treated as reduced by 100 per cent BPR, there being no provision in the legislation for apportionment. The taxpayer also argued that because the whole of the exterior of the house was viewed by the public and because the whole structure of the house had a protective function to the parts open to the public the house was indivisible in this case, even though a freehold property might be divisible for other cases.

The Special Commissioners held that the whole of the freehold of Ragley Hall was a single asset owned by the Ninth Marquess and that the part which was the subject of the lease back to his father formed part of that single asset, even though he was not in possession of it. It was not possible to divide the building in any sensible way:

> ... what finally decided me that the appeal should be allowed was the nature of the business in this case and the part that the physical structure of the hall played in it. It is plainly important as a single structure and the whole building is a vital backdrop to the business carried on. The whole of the exterior is essential to the business.

One wonders if by analogy it is possible that the current view of the Inland Revenue, that agricultural property relief (APR) should be disallowed in respect of the residential parts of farmhouses, is unsustainable. The valuation of farmhouses and the application of a 30 per cent discount for residential use is a practical problem with high value houses.

Is the asset relevant business property?

Relief under s.104 of the IHTA 1984 is given where the value transferred by a transfer of value is attributable to 'relevant business property'. There are six types of relevant business property, attracting relief at the rates shown in Table 9.4.

Table 9.4   Relief rates of relevant business property

1.	A business or an interest in a business	100%
2.	A controlling shareholding in an unquoted company	100%
3.	A minority shareholding in an unquoted company	100%
4.	A controlling shareholding in a quoted company	50%
5.	Land, buildings, machinery or plant used wholly or mainly in a business carried on by a company controlled by the transferor or by a partnership of which he is a partner	50%
6.	Land, buildings, machinery or plant in which the transferor has an interest in possession and which is used in his business	
	If transferred with the business:	100%
	If not	50%

The definition of 'unquoted' has varied over the years since IHT was introduced. The current definition, which has applied since 10 March 1992 is 'not quoted on a recognised stock exchange'. Shares dealt in on the USM and AIM are unquoted. All companies whose shares are traded on the NASDAQ market are quoted.

Has the minimum period of ownership been met?

In general, relief is not confined to property situated in the UK but the transferor must have owned it for at least two years before the transfer (s.106, IHTA 1984). This requirement is adapted where, within the two-year period, the property has replaced other business property, or there have been two transfers, one of which was on death.

Where one spouse transfers a business asset to the other during his lifetime, the recipient spouse must own the asset for at least two years before being able to benefit from BPR. This does not normally apply in a death situation: if the recipient spouse dies or makes a gift of the assets within the two-year period; or if the transferring spouse dies and his period of ownership together with the recipient's period of ownership exceeds two years, BPR is usually available (ss.106, 108 and 109, IHTA 1984).

> **Example**
>
> If A leaves shares on his death to B, a subsequent transfer of the shares by B can qualify for relief even if made less than two years after A's death. Similarly if X makes a lifetime transfer to Y, business property relief can be claimed on Y's death (subject only to either X or Y having held the asset for at least two years).
>
> Note that the basic difference between s.108 (where spouses are involved) and s.109 is that for the purposes of the former there is full tack on (i.e. the two-year period is satisfied if in aggregate the period is satisfied); for s.109 (i.e. non-spouse situations) the tack on requires the donor alone to have satisfied the two-year period.

Relief under s.104 of the IHTA 1984 is given automatically where it is due. It is given after agricultural property relief (if that relief applies) and before available exemptions e.g. surviving spouse exemption.

In practice, the benefit of the relief is obtained by making an appropriate deduction (with accompanying explanation) in the account by which a transfer of value is notified to the Revenue. So far as transfers on death are concerned, this is done on Sched.D14 of the IHT200 form.

9.3 AGRICULTURAL PROPERTY RELIEF (APR)

Basic principles

APR is available to the extent that the value transferred by a transfer of value is attributable to the agricultural value of agricultural property. It must not be subject to a contract for sale and the ownership and occupation conditions must be satisfied.

The relief only relates to agricultural property that is situated within the UK, even if the taxpayer is domiciled in England and Wales, the Channel Islands and the Isle of Man.

If agricultural property is identified, the relief will be given at the rate of 100 per cent, if the land was valued with vacant possession or was let on a tenancy beginning on or after 1 September 1995. Otherwise, only 50 per cent relief applies.

'Agricultural property' means agricultural land or pasture and includes woodlands and other buildings used in connection with the intensive rearing of livestock or fish if the woodlands or building are occupied with agricultural land or pasture and the occupation is ancillary to that of the agricultural land or pasture. It also includes such cottages, farm buildings and farmhouses, together with the land occupied with them, as are of a character appropriate to the property (s.115(2), IHTA 1984).

The breeding and rearing of horses on a stud farm and the grazing of horses in connection with those activities is to be taken to be agriculture and any buildings used in connection with those activities to be farm buildings (s.115(4), IHTA 1984).

Livestock, deadstock and farm plant and machinery are not included, but these may qualify for business property relief, as may the value of land in excess of its agricultural value and milk quota where it is valued separately (*Tax Bulletin*, February 1993, p.51).

From 6 April 1995, land used for short rotation coppice will count as agricultural property and qualify for either 100 per cent or 50 per cent relief depending upon the circumstances, as will buildings used in the cultivation, which will be regarded as farm buildings. Similarly, farmland and buildings used for the management of habitat land (land dedicated under the Government's habitat scheme) counts as agricultural property for the purpose of relief at 100 per cent or 50 per cent.

Nature of relief

The relief applies only to the agricultural value of the property and this is ascertained on the basis that the property is subject to a permanent covenant prohibiting the use of the property for any other purpose. Tax on lifetime transfers that are not PETs will be calculated subject to the relief, which is given by way of a percentage reduction in the value of the property.

Minimum period of ownership

The property must have been either:

- occupied by the transferor for the purposes of agriculture throughout the period of two years prior to the date of the transfer; or
- owned by the transferor and occupied by him or someone else for the purposes of agriculture throughout the period of seven years prior to the date of the transfer.

Periods of ownership by individual spouses can be cumulated where one inherits on the death of the other. Also, if the transferor controls a company which occupies the property he will be treated as occupying personally. Where the property transferred is occupied by the transferor and replaces other agricultural property owned by him, the periods of ownership can be added together for the purposes of meeting the requisite ownership period (two out of last five years of ownership or five out of seven).

Table 9.5 Tax on lifetime transfers that are not PETs

1.	Where the transferor immediately before the transfer enjoyed either the right to vacant possession or the right to obtain it within the next 12 months	100%
2.	The transferor was beneficially entitled to his interest since before 10 March 1981 and (i) if he had disposed of it by a transfer of value immediately before that date, he would have been entitled to claim the 50% relief available between 6 April 1976 and 10 March 1981; and (ii) that relief would not have been restricted by reference to the limits of £250,000 or 1,000 acres (whichever was the more favourable to the taxpayer) which applied between those dates; and (iii) the interest did not in the period from 10 March 1981 to the date of the transfer, give him the vacant possession rights in (1) above and did not fail to give him those rights because of any act or deliberate omission by him during that period	100%
3.	Where transfer of value relates to farmland which was let for periods exceeding 12 months let on or after 1 September 1995	100%
4.	Transfers of value of farmland and related buildings that have been dedicated to wildlife habitats on or after 26 November 1996 which meet the usual ownership criteria	100%
5.	In relation to transfers of value made and other events occurring after 9 March 1992 not covered by (1) to (4) above	50%

Charges

A basic rule of IHT is that assets are valued after the deduction of charges secured against them and tax is paid on the balance. This means that any secured loans against business or agricultural property also reduce its value for the purposes of the relief. If possible loans should be secured against assets that do not have the benefit of the relief so as to maximise eligibility.

Binding contracts for sale

For both BPR and APR the effect of a binding contract over relevant property is to remove eligibility for the relief.

Farmhouses

For a house to be eligible for treatment as a farmhouse, and therefore to potentially obtain 100 per cent relief upon it for IHT purposes there are three key stages.

1. Is the house 'agricultural property'?
2. Even if it is agreed that the house is 'agricultural property' is it of a 'character appropriate' to that agricultural land?
3. Has it been occupied for the purposes of agriculture for the requisite period?

There has been difficulty in recognising whether any dwelling house qualified for APR since the current legislation came in, in 1981 culminating in the leading case of *Lloyds TSB as Personal Representative of Rosemary Antrobus Deceased* v. *IRC* [2002] WTLR 1435.

The house in this case, Cookhill Priory, was a six-bedroom house dating back to the mid-sixteenth century. A Georgian extension had been added in about 1765 and 20 years later the Chapel of Nuns was rebuilt. The deceased's father had bought the Priory in 1907 together with 126 acres of land. He farmed the land himself until 1942, dying in 1943. His widow died in 1959 and Miss Antrobus, having had a tenancy over most of the land since 1942, acquired the property on her mother's death. The house was Grade II listed because of its historical interest.

Miss Antrobus was a farmer, both arable and livestock. She showed losses in her accounts between 1995 and 2001 although previously profits had been made. She died on 22 June 2001 and all the land and buildings were agreed to be agricultural property except for two let houses and Cookhill Priory. It was agreed that the Priory was a farmhouse, the only issue was whether it was of a character appropriate to the agricultural property.

To decide, the Special Commissioner applied five tests.

1. Whether the house is appropriate by reference to size, content and layout, with the farm buildings and the particular area of farmland being farmed (*Korner & Others* v. *IRC* (1969) 45 TC 287).
2. Whether the house is proportionate in size and nature to the requirements of the farming activities conducted on the agricultural land or pasture in question (*Starke* v. *IRC* [1994] STC 295).
3. The 'know it when you see it' test (one of the tests applied in *Dixon* v. *IRC* [2002] WTLR 175).
4. Whether the educated rural layman would regard it as of a character appropriate, in particular whether it was a dwelling house with land, or a farmhouse with a farm (the second test in *Dixon*).
5. Whether the house has been historically associated with the agricultural property and whether there was a history of agricultural production (the third test in *Dixon*).

Expert evidence was brought on behalf of the estate, in which evidence of 27 comparable buildings in the locality indicated it was of a character appropriate. The Inland Revenue argued that although it was a farmhouse it had a dual purpose as having become the dwelling of a prosperous person surrounded by parkland, and on economic grounds the holding was not economic.

The Special Commissioner, applying the five tests, found in favour of the taxpayer. Considerable weight was attached to the expert evidence of comparables.

9.4 INTEREST IN POSSESSION TRUSTS

The creation of such a settlement during the settlor's lifetime is a PET.

On the death of the life tenant the underlying capital value of the trust fund will be added to his free estate for the purposes of calculating the IHT due on the trust fund on the death of that life tenant (s.49, IHTA 1984).

The trust may contain powers to advance capital or appoint it either to the beneficiary during his lifetime or to be given to the beneficiary to appoint the fund in favour of others after his death. The termination of a life interest will generally be a PET by that beneficiary (ss.51 and 52, IHTA 1984).

On any *inter vivos* termination of an interest in possession the beneficiary may give notice to the trustees of the settlement of the availability of his annual exemption or the fact that he is making a gift in consideration of marriage, and these reliefs may be claimed.

There will be no charge to IHT on a beneficiary's interest in possession coming to an end other than on death where the beneficiary becomes absolutely entitled, e.g. he satisfies a contingency.

Example: the Llewellyn trust

This trust was created under the will of Frederick Llewellyn who died on 1 January 1989. He appointed his two daughters as his executors and trustees.

His widow, Elizabeth was the life tenant of the trust fund and died on 22 November 2004, domiciled in England and Wales. The trust provided that the income should be paid to Elizabeth during her lifetime and then the capital should pass to the two daughters, Jane and Angela, equally. There was a substitute for grandchildren but both Jane and Angela were living at the relevant date.

On Mrs Llewellyn's death the IHT was calculated as follows.

	Gross £	Tax £
Free estate	256,000.00	
Llewellyn trust	694,100.00	
	950,100.00	
Less nil rate band at date of death	(263,000.00)	
Total at 40%	687,100.00	274,840.00
Payable by:		
PRs of Elizabeth Llewellyn decd.		
256,000/950,100 × 274,840		74,054.35
Trustees of Llewellyn trust		
694,100/950,100 × 274,840		200,785.65

9.5 DISCRETIONARY TRUSTS

Lifetime transfers into discretionary trusts are not PETs so transferring assets into such trusts without the settlor incurring a liability to IHT relies on the availability and applicability of the lifetime exemptions and reliefs set out earlier in this chapter.

Apart from the possibility of a charge to IHT on transferring assets into such a trust (20 per cent rate of tax applies on lifetime transfers) there are two other occasions of charge, i.e. the 10-yearly charge and distributions from the settlement.

The 10-yearly charge arises on the tenth anniversary of the creation of the trust, and then at the end of each subsequent 10-year period during the life of the trust (s.64, IHTA 1984).

This is calculated as though a transfer of value is made of the property in the settlement on the tenth anniversary of its creation, together with any related property and by a settlor who had a cumulative total equal to the value of the chargeable transfer made by the settlor in the seven years prior to the creation of the trust, plus the amounts upon which IHT has been charged on any distributions from the settlement in the previous 10 years.

Tax is charged on the value of any relevant property (taking into account any BPR or APR due) in the trust immediately before the anniversary. Tax is calculated assuming the value of the relevant property includes in addition the total of all chargeable transfers made by the transferor (in lifetime settlements) in the previous seven years. The rate of tax is 30 per cent of 20 per cent of the amount by which the total exceeds the nil rate band (NRB) calculated as follows:

$$([\text{Relevant property} - \text{current NRB}] \times 20 \text{ per cent}$$
$$- [\text{cumulative total} - \text{current NRB}] \times 20 \text{ per cent}) \times 30 \text{ per cent}$$

On the basis of the current lifetime tax rate of 20 per cent, the rate of tax charged on each anniversary can never be more than 6 per cent.

Distributions from the settlement are charged at a proportionate rate of tax – either one-fortieth (for each complete quarter which has elapsed since the inception of the trust or since the last 10-yearly anniversary) of the effective rate (if the trust has passed its first 10-year anniversary), or the rate fixed on inception (if the distribution is within the first 10 years) (s.69, IHTA 1984).

Where the settlor has made no prior transfers in the previous seven years and the value transferred is within the nil rate band there will be no charge to IHT on distributions made within the first 10 years of the trust or on its first 10-yearly anniversary. Thereafter, it will depend on whether the value of the assets in the fund exceeds, at the relevant dates, the nil rate band threshold at the time.

For this reason, it is sometimes the case that a settlor will be advised to make several unrelated discretionary settlements on separate days by placing assets likely to grow in capital value into different discretionary trusts so that any growth will be divided up and each trust will have an entitlement to its own nil rate band. Obviously the 'clock' for each subsequent settlement has to take into account the earlier gifts, but even so more value can be transferred overall without a charge to IHT.

Note that the *Ramsay* principle means that care should be taken to have differently constituted trusts with different beneficiaries, varying accumulation and perpetuity periods, even differing governing laws. However, bear in mind that in practical terms, too many trusts can be unwieldy to manage.

'Related settlements' are other settlements made on the same day by the same settlor unless the property is held for charitable purposes only (s.62, IHTA 1984). Where two or more settlements are related to one another, whether or not they are discretionary settlements, the property comprised in them immediately after they commence will be taken into account when calculating the IHT on any 10-year anniversary or distribution from any which are discretionary. Thus a settlor should not create a discretionary settlement on the same day as any other trust. This can be a practical problem when including trusts in wills since it is common to include at least one discretionary trust over the nil rate band and possibly other trusts. All trusts in the will are treated as having the same commencement date for IHT purposes, i.e. the date of death of the settlor. Fortunately, where the trust is an interest in possession trust in favour of the deceased's spouse, then it will not be treated as a related settlement for these purposes (s.80, IHTA 1984).

Given the special way in which IHT is calculated on discretionary trusts it is preferable to ensure that, when the settlor is making lifetime gifts, any discretionary trust pre-dates any PETs as this will help to avoid the complexity of the settlor's prior cumulative total on death subsequently affecting the correct tax rate on the 10-yearly anniversaries or on distributions from the trust.

For useful worked examples and further information, see IHT16 (obtainable free from a Tax Enquiry Centre or Tax Office).

The death of any of the class of beneficiaries including the surviving spouse will not give rise to a potential charge to IHT on the fund. Neither will it be aggregated with any beneficiary's free estate. The trustees would also have the discretion to deal with the different beneficiaries' needs in appropriate ways.

Example: the Ashburton trust

Jocelyn Ashburton created the Ashburton trust on 6 April 1990 by transferring assets worth £500,000 into a discretionary trust (to include the IHT due which he paid personally). Jocelyn's gross chargeable transfers in the preceding seven years totalled £100,000. He had no available annual exemptions or other reliefs.

Under the terms of the trust deed the trustees have discretionary power to pay income to any of the named beneficiaries and to accumulate any income that is not so applied. The accumulation period is 21 years and the perpetuity period is 80 years.

A distribution of £10,000 was made by the trustees (Ian Fleece of Fleece, Grabbit & Run, solicitors and John Pound of Pound, Shillings and Pence, accountants) to Alastair Ashburton, a grandson of the settlor, on 6 April 1995, subject to payment of the tax due out of that amount.

The market value of the trust fund was £775,000 on 6 April 2000.

On 27 May 2005 the trustees made a distribution of £25,000 to Janine Ashburton, the settlor's daughter, paying the tax due out of the remainder of the settled fund.

Tax position of settlement (settlor having paid the tax)

	Gross £	Tax £
Deemed cumulative total – settlor's previous transfers	100,000	–
Deemed chargeable transfer – initial value of trust fund	500,000	96,400
	600,000	89,200

(*600,000 −154,000 = 446,000 @ 20%)

Effective rate $= \dfrac{89,200}{500,000} = 17.84\%$

Actual rate is 30 per cent of effective rate, i.e. 5.35%

6 April 1995 – distribution to Alastair

Exit charge on distribution
Amount chargeable: £10,000
Actual rate: 5.35 per cent
Number of complete quarters between 6 April 1990 and 6 April 1995 = 20
The charge is 20/40th of 5.35 per cent of £10,000, i.e. £267.50

6 April 2000 – 10-yearly charge

	Gross £	Tax £
Settlor's previous transfers within seven years of trust set-up	100,000	
Distributions subject to exit charges in previous 10 years	10,000	
	110,000	
Value of relevant property at 5 April 2000	775,000	130,800
	885,000	130,800

(*885,000 −231,000 = 654,000 @ 20%)

Effective rate $= \dfrac{130,800}{775,000} = 16.87\%$

Actual rate is 30% of effective rate, i.e. 5.06%
Tax payable by the trustees is £775,000 × 5.06% is £39,215

27 May 2005 – distribution to Janine

Exit charge on distribution to Janine

Actual rate at previous 10-year anniversary: 5.06%

Number of complete quarters between 5 April 2000 and 27 May 2005 = 20

Rate of exit charge applicable:

5.06% × 20/40th = 2.53%

Distribution of £25,000 net, gross equivalent:

$$25,000 \times \frac{100}{97.47} = £25,648.92$$

Exit charge payable by trustees is £25,648.92 × 2.53% i.e. £648.92

9.6 ACCUMULATION AND MAINTENANCE TRUSTS (A&M TRUSTS)

A&M trusts were introduced in 1975 with the introduction of capital transfer tax (CTT). CTT charges were high so the extension of these to discretionary trusts made them immediately less attractive as tax mitigating tools. Although adult beneficiaries could be given outright gifts or interest in possession gifts instead, the changes to CTT did disadvantage minor beneficiaries for whom outright gifts or gifts on interest in possession trusts are less appropriate. Unborn beneficiaries were also clearly prejudiced by this change as obviously they could not recieve outright gifts!

To address the position of unborn and minor children, the Finance Act 1975 made provision for the creation of trusts which are now known as A&M trusts. This encouraged appointments out of old discretionary trusts to A&Ms because of their favourable IHT treatment. An A&M trust is a special form of discretionary trust – special because there are IHT benefits by comparison to the IHT regime for discretionary trusts.

Although there are three main ways of giving property to children (by bare trust, life interest trust or A&M trust) the creation of A&M trusts remains popular because it is largely an IHT-free zone. Bare trusts have been disadvantaged by the Finance Act 1999, as far as trusts created by parents are concerned. Life interest trusts give rise to a charge to IHT when the life tenant dies or will be treated as a PET if the trust is broken up before the life tenant's death.

An A&M trust is also a hybrid trust between an interest in possession trust, where someone has the right to receive income as it arises, and a non-interest in possession trust, where the beneficiaries have no particular right to any interest in the trust, merely the hope that the discretion vested in the trustees will be exercised in the particular beneficiary's favour. This is because the A&M trust is one where the property is held on trusts such that no one is *entitled* to an interest in possession but one or more beneficiaries will on or before attaining the age of 25 *obtain* an interest in possession. The income meanwhile is to be accumulated so far as not applied for the maintenance, education or benefit of a beneficiary.

The A&M trust is a hybrid because as and when a beneficiary satisfies any age contingency over income, that beneficiary will have a right to receive the income then arising as it arises even if the beneficiary has not as yet gained entitlement to the capital. Also, there may well be a class of beneficiaries who have yet to reach the vesting age for income and so as yet they have no right to anything. This can arise because the trust deed specifically sets different ages for entitlement to income and capital or, more likely, because the provisions of s.31 of the Trustee Act 1925 apply to grant the right to receive the income to beneficiaries at the age of 18, but who have up to that point had no vested interest in the income, whilst the trust provides entitlement to capital at, say, the age of 25.

A&M trusts are creatures of legislation – they exist if the terms of the trust are within the provisions of s.71 of the IHTA 1984 and are automatically affected by s.31 of the Trustee Act 1925 unless for some reason this section has been expressly excluded. Section 31 can be excluded but then the trustees will undoubtedly wish to have the express power to accumulate given to them, since without this there is no power to accumulate income without s.31 being in operation. Most draftsmen will leave s.31 of the Trustee Act 1925 to apply as a shorthand way of enabling the trustees to use the income arising for the benefit of beneficiaries who are not yet entitled to it as of right, and requiring them to accumulate any surplus.

There are, in practice, three main types of A&M trust.

1. A trust for a single beneficiary.
2. A trust for a known and fixed number of beneficiaries who are all alive at the time of the trust's creation.
3. A trust for a class of beneficiaries which is not limited to those who are alive but will include children born afterwards.

The drafting of the third type is very tricky mostly because of the effect of the prohibition on accumulating income beyond 21 years from the date of commencement of the trust, apart from the limited extension afforded by s.31 of the Trustee Act 1925.

There are three main IHT advantages for A&M trusts.

1. A gift to an A&M trust is a PET.
2. No periodic or exit charges arise, as they do under the discretionary trust regime.
3. There is no exit charge to IHT on a beneficiary attaining an interest in possession on or before attaining the age of 25.

On creation

If an A&M trust is created during the lifetime of the settlor rather than in a will then the transfer into trust is a PET from an IHT point of view. This means that no tax is paid at the time the trust is created. Instead, we wait and see if the settlor lives for seven years following the creation. If so, then the PET will not be subject to IHT on the death of the settlor.

If the settlor does die within seven years of creating the trust then, as with any other PET, the date when it was created will be relevant. PETs that become chargeable are cumulated on a strict chronological basis, i.e. go back the full seven years and work forward to date of death. The earlier the PET and the lack of other prior PETs which have become chargeable make it likely that the nil rate band available on death will cover the PET. This means that even though the PET has become chargeable, if its value at the time of the gift proves to be within the available nil rate band on death there will be no IHT to pay in respect of the PET, as the effective rate of IHT on it will be 0 per cent.

To the extent that the PET exceeds the available nil rate band it will be taxable at the death rate on the value of the gift to the trust at the time when the PET was made. If special assets were included in the gift, such as business or agricultural property, then at the time the trust was created 100 per cent BPR or APR may have been available but by the time the PET becomes chargeable these generous rates of relief may well have decreased. In this case it will be the rate of relief applicable at the time the PET becomes chargeable which will be relevant when calculating the IHT due in respect of the chargeable PET. Since 10 March 1992, transfers of business and agricultural property into an A&M trust may be eligible for 100 per cent or 50 per cent relief.

Remember that for the trustees to be eligible for BPR/APR they must satisfy the relevant conditions, in particular the minimum periods of ownership, so that until the trustees have owned the assets for that period they will not be eligible for the relief should they choose to transfer the assets to a beneficiary.

A particular problem for A&M trusts is where the settlor dies within seven years of making the trust gift so that the clawback provisions for BPR/APR have to apply (s.113A, IHTA 1984 for BPR and s.124A, IHTA 1984 for APR). The basic rule is that where a transfer occurs for IHT purposes, such as death of the settlor, BPR/APR may be lost unless certain conditions are met:

1. the original property or any replacement property was owned by the transferee throughout the period beginning with the date of the chargeable transfer and ending with the death of the transferor; and
2. that in relation to a notional transfer of value made by the transferee immediately before the death, the property would qualify for relief (in the case of BPR but for the operation of s.106); and
3. that the property transferred was relevant business property/agricultural property at the time of the transfer.

If a beneficiary has attained an interest in possession between the date of commencement of the trust and the settlor's death, the clawback provisions would apply to treat that beneficiary as the 'owner' of these special assets and therefore the change from ownership by the trustees will trigger the clawback of the relief as far as that beneficiary's share is concerned. As far as the rest of the fund is concerned, the trustees will still be regarded as the owner and appear to be safe from clawback.

On termination of the trust

Once the trust is up and running if s.71 of IHTA 1984 applies then there is no charge to IHT when the assets vest in a beneficiary and no 10-year anniversary charge, which would be the case if the trust were simply a discretionary trust. Instead the beneficiary receives his share of the assets IHT free.

Where the trust was created on or after 15 April 1976 and where the beneficiaries are not all children of a common grandparent there is an exception to this important rule. In such a case after the expiration of 25 years IHT is chargeable at the rate of 21 per cent: being a rate of 10 per cent for the first 10 years plus 8 per cent for the next 10 plus 3 per cent for the next five years giving a cumulative rate of 21 per cent (s.71(3), (5) and s.70(6)).

If the settlor was UK domiciled, the entire fund will incur this 21 per cent charge, there is no nil rate band to apply although APR/BPR will apply if appropriate. If the settlor was not UK domiciled, the tax charge will apply to just the UK situs assets.

On the 25th anniversary of the trust it will cease to be an A&M trust and will become an ordinary discretionary trust incurring the usual 10-yearly periodic charges and exit charges from the date of that anniversary.

Avoiding the IHT charge

The charge to IHT at the end of the 25-year period can be avoided if the beneficiaries acquire an interest in possession, since where an A&M trust ceases to qualify as such by reason of a beneficiary acquiring an interest in possession prior to or on attaining the age of 25 no charge to IHT arises (s.71(4), IHTA 1984).

To implement this change at the necessary time, the trustees need to have appropriate powers of appointment. The trustees will need to exercise their powers giving the beneficiaries an outright entitlement or an interest in possession in all the assets that will be subject to the charge.

Check the powers of appointment granted to the trustees. Many of the early A&M trusts were restrictive in nature and draftsmen were anxious not to let such a favoured trust get outside the s.71 regime and so some will not afford the trustees the necessary powers. Section 32 of the Trustee Act 1925 will, in its unamended form, allow trustees to exercise a power to advance up to half the fund, but this will leave the remainder in charge to tax. Frequently, of course, the wording of s.32 of the Trustee Act 1925 is altered to allow for the whole of a beneficiary's interest to be advanced and this will overcome the problem.

The position is complicated where the assets in the trust fund comprise land and unquoted shares, i.e. assets that are not easily divided between the beneficiaries by virtue of what has become known as the rule in *Crowe* v. *Appleby* [1975] STC 502.

In this case, the trustees of a will held freehold property in equal undivided shares. While one of the shares had vested absolutely, the remaining shares were held in trust for the children of the deceased for their lifetimes. When one of the children died, so their share vested absolutely in their own children, the Court of Appeal held that the children had not become absolutely entitled against the trustees, since there were still shares in the property held in trust.

The effect of this rule is therefore that absolute entitlement to such undivided assets may not arise until all the presumptive beneficiaries have attained the vesting age.

This is unfortunate as in order to be able to hold over the inevitable gain arising on the 'disposal' of the trust fund to the beneficiaries, capital vesting must occur at an age no later than 25 as otherwise the exemption in s.71(4) of the IHTA 1984 would not apply so that the s.260(2)(d), TCGA 1992 holdover relief would not be met. Without this relief this would give rise to a gain assessable on the trustees.

If the class of beneficiaries eligible to be considered for benefit under the trust has not closed at this point this will inevitably be a problem. If the trustees are able to use wide powers of advancement to effectively close the class by advancing the capital out of the trust fund on to new trusts in favour of the existing beneficiaries, this might be a solution to the problem.

On death of beneficiary

The trust fund will not form part of the beneficiary's estate for IHT purposes if he dies before attaining an interest in possession.

Once the child has attained an interest in possession, the child's interest in the trust is no longer in an A&M trust for IHT purposes, with the result that if the beneficiary dies after attaining the interest in possession his share of the trust will be taxed along with his free estate, in the same manner as any other interest in possession. The trust fund's assets will of course pass under the terms of the trust though rather than under the deceased beneficiary's will or intestacy.

On variation of the shares

Trustees may be given power to vary the size of the shares to which beneficiaries will become entitled either absolutely or to an interest in possession by age 25. If such a power is exercised before a beneficiary attains an interest in possession, this is not a transfer of value for IHT purposes. However if the power is exercised at a time when a beneficiary does have already an interest in possession and that interest is revoked, such a revocation will be a PET or a chargeable transfer, depending on whether the revocation is absolute or on discretionary trusts.

CHAPTER 10

Capital gains tax

10.1 INTRODUCTION

Capital gains tax (CGT) was introduced with effect from 6 April 1965. The legislation was consolidated in the Taxation of Chargeable Gains Act 1992 (TCGA 1992) and has been significantly amended since.

CGT arises when 'chargeable assets' are 'disposed' of. Chargeable assets are all forms of property unless specifically exempt. Examples of exempt assets are an individual's only or main residence (s.222, TCGA 1992), chattels worth less than £6000 (s.262, TCGA 1992), private motor cars (s.263, TCGA 1992), and prizes and betting winnings (s.51, TCGA 1992).

A disposal can be by way of a gift or sale or, for example, if insurance proceeds are received for damage to an asset.

10.2 CGT COMPUTATION

Gains and losses are calculated on each asset and are calculated in the following way.

	£	£
Sale proceeds/market value		X
Less:		
Market value at 31/3/82 or original cost	A	
Indexation allowance (frozen at 5/4/98)	B	
Costs of disposal	C	
		(Y)
Gross gain		Z
Taper relief applied to Z		
Less: Annual exemption		(4,250) (2005/06)
(one-half an individual)		
Net gain		£ D

Irrespective of the type of trust, the trustees will suffer capital gains tax at 40 per cent (34 per cent on or before 5 April 2004) on their actual and deemed disposals of property during the continuance of the trust.

Trustees have one-half of the annual exemption of an individual and therefore for 2004/05 the annual exempt amount is £4,100 and for 2005/06 it is £4,250. If there are related settlements, this exemption is shared between all the related settlements.

The charge to CGT is based on disposals and deemed disposals and tax is calculated in the same way as for an individual, with indexation allowance being available from 31 March 1982 re-basing (for which there may be an estate election re-basing all the assets to the value at this date) to 5 April 1998, when indexation was stopped.

Shares are dealt with differently in that 'pools' of the same type of share-holding in the same company are created and indexation was given, up to 5 April 1998, on the occasion of any additions or exits from the pool. It is also necessary to remember that bonus, scrip and rights issues add to a pool. The effect of pooling is that individual acquisitions lose their identity in the pool, which is treated as a single asset with an overall average cost per share.

The introduction of CGT taper relief means that pooling ceased for acquisitions on or after 6 April 1998. This is necessary so that the time of each acquisition can be recorded and retained and each treated separately from other acquisitions.

Different rules for identifying shares disposed of with those acquired apply for disposals after 5 April 1998, which are identified with acquisitions in the following order.

1. Same day acquisitions.
2. Acquisitions within the following 30 days.
3. Previous acquisitions after 5 April 1998, identifying the most recent acquisitions first (a last-in-first-out basis).
4. Any shares comprised in the pool at 5 April 1998.
5. Any shares held at 5 April 1982.
6. Any shares acquired before 6 April 1965.

If the above identification rules fail to exhaust the shares disposed of, they are to be identified with subsequent acquisitions.

10.3 OCCASIONS OF CHARGE

The gift to a settlement, of whatever type, may give rise to a charge to CGT for the settlor. In addition, the appropriate percentage of taper relief will apply depending on whether the settlor is settling business or non-business assets.

Alternatively a claim for holdover relief under either s.165 of the TCGA 1992 (gifts of business assets) or s.260 of the TCGA 1992 (gifts chargeable to IHT, etc.) may be made to postpone the charge, in which case the trustees will acquire the settled assets at the indexed base cost of the settlor. On any subsequent disposal of those assets the trustees will suffer CGT not only on the gain accruing during their period of ownership but also on that accruing during the ownership of the settlor. Restrictions on the use of holdover elections were introduced in s.22 of, and Sched.21 to, the Finance Act 2004. These restrictions relate mainly to settlor interested trusts and discretionary trusts where relief may be claimed in the future under ss.222–225 of the TCGA 1992.

It may be possible to pay any tax due by instalments under s.281 of the TCGA 1992.

Interest in possession trusts

(1) Life interest terminates other than on death

When a life interest terminates other than on the death of the life tenant and on such a termination some person becomes absolutely entitled to the trust assets, the trustees will (under s.71 of the TCGA 1992) be deemed to dispose of the assets forming part of the settled property to which the person becomes absolutely entitled and to reacquire that property as nominee for the person so entitled within s.60. Such an occasion will arise, for example:

1. When a beneficiary satisfies a contingency and becomes absolutely entitled to the settled property.
2. By an arrangement between the life tenant and the remainderman whereby the life interest is surrendered in favour of the remainderman or the remainderman disposes of his interest to the life tenant.
3. Where the trustees (if they have the requisite power) advance assets to the life tenant (or the remainderman) free of the trusts.

All these occasions give rise to a CGT charge for the trustees on the difference between their acquisition cost of the assets held (subject to indexation to 5 April 1998) and the market value of those assets at the time of the deemed disposal; and with the application of taper relief.

Where the assets concerned are 'business assets' within s.165 of the TCGA 1992, an election may be made by the trustees and the person who becomes absolutely entitled to hold over any gain arising so that that person acquires them at the trustees' base cost. The transfer of the assets to the beneficiary may not occur at that stage but, since the trustees now hold as nominee for the beneficiary, in the future CGT will be charged as though the trust property was owned by the beneficiary absolutely.

The election for holdover relief is available even on a deemed disposal.

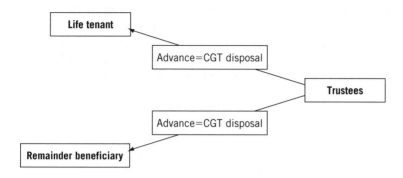

Figure 10.1 CGT when life interest terminates other than on death

(2) Life interest terminates but trust continues

If a life interest terminates, other than on the death of the person entitled to it, there will not be a deemed disposal by the trustees if there is no person to become absolutely entitled to the settled property. This, of course, assumes that the settled property concerned continues to be held by the same settlement for CGT purposes so no tax will arise. This would be the case, for example, where a life tenant surrendered his life interest prematurely and a succeeding life tenant's interest fell into possession.

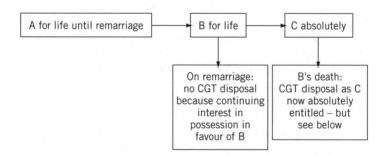

Figure 10.2 CGT when life interest terminates but trust continues

(3) Death of life tenant

On the death of the life tenant (whether the interest in the settled property terminates at that time or not) the assets held in the settlement will be deemed to have been disposed of by the trustees (s.72, TCGA 1992). If the assets remain settled property they are deemed to have been immediately reacquired by the trustees at their market value at the date of death; however no chargeable gain will accrue on the disposal. If the assets do not remain settled

159

property but, following the termination of a life interest by the death of the life tenant, are held for someone absolutely or free of the trusts of the settlement, the trustees are deemed to dispose of those assets and reacquire them as a nominee for a consideration equal to their market value (s.71, TCGA 1992). Again, by virtue of s.73, no charge to CGT will arise.

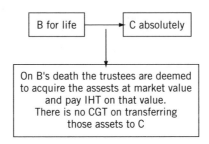

Figure 10.3 On death of a life tenant

(4)   Clawback of heldover gain

One important distinction to be drawn is between the CGT-free uplift on death which applies where a person is absolutely entitled to the assets (s.62, TCGA 1992) and the uplift available on the death of the life tenant which arises from the provisions of s.74 of the TCGA 1992.

On the death of a person absolutely entitled to assets which at the time were the subject of an election for holdover relief, all unrealised gains (accruing during the ownership of both the donor and the donee) will not be subject to CGT since the deceased donee makes no disposal. The donee's PRs acquire those assets at their market value at the date of death, thereby washed of unrealised gains.

Section 74, however, prevents assets in a settlement, which were the subject of a holdover election under either s.79 of the Finance Act 1980 or ss.165 or 260 of the TCGA 1992 when transferred to the settlement, being washed of the gains so held over on the death of the life tenant.

Relief under s.260 to defer the charge to tax will not always be available, because the relief will not apply where an exempt transfer arises after the life interest ceases.

For example, it would *not* be applicable where a surviving spouse held the succeeding interest and full relief under s.18 of the IHTA 1984, was available; or where the succeeding interest was held by a UK charity, so that exemption would be available under s.23 of the IHTA 1984.

Where holdover relief is available on both gifts into and distributions by the trustees out of settlements, consideration should be given, if within the trustees' powers, to the distribution of assets incorporating large gains to a life tenant. Those assets then form part of the life tenant's estate on death and

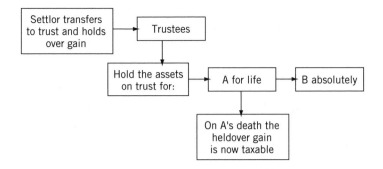

Figure 10.4 Clawback of heldover gain

are completely washed of gains at his death. The IHT consequences of the assets forming part of the life tenant's estate on death may not be a disadvantage, since IHT would in any case otherwise be charged on the settled property as though it was owned by the life tenant and he had made a transfer of it immediately before his death.

Sections 72 and 73 of the TCGA 1992 do not apply to interests which are in possession but which are not life interests, e.g. an interest in possession which will come to an end when the income beneficiary attains a certain age. Thus such trusts are disadvantaged in that the death of the beneficiary will technically result in a CGT charge (where the settled property is then held absolutely) or no uplift in base cost (where the property continues to be held in trust).

In order to ensure that such trusts were brought into line with life interest trusts, the Inland Revenue issued a concession that ss.72 and 73 will apply in these circumstances in the same way as for life interest trusts (D43). This was put on a statutory footing by the Finance Act 1996 for deaths occurring after 5 April 1996.

Discretionary trusts

For CGT purposes the creation of a discretionary settlement will be a disposal and a charge to CGT may arise on the gains arising on the assets settled. However, an election for holdover relief under s.260 of the TCGA 1992 may be made regardless of the nature of the assets transferred. The Finance Act 2004 introduced restrictions to the use of this holdover relief if it is possible the principal private residence relief may be claimed in the future. Put simply, it is no longer possible to claim both holdover relief and principal private residence relief on the same property.

At the moment it is possible for holdover relief to apply where transfers are made within the settlor's nil rate band.

A charge to CGT will subsequently arise in discretionary settlements on any distribution, appointment or other occasion, such as the end of the settlement period, on which one or more beneficiaries become absolutely entitled to the whole or part of the trust property. At that time the trustees will be deemed to have disposed of the assets to which a beneficiary has become so entitled and to reacquire them as nominees or bare trustees for that beneficiary. Here again an election for holdover relief under s.260 will usually be available.

Whilst any settlement continues, the trustees will be liable to CGT on realised gains at 40 per cent (34 per cent on or before 5 April 2004) subject to taper relief and their annual exemption. (The annual exemption is half of the amount available to an individual, or a smaller proportion if the settlor has created more than one settlement, subject to a minimum of one-tenth of the individual's exemption if the settlor has created five or more settlements.)

A&M trusts

The charge to CGT is calculated as if the disposal had been made at market value at the date the beneficiary became absolutely entitled (s.71(1), TCGA 1992). If the trustees retain the legal title to the assets beyond the vesting date, perhaps because it is not easy to subdivide the assets and transfer title to one beneficiary at this stage, then the rule is that the trustees will then be holding the assets as bare trustees for that vested beneficiary until transfer. This will mean that any subsequent actual transfer to the beneficiary is a non-event for CGT – any disposal of the asset will be treated as being made by the beneficiary and not the trustees (s.60, TCGA 1992). The effect of this is that any growth in its value from the date of vesting to the date of disposal will be assessable on the beneficiary at his appropriate rate of tax.

Sometimes it will be possible to hold over the gain at the time of vesting even if the assets are not business assets, due to the application of s.260 of the TCGA 1992 to the situation. Provided that the vesting age for both capital and income is the same (e.g. 25) the beneficiary and the trustees can elect for holdover so that no charge to CGT arises. Instead, the beneficiary is treated as receiving the assets pregnant with gain so that as and when the beneficiary decides to dispose of them himself there will be a potential charge to CGT on him at that time.

Normally, s.260, TCGA 1992 relief is only available where the same event gives rise to an immediate charge to IHT and CGT but there is a special provision in s.260(2)(d) of the TCGA 1992 which says that holdover is available where a beneficiary obtains an interest in possession in an A&M settlement for which relief is given by s.71(4) of the IHTA 1984. The relief will not apply if at the time of achieving the vesting of capital the beneficiary is already entitled to an interest in possession in it.

Where trustees can use s.260 holdover they should think about the risk of the clawback provisions applying in the future which would mean the gain would become assessable on the trustees. This would occur for example if the beneficiary who received the assets subject to a holdover claim became non-resident within the six years following the year of his acquisition. In such circumstances it is possible for the trustees to retain legal ownership of the assets as security as bare trustees whereas the beneficiary would have a vested interest in the equities.

CGT arises when the age at which a beneficiary becomes entitled to the income of the trust fund (i.e. the age at which they get an interest in possession) differs from the age at which the beneficiary becomes entitled to the capital of the trust fund. A&M trusts are vulnerable to having a difference in these two ages because the temptation when drafting is to focus only on the need to achieve a specified age up to and including 25 by which a vested interest in capital is achieved, instead of considering capital and income separately. If no reference is made to when income vests then s.31 of the Trustee Act 1925 will apply and vest the income at age 18. The result will be that when the capital vests later CGT will be payable on the disposal of the share in the fund to the beneficiary. The time bomb explodes in the trustees' collective face!

On a beneficiary becoming absolutely entitled to the whole or part of the trust property, the trustees will be deemed to dispose of and reacquire the trust property at its market value on behalf of the beneficiary as his nominee or bare trustee. Any gains arising will be subject to CGT at 40 per cent in the trustees' hands (less exemptions and taper relief).

10.4   SPECIFIC RELIEFS

CGT can be reduced in the following ways.

1. By a full or partial exemption, e.g. annual exemption or taper relief. This is where the actual gain is reduced by the amount of the relief on a once and for all basis.
2. By a deferral of the liability, with the possibility of future liability facing the same taxpayer, e.g. replacement business assets, where the amount of gain generated by a disposal is not currently taxed. Instead, the base cost of the new qualifying asset is reduced by, in simple terms, substituting the base cost of the original qualifying asset so that the gain on the disposal of the new asset in future will be that much greater.
3. By a deferral of the liability and with the possibility of future liability falling on the recipient of the gift, not the donor, e.g. business asset relief or s.260, TCGA 1992 relief. Again the donee's base cost is effectively reduced from market value at the time of the gift to the donor's base cost at acquisition.

The crucial difference between (2) and (3) is the change of taxpayer. In (3) the recipient becomes the potential taxpayer (although there are provisions for clawing back relief under s.260 and assessing subsequent gains on the donor) instead of the donor.

Often the trick with CGT is to utilise a combination of exemptions and reliefs to mitigate the overall tax bill, making the disposal less painful as a barrier to reducing the donor's estate during lifetime in order to, in turn, minimise his IHT bill on death.

Given that many trusts created during a settlor's lifetime will be part of this planning process, the trust administrator needs to be aware of the key reliefs. These reliefs are not just relevant to the settlor but may also affect trustees in the day-to-day administration of their trusts as beneficiaries become absolutely entitled to trust assets, by appropriation, appointment, advancement or satisfying a contingency.

Similarly, the trust administrator must be mindful of the anti-avoidance provisions which exist where the trust is settlor-interested.

1 Gifts of certain assets

For CGT a gift of a chargeable asset is regarded as a disposal at open market value (except for husband/wife transfers) and the chargeable gain or allowable loss is computed in the usual way, with indexation allowance (until 5 April 1998) and taper relief being taken into account to reduce or eliminate gains.

Gifts which qualify for relief are:

1. Business assets:

    (a) assets used in the trade, profession or vocation carried on by the trustees making the disposal or a beneficiary who had an interest in possession in the settled property immediately before the disposal; or

    (b) shares and securities in an unlisted trading company or a holding company of a trading group and shares in a listed company provided that the trustees hold 25 per cent of the votes (s.165 and Sched.7, TCGA 1992).

2. Gifts which are *immediately* chargeable to IHT (s.260, TCGA 1992). Where a gift attracts IHT immediately (e.g. assets leaving a discretionary settlement) then holdover relief under s.260 can be claimed on the associated disposal for CGT purposes.

Loss of holdover relief to settlor-interested trusts (Sched.21, Finance Act 2004)

With effect from the date of the press release on 21 October 2003, s.165 gifts relief is denied on a transfer of shares or securities to a company. The remaining provisions affect disposals on or after 10 December 2003.

The Pre-Budget Report announced that where the new provisions inserted in ss.169B to F of the TCGA 1992 apply there is no longer the opportunity to use CGT holdover relief under either s.165 or s.260 of the TCGA 1992 where the settlor retains an interest in the recipient trust.

A settlor-interested trust is defined in the new s.169F(2) as:

> any property which may at any time be comprised in the settlement or any derived property is or will or may become payable to or applicable for the benefit of the individual or his *spouse* in any circumstances whatsoever. (emphasis added)

'Spouse' in this context does not include a separated spouse or widow or widower. This will affect trusts used to maximise retirement relief and restart taper relief for CGT and where the assets were pregnant with gain.

Section 165 of the TCGA 1992 applies to gifts of business assets and therefore could be used to shelter gains arising on the disposal of such assets to a trust of any type. Section 260 of the TCGA 1992 is a generous relief which provides for a chargeable gain to be deferred on the disposal of any type of chargeable asset by way of a gift where the same event is immediately chargeable to IHT.

A settlor who wished to make estate planning arrangements to move assets of value which might be likely to grow in the future out of his estate could transfer them to a discretionary trust (an immediately chargeable transfer for IHT) or to an A&M or interest in possession trust if he gave business assets. Despite there being a possible gain arising on that disposal, the settlor could hold over any gain such that the trustees of the receiving trust would be deemed to acquire those assets, not at their market value at the date of the transfer but rather at the value at which the settlor acquired them (together with any eligible indexation allowance).

The beauty of this arrangement was that the settlor might be able to effectively wash out these 'pregnant' gains of his if the trust he gifted the assets to was one that had unused losses and which had him as one of its beneficiaries. In this case the trustees could themselves acquire the assets from the settlor at his low base cost and subsequently sell them to a third party in an arm's length transaction at market value, realising the full gain against which the trust's unused losses could be set, thereby reducing the gain or even extinguishing it.

If the settlor was a beneficiary of this settlement the proceeds of sale of the asset could even be given to him in whole or in part by way of an appointment out of the trust. Although in the case of a discretionary trust this would be subject to an exit charge for IHT, this would be at a rate of no more than a proportion of 6 per cent.

The other example of where CGT would now be chargeable would be where the settlor has reserved a right to revoke the trust or is the person who is entitled to the reversionary interest after the expiration of, say, 100 days. This effectively prevents the use of what became known as the *Melville Mark II* schemes (for an explanation of *Melville* see p.33, **para.2.3**).

Note that an individual will no longer able to rely on ss.165 or 260 of the TCGA 1992 to transfer assets to a trust where the settlor *or his spouse has an interest or acquires an interest within six years.* This obviously allows for the addition of the settlor or his spouse by operation of powers to add beneficiaries to a trust. Great care is therefore needed when operating such powers.

The result of this immediate change is that there will now be a real gain on which CGT will be charged unless the trust was set up as a trust for a disabled person or to maintain historic buildings. This coupled with the increase in the trust rate of CGT to 40 per cent as from 6 April 2004 means that the cost to the trustees of dismantling any trust in which the settlor or his spouse is interested may be equally high.

Holdover relief under ss.165 and 260 will still be available where the recipient trust is not settlor-interested (and does not become so within six years of the gift to it) and where the trustees are making a transfer out of the trust, except where this involves the interaction with principal private residence relief.

2 Taper relief

For disposals after 5 April 1998, a chargeable gain will be progressively reduced (tapered) according to the length of time the asset has been held. The reductions for gains on business assets are more generous than for those on non-business assets. However, since the relief's inception in the Finance Act 1998, subsequent Finance Acts have made significant changes. The relief has become more complex, and care needs to be taken by practitioners. In particular it should be noted when definitions have changed, since this could mean a change in eligibility from, say, non-business asset taper to the more favourable business asset taper. Such a change may entail the application of the apportionment rules (see Figure 10.5 below).

Initially, all assets held on 17 March 1998 (Budget Day) were deemed to have been held for one complete year as from 6 April 1998 when taper relief came into effect. When the arrangements for business asset taper came into effect for disposals after 6 April 2000, the 'bonus year' was dropped for business assets but is retained for non-business asset purposes.

Gains on business assets

No. of complete years for which asset held	Disposals after 6/4/02	Equivalent tax rates for higher rate taxpayer
0	100	40
1	50	20
2 and over	25	10

No. of complete years for which asset held	Disposals after 5/4/00 and before 5/4/02	Equivalent tax rates for higher rate taxpayer
0	100	40
1	87.5	35
2	75	30
3	50	20
4 and over	25	10

No. of complete years for which asset held	Disposals after 5/4/98 and before 6/4/00	Equivalent tax rates for higher rate taxpayer
0	100	40
1	92.5	37
2	85	34
3	77.5	31
4	70	28
5	62.5	25
6	55	22
7	47.5	19
8	40	16
9	32.5	13
10 and over	25	10

Gains on non-business assets

No. of complete years after 5/4/98 for which assets held	Percentage of gain chargeable	Equivalent tax rates for higher/basic rate taxpayer
0	100	40/20
1	100	40/20
2	100	40/20
3	95	38/19
4	90	36/18
5	85	34/17
6	80	32/16
7	75	30/15
8	70	28/14
9	65	26/13
10	60	24/12

Figure 10.5 Taper relief

Losses are set against gains before applying the percentage reduction, losses being allocated to gains on the basis that is most beneficial to the taxpayer. As seen in **para.10.2**, the annual exemption is deducted from the net tapered gains. However, losses brought forward are used to reduce the pre-taper gain to an amount equal to the annual exemption, so the benefit of taper may be lost.

Where an asset has been transferred to trustees who have acquired the assets from the settlor by virtue of a holdover election the trustees will lose any accumulated period of ownership of the settlor. The taper relief period always starts again from zero and needs to be built up by the trustees.

Crucial distinction between business and non-business assets

A chargeable gain on the disposal of an asset qualifies for the business asset rate of taper if the asset is a business asset of the person making the disposal throughout the relevant period of ownership. There are separate business asset tests for shares and securities (para.4, Sched.A1, TCGA 1992) and for other assets (para.5, Sched.A1, TCGA 1992).

It should be noted that the definition of business assets changed on 5 April 2000, on 17 April 2002 and again from 6 April 2004. The changes widen the definition of business assets. It will be important to check whether any assets currently qualifying as business assets have been qualifying business assets since 6 April 1998 or since the date of acquisition, if later.

Shares and securities

Shares and securities in a company are business assets at any time if at the time they are shares in a 'qualifying company' of the trustees of a settlement.

A 'qualifying company' is currently defined (after 6 April 2000) as a *trading* company or holding company of a trading group where one of the following applies.

1. The company is unlisted so trustees holding any size of shares will qualify no matter how large or small the holding.
2. The company is a quoted company and there is an 'eligible beneficiary' who is an officer or employee (full or part-time) of the company.
3. The company is a quoted company and at least 5 per cent of the voting rights in the company are exercisable by the trustees.

A company is also a qualifying company if the company is *non-trading* provided that:

1. there is an 'eligible beneficiary' who is an officer or employee (full or part-time) of the company; *and*
2. the individual or the trustees do not have a 'material interest' in the company.

For the period between 6 April 1998 and 6 April 2000 a company is a qualifying company if it is a trading company or the holding company of a trading group and the trustees hold at least 25 per cent of the voting rights.

If trustees own shares for the period between 6 April 1998 and 6 April 2000 the company must be a trading company or the holding company of a trading group and they must control at least 25 per cent of the voting rights, or at least 5 per cent of the voting rights and an eligible beneficiary is a full-time working officer or employee of the company or a connected company.

For disposals after 16 April 2002 there is a new definition of 'trading company' as a company carrying on 'trading activities' whose activities do not include to a substantial extent activities other than trading activities. Trading activities mean those activities carried on by a company:

1. in the course of or for the purposes of a trade being carried on by it; or
2. for the purposes of a trade that it is preparing to carry on; or
3. with a view to its acquiring or starting to carry on a trade; or
4. with a view to its acquiring a 'significant interest' in the share capital of another company that is itself a trading company or the holding company of a trading group.

The old definition of 'trading company' was a company that was either:

1. a company existing wholly for the purpose of carrying on one or more trades; or
2. a company that would fall in paragraph (a) above *apart from any purposes capable of having no substantial effect* on the extent of the company's activities (emphasis added).

The Inland Revenue issued guidance on that definition in *Tax Bulletin* No.53, June 2001. Basically, they will consider the following retain the badge of 'trading' if:

1. The proportion of income from non-trading activities is 20 per cent or less of the total.
2. The net asset value of the business is represented by 20 per cent or less of non-trading assets.
3. The amount of time spent by the directors and employees on the different activities of the company is no more than 20 per cent spent on non-trading activities.

If any of these activities breach the 20/80 split there is a real danger that the shares will not qualify for the business asset rate of relief.

The Inland Revenue has confirmed that investments made of surplus working capital that is required for future use, and funds set aside for future capital investment, should not jeopardise the business asset status of the company.

If a company fails this trading test, the shares in it will only qualify for non-business asset taper unless, in the case of a trust, there is an eligible beneficiary working in the company and that person (together with the trustees) does not have a *material interest* in the company.

A person or trust would have a material interest if they held or were entitled to acquire:

1. more than 10 per cent of any class of share or security of the company; or
2. more than 10 per cent of the voting rights in the company; or
3. a right to more than 10 per cent of the profits of the company that are available for distribution; or
4. entitlement to more than 10 per cent of the assets of the company on winding up or in other circumstances.

For the 'material interests' test, the rights of connected persons (such as spouse, relatives and certain trusts and companies) would be added to the individual's rights.

There is a second test in para.11 of Sched.A1, which relates to a situation where the company changes its activities. The consequence of a change in ownership of investments by a company was that the shares failed to meet the business asset definition and the taper relief clock started again from scratch. For example, this change would occur if a close company began to trade or a company began the business of holding investments or if the company increased the size of its investment business. This could easily happen if the major shareholder was looking to retire and started to use profits in the company to purchase an investment property. Alternatively, if the company originally manufactured widgets but then stopped manufacturing widgets and started to repair 'whatdoyoucallits' instead, this would be a change in activity, even though both activities are trading.

Fortunately, the definition of 'trading company' and 'holding company' changed for disposals on or after 17 April 2002 and for holding periods commencing on 17 April 2002. The effect of the changes to the definition of 'trading company' is to base this definition on the company's *activities* and not its purpose. So that the period when the company's activities disallows business asset status will simply be a non-eligible period rather than wiping out any prior period when it did qualify.

Where a close company becomes inactive or changes its activities the period when the company was inactive or not eligible will not count towards the taper period, but it will not trigger a resetting of the prior period when the company did qualify.

Assets other than shares

For disposals of assets after 5 April 2004 the arrangements have been simplified. If the disposal is made after 5 April 2004, the asset will be a business asset if at that time it was being used wholly or partly for the purposes of a trade carried on by any individual, the trustees of a trust, the PRs of a deceased person or a partnership whose members then included:

1. an individual or a company or holding company which is the individual's qualifying company; or
2. the trustees or any one or more of them acting as trustee of a company or holding company which is the trustees' or an eligible beneficiary's qualifying company; or
3. an individual's PRs or any one or more of them acting as PR or the PRs' qualifying company or holding company.

Prior to 6 April 2004 the arrangements were more complicated.

In the case of trustees, it was necessary to ascertain whether the asset was being used at the time of the disposal, wholly or partly, for one or more of the following purposes.

1. The purposes of a trade carried on by the trustees of the settlement.
2. The purposes of a trade carried on in partnership by the trustees or including any one or more persons who are trustees acting in their capacity as such.
3. The purposes of a trade carried on at that time by an eligible beneficiary or by a partnership of which an eligible beneficiary was at that time a member.
4. The purposes of any trade carried on by a company which at that time was a qualifying company by reference to the trustees of the settlement or an eligible beneficiary.
5. The purposes of any trade carried on by a company which at that time was a member of a trading group the holding company of which was at that time a qualifying company by reference to the trustees of the settlement or any eligible beneficiary.
6. The purposes of any office or employment held by an eligible beneficiary to which he is required to devote substantially the whole of his time (i.e. at least 75 per cent of normal working hours (Inland Revenue *CGT Manual* at CG 17954)).
7. The purposes of a non-qualifying office or employment in a trading company by an eligible beneficiary if before 6 April 2000 the eligible beneficiary was a full-time working officer or employee, or after 5 April 2000 was any officer or employee.

The interesting, and somewhat odd, result of this definition was that if a set of trustees owned a building and let it to an unlisted trading company the trustees would be eligible for business asset taper in respect of that asset. However if the trustees let the site to a neighbouring business for the businessman's sole trade, the trustees would get no business asset taper since the asset was not being used in the *trustees'* trade. It did not matter in the let to the company that the trustees owned no shares in the company that rented from them nor that the members of the company had no interest in the trust!

Treatment where a part period of ownership only qualifies for business taper

Where an asset has not been a business asset throughout the whole of the relevant period of ownership, for the purpose of the relief the chargeable gain has to be apportioned into separate gains treated as arising on the disposal of a business asset and a separate non-business asset.

This treatment will inevitably arise where the change in categorisation of certain shareholdings or assets has moved from not being eligible at 6 April 1998, when taper relief was introduced, to becoming eligible at a later date when definitions changed.

Strange results arise from the apportionment of the gain between business and non-business asset treatment. The stages to computing the gain will be as follows.

1. Compute the untapered gain first.
2. Apportion the period of ownership between a portion when it was non-business ownership and a portion when it was in business ownership – ignore the 'bonus year' but take into account complete months of ownership
3. Apportion the gain in (1) in accordance with (2).
4. Apply the relevant amount of taper relief to each portion of the gain (this works on the number of complete tax years of ownership since 6 April 1998), but in the case of non-business asset taper relief remember to add in the 'bonus year'.

Trustees owning assets which were previously not eligible for business asset treatment or shareholdings which prior to 6 April 2000 were not eligible but which have now become eligible are also subject to the apportionment treatment on disposal by the trustees.

Example: Mad Hatter Ltd

The trustees of a trust hold 4 per cent of the shares in Mad Hatter Ltd, an unquoted trading company. They acquired these shares on 16 March 1998. The trustees dispose of the shares on 6 November 2004.

The *number of years of ownership* by the trustees that are relevant for calculating the rate of taper relief is calculated from the qualifying holding period of 6 April 1998 to 6 November 2004. Since only whole years count for determining the rate of the relief, there are six whole years available (6 April 1998–6 April 2004).

The *relevant period of ownership* by the trustees would be from 6 April 1998 to 6 November 2004, i.e. six years seven months, making a total of 79 months, and it is this period that is used for apportioning the gains between business and non-business asset treatment.

Since to be eligible for business asset taper at the time of the trustees' acquisition the trustee would have had to have 25 per cent of the voting rights in Mad Hatter Ltd the shares in the company would be treated in the trustees' hands as non-business assets until 6 April 2000. Thereafter they will be business assets for the period to disposal on 6 November 2004.

Thus, of the total relevant period of ownership by the trustees, two years will be non-business assets ownership and four years seven months will be business asset ownership.

The gain will therefore be apportioned as to 24/79th to non-business asset taper treatment and 55/79th to business asset taper treatment. Thus the non-business asset portion of the gain would be treated to seven years taper (the six whole years of ownership plus the bonus year for non-business assets held at 17 March 1998) and the business asset taper portion of the gain will be treated to six years taper.

Trustees pay CGT at 40 per cent. Where the non-business taper is seven years the percentage of the gain remaining chargeable is 75 per cent. This means that 25 per cent relief is given on 24/79th of the gain and the trustees will pay tax at 40 per cent on this. The business asset taper is six years and therefore given the maximum percentage relief of 75 per cent, so 25 per cent remains in charge to tax.

Calculation

If the overall net gain before taper were calculated was £100,000, the trustees would pay:

Non-business asset
(75% × 24/79th of £100,000   =   (75% of £30,379.75)
                                     =   £22,784.81

Business asset
(25% × 55/79th of £100,000   =   (25% of £69,620.25)
                                       =   £17,405.06

Total CGT due
40% [£22,784.81 + £17,405.06
−£3,750 (annual exemption)]   =   £14,575.95

The key question for individuals might be how to 'wash out' the period of ownership that does not qualify for business asset taper, so avoiding for the future the need to apportion the period of ownership between the two types of relief. For some taxpayers the solution was to settle the asset upon interest in possession trusts for themselves under an s.165, TCGA 1992 holdover election for CGT. This method was used for the crystallisation of the best rate of retirement relief as its phasing-out period began. This tax planning opportunity was blocked in s.116 of, and Sched.21 to, the Finance Act 2004. It is no longer possible to hold over gains under s.165 of the TCGA 1992 when assets are transferred to a settlor-interested trust.

Trusts where beneficiary qualifies personally for business taper

For trustees to obtain business asset taper treatment it is not always necessary for the trustees to qualify in their own right. Paragraph 5(3) of Sched.A1 to the TCGA 1992 permits a set of trustees to benefit if an asset is used for the purposes of a trade that 'was carried on at that time by an eligible beneficiary by a partnership of which an eligible beneficiary was at that time a member'. It also provides relief for assets used by a qualifying company not only of the trustees but also of an 'eligible beneficiary'. So who will be an eligible beneficiary?

In para.7 of Sched.A1 to the TCGA 1992 we are told that an eligible beneficiary is an individual having a relevant interest in possession under the settlement in either:

1. the whole of the settled property; or
2. a part of the settled property that is or includes the asset.

A 'relevant interest in possession' is any interest in possession other than a right under the settlement to receive an annuity or a fixed-term entitlement.

A 'fixed-term entitlement' is apparently one where the interest is limited to a fixed period where at the end of that period the beneficiary does *not* gain an absolute interest. This does not exclude the vast majority of interest in possession trusts where the interest is 'for life' since that is not a fixed, determinate, term. It would apply to interest in possession trusts of short, say six months, duration.

Paragraph 8 of the Schedule goes on to explain that where there are non-qualifying and qualifying beneficiaries in relation to a particular asset, any gain on disposal of the asset is apportioned by reference to the beneficiary's entitlement to the income of the trust fund. For example, there are three beneficiaries only one of whom qualifies for business asset taper. They share the income of the trust equally, so one-third of the gain will be attributable to each of them for taper relief purposes only. Only one-third of the gain will be eligible for business asset taper in the trustees' hands because that is the proportion of the interest of the eligible beneficiary in the trust; whereas the remaining two-thirds of the gain will be taxed on the trustees with only non-business asset taper relief.

Summary

1. Check the date of acquisition of assets.
2. Establish whether there has been a change of status in the asset over the period of ownership and consider the effect of the apportionment rules.
3. Be aware that it is only periods of ownership since 6 April 2000 or 6 April 2004 that will count if the asset did not qualify for business asset status before either date.
4. Remember to review the 'trading' status of any company whose shares are held and be vigilant about any alterations to the nature of the company's activities.
5. Be clear in trusts as to whether you have an eligible beneficiary in relation to a particular asset and if so to what extent, based on the beneficiary's entitlement to the income of the trust fund. This may mean reviewing the trading status of any company using the assets.
6. In relation to quoted shareholdings, remember the changes to the matching provisions on the disposal of shares, which the introduction of taper relief inevitably brought about.
7. Detailed and accurate record keeping becomes ever more important.

Principal private residence (PPR) relief

Trustees of a trust who permit a beneficiary of the trust to occupy a trust property as that beneficiary's principal private residence gain the advantage of PPR relief on any disposal of that property in much the same way as an individual owner (s.225, TCGA 1992).

This useful extension of PPR relief to trustees applies to both interest in possession trusts and discretionary trusts since the case of *Sansom* v. *Peay* confirms it applies whenever trustees 'permit' a beneficiary to occupy.

Note, however, that Sched.22 to the Finance Act 2004 inserts s.226A into the TCGA 1992 to apply to disposals on or after 10 December 2003. Essentially, the effect of this is to prevent the application of *both* PPR relief and s.260 holdover to the same set of assets.

For example, it was a popular and well-used procedure for a settlor to transfer a second home, worth less than the IHT nil rate band, not eligible for PPR relief, into a discretionary trust. The settlor would hold over the gain on this disposal under s.260 and the trustees would subsequently either permit a beneficiary to occupy the property as the beneficiary's PPR so enabling the trustees to subsequently sell it with the benefit of PPR relief under s.225 of the TCGA 1992; or the trustees would eventually transfer the property to the beneficiary for the beneficiary to occupy as his PPR such that the beneficiary, on any subsequent sale by him would have wiped out all the inbuilt capital gains by virtue of applying his PPR relief to the proceeds of sale.

The new restriction means that if the settlor claims s.260 holdover on the transfer of the chargeable property to the trust it will not be possible to claim PPR relief on the disposal of the property by the trust or by the ultimate beneficiary.

Clearly, if the settlor was a beneficiary of the trust which received the property the new arrangements in Sched.21 to the Finance Act 2004 would mean that s.260 of the TCGA 1992 was not available to the settlor on the transfer into the trust, but the PPR relief could then be available on the sale.

Discretionary trusts in the awkward position of having a property transferred using holdover with the trustees holding it with a low base cost must note that there are some transitional rules available. PPR relief will be available for the part of any gain which arose (on a time apportionment basis) before 10 December 2003.

Only the part of the chargeable gain attributable to the portion arising after 10 December will be without relief. Practitioners should therefore review whether there is a need to act sooner rather than later in selling such a property to maximise the PPR relief available.

10.5   CONCLUSION

In outlining the main reliefs and exemptions this overview has been kept as straightforward as possible. There may well be trusts where Enterprise Investment schemes apply, old retirement relief was relevant or the old re-investment relief applied. A specialist text on the taxation of trusts is recommended for a more detailed analysis, such as Hutton and Ferrier, *Tolley's UK Taxation of Trusts*, 14th Edn (LexisNexis, 2004).

What is immediately apparent is the need for excellent record keeping in order to correctly assess a particular trust's CGT liabilities. It is recommended that the trust administrator ensures that the system employed maintains an accurate assets register within the investment file, in which acquisition dates are logged together with acquisition values.

Where the settlor or the trustees claim a form of holdover relief it will be necessary to keep in the permanent tax file or in the investment file details of the agreed holdover which has been accepted by HMRC and any similar significant decisions relevant to future disposals.

CHAPTER 11

Income tax

11.1 INTRODUCTION

Before a discussion of income tax, it is useful to consider a few general items that underlie the income tax system in the UK.

1. *The tax year* runs from 6 April in one year to 5 April in the next; for example, the tax year from 6 April 2005 to 5 April 2006 is known as the 2005/06 tax year.
2. *Total income* is broadly calculated by adding together the amounts of income received from trading income, employment income, pension income, social security income, property income, savings and investment income and miscellaneous income. This approach has replaced the so-called schedular system which had applied since 1803. It came about as a result of the tax rewrite project. It is necessary now to refer to the Income Tax (Trading and Other Income) Act 2005 (ITTOIA 2005) for most income receipts save for income taxable under the Income Tax (Earnings and Pensions) Act 2003.
3. *Taxable income* is the result of deducting allowable expenses from total income, together with a deduction of relevant personal allowances. In the case of trusts there is no personal allowance that relates to trustees.
4. *Tax collection:* tax on bank and building society interest is deducted at source; similarly, a tax credit is also given in respect of dividend income. Trustees do have to complete a Self Assessment Tax Return – the SA900. Tax is then paid by the trustees direct to HMRC in two half-yearly instalments on 31 January and 31 July following the tax year to which it relates, under the self-assessment system.

11.2 RATES OF TAX

Except where they are liable at 'the rate applicable to trusts', trustees are normally liable at the lower rate of income tax (20 per cent) on savings income and the basic rate (22 per cent) on other income, the trust income being determined using the principles applicable to each source. Effectively, any income taxable by direct assessment is taxed at 22 per cent. Before 6 April 1996, the lower rate applied only to dividend income but this was widened to include bank and building society interest.

If a tax recovery is possible (i.e. where the ultimate beneficiary is a non-taxpayer) then tax deducted at source or given by tax credit may be repaid, in certain circumstances.

The Finance (No.2) Act 1997 provisions relating to the tax treatment of dividend income affects trusts from 6 April 1999. The provisions both altered the rate of tax credit from 20 per cent to 10 per cent and also made it not repayable, so the credit cannot be used to frank distributions to beneficiaries.

The tax credit inclusive dividend income of trustees of interest in possession trusts is taxed at 10 per cent with an equivalent tax credit. The tax credit is passed on to the life tenant as a non-repayable tax credit, so the life tenant is taxed in the same way as if the dividend had been received directly.

For trusts without an interest in possession, the tax credit inclusive dividend is taxed at 32.5 per cent (25 per cent before 6 April 2004), called the dividend trust rate (ITTOIA 2005, Sched.1, Pt 1, paras. 3 and 277). Other income will remain chargeable at 40 per cent (34 per cent before 6 April 2004), which will still be called the rate applicable to trusts. In addition, such trusts will not have to pay tax at the rate applicable to trusts on the first £500 of income from 6 April 2005.

11.3   EXPENSES

There is no specific relief for trust expenses since each source of income is assessed according to the rules of that source and 'trust' expenses are not an allowable deduction under any of those rules. It follows that they are an expense payable out of income that has already borne tax, to the extent that they are not payable out of capital.

Expenses legitimately chargeable against particular sources of income, such as property management expenses, will be deductible from rental income. However trust management expenses have to be paid out of the net taxed income and will reduce the amount of tax due only on trusts with no interest in possession.

Expenses connected with the trust fund as a whole are chargeable against capital, e.g. legal fees. Section 686(2)(a) of the ICTA 1988 limits the expenses to those 'which are properly chargeable to income or would be so chargeable but for any express provisions of the trust'. In other words, the trustees must not expect 'expenses' to include life premiums paid out of income by reason of a special clause in their trust deed, nor any other expenses which are not normal.

The Trustee Act 2000 permits trustees to choose whether to pay expenses out of income or capital. This development means there is a distinction between the trust accounting treatment of expenses and the tax treatment of expenses.

Both the tax treatment of expenses and the trust treatment are under review. For details of the tax treatment see the Inland Revenue manual **TSEM 3500 (www.hmrc.gov.uk/manuals/tsemmanual/tsem3500.htm)**. For details of the trust review see the Law Commission Consultation Paper No.175, *Capital and Income in Trusts: Classification and Apportionment* (**www. lawcom.gov.uk/files/cp175.pdf**).

Trust management expenses will reduce the amount of tax when calculating the additional charge under ss.686 and 687 of the ICTA 1988 on discretionary and A&M trusts. The expenses of an A&M trust or of a discretionary trust are *not* available to the beneficiaries whether by way of income distribution or as capital when accumulations are paid out, and so income used to pay those expenses does *not* suffer any additional tax (s.686(2AA), ICTA 1988).

In general, accountants automatically charge fees against income in the trust accounts. Banks do the opposite (supported by the instructions in their standard charging clauses). Solicitors are generally somewhere in the middle. The amount of the expenses can have a significant effect on the additional tax payable by virtue of the rate applicable to trusts.

If income is mandated to the life tenant of an interest in possession trust the trustees cannot deduct expenses from it; they will have to pay expenses from capital.

The outcome of HMRC's review of the tax treatment of expenses allowed against income is awaited with interest but in any event it is necessary to be able to demonstrate that the particular expenses are genuinely income expenses to be deductible.

Expenses must always be deducted against income in a strict order and be grossed up at the applicable rate as shown in Table 11.1.

Table 11.1 Deduction of expenses

	Dividends	Bank interest	Rent
Gross income taxable	10%	20%	22%
Order of set-off of expenses	1	2	3
Grossing up rate for expenses	100/90	100/80	100/78

11.4 ACCRUED INCOME SCHEME

This complex scheme came into being on 28 February 1986 to address a problem for the Inland Revenue. Pension and other large institutional investors were making tax savings through the purchase of gilts with interest, thus converting income to capital in the process. Unfortunately, the small investor was not excluded from the operation of this scheme and particular rules therefore apply to the buying and selling of 'securities'.

Trust law requires the cost of securities bought 'cum' interest to be paid out of capital and the proceeds of sale to be a capital receipt. The aim of the accrued income scheme is to ensure that each person pays income tax on the interest on securities which accrues during his period of legal owner-ship – i.e. on an accruals basis by reference to a legal rather than beneficial ownership.

When trustees purchase interest-bearing securities cum interest they are deemed to have purchased the interest which had accrued by the settlement day of the transfer: the 'rebate amount'. When trustees sell cum interest they are deemed to have received the accrued interest as income: the 'accrued amount'.

Any contract note for the sale and purchase of these securities should have the amount of accrued interest itemised. The accrued amount is assessable on the trustees. Relief is given in respect of any rebate amount, either against the next interest received on the security or against the accrued interest on the sale, whichever is the sooner.

Accrued income charges and reliefs are taken into account in the tax year in which the next interest payment date falls after the settlement date. (There should be no problem with the settlement date as government stocks and local authority loan stocks are normally for settlement on the day following the transaction.) Accrued income relief is given by reducing the assessable interest. Charges and reliefs are not netted off unless they relate to the same kind of stock with the same interest payment dates.

When trustees are assessable upon the accrued interest on sale they bear tax at the rate applicable to trusts (40 per cent) whether or not there is an interest in possession. Trust law requires the proceeds to be received as capital so the tax due on it will have to be paid out of capital. It is only when s.687 of the ICTA 1988 applies that the tax can *reappear* as tax on the income of an individual (because it becomes part of the tax pool).

> **Example**
>
> 25 May 2004, trustees purchase £10,000 8¾ per cent Treasury Loan 2017. Accrued interest is £213 (26/2/2004 to 25/5/2004).
>
> On 25 August 2004, £437.50 of gross interest is received on the investment. Relief of £213 is given leaving £224.50 net income for tax purposes. If the investment was sold on say 25 June 2004 (i.e. before the interest was paid out in September) then if the accrued interest on the sale was £288 (for 120 days) the amount of income assessable would be £75 (i.e. £288 less the £213).

11.5   INTEREST IN POSSESSION TRUSTS

A beneficiary entitled to the income from settled property will be charged to income tax on that income at the rates applicable when the income from the settlement is aggregated with his own income. The income may be mandated directly to the beneficiary (in which case it may be unnecessary for the trustees to submit returns as regards the income concerned) or may be received by the trustees and subsequently paid over to the beneficiary. The trustees will account for basic rate tax on the whole of the trust fund (with no deduction for expenses). After deduction for expenses, the income paid over to the life tenant will be treated as being a net amount from which income tax at the basic rate has been deducted.

11.6   SETTLEMENTS WHERE THERE IS NO INTEREST IN POSSESSION

The administration of the collection of income tax in A&M and discretionary trusts is greater than that for interest in possession trusts. This is because of the special rates of income tax which apply. In order to self-assess the trust income, the trustees must complete a SA900 Trust and Estate Tax Return each year and pay the additional tax due to HMRC.

Trustees will be liable to income tax at the rate applicable to trusts (i.e. 40 per cent but 34 per cent up to 5 April 2004) since, even if they have no power to accumulate, they will have discretion as to the distribution of income amongst the beneficiaries.

The beneficiaries to whom the trustees decide to distribute income will receive a net amount from which income tax at the rate applicable to trusts has been deducted. They may recover this tax in whole or in part if their personal rates of income tax are less than 40 per cent.

To make it possible for a beneficiary to make a tax recovery the trustees must provide a tax certificate (R185) to the beneficiary showing tax deducted on the income distributed. There is also a complex tax pool system which must also be maintained by the trustees.

Where trustees do have the power to accumulate income, some trust deeds also include power to distribute accumulated income as though it were income of the year in which it is so distributed. This can be a useful power since it means the trustees can decide in a particular case whether a beneficiary would benefit more from an income distribution (e.g. where the beneficiary is a non-taxpayer) or from a capital distribution (e.g. where the beneficiary is a higher rate taxpayer). If an income distribution is made, the ability to utilise the credit for the tax paid by the trustees will not be lost and accumulated funds may subsequently be distributed as income rather than capital.

Payments received by a beneficiary from trustees of a discretionary settlement which form part of the beneficiary's income do not suffer an IHT charge on distribution to him (s.65(5)(b), IHTA 1984). This power to convert capital back to income may be valuable if:

1. the tax paid by the trustees may thereby be recovered; or
2. it is used to distribute accumulated income from a discretionary trust prior to a 10-year anniversary without incurring an inheritance tax charge, thereby reducing the property in the settlement for the purposes of that 10-yearly charge.

If the trustees have power to retain undistributed income, it should not be necessary to distribute that income prior to a 10-year anniversary. Any undistributed or unaccumulated income will not suffer a charge to IHT at that time although accumulated income will do so (Statement of Practice SP 8/86).

Conversely, of course, the beneficiaries' personal rates of income tax may suggest that income should be capitalised and paid out as such. Provided regular payments are not made, the beneficiaries should not suffer an income tax charge on payments of capital.

The income tax consequences for a parent creating an A&M settlement need careful consideration. To the extent that capital or income is applied for an unmarried child aged under 18, the income of the settlement will be treated as the settlor's income (s.629(1), ITTOIA 2005).

If, however, the income is accumulated and no payments of capital are made under an irrevocable settlement, no income tax charge will fall upon the parental settlor (s.631(1)–(3), ITTOIA 2005). A parent will, therefore, normally wish all income to be accumulated until the beneficiaries have attained 18 and will be chargeable to income tax in the hands of the trustees at the rate applicable to trusts under s.686 of the ICTA 1988.

On a distribution of income from an A&M settlement the recipient beneficiary will be treated as receiving a net amount from which income tax at the rate applicable to trusts has been deducted (s.687, ICTA 1988). The amount of tax which is treated as having been deducted may (in whole or part) be reclaimed if the beneficiary's personal rates of income tax are lower than 40 per cent.

Grandparent settlors (and parents whose children are aged over 18) do not suffer such problems. Income tax at the rate applicable to trusts is charged on the income in the trustees' hands and, if distributed to beneficiaries, the income will again be treated as being a net receipt from which income tax at 40 per cent has been deducted. Tax will be paid or reclaimed by them according to their personal circumstances. In this way settlements by grand-parent settlors enable the use of grandchildren's personal allowances (which might otherwise be unused). Such settlements may, therefore, be particularly efficient if regular payments out of the settlement are to be made, for example to meet school fees.

Apparently, there are a large number of A&M trusts and discretionary trusts where the income received each year is below £500. Despite the small nature of the trust income these burdensome rules still apply so that in reality the costs of administration may in some cases almost account for the whole of the income. For this reason HMRC has introduced in s.14 of the Finance Act 2005 provisions to allow for a basic rate band of income in all such trusts which will not be subject to the rate applicable to trusts or the dividend trust rate (formerly the Schedule F dividend rate).

In s.14(1), a new section is introduced after s.686C of the ICTA 1988. The new section is to be s.686D of the ICTA 1988 and in (3) it says:

> So much of the special trust tax rate of income as does not exceed £500 is not chargeable to income tax at the dividend trust rate or the rate applicable to trusts (but is instead chargeable to income tax at the basic rate, the lower rate or the dividend ordinary rate, depending on the nature of the income).

Subsections (4)–(8) explain that for the purposes of deciding how much income tax applies to incomes arising or treated as arising of different types which is received by the trustees, up to £500 of income which has been taxed already before receipt by the trustees at the dividend ordinary rate (stock divi-dends), the basic rate (offshore income gains, employee share ownership trusts and guaranteed returns on futures and options) and the lower rate (transfers of securities, profits from deeply discounted securities and gains from contracts for life assurance) will be treated as having borne sufficient tax. The rate applicable to trusts and the dividend trust rate will only be applied to the excess income over £500.

For s.687 purposes the amount of the income which bears only the lower or basic rate or the ordinary dividend rate instead of the rate applicable to trusts or the dividend trust rate is not deducted against the tax assessment on the trustees in respect of the distribution to beneficiaries. This is obviously because a tax advantage has been provided to the trustees on receipt of the income and it should not be effectively given a double relief.

These rules apply to income arising to trustees of A&M trusts and discretionary trusts from 6 April 2005.

11.7 THE RATE APPLICABLE TO TRUSTS

In trusts where the income may be accumulated the special rules referred to for the income tax treatment of income are set out in ss.686 and 687 of the ICTA 1988 (despite the tax rewrite project these references remain).

Sections 686 and 687 of the ICTA 1988 are designed to ensure that trust income which can be accumulated is taxed at something higher than basic rate but without double taxation. Double taxation is avoided by giving credit for the additional tax collected by s.686 when income is distributed. Income of a discretionary trust is also affected because the ability to exercise discretion is also an ability to defer distribution. Section 686 charges the income received by the trustees; whilst s.687 passes on the tax credit to the beneficiaries.

The rate of tax charged under s.686 is the rate applicable to trusts. It used to be called 'the additional rate' since it was simply 10 per cent more than the basic rate of tax. This linkage with the basic rate was lost with the introduction of self-assessment.

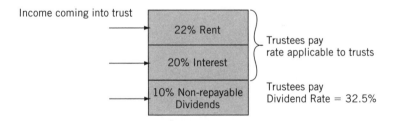

Figure 11.1 ICTA 1988, s.686

Section 687 is drafted as an independent charging section. It charges tax at the rate applicable to trusts on any payment made by the trustees under a discretion, where the payment is income in the hands of the recipient.

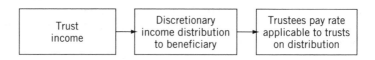

Figure 11.2 ICTA 1988, s.687

Having decided that a payment is within s.687 it is then grossed up at the rate applicable to trusts. The beneficiary receives a tax voucher showing a deduction of the tax and the trustees are assessed on the like amount.

Section 687(3) sets up a 'tax pool' which, with minor variations, is the tax paid or credited under the normal rules of assessment plus the extra which makes the basic or dividend trust rate or the lower rate up to the rate applicable to trusts. The tax pool is set against any tax assessable under s.687 when the payments are made to the beneficiaries. Provided that the net payments to the beneficiaries are within the net income, taking one year with another, there should be no tax to pay under s.687. With the changes from 6 April 1999 to the treatment of dividend income, there has to be care taken not to over-distribute if tax pools are not in existence, since the charge to tax on dividend trust income is 32.5 per cent (25 per cent before 6 April 2004) whereas the tax credit is only 10 per cent and is non-repayable and therefore cannot be added to the tax pool.

Figure 11.3 The tax pool

The principal components of a tax pool are as follows.

1. Any balance brought forward from prior years.
2. The rate applicable to trusts on the normal income of the trust assessed under s.686.
3. 22.5 per cent (15 per cent before 6 April 2004) of dividends.

In older settlements the tax pool going forward will bear no resemblance to the undistributed income shown in the accounts because tax rates will have changed between one tax year and another. The coming of age of an infant beneficiary produces other mismatches, in that the beneficiary will take his share of the trust fund but the tax pool will not alter. The inclusion of amounts under the accrued income scheme also adds to the differences.

Stripping the tax pool is important in the years before an A&M settlement ceases to be such. The tax pool only exists as long as s.687 applies to the payments made by the trustees (i.e. exercising discretion over income). As A&M trusts change into either interests in possession (beneficiaries attain the age of 18) or absolute interests are achieved, then s.687 will no longer apply and the tax pool will disappear, and with it the possibility of recovering the difference between the rate applicable to trusts and the basic and lower rates.

The current modernisation review of the trust tax system is likely to end up abolishing the tax pool system. It is anticipated that it will be phased out over a short period of years.

It is important to remember the following points.

1. The trust income is that which is assessable for the year in question and not necessarily the amount received.
2. The expenses are those incurred in the tax year, not those paid: i.e. it works on an accruals basis.
3. Interest paid is an expense for the purpose of the calculation of the additional tax due even if it is not allowable as a deduction from the source income itself under general tax principles. This includes interest on late payment of tax.
4. Expenses are those payable out of trust income and not trust capital.
5. Expenses are deducted first from income taxed at 10 per cent, then from income taxed at 20 per cent and thereafter from that taxed at 22 per cent and the rate applicable to trusts.
6. The gross income paid to beneficiaries with interests in possession is deducted, as is the gross income treated as that of the settlor (if any).
7. Accrued income and certain capital receipts which are deemed as income for general tax purposes are not within the scheme and are deducted.

Example: Discretionary trust – rate applicable to trusts: the Forster trust

John Forster created a trust on 6 April 1990 by *inter vivos* settlement. The trust income each year must be either distributed or accumulated as the trustees think fit for the benefit of his nieces and nephews. The assets placed into the trust consisted of certain properties let unfurnished on landlord's repairing short leases; cash on bank deposit; and quoted and government investments.

At 6 April 2004 the tax pool brought forward under s.687 of the ICTA 1998 was £1,150. For 2003/04 the amount of income tax paid on account equalled the liability for the year of £3,478. The receipts and payments of the trust for 2004/05 were as set out below.

Receipts and payments for Forster trust example

	2004/05 £
Receipts	
Rents receivable	11,300
Interest on £10,000 9% government stock (gross)	900
Bank interest (gross)	900
Dividends from UK quoted companies (including tax credits)	3,200
Payments	
Trustees' expenses properly chargeable to income	450
Loan interest (to finance an extension to let property)	350
Repairs to let properties	200
Discretionary payment to Anne	3,060

Statement of trust income for Forster trust example 2004/05

			Gross	Tax deducted
Non-savings income				
Schedule A				
Rent receivable			£11,300.00	
Less expenses	Repairs	−£200.00		
	Loan	−£350.00		
	Interest		−£550.00	
			£10,750.00	
Savings income				
Interest on government stock			£900.00	£180.00
Bank interest			£900.00	£180.00
Equities				
Dividends			£3,200.00	£320.00
Net total income of the trust			£15,750.00	£680.00

Tax thereon:

	Total	Income taxed at Dividend rate	Savings rate	Basic rate
	£	£	£	£
Rental income	10,750			10,750
Savings income	1,800		1,800	
Dividend income	3,200	3,200		
	15,750	3,200	1,800	10,750
Less: Expenses – grossed up using dividend rate (£450 × 100/90)	−500	−500		
Trust income after expenses	15,250	2,700	1,800	10,750
Tax at dividend rate of 10%	320.00	320.00		
Tax at savings rate of 20%	360.00		360.00	
Tax at basic rate of 22%	2,365.00			2,365.00
Further tax to dividend trust rate – 22.5% (that is 32.5% −10) on £2,700.00	607.50	607.50		
Further tax to rate applicable to trusts – 20% (that is 40 −20)	360.00		360.00	
Further tax to rate applicable to trusts – 18% (that is 40 −22)	1,935.00			1,935.00
Total tax	5,947.50	927.50	720.00	4,300.00
Less: Tax deducted at source	−680.00	−320.00	−360.00	
Tax payable by self-assessment	£5,267.50	£607.50	£360.00	£4,300.00
Payments on account for 2004/05				
31 January 2005 – ½ × £3,478		1,739.00		
31 July 2005		1,739.00		
Balance due for 2004/05	1,789.50			
First payment on account due for 2005/06	2,633.75			
Total tax due 31 January 2006		4,423.25		

Income available for distribution

Trust income after expenses	15,250.00
Less: tax at rate applicable to trusts	− 5,947.50
Available for distribution	9,302.50
Actually distributed	−3,060.00
Leaving undistributed income of	6,242.50

Trust's position under s.687, ICTA 1988

Tax paid under self-assessment	5,267.50
Repayable tax deducted at source	360.00
	5,627.50
Unutilised tax b/f	1,150.00
Total tax pool	6,777.50
Utilised in 2004/05 (see below)	−2,040.00
Tax pool carried forward	£4,737.50

Calculation of tax utilised in 2004/05

Net distributions made to benefiaries	3,060.00	
Gross distribution made to beneficiaries – always at the main rate applicable to trusts therefore × 100/60	5,100.00	
Tax attaching to distributions – already accounted for by trustees on trust income chargeable under s.686 at rate applicable to trusts i.e. 40% or 32.5% for dividend income	2,040.00	(Alternative way of calculating this figure is 3,060 × 40/60)
Amount due from trustees under s.687, ICTA 1988.		£0.00

11.8   INCOME TAX CERTIFICATES TO BENEFICIARIES

To ensure that each beneficiary has evidence of his income entitlement in any particular tax year (which is particularly important under self-assessment) at the end of the tax year the trustees of the trust should provide a certificate in form R185 (Trust Income). For an example, see Appendix 1.9 and 1.10.

This certificate will show the income and the income tax paid. The beneficiary will include the income shown on the certificate in his own statutory income and utilise any unused personal allowances or lower rate band to claim an income tax repayment. If the beneficiary's income already exceeds the basic rate threshold, the certificate will be evidence of tax already paid so only an assessment to higher rate on the excess will be due.

From June 2003 the previously separate R185 forms for discretionary and non-discretionary trusts are combined to produce one form for both types of trust. The R185 (Trust Income) form is available online (**www.hmrc.gov.uk/pdfs/r185_ti.pdf**).

11.9   SELF-ASSESSMENT FOR TRUSTEES

Have you got the right tools?

1. Under self-assessment, the trustees as taxpayer must complete the Trust and Estate Tax Return for each trust where a return is issued or where there is income and gains arising which are not to be shown on, say, the life tenant's tax return by agreement with the Inspector of Taxes. Supplementary schedules may need to be completed in a particular trust depending upon the nature of the income and any chargeable gains. These separate schedules and any self-assessment forms and leaflets may be ordered through the Self-Assessment Order line which is available seven days a week from 8a.m. to 10p.m. (contact details are provided at the end of this Chapter; alternatively, the forms may be downloaded from **www.hmrc.gov.uk**).

2. Have you registered as a taxation practitioner or agent with a UK tax office? This enables you to receive information on self-assessment and other taxation matters.

3. It will be important to subscribe to HMRC's *Tax Bulletin* or view it on HMRC's website (**www.hmrc.gov.uk**). The Tax Bulletin provides the views of HMRC's technical specialists on particular issues. It does not replace formal Statements of Practice but it does provide HMRC's view of the law.

4. Have you authority to act as the agent of the trustees of a trust? HMRC normally requires tax agents to complete Form 64-8, which is authority

from the taxpayer for HMRC to liaise with the tax agent. (An example is shown at **Appendix 1.5**.)

5. Clients may need to be educated about the way in which self-assessment works. Prepare information explaining the basics, not least the record-keeping requirements. A HMRC guide is available free from the Order line: *A General Guide to Keeping Records – SA/BK4* and it may be useful to ensure that your clients receive a copy.

6. Prepare a precedent letter to send to clients setting out when a return needs to be requested, the importance of providing you with all the information needed to complete the return within a specified period, the dates for payment of tax, and the sanctions for failing to request and complete a return or pay the tax on time. It is important to stress that HMRC requires full disclosure and that this is the only basis upon which you can accept instructions.

7. Set yourself a clear work programme allowing sufficient time to complete and submit all your trust returns on time and issue statements of income to beneficiaries early enough for them to submit their own returns by 30 September following the end of the tax year, if they wish. The advantage of submission by 30 September is that HMRC will calculate the tax liability for the taxpayer. The HMRC calculations should always be checked. It is often necessary in smaller practices to arrange for some extra help during the period September to January when the trust administrator is still administering the trusts but in addition needs to ensure all the tax returns are in on time. This may entail outsourcing the preparation of accounts and tax returns if there is insufficient capacity within the office to meet the deadlines.

8. The use of IT is increasingly essential. It enables you to collect data and subsequently carry forward repetitive information to future years without re-entering the data. This improves accuracy and enables you to make a speedier response to queries than a manual approach. See further **Chapter 16**.

Basic principles

What was new about self-assessment?

A seismic shift occurred on 6 April 1996. From the tax year 1996/97 onwards, the trustees as taxpayer must decide how much tax is payable on the income and gains of the trust and pay the correct amount of tax accordingly. HMRC expects the taxpayer to get it right first time. There is a single tax return for all trustees and PRs (SA 900).

Trustees need to determine the following.

1. Whether they are liable at the rate applicable to trusts.
2. Whether they are resident in the UK for tax purposes.
3. The correct level of CGT annual exemption.
4. The correct trust status for tax purposes.

On receipt of the tax return, HMRC simply processes it to see if it is valid (e.g. has it been signed? Are there any obvious arithmetical errors?). Later, HMRC will check it and compare it with information from other sources. If there is a risk that the return is incorrect, HMRC will start an enquiry. Some returns will be investigated on a random basis. HMRC expects to select between 5,000 and 10,000 cases a year for random enquiry.

Basis of assessment

Under the self-assessment system the current year basis of assessment is used for all income and gains, so all taxpayers pay on a fully current year basis, i.e. income tax will be charged on the income or profit arising in the tax year itself, or on the profits arising in the 12-month accounting period ending in that year.

Time limits

Notification of the receipt of gross income or chargeable gains

Trustees must indicate if there is any chargeability in the trust within six months of the end of the tax year. This means requesting a tax return if none has been issued. For the tax year 2004/05, this would mean notifying HMRC of chargeability by 5 October 2005 and requesting an SA900 by that date.

Amendments

Amendment of a self-assessment can be made at any time up to 12 months following the filing date of the return but not if the return is already under enquiry. Changes should always be notified to HMRC but settlement may not always be agreed without a sanction applying if the amendment is notified outside the 12-month period. Where an amendment is submitted the 12-month enquiry period starts from the end of the tax quarter in which the amendment is submitted.

Dates for submission of tax returns

1. 30 September following the end of the tax year if trustees want HMRC to calculate the tax for them.
2. 31 January following the end of the tax year if the trustees are to calculate their own tax.
3. If the return is issued late (for example the trustees had to request a return to notify chargeability) then the taxpayers must submit it within two months of the date of issue if they want HMRC to calculate the tax, or within three months if they will calculate the tax themselves.

Tax is payable on two dates

1. 31 January each year, when the money due comprises:

    (a) payment of final payment for the previous tax year for income tax;
    (b) the whole of any CGT for that year; and
    (c) the first payment on account of income tax due for the current tax year (50 per cent of the previous year's tax).

2. 31 July each year, when the money due comprises:

    (a) the second payment on account of income tax due for the previous tax year (50 per cent of the tax of the previous tax year).

For example:

31 January 2005	*31 July 2005*
• Any outstanding income tax for 2003/04	• 50 per cent of income tax of 2003/04 as second payment on account of income tax for 2004/05
• Any CGT for 2003/04 • 50 per cent of income tax of 2003/04 as second payment on account of income tax for 2004/05	

There is a *de minimus* test – no payments on account need be made if the previous year's tax is less than £500 or the proportion of the previous year's tax which was deducted at source was more than 80 per cent of the total tax for that year.

Sanctions

Interest is charged on tax paid late for whatever reason and upon unpaid surcharges. Interest runs from the relevant due date (i.e. 31 January or 31 July) until the date of payment.

Surcharges are charged on top of interest on the balancing tax payments to encourage timely payment. Five per cent of the tax due is charged on all tax paid more than 28 days after the due date, i.e. 31 January following the tax year or 30 days from agreeing any increased liabilities (if later). Thus, a surcharge would be payable within 58 days of fixing any increased liabilities. A further 5 per cent is charged should the tax be six months late. Interest is charged on unpaid surcharges.

Penalties of up to 100 per cent of the tax fraudulently or negligently understated can be charged, just as before. A maximum penalty of £3,000 per annum can also be charged if the records required for self-assessment have not been retained by the taxpayer: see *A General Guide to Keeping Records – SA/BK4* available free from the Order line.

There is an automatic penalty of the greater of £100 or the amount of tax outstanding if the tax return is submitted late. A further penalty of £60 per day may be imposed at the direction of the Tax Commissioners. A further £100 is charged if it is still not filed by the following 31 July. If the return remains outstanding on the anniversary of the filing date, the whole amount of the tax charged can be applied as a penalty.

Enquiries

If there are any queries on the return, when submitted, a Notice of Intention to raise queries has to be issued by HMRC within 12 months of the filing date for the return. There is a leaflet 'Code of Practice 11' entitled *Enquiries into Tax Returns by Local Tax Offices* and a copy can be obtained from the Order line. There are separate codes for specialist tax offices, for example where serious fraud is suspected. If you receive one of these with the Notice, ensure that you take specialist advice from a practitioner familiar with tax investigations or criminal practice before you make any response.

HMRC has the explicit right to enquire into the completeness and accuracy of any tax return without justifying that enquiry by identifying particular aspects of the return that give cause for concern. This right will cover all enquiries, from straightforward requests for further information on individual items, through to a full examination of all the underlying records.

In the 12-month period that HMRC has to raise enquiries on a return, all matters relevant to that return must be raised during the enquiry correspondence, whether trivial or significant.

The formal Notice of Enquiry, under s.9A of the Taxes Management Act 1970, goes to the trustees and it will contain the actual enquiries that HMRC wishes to make. If your firm is on the record as agent for the trustees, then a copy of the Notice will come to the firm.

Full disclosure

The Tax Inspector is assumed to have knowledge of:

(a) information contained in the tax return and its enclosures;
(b) information in a claim made on behalf of the taxpayers and the enclosures accompanying it; and
(c) information, the existence and relevance of which are notified to the Inspector or could reasonably be expected to be inferred from the information in the return, enclosures and claims.

Information is available to an Inspector if it is contained in the return for the current tax year or the two preceding chargeable periods. It therefore follows that if you wish the Inspector to rely on an understanding of the particular treatment of the estate or trust based on documents provided initially, these documents may need to be resubmitted every three years to enable this assumption to apply.

The assumption is based on the test that the Inspector is deemed to know what a reasonably competent Inspector would be expected to conclude on the basis of the information available. This means the information must be reasonably clear in the return, so the onus is on the trustees to draw attention to any important information that is relevant to a tax liability, especially if there is some doubt as to how a particular piece of information might be interpreted. The professional bodies advise practitioners to follow a policy of full disclosure to HMRC. The final decision on any particular matter to be disclosed will rest with the trustees, but the professional should query the instruction not to disclose something that you feel is required to be disclosed.

There is no definition of what would constitute 'full disclosure'. Most taxation practitioners believe that it is a level of disclosure that is sufficient to ensure that no s.29 of the Taxes Management Act 1970 assessment could be made on the grounds of incomplete disclosure. This means that the Inland Revenue must receive sufficient detail to be able to be treated as deemed to have been able to understand the position taken by the tax practitioner.

You will have to consider with the trustees, the appropriate level of disclosure in any particular case. Too much disclosure may attract unnecessary and potentially costly enquiries by HMRC that will give rise to fees that may be difficult to justify. Insufficient disclosure will mean that the return 'even if completely accurate' can be challenged by HMRC after the normal time limit for enquiries has passed.

For trusts, consider submitting:

(a) a copy of the trust deed to support the reported income tax treatment, and
(b) income account details where these provide additional information in support of the tax treatments reported.

Estimates and valuations

HMRC accepts that in some circumstances it may be necessary to enter a figure on to a tax return that is not completely certain in order to complete the return by the statutory deadline.

Where trustees expect to be able to provide a more accurate figure later, provisional figures will be entered and the relevant box on the tax return must be ticked in order to indicate that the figures are provisional. Further details will have to be supplied and HMRC should be directed to those under the 'Additional Information' box at the back of the tax return. This will result in an automatic Notice of Enquiry received from HMRC in order that it may keep the matter open until you have submitted the final figure. Do not delay notifying the final figure as penalties may arise.

Where there is no way of arriving at a more accurate figure (for example where there is only a proportion of an expense which is deductible for tax) then this figure will be an estimate and HMRC's attention should be drawn to it, otherwise there may be a possible dispute over whether or not there has been full disclosure. The tax return actually states:

> if you are including an estimate which, while not a precise figure, is sufficiently reliable to enable you to make an accurate Tax Return, there is no need to make specific reference to it.

Valuations

Some figures are a judgement and, in the case of professional valuations, have probably been arrived at through a detailed process of valuation by professionals such as a land agent or specialist accountant.

In general terms, HMRC treats valuations in the same way as estimates so trustees must make a specific disclosure if the figure provided is not sufficiently reliable for the tax return to be treated as accurate.

For CGT purposes, even if a professional has produced the valuation, HMRC must be notified that it is a valuation. HMRC has said that it will not challenge proper professional valuations that fall within the range of possibilities for negotiated valuations between fully briefed professionals.

Avoid making 'stabs in the dark'. HMRC views a failure to take professional valuation advice as constituting neglect, which gives them the opportunity to reopen enquiries after the due dates. Negligently inserting an inadequate estimate or valuation will expose the trust to possible penalties.

The requirement to make sufficient disclosure was considered in the recent case of *Langham* v. *Veltema* [2004] STC 544. There has been much comment on the outcome of this case and whether it increases HMRC's powers to claim discovery. It is essential to draw attention to any valuation submitted by setting out the details in the 'Additional Information' box at the end of the tax return.

Record keeping

All taxpayers, whether trusts, estates or individuals, must keep the records which are required by the self-assessment legislation. See *A General Guide to Keeping Records – SA/BK4*. The record-keeping obligation is entirely separate from making a return. Whether or not a tax return needs to be submitted does not obviate the need to keep all the necessary records that will be required to make a tax return or make a claim under the tax system.

The originals of some records have to be kept, such as records relating to tax deductions and credits, particularly if they are needed to justify a repayment of tax (s.12B(4A), Taxes Management Act 1970). Otherwise, keeping copies can satisfy the obligation. Where details are transferred on to a computer, the original paper documents must be kept unless they are microfilmed (s.12B(4), Taxes Management Act 1970).

Record keeping includes creating records such as working sheets to support the payment of residuary income to beneficiaries in an estate.

When considering CGT, it is suggested that correspondence relating to the sale or purchase of the item that is subsequently disposed of is helpful if there is any doubt as to when beneficial ownership of the asset actually passed between the owners.

Generally, records of income tax and CGT need to be kept for 22 months after the end of the tax year to which they relate. Where CGT is involved, clearly some records relating to the acquisition of the asset will have to be kept until the asset is disposed of, which could be much longer than the 22-month period. For those trusts involved in trading or partnerships, the records need to be kept for five tax years after the fixed filing dates.

Duties and responsibilities of trustees

Trustees need to make a self-assessment by the same filing dates and subject to the same rules as other taxpayers. They must notify liability and pay tax.

Which trustees are liable? The 'relevant' trustees are defined in s.7(9) of the Taxes Management Act 1970 as those who are trustees:

1. when the income arises;
2. in the tax year when a gain arises (which is not necessarily the same thing); and
3. all those who subsequently become trustees.

It is therefore particularly important to ascertain the liability to pay tax or any sanctions for late submission of a return or tax payment when advising outgoing and incoming trustees. The relevant trustees are liable to the tax of the trust and any interest for late payment. An incoming trustee is liable for all past tax and interest and an outgoing trustee remains liable in respect of all tax and interest in relation to income arising up to the date of retirement and capital gains arising up to the end of the tax year of retirement.

A trustee is only liable to a penalty or surcharge if he was a trustee at the time when the default occurred (s.107A(2),(3), Taxes Management Act 1970). Hence an incoming trustee will not be liable for surcharges and penalties in relation to defaults occurring before he became a trustee. An outgoing trustee will remain liable in respect of all surcharges and penalties in respect of income arising up to the date of his retirement and capital gains arising up to the end of the tax year in which he retired.

A tax return can be issued to any of the relevant trustees but the obligation to file it is imposed on all of them (s.107A(1), Taxes Management Act 1970).

11.10 ADDRESSES AND CONTACTS

Self-Assessment Order line:	Telephone: 0645 000 404 Fax: 0645 000 604 Postal Address: SA Order line PO Box 37 St Austell PL25 5YN **www.hmrc.gov.uk/contactus/staustellform.htm**
Electronic Lodgement Service:	Revenue ELS Business Support Team Room 116, Accounts Office Shipley West Yorkshire BD98 8AA Telephone: 01274 539301/539325
Capital Taxes Office:	Ferrers House PO Box 38 Castle Meadow Road Nottingham NG2 1BB DX: 701201 Nottingham 4
Nottingham Trust District: (Responsible for all the counties in England and Wales which are not covered by HMRC Trusts Truro.)	Huntingdon Court 90–94 Mansfield Road Nottingham NG1 3HG Telephone: 0115 911 6500

FICO (Trusts and Charities): St Johns House
Bootle
Merseyside L69 9BB
Telephone: 0151 472 6238
Fax: 0151 472 6004

FICO International
(Non-residents):

72 Maid Marion Way
Nottingham NG1 6AS
Telephone: 01602 242299
Fax: 01602 504374

HMRC Trusts Edinburgh:
(Responsible for Scotland
and Northern Ireland and
any trusts under Scottish
law or with a corporate
trustee.)

Meldrum House
15 Drumsheugh Gardens
Edinburgh EH3 7UL
Telephone: 0131 777 4030

HMRC Trusts Truro:
(Responsible for all the
London Boroughs and
the counties of Devon,
Cornwall, Somerset,
Dorset, Gloucestershire
and Wiltshire.)

Lysnoweth
Infirmary Hill
Truro
Cornwall TR1 2JD
Telephone: 01872 245403

CHAPTER 12

Trusts with a vulnerable beneficiary

12.1 INTRODUCTION

As part of the modernisation of the system of trust taxation a form of relief has been introduced in ss.23–45 of, and Sched.1 to, the Finance Act 2005 for trusts with a vulnerable beneficiary. As the explanatory notes to the Bill said:

> clauses [23–45] . . . create a new tax regime for certain trusts with vulnerable beneficiaries. They determine which trusts and beneficiaries will be able to elect into the regime and, where a claim for special tax treatment is made for a tax year, provide for no more tax to be paid in respect of the relevant income and gains of the trust for that year than would be paid had the income and gains accrued directly to the beneficiary. The changes will take effect from 6 April 2004.

Please note therefore that although the rate applicable to trusts and the dividend trust rate were increased from 6 April 2004 these provisions apply to that income which will be the subject of tax returns for 2004/05. In this way these special trusts and beneficiaries will not bear the new higher rates on their income.

12.2 WHO IS A VULNERABLE PERSON?

There are two types of 'vulnerable person': a disabled person and a relevant minor.

A 'disabled person' is defined in s.38(1) as:

(a) a person who by reason of mental disorder within the meaning of the Mental Health Act 1983 is incapable of administering his property or managing his affairs, or

(b) a person in receipt of attendance allowance or of a disability living allowance by virtue of entitlement to the care component at the highest or middle rate.

The definition is extended in s.38(2) to people who would otherwise meet the criteria for the receipt of attendance allowance or disability living allowance if they were to meet the prescribed conditions as to residence under the relevant rules. This would allow non-resident beneficiaries who met the criteria, other than residence, to be treated as a vulnerable beneficiary for these purposes.

Subsection (3) provides that the special provisions do not cease to apply if the sole reason that the person is no longer in receipt of the allowance in question (or would no longer be in receipt of it if the relevant residence requirements were to be met) is because that person is undergoing treatment for renal failure in a hospital or is being provided with certain accommodation.

A 'relevant minor' is defined in s.39 as someone who:

(a)   has not yet attained the age of 18, and
(b)   at least one of his parents has died.

At least the actual definition of 'relevant minor' no longer discriminates between children of testate or intestate parents, which the consultation documents did. It also is not so draconian as to require the loss of both parents, which would only then apply to a relatively small group of children.

It will be noted that for these purposes the definition is not so wide as to take in other types of people who might be regarded as vulnerable, such as people subject to addictions.

12.3   WHICH TRUSTS QUALIFY?

In the case of a disabled person, a qualifying trust is one where a vulnerable person election has been made and is effective for that tax year (s.40) and which satisfies the following conditions during the lifetime of the disabled person or until the termination of the trusts, if that occurs before his death (s.34(2)):

(a)   if any of the property of the trust is applied for the benefit of a beneficiary, it is applied for the benefit of the disabled person, or
(b)   either that the disabled person is entitled to all the income (if there is any) arising from any of the property or that no such income may be applied for the benefit of any other person.

Subsection (3) provides that the trusts on which property is held are not to be taken to fail to meet the conditions set out above solely by reason of the fact that s.32 of the Trustee Act 1925 confers powers of advancement on the trustees.

In the case of a relevant minor a qualifying trust is a trust established under ss.46 and 47(1) of the Administration of Estates Act 1925 (statutory trusts operating on intestacy), or established under the will of a deceased parent of the relevant minor or established under the Criminal Injuries Compensation Scheme and where the following conditions are met (s.35(3)).

1.   That the relevant minor will, on attaining the age of 18, become absolutely entitled to the property, any income arising from it and any

income that has arisen from property held on the trusts for his benefit and been accumulated before that time.

2. That, until that time, for so long as the relevant minor is living, if any of the property is applied for the benefit of a beneficiary, it is applied for the benefit of the relevant minor.

3. That, until that time, for so long as the relevant minor is living, either:

   (a) the relevant minor is entitled to all the income (if there is any) arising from any property, or
   (b) no such income may be applied for the benefit of any other person.

Just as for disabled persons, trusts for relevant minors are not to be treated as being outside these conditions simply because the trustees enjoy the powers of advancement conferred by s.32 of the Trustee Act 1925.

In each case it is possible that only part of an asset belongs to a trust which complies with the conditions to qualify for the special treatment. In just the same way as the whole asset and any income arising or treated as arising would qualify, so too will that part of the asset which qualifies and any income arising from it or treated as arising from it.

12.4 HOW IS A CLAIM MADE FOR SPECIAL TAX TREATMENT?

A 'vulnerable person election' must be made jointly by the trustees and the vulnerable person in such form as HMRC (as they are now known) announces (s.37). It will specify the date from which it is to have effect.

It will also be made by notice to HMRC no later than 12 months after 31 January next following the tax year in which the effective date falls, or within such further time, if any, as the Board of HMRC may by notice have allowed; and contain the following.

1. Such information as the Board of HMRC may require, including particular information relating to the trusts, the trustees, the vulnerable person and his entitlement under the trusts and any other person connected with the trusts.

2. A statement that the trusts in relation to which the election is made are qualifying trusts.

3. A declaration that all the information contained in the election is correct to the best of the knowledge and belief of the trustees and the vulnerable person.

4. A declaration by the vulnerable person that he authorises the trustees to make any claim for any tax year as they consider appropriate.

5. Such other declaration as the Board of HMRC may reasonably require.

The election is irrevocable.

The election will continue from the effective date until one of the following events occurs (s.37(5)):

1. The vulnerable person ceases to be a vulnerable person.
2. The trusts in relation to which the election is made cease to qualify.
3. The trusts are terminated.

It is the duty of the trustees to inform HMRC that the vulnerable person election has ceased to have effect and this must be done by notice, within 90 days of them becoming aware that such an event has occurred, containing the particulars of that event.

The Act is strangely silent on who should join in the election with the trustees on behalf of the vulnerable person where the vulnerable person is not competent to make the election himself. In the consultations, some respondents felt it would be best to stipulate which persons could act on the vulnerable person's behalf, e.g. parent, guardian, legal representative, etc., but the Act does not say. In the absence of specific guidance then the provisions of the Taxes Management Act 1970 will presumably apply. There may be cases where the trustees are the same persons as those who have authority to act on the vulnerable person's behalf.

12.5   WHAT IS THE INCOME TAX TREATMENT?

First of all, the special tax treatment only applies if the election has been made and the income on the qualifying trusts arises or is treated as arising in the hands of the trustees and not the settlor under s.624(1) of the ITTOIA 2005. In other words, the trust must not be settlor-interested.

The trustees' liability to income tax will be reduced by an amount equal to the amount by which the sum determined in accordance with s.27 (income tax liability of the trustees in respect of the qualifying income) exceeds the amount determined in accordance with s.28 (extra tax to which the vulnerable person would be liable if qualifying trusts income were actually his).

Trustees' liability

Unless only part of the income of the trust is qualifying trust income, the trustees' liability will be the amount of income tax chargeable on the trustees' total income less management expenses which are properly chargeable to total income or would be so chargeable but for any express provisions of the trust.

Where only part of the trust's total income is eligible for qualifying trust status, then such part of the trust's expenses which are applicable to total income will be disregarded in computing the trustees' liability as the proportion that non-qualifying income bears to the total income of the trust.

For example, consider a trust with two beneficiaries, one of whom quali-fies as a vulnerable beneficiary but the other does not. If the total income for the year was £6,000 and the management expenses referable to that total income were £200, then £100 of those expenses would be ignored in the computation of the trustees' liability in respect of the qualifying income.

$$\frac{3,000}{6,000} \times £200 = £100$$

Vulnerable person's liability

The vulnerable person's liability is calculated by working out what his total tax liability would be if you included in his income the qualifying trust income and deducted the total income tax and CGT liability of the vulner-able person (without the qualifying trust income which was distributed to him and excluding any relief given to him, by way of income tax reduction).

There are special rules applicable to vulnerable persons who are non-resident in the UK during the tax year – see ss.28(4), 41(2) and para.3, Sched.1.

Example

The Castle Discretionary Trust received gross income from all sources in 2004/05 of £10,000. The management expenses referable to income amounted to £200 gross. Mr Rook is the prime beneficiary of the trust which is a qualifying settlement by virtue of the fact that Mr Rook is a vulnerable person. Mr Rook's total income for 2004/05 amounted to £6,000 and he realised no chargeable gains.

The trustees resolve for 2004/05 that all the available income shall be accumulated.

The trustees' liability (assuming there is no income from dividends):
40% £(10,000 − 200) = 40% £9,800 i.e. £3,920

Mr Rook's personal tax liability, ignoring the trust's distribution:

	£	£
Total income	6,000.00	
Less: personal allowance	(4,745.00)	
Taxable income		1,255.00
Tax thereon	First £2,020 is at 10%	125.50

Mr Rook's personal tax liability, adding in the trust's income:

	£	£	£
Personal income	6,000.00		
Trust's income, after expenses	9,800.00		
Total income		15,800.00	
Less: personal allowance		(4,745.00)	
Taxable income			11,055.00
Tax thereon	First £2,020 is at 10%	202.00	
	Next £9,035 is at 22%	1,987.70	
			2,189.70

Therefore, applying the formulae from ss.26–28, the trustees' tax relief on the trust's qualifying income is: TQTI − VQTI

where:

- TQTI is the amount of income tax to which the trustees would ordinarily be liable in respect of the qualifying trusts income arising or treated as arising, i.e. in the example £3,920.00.
- VQTI is the *extra* tax which the vulnerable person would be liable to pay if the qualifying trust income were his income, i.e. in the example £(2,189.70 − 125.50) = £2,064.20

The trustees' tax relief will therefore be £(3,920.00 − 2,064.20) = £1,855.80.

Where the vulnerable person election only has effect for part of the tax year, the above formulae are modified as follows.

1. The trustees' qualifying trusts income will be the income arising to them in the elected part of the tax year.
2. The trustees' income arising and expenses are treated respectively as references to the income arising and expenses arising in that elected part of the tax year.

12.6   WHAT IS THE CGT TREATMENT?

Sections 30–33 set out the provisions relating to CGT. The following conditions have to be met in order for the trustees of the qualifying settlement to receive the special CGT treatment on trust gains.

1. Chargeable gains arise in the tax year to the trustees on the disposal of trust property held on the qualifying trusts for the benefit of a vulnerable person.
2. The trustees would be chargeable to CGT in respect of those gains were it not for the application of Chapter 4 of the Finance Act 2005.
3. The trustees are resident in the UK during any part of the tax year or ordinarily resident in the UK during the tax year.
4. The trustees make a claim for special tax treatment for the tax year.

If these conditions are met the special CGT treatment applies unless excluded by s.30(3), which says that s.30 does not apply in relation to the tax year in which the vulnerable person dies.

If the vulnerable person is UK resident, the treatment is set out in accordance with s.31, whereas if the vulnerable person is non-UK resident during the tax year, the special CGT treatment applies in accordance with s.32.

The resident vulnerable person is basically treated as though he were the settlor of the settlement and is taxed on the trust's disposal as though he had retained an interest in the settlement. Essentially, s.31 provides for ss.77(1), 78 and most of s.79 of the TCGA 1992 to apply. Any chargeable gains which, apart from this provision, would be charged on the trustees is reduced first by any allowable trustees' losses and then the vulnerable person is able to recover from the trustees the amount of any CGT which consequently becomes chargeable on him.

Where the vulnerable person is non-resident there is a complicated formula for calculating that person's liability to CGT on the basis of ss.32–33 and Sched.1.

12.7 WHAT ENQUIRIES CAN HMRC MAKE?

By virtue of the powers set out in s.40 HMRC may by notice require the trustees or the vulnerable person to furnish it with such particulars as it may reasonably require for the purposes of determining whether the vulnerable person meets the definitions of the Act and whether the trust is therefore a qualifying trust, and whether an event has occurred whereby the trust or the vulnerable person no longer qualify for this special tax treatment.

The notice which HMRC serves must specify the time within which the information must be supplied and this must be a period of not less than 60 days.

HMRC may as a result determine that the case for special tax treatment is incorrect or the period of application has ceased from the date which it specifies in the notice. Any such notice of determination may be appealed by notice to the General Commissioners. An appeal notice must be given to the Board of HMRC within 30 days after the notice of the determination was given.

12.8 WHICH PENALTIES MAY APPLY?

A failure to supply the information requested in a notice issued by HMRC will result in an automatic fine of £300 with the possibility of this being increased by £60 per day (s.98(1), Taxes Management Act 1970).

Where a person fraudulently or negligently furnishes, gives, produces or makes any incorrect information, certificate, document, record or declaration of a kind mentioned in any of the provisions specified in the table to s.98, he shall be liable to a penalty not exceeding £3,000.

PART FOUR

Practical trusts

CHAPTER 13

Dealing with various events

13.1 INTRODUCTION

In the course of administering trusts a number of events occur on a regular basis and the actions to be taken should become familiar. A common issue is whether or not the trust can be brought to an end earlier than its normal finish date. The reasons why a trust has outlived its usefulness are many and varied, but for small trust funds a regular problem for beneficiaries and administrators alike is that the costs of running the trust properly may come to outweigh any benefits to the beneficiaries.

In this Chapter consideration is given to whether it is wise to break up a trust early and it then goes on to consider what powers may be needed to do so. Later in the Chapter there is a review of the key events which occur in the usual trusts necessitating either a winding up of the trust or a major distribution from it.

13.2 WHEN TO LEAVE EXISTING TRUSTS ALONE

Life interest settlements

CGT – death of life tenant

Many interest in possession trusts are said to benefit a particular person for that person's lifetime. This form of interest in possession trust was popular in the past to secure a life interest for the surviving spouse whilst preserving the underlying capital value for the children after the surviving spouse's own death.

In **Chapter 9** the IHT consequences of the death of the life tenant confirmed that the trust fund is taxed as though it were part of the life tenant's estate. This is often not desired by the beneficiaries of both the trust fund and the life tenant's own estate. As a result, the trustees are asked to consider bringing the interest in possession trust to an end whilst the life tenant is alive.

It is, however, advantageous from a CGT point of view to leave the trust fund intact until the life tenant's death because of the uplift in the base cost of the trust's own assets to the market value at the date of the life tenant's death. Each case needs careful consideration to see whether the CGT advantages of leaving the assets in trust until after the death of the life tenant outweigh the IHT disadvantage.

If the trust assets are not intended to be sold and are pregnant with gain probably the best option is to leave the assets in trust to get benefit of CGT uplift to market value at the date of death of the life tenant, particularly if they carry 100 per cent business property relief or agricultural property relief for IHT purposes.

When reorganising old, inflexible settlements it is vitally important not to unintentionally cause a new settlement to arise for CGT as otherwise there will be a deemed disposal and reacquisition by the trustees giving rise to a charge to CGT under s.71 of the TCGA 1992.

Surviving spouse exemption from estate duty

A few settlements still exist which enjoy the surviving spouse exemption from estate duty (that is where on the death of the first spouse to die, estate duty was paid rather than exemption claimed at that time). The exemption has the effect of protecting the trust fund from taxation on the death of the second spouse. It is wise not to untangle such a trust, because the whole trust fund will be free of IHT when the life tenant dies, instead of being taxable, which will be a huge advantage to the remainder beneficiaries. Subject to the needs of the life tenant it is a good idea to invest for capital growth in the trust so that as much capital value as possible will pass to the remainder beneficiaries without a charge to IHT.

Assignment of reversionary interests

Under s.47 of the IHTA 1984 the interests of the remainder beneficiaries are regarded as 'excluded property' for IHT purposes, whilst the life tenant is still alive. A good way of tax planning to ensure there is no likelihood of a charge on a transfer of value is to assign the benefit of the reversion as remainderman whilst the life tenant is alive to a chargeable beneficiary, such as the remainderman's own children. The assignment is not a PET nor is it a chargeable transfer, so there is no need to survive seven years from the date when it is made to ensure it will not be taxed. This is because the reversionary interests are outside the scope of IHT altogether. Where the reversionary beneficiary would like to make the most of this benefit it is worth considering keeping the trust going, at least until after the assignment.

Discretionary

Where discretionary trusts were made pre-18 March 1986 it was possible for the settlor and/or the settlor's spouse to have been included in the class of beneficiaries or to be the subject of a discretionary power which could be exercised in the settlor's favour without the transfer into the trust being treated as a gift with reservation of benefit. This type of reservation was permissible under capital transfer tax. It is now no longer permissible with the result that the settlor is taxed on the income and capital gains of the trust fund.

Up until the first 10-yearly anniversary it was probably not necessary to alter these trusts for IHT purposes but it should be considered before the settlor's death and before the next 10-year anniversary.

13.3   BREAKING UP A TRUST EARLY

Types of powers

In order to break up the trust, short of court proceedings under the Variation of Trusts Act 1958, certain powers need to be contained within the trust deed unless it is a *Saunders* v. *Vautier* [1841] 4 Beav 115 situation. That is, all the beneficiaries are competent adults who together are absolutely entitled to all the property in the trust, in which case they can direct the trustees to distribute the assets in the trust to them, partition it, or require the funds to be held on fresh trusts.

Discretionary trusts will provide the trustees with a wide power of appointment and usually with the discretion to resettle trust assets as required. It is therefore the very essence of a discretionary trust that the trustees decide when and if to make distributions out of the trust. If the trust is no longer needed or wanted, then all the trustees have to do is to agree to distribute all the remaining funds to the beneficiaries absolutely or on other trusts for the beneficiaries.

It is much more common for there to be a dilemma about whether a trust can be broken up early where the trust is an interest in possession trust or an A&M trust.

For an A&M trust to be brought to an end early the class of potential beneficiaries would need to have closed and those which remain within the class would have to be 18 years of age or more and have full mental capacity. The trust could in those circumstances be broken up under the *Saunders* v. *Vautier* decision, if all the beneficiaries agree.

Often, there will be powers granted to the trustees providing flexibility if the beneficiary has achieved an interest in possession. Modern interest in possession trusts and A&M trusts will usually contain powers suitable to achieve a reorganisation of the trust funds by the trustees, rather than using the blunt instrument of *Saunders* v. *Vautier*.

The type of powers which will be needed to reorganise a trust will be the following.

1. Power of appointment – which would permit the creation of new trusts for the beneficiaries.
2. Power of resettlement – which permits the transfer of funds to a new settlement.
3. Power of advancement – which permits the application of capital for the benefit of a beneficiary.

Nature of the power

The question to ask is: is the nature of the power administrative or dispositive? It needs to be dispositive in order to be used on a reorganisation. There is a series of cases which demonstrates the nature of different powers.

Roome v. *Edwards* [1981] 54 TC 359, HL, expressed the view that where a special power of appointment is exercised, it would not be correct to say that a separate settlement had been created if it were found that provisions of the original settlement still continued to apply to the appointed funds or those funds were liable to fall back into the original fund.

In *Ewart* v. *Taylor* [1983] 57 TC 401, Ch D, everything was kept separate including the management powers; there were different trustees and the accountants prepared separate accounts for the new trust, which was held to be separate from the original fund.

In *Bond* v. *Pickford* [1983] STC 517, CA, a distinction was made between powers which were said to be in the 'wider form' and therefore the exercise of them would mean the removal of assets from the original settlement and thus a new settlement, and those which were said to be in the 'narrower form', the exercise of which would not create a new settlement.

Extent to which it is being used

Even where there is a wider form power of appointment, it does not follow that the exercise of such a power will result in a new settlement being created. Instead it is necessary to establish the intent behind the exercise of the power (*Swires* v. *Renton* [1991] STC 490, Ch D).

External evidence to show a new trust created

There is a Statement of Practice SP7/84 in which HMRC sets out the circumstances in which it will *not* treat the appointment as a deemed disposal. If:

1. the appointment is revocable; or
2. the trusts are not exhaustive so it is possible that assets will return to the original fund; or
3. the duties of trustees still fall on the original trustees

HMRC will not regard the appointment as a deemed disposal. This applies whether the power exercised relates to the whole or part of a trust fund. It will be up to the taxpayer to bring evidence to show that the exercise falls within the Statement of Practice.

Using the *Saunders* v. *Vautier* rule

Where an interest in possession trust is to be broken up with all the beneficiaries' consent there are a number of options open to the parties.

(a) Partition of the fund between the beneficiaries

This method envisages a division of the assets in the trust between the life tenant and the remainder beneficiaries. In order to achieve a fair and reasonable division it is usual to obtain an actuarial valuation of the different beneficial interests. Obviously, the older and frailer the life tenant, the less value will be attached to that person's interest in the trust and the greater value will be allocated to the remainder beneficiaries' interests.

There is a clear IHT advantage to a partition if the life tenant is likely to live for more than seven years following the partition. This is because the share of the trust fund passing to the remainder beneficiaries is treated as a PET by the life tenant, and as such the transfer is not subject to IHT at the time of the partition. It has the advantage too, of passing out of the trust what might be appreciating assets and so reduces the impact of any assets being still held in the trust which would otherwise be taxable in conjunction with the life tenant's estate upon death.

Often, a reducing term whole life assurance policy is taken out on the life of the life tenant to provide a fund to meet any IHT bill should the life tenant die within the seven-year period.

However, the partition will result in both the life tenant and the remainder beneficiaries becoming absolutely entitled to a share of the trust fund, which triggers a disposal for CGT. It may be that a relief could apply to reduce the impact but if there remains a chargeable gain then the trustees must remember that they are accountable for the CGT and ensure that they have the means to meet this bill before passing all the assets permanantly out of their control.

(b) Release of the life tenant's interest by surrender to the remainder beneficiaries

Sometimes a life tenant has adequate resources and does not want his own estate affected by the coupling with the trust fund for IHT. Also, a life tenant may wish to help the remainder beneficiaries immediately, rather than leaving them to wait for his death.

If the life tenant has no need of any part of the trust fund then the life tenant can surrender his interest. This operates in the same way as (a) for IHT in that it will be a PET by the life tenant and will pass potentially appreciating assets early to the remainder beneficiaries. It is also a disposal for CGT, as in (a) above.

(c) Enlargement of the life tenant's interest by gift from the remainder beneficiaries

In some cases it is the remainder beneficiaries who have no need of the trust fund and they choose to gift the remainder interests to the life tenant, who may be finding it difficult to manage on just the income from the trust.

Where the life tenant acquires the remainder interests as a gift from the remainder beneficiaries, the IHT consequences are different from those discussed in (a) and (b). Whilst the life tenant is alive any assignment of the reversion will be 'excluded property' for IHT so there will be no PET and no charge for IHT.

For CGT it will still be a disposal by the trustees, as now the life tenant will become the sole owner of the trust's assets freed and discharged from the terms of the trust.

(d) Enlargement of the life tenant's interest by purchase from the remainder beneficiaries

The difference between (c) and (d) is that there is no gift but rather consideration in money or money's worth passing between the life tenant and the remainder beneficiaries for the transfer to the life tenant of the reversionary interests. It is not therefore possible to rely on those reversionary interests as being 'excluded property'. They are not excluded property because they have been purchased.

In IHT terms the monetary consideration paid by the life tenant is effectively a PET – a gift of the purchase price (s.55(1), IHTA 1984). Again, it will be a CGT disposal by the trustees.

Note that if the trust assets contain land, a land transaction will also have occurred for which consideration has been paid, so it will be important to assess the liability, if any, to SDLT and account for it appropriately.

(e) Assignment to third parties by remainder beneficiaries

It may be that the life tenant and the remainder beneficiaries are all adequately provided for but a remainder beneficiary would like to reduce the risk of IHT in his estate by removing his entitlement to the interest in the trust. An assignment of his reversionary interest by way of gift to any person or persons of his choosing will be a gift of 'excluded property' and so outside the scope of IHT.

Assuming it is an English trust, rather than one offshore, then the disposal of the interest in the trust will be exempt from CGT under s.76(1) of the TCGA 1992.

(f) Disclaimer of life interest which has not yet arisen

Consider a trust with consecutive life interests, such as to Fred for life and then to June for life and then to Alistair absolutely; June's interest is not yet in possession all the time Fred is alive.

In the event that June disclaims her interest Alistair will receive the reversion in her place on Fred's death.

The act of disclaimer by June is not a taxable event for IHT because at the time the interest was disclaimed there was no actual interest in possession for her. Similarly, because she was not in possession at the time it will not be a disposal for CGT purposes.

13.4   TAX CONSEQUENCES

It should therefore be apparent that a major consideration when dealing with the break up of the trust or the distribution of assets out of the trust will be the taxation consequences of the alternatives under consideration.

IHT considerations

1. If the trust is an interest in possession trust, the termination of the trust will result in the life tenant being treated as though he made a transfer of value of the amount of the trust fund or at least the value of that part in which his interest terminates. This is so whether or not the transfer is made by himself assigning or surrendering his life interest or from the operation of the terms of the trust.

    If the life tenant becomes absolutely entitled to the funds there will be no charge to IHT as he is in no different position (from an IHT point of view) than when he was life tenant. Before the trust interest terminated he was treated as owning the capital value of the trust fund (s.49, IHTA 1984), and as a result of the transfer of the trust fund to him he now actually owns that value personally. The effect is clearly that his estate has not been diminished by the transfer out of the trust thus so as far as the interest transferred to the life tenant is concerned it is IHT neutral.

If someone else benefits as a result of the transfer or if the transfer is into A&M trusts the life tenant will be regarded as making a PET because his estate will be going down by the amount of value passing out of the trust fund.

2. With discretionary trusts, the exit charge regime applies so that a charge to IHT will arise on the value of the fund that is leaving the trust.

3. An A&M trust will gradually come to an end as each beneficiary attains an absolute interest or interest in possession. Provided the vesting is within the requirements of s.71 of the IHTA 1984 it should not give rise to a charge to tax. Where the size of the share of each beneficiary alters (e.g. if the trust is worded to include beneficiaries who are yet unborn it is possible that the size of a beneficiary's share will alter as the size of the class changes), then it should not give rise to a transfer of value by the original beneficiary if the alteration occurs *before* he attains an interest in possession. However, care is needed if the alteration is likely to arise after an interest in possession has been achieved, when it will constitute a transfer of value by the original beneficiary.

Table 13.1 IHT on termination of trusts

	PET	Chargeable
Interest in possession trust	Yes, if termination is other than on death s.3A(7), IHTA 1984 and to another individual, another interest in possession settlement, to an A&M trust or to a disabled trust	Yes, if termination of interest in possession arises on the death of the life tenant. Subject to the application of BPR and APR where appropriate.
A&M trust	No	No on a beneficiary becoming entitled to settled property or to an interest in possession in it by reaching 25 or any earlier specified age; not on death of a beneficiary before reaching the qualifying age: s.71(4), IHTA 1984.

Discretionary trust	No	Exit or proportionate change unless excluded property; or, made within first quarter since creation or first quarter following a 10-yearly charge; or is made to trust which has exemption, e.g. employee trusts – s.75, IHTA 1984.
		Subject to the application of BPR and APR, where appropriate.

CGT considerations

From a CGT perspective a charge to CGT arises on the termination of a life interest trust where the life tenant is still alive if someone becomes absolutely entitled to the settled property. As long as the property remains settled after the termination of the life interest, there should be no charge to tax.

If assets leave the original trust on the exercise of a special power, is the exercise of that power wide enough to create a new trust or for someone to acquire an absolute interest, or is it effectively carving out a separate fund *within* the same original trust? If it can be shown that the exercise of the power is creating a sub-fund of the original trust it should be possible to elect for both the original trust and the sub-fund to be taxed for CGT purposes as one settlement, which will save a deemed disposal occurring on the creation of the sub-fund.

In many cases the only way it can be cost effective to dismantle a trust from a CGT point of view is to rely on a combination of exemptions and reliefs. For s.165 of the TCGA 1992 the assets must be business assets, whereas s.260, TCGA 1992 holdover relates to any type of property provided the same disposal is also a chargeable transfer for IHT purposes: i.e. you are transferring into or out of a discretionary trust. Taper relief is important and in an interest in possession trust, principal private residence relief may help, where appropriate (see **para.10.4**).

Always take care to consider s.71 of the TCGA 1992 which introduces the concept of a deemed disposal by the trustees and reacquisition at market value in certain circumstances. These provisions will catch out the unwary when trying to break up a trust!

Table 13.2 CGT on termination of trusts

	Business assets	Property occupied by beneficiary as principal private residence	Other property
Interest in possession trust	• s.165, TCGA 1992 holdover. • Revised enterprise investment relief can apply to disposals where the gain is reinvested in shares in an unlisted trading company and the beneficiaries are all individuals. • Taper relief for business assets – eligible beneficiary will help.	• ss.222, 225, TCGA 1992 exempt.	• Chargeable, subject to indexation allowance until 5 April 1998; taper relief for non-business assets.
A&M trusts	• s.165, TCGA 1992 holdover when beneficiary attains vested interest. • s.260(2)(d), TCGA 1992 may apply if vesting age for income and capital the same.	• If any beneficiary falls within ss.222, 225, TCGA 1992 exempt. • s.260(2)(d), TCGA 1992 may apply if vesting age for income and capital the same.	• s.260(2)(d), TCGA 1992 may apply if vesting age for income and capital is the same. • Holdover not available under s.260, TCGA 1992 if the beneficiary already has a life interest or the contingency is an age greater than 25.

Table 13.2 CGT on termination of trusts – cont.

	Business assets	Property occupied by beneficiary as principal private residence	Other property
	• Taper relief for business assets.		• Watch out for crystallisation of a holdover gain which arose when the trust was created. • Taper relief for non-business assets.
Discretionary trusts	• s.165, TCGA 1992 holdover. • Taper relief for business assets.	• ss.222, 225, TCGA 1992 exemption, *Sansome v. Peay* [1976] SP 10/79.	• s.260, TCGA 1992 exemption. • Taper relief for non-business assets.

13.5 INTEREST IN POSSESSION TRUST ENDS ON DEATH OF LIFE TENANT

When the life tenant dies and there is no succeeding life interest, the trust comes to an end and the assets have to be disbursed to the remainder benefi- ciaries. Given the taxation consequences for IHT set out in Chapter 9, it is inevitable that the trust administrator will need to liaise with those dealing with the personal or 'free' estate of the deceased life tenant.

The following actions are therefore required of the trust administrator.

1. Produce bill for the trust administration up to the date of death of the life tenant.
2. Obtain a copy of the death certificate from the PRs in the free estate.
3. Complete IHT100 (see **Appendix 2.1**) and send it, if possible, to the PRs in the free estate for them to submit to IR Capital Taxes with the IHT200 in respect of the free estate. It is not always possible to submit the IHT100 and IHT200 together but obviously it helps in agreeing the IHT calculations if this can be done. Sometimes relations between the trustees and PRs are not good, for whatever reason, and the trustees may be frus- trated in trying to calculate their tax bill in the absence of information about the free estate. In those circumstances, the trustees should submit the IHT100 completed as far as possible, with a covering letter explaining the position and asking for further directions.

    The clearance certificate for the free estate will not be issued until the tax on the trust has been paid and vice versa. Clearance for the trust is obtained using the same clearance form as for an estate (IHT30).
4. In order to complete the IHT100 it will be necessary to obtain a probate valuation of the investments in the trust fund at the date of death of the life tenant and the value of the bank and building society accounts and other assets.
5. It will be necessary to consider from where the IHT is to be paid. Unlike the personal accounts of an individual, the trust funds are not frozen with the death of the life tenant. Before the trustees decide to sell any particular assets to meet the IHT bill it is a good idea to liaise with the remaindermen as they may wish to take their interest *in specie*.
6. The IHT100 must be rendered to IR Capital Taxes within 12 months of the life tenant's death. Tax will be due:

    (a) where the death occurs after 5 April and before 1 October – on 30 April in the following year;
    (b) where the death occurs during the rest of the fiscal year – six months after the end of the month when the death occurred.
7. Tax paid late is subject to interest and that interest is not deductible for income tax purposes. Thus it can be expensive to delay the filing of an account, even though the date for filing the account may not be due.

8. Cancel any standing orders transferring income to the life tenant on a regular basis and divert the income where appropriate, e.g. to the trust's bank account or your client account. It may be necessary to apportion the income between the interest of the trust and the free estate. This will depend upon whether or not the rules regarding apportionment apply. In many modern trust documents and professionally prepared wills the operation of the Apportionment Act 1870 and the equitable rules of apportionment are excluded. For example, clause 8 of the STEP standard provisions (1st edition) says 'Income and expenditure shall be treated as arising when payable, and not from day to day, so that no apportionment shall take place.' In the absence of a similar provision the calculations are complicated and therefore time consuming.

9. Advise the remaindermen of the death of the life tenant and enquire as to whether they want to receive cash or, if appropriate, their interest *in specie*. It will be necessary to explain the CGT uplift to the date of death of the life tenant and that the trustees now hold the fund as bare trustees for the remainder beneficiaries, so that should a trust asset be sold each beneficiary will be assessable on his share of any gain arising on the difference between the sale price and the value at the life tenant's death. Beneficiaries who are non-resident or who have large personal CGT losses may be unconcerned at this prospect, whereas a beneficiary who has already utilised his personal annual exemption and pays CGT at a marginal rate of 40 per cent may prefer that either no sale takes place or that it should be delayed to a later tax year when he would have a fresh annual exemption.

10. When the free estate is ready, submit the IHT100 to HMRC Capital Taxes via the free estate's solicitors, where possible.

11. Pay any IHT when assessed.

12. Advise the trust income tax office of the date of death of the life tenant and agree the income and CGT of the trust to the date of death of the life tenant. This may have been shown on the life tenant's tax return by agreement. Income and capital gains arising from the date of death until the trust is distributed will be shown on the trust's tax return. Ask the trust tax office to confirm that it is closing its file.

13. Submit the IHT30 for clearance in duplicate and where possible cross-refer to the free estate's Capital Taxes Office (CTO) reference.

14. Prepare a bill of your costs since the date of death of the life tenant, to anticipate closure of the trust.

15. Prepare and obtain approval to the closing accounts of the trust from the trustees.

16. Deal with any transfers of real property and s.16 of the Trusts of Land and Appointment of Trustees Act 1996 discharge from the trust for the trustees.

17. Distribute the trust fund in accordance with the accounts and any agreements obtained from the beneficiaries, and obtain receipts.
18. Where the settlement was created *inter vivos* then the trustees need to find a way of being informed of the settlor's death, should that occur within seven years of the gift into the settlement. The trustees will be expected to pay the tax arising by virtue of the death, but the PRs of the deceased settlor can also be liable if the tax remains unpaid. The assessments to tax for trusts in these circumstances frequently include errors so any assessment received from the CTO should be checked.
19. Archive your file.

13.6   BENEFICIARY SATISFIES AGE CONTINGENCY IN A&M TRUST

In A&M trusts the beneficiary has to reach a specified age before his entitlement vests. Common choices of age are 18, 21 or the maximum 25 years of age. If the trust administration system has been set up properly, a trust diary will have recorded the date when each beneficiary will attain the specified age. It would hopefully also include an 'early warning' message, say six months before the vesting date, to allow the trust administrator time to review the file and to take some preparatory steps.

Depending on the wording of the trust, the beneficiary may be receiving an absolute interest, in which case a portion of the trust fund will need to be transferred to that beneficiary absolutely, freed and discharged from the terms of the trust. Alternatively, the beneficiary may simply be moving from a contingent interest to an interest in possession, in which case a trust still continues but the nature of the interest and the tax treatment of the income changes completely (see **Chapter 11**).

In the event that the beneficiary receives an absolute entitlement on achieving a specified age, the trust administrator should take the following steps.

1. Write to the trustees and the beneficiary at least one month before the age at which the minor attains the relevant age under the trust, advising of any action to be taken, the likely timescale, and if there are any assets that can be taken *in specie* or which will need to be sold.
2. Value the investments at the market price on the vesting day and identify the balances on bank and building society accounts on that day.
3. You will need to consider any tax implications with the trustees. An A&M trust for IHT purposes is one which complies with s.71 of the IHTA 1984, so when a beneficiary becomes absolutely entitled to his share of the fund there is no charge to IHT (s.71(4), IHTA 1984).

    There is an exception to this rule where the trust was created on or after 15 April 1976 and the beneficiaries are *not* all children of a common grandparent. The position is also complicated where the assets in the trust fund comprise land or unquoted shares. These assets are not easily divided because of the rule in *Crowe* v. *Appleby* [1975] STC 502. For more on these complications, see Chapter 9.

A charge to CGT will arise on a beneficiary achieving an absolute interest on attaining the specified age. The charge is calculated as if the disposal to the beneficiary had been made at market value at the date when the beneficiary satisfied the age contingency.

If the trustees and the beneficiary agree and the trust provided for the same specified age for the vesting of the income and capital entitlements then it is possible to hold over this gain under s.260(2)(d) of the TCGA 1992. Trustees should think carefully about agreeing to hold over the gain as there are clawback provisions which will apply where the beneficiary becomes non-resident within the six years following the year of his acquisition.

4. Prepare a statement for the beneficiary and the trustees showing the beneficiary's entitlement under the trust.
5. Prepare a bill of your costs for approval by the trustees.
6. Obtain the trustees' approval to the distribution statement and your costs.
7. Distribute the assets to the beneficiary with an appropriate tax deduction certificate in respect of any income.
8. Obtain an indemnity or better security from the beneficiary in favour of the trustees if there is any likelihood of a further charge to tax, e.g. a clawback of any CGT which is held over.

13.7 TRUSTEES MAKE APPOINTMENT OUT OF DISCRETIONARY TRUST

When the trustees of a discretionary trust decide to make an appointment out of the capital of the trust fund to a beneficiary, this constitutes an occasion of charge for IHT. An exit or proportionate charge must be calculated and reported to HMRC Capital Taxes.

It may be an appointment of cash from the trust in which case there will be no CGT to account for. If, however, assets are appointed out of the trusts, e.g. if the trust was being brought to an end and all the assets were being appointed out of the fund, and if any of those assets are chargeable assets there will be a disposal for CGT which will have to be accounted for by the trustees unless the trustees are willing to hold over the gain under s.260 of the TCGA 1992.

The following actions should therefore be instigated by the trust administrator.

1. Ensure that the trustees have minuted their resolution to make the proposed appointment and prepare a written resolution confirming it for signature by the trustees if no meeting has taken place.
2. Identify which assets are to be appointed to the beneficiary and obtain valuations if they are to be transferred *in specie* rather than encashed.
3. Consider the IHT and CGT implications of making this appointment.
4. Calculate the exit charge for IHT and any CGT which will be payable on the disposal of chargeable assets.
5. Discuss with the trustees from where the taxes are to be met. If the trust is to continue and this is only an appointment of part of the fund, is the fund to bear the tax or is the appointed fund to bear it? The choice will affect the calculations.
6. Make appropriate arrangements for meeting the payment of the tax and submit the IHT100 in respect of the appointment to HMRC Capital Taxes.
7. Pay the IHT and obtain clearance on IHT30 from HMRC Capital Taxes.
8. The trustees will need to include the disposal on the trustees' SA900 tax return for the tax year of the disposal. If the trust is being wound up, a tax return can be asked for and completed early. If the disposal is not of the whole fund but does consist of assets which require valuation, the trustees should submit CG34, a form on which the taxpayer presents his calculation of the CGT liability arising on the disposal for early approval by the Inspector of Taxes. The advantage of submitting this form early in the tax year is that any valuations which need the involvement of the District Valuer or Share Valuation Division can be undertaken straight-away, thus minimising the risk that the tax is paid late because the tax bill was not agreed in time.
9. The trustees and the beneficiary may be willing to hold over any gain under s.260 of the TCGA 1992. If so, this needs to be calculated and the holdover claim submitted.
10. Your fees for dealing with these tasks will usually be over and above your usual administration fees, and so should be assessed and agreed with the trustees.
11. Any deed of appointment necessary should be prepared for signature by the trustees.
12. If any real property is being transferred, the usual conveyancing documents will need to be prepared transferring legal title from the trustees to the beneficiary. Note that a deed of discharge under s.16 of the TLATA 1996 will be needed by the beneficiary.
13. For other assets which are to be transferred, the relevant title documents will be necessary.
14. Where the trust continues, the trust records will need to be updated to reflect the appointment.

13.8   DEATH OF A DISCRETIONARY BENEFICIARY

If a discretionary beneficiary dies, this is not a trigger for the trust to come to an end automatically like the death of the life tenant under an interest in possession trust. Instead it is an opportunity to reflect whether the main purpose for having the trust has ended, and all things considered, it might as well be wound up.

The trust administrator should consider the following actions.

1.   Obtain a death certificate for the deceased for the trust records and update those records.
2.   As there is no aggregation with the free estate of the deceased beneficiary, the trustees need to consider who, if anyone, is to benefit from the fund in future.
3.   Consider whether it is more cost effective to break the trust now rather than to continue.
4.   If the trust is to come to an end, the considerations will be similar as for when an appointment is to be made out of the trust (see **para.13.7** above).

13.9   RISK MANAGEMENT

When a trust is being administered the trust systems used should act as a check and a balance against risk. For the trust manager or head of department these procedures should be kept under review to see if they:

1.   are being followed;
2.   are still relevant in the light of current law and practice;
3.   are understood by everyone in the team.

Good risk management should reduce the likelihood of a high impact mistake affecting both the reputation of the firm and also the finances of the partners. If the firm can demonstrate to their insurers that they take risk management seriously, then hopefully this will make it easier to obtain professional indemnity insurance on competitive terms.

For the benefit of department heads everywhere, Table 13.3 lists some suggested possible risks arising when a trust is about to be wound up, with a recommended preventative step which could be accommodated within the team's administrative systems.

Table 13.3 Suggested list of possible risks

Event	Risk	Preventative step
Vesting of income or capital	No record of vesting date.	Maintain central diary.
Decision to appoint assets out of the trust	Tax inefficient date chosen.	Improve knowledge and take relevant expert advice before taking step if unsure of tax consequences.
Contacting beneficiaries	Who is entitled and where they are is unknown or unclear leading to incorrect distribution.	Maintain correct records and utilise the services of expert agent if need to trace 'lost' beneficiary.
Obtaining valuation of assets	Incorrect valuation obtained at the wrong time.	Market value required: • at the date of vesting in A&M trusts, on beneficiary's share; • at the date of death of the life tenant on the whole value of the fund in interest in possession trust; • at date of appointment on assets appointed from discretionary trust.
Realisation of assets	Indivisible assets will not vest at usual time in A&M trusts – real property and private company shares are subject to the rule in *Crowe* v. *Appleby* and vest only at the vesting age of the youngest beneficiary.	Check powers of appropriation and powers to change the nature of the trust.
Preparation of accounts	Insufficient records to prepare proper set of accounts.	Maintain accurate records and draw up an annual set of accounts.

Table 13.3 Suggested list of possible risks – cont.

Event	Risk	Preventative step
	Trustees fail to approve them.	Check proper terms of business in place and you are charging only in accordance with these. Implement proper client complaint handling procedures.
	Beneficiaries unhappy with the results.	Seek expert advice on what may now become a contentious matter. Ascertain source of the complaint – if linked to performance of the fund have in place correct agency agreement and policy statements with financial advisers and ensure annual review of their performance at least; remove those who are not performing.
Income tax	Failing to distinguish correctly between capital and income.	Prepare annual accouants.
	Not submitting the SA900 on time and incurring tax penalties.	Diary date for 31 January following the end of the tax year in which income received and, say, one month before warning of deadline.
	Not correctly assessing the tax bill giving rise to extra work which cannot be charged for and possible interest and penalties.	Improve know-how of staff or outsource to competent expert.
	Not paying the tax bill on time giving rise to potential interest and penalties.	Identifying the due dates for payment of income tax as it applies to the particular trust and recording in diary system.
	Not providing tax certificates to the beneficiaries.	Use IT to help provide relevant paperwork.

Table 13.3 Suggested list of possible risks – cont.

Event	Risk	Preventative step
IHT	Incorrect sum calculated on termination.	Improve knowledge of chargeable events and the appropriate formula to apply.
	Not returned on time to HMRC Capital Taxes incurring penalties.	Maintain diary records.
	Not paid on time, incurring penalties.	Maintain records for the due dates of payment.
	Incorrect form used to notify of the chargeable event.	Use IHT100 and obtain practitioner's guide to its completion from HMRC.
CGT	Deemed disposal missed or gain not returned to HMRC on time incurring late payment and penalty.	Improve know-how – due date for receipt of return 31 January following the end of the tax year of disposal.
	Incorrect amount of tax calculated.	Use CGT34 to obtain HMRC agreement and if the gain is to be held over use IR295 helpsheet.
	Tax not paid on time resulting in interest and penalties.	Improve knowledge of due dates – 31 January following the tax year in which disposal made.
	Disposals made by continuing trustees in same tax year as you retired – if not returned and tax paid you remain liable trustee.	Obtain indemnities for tax on retirement and retire if possible at end of tax year.

Table 13.3 Suggested list of possible risks – cont.

Event	Risk	Preventative step
Documenting transfers of assets	Some assets missed so trust continues when it was thought it was terminated.	Maintain accurate record of trust investments.
	All procedures to effect transfer not complete with possible resultant tax problems and unhappy beneficiaries.	Improve know-how for different transfer requirements for different assets.
		Ensure file management procedures in place to avoid administrative errors.
Billing	Estimating costs inaccurate causing undercharging or complaints from client for charging more than anticipated.	Follow Rule 15 procedure and maintain good costs controls.
	Having insufficient cash available to pay fees from trust funds – e.g. debt scheme.	Anticipating likely needs and agreeing appropriate procedure with trustees.
	Writing off chargeable time in large quantities.	Proper supervision of staff and identification of learning needs before a problem arises.

231

CHAPTER 14

Nil rate band discretionary trust debt scheme

14.1 INTRODUCTION

In a book for practitioners, it seems essential to highlight one type of discretionary trust which has become commonplace in will drafting over the past 10 to 15 years and therefore is likely to be a frequent addition to the trust administration teams' caseload: the nil rate band discretionary trust debt scheme (NRB trust).

Approximately 20 years ago a client of mine asked if there was anything which could be done to mitigate the overall IHT bill on his parents' joint estate following his father's death, when the only asset of any real value was their home. His mother wanted to remain in the matrimonial home. The client was an accountant and together we poured over the IHT legislation and came up with an arrangement whereby the father's will would be varied to include a NRB discretionary trust and instead of transferring half the house to the trust we would replace that with a debt due from the surviving spouse to the discretionary trustees. When the client's mother died, we met with no difficulty in reducing the value of her estate for IHT by the amount of the debt owing to the discretionary trustees.

My client and I rather naively thought it was a job well done. Little did we realise that it would in future become the normal way of dealing with the family home. Credit for the published precedents goes to Richard Oerton of Speechley Bircham and James Kessler QC, both of whom have done much to help practitioners with the drafting of wills containing suitable clauses. Mr Oerton was, I believe, responsible for the clauses in Butterworths' *Wills, Probate and Administration Service* and James Kessler QC continues to expand and develop all sorts of threads in updating the Butterworths work and in his own seminal text *Drafting Trusts and Will Trust,* 7th Edn (Sweet & Maxwell, 2004) as well as supplements on his website (**www.kessler.co.uk/dtwt/articles/index.html**).

The NRB trust is a clause in a will containing a settled legacy of a cash sum equivalent to the largest sum the deceased can give without IHT arising on the deemed transfer of value which is treated as taking place on death. It is expressed as a cash gift instead of making a gift of a share in the matrimonial home to the discretionary trust. This is because one of HMRC's arguments, where an interest in a property is held in what is said to be a discretionary trust but occupied by one of the beneficiaries, has been that the occupation of the beneficiary creates an interest in possession instead (see further SP10/79).

The effect of this argument by HMRC is that on the surviving spouse's death, the second spouse treated as owning the whole of the trust fund (i.e. the first spouse's interest in the matrimonial home) in addition to their own assets (including the second spouse's interest in the matrimonial home) (s.49, IHTA 1984). The IHT consequence is that no use has then effectively been made of the NRB of the first spouse to die. Instead, the whole value of the matrimonial home is charged to IHT on the second death, something which the use of the discretionary trust was trying to avoid.

After the NRB trust clause, the residue of the estate is left either to the surviving spouse absolutely or to a flexible interest in possession trust for the benefit of the surviving spouse for life.

When the first death of one of the spouses occurs in cases where the wills contain these provisions this will necessitate having to deal with the implementation process associated with them. Care is needed to ensure that the correct approach is taken in the circumstances.

For the trust administrator, the initial set up work to implement the terms of the will are often undertaken by the probate practitioner. The trust practitioner will then be asked to manage what may seem a rather strange discretionary trust where quite possibly the only asset is an IOU or an equitable charge. It is therefore important for the trust practitioner to appreciate how he comes to be holding one or the other and some of the consequences of that.

14.2   TWO SCHEMES OR ONE?

The popular wording for will precedents includes two options.

1. *Debt scheme* – where the residuary beneficiary undertakes a personal liability to the trustees of the discretionary trust for the payment of the NRB sum to them when asked.
2. *Charge scheme* – where the deceased's executors charge the deceased's equitable interests in the matrimonial home with the value of the settled legacy in favour of the trustees of the discretionary trust and there is no personal liability on the residuary beneficiaries to repay this loan personally.

The debt scheme – promise or IOU

In its simplest form the promise of payment will be in the form of a promissory note or IOU made by the surviving spouse to the trustees of the discretionary trust. This is not secured on the deceased's property or the surviving spouse's property but is a simple debt against the surviving spouse's estate which is owed personally to the trustees.

In the more complex case, where the will is seeking to avoid the problems posed by s.103 of the Finance Act 1986 (see **para.14.3** below) by giving a gift of the residue not to the surviving spouse absolutely but to an interest in possession trust in that spouse's favour, the promise of payment will be made by the trustees of the residuary interest in possession trust in favour of the discretionary trustees.

The popular version of this IOU is in the form of a Deed of Covenant. See, for example Form 4.5A (surviving spouse) and Form 4.5B (interest in possession trustees) in Butterworths' *Wills, Probate and Administration Service.*

Clearly an IOU provides little security for the NRB discretionary trustees since the residuary beneficiary may have insufficient assets at the time the debt is called in by the trustees, to repay the loan. The trust administrator may feel that it would be prudent for his trustees to require better security for the debt than a simple IOU. The wording of the precedent will clauses does allow the NRB discretionary trustees to insist on a legal charge. The legal charge will be secured over the family property which by then will either be owned by the surviving spouse absolutely or held on trust by the surviving spouse for himself and any trustees of a residuary trust. The effect is still the same: someone or some body of trustees is liable personally to see to the repayment of the monies secured by the legal charge, but at least the NRB discretionary trustees have some independent security for the loan.

The charge scheme – an equitable, non-recourse charge

The legal title of a house owned equitably by two spouses as tenants in common in equal shares passes to the survivor alone by right of survivorship of joint tenants of the legal estate, on the first death. This means that the deceased's PRs have ownership only of the deceased's equitable share (usually one-half) of the property and will need to assign the ownership of this to the surviving spouse or the residuary interest in possession trustees, as part of administering the deceased's estate.

Where there is no problem with s.103 of the Finance Act 1986, the charge may be either a legal charge over the property or an equitable charge over the beneficial interests in the property. If s.103, Finance Act 1986 problems arise then any such a charge can be no more than an equitable, non-recourse charge such that the surviving spouse who made those lifetime gifts will have no personal responsibility for its repayment. Rather, the arrangement will be undertaken by the PRs and the discretionary trustees *before* the assignment of the equitable interest of the deceased takes place. Thus when the assignment is done it will be done subject to the charge but without recourse to the surviving spouse for its repayment. Instead, repayment will take place on a sale of the property. (For a published precedent for the preparation of an equitable non-recourse charge, see Form 391 in Butterworths' *Encyclopaedia of Forms and Precedents*, volume 42(1).)

14.3 BACKGROUND ISSUES ON IMPLEMENTATION

Anti-avoidance

If *at any time* during the joint lifetimes of the spouses, property has passed by gift from the surviving spouse to the first to die (albeit spouse exempt for IHT purposes), a deduction for any debt incurred on or after 18 March 1986 is denied for the liability in the survivor's estate by s.103 of the Finance Act 1986 to the extent of the amount of such gift or gifts:

> 103 (1) Subject to subsection (2) below, if, in determining the value of a person's estate immediately before his death, account would be taken, apart from this subsection, of a liability consisting of a debt incurred by him or an incumbrance created by a disposition made by him, that liability shall be subject to abatement to an extent proportionate to the value of any of the consideration given for the debt or incumbrance which consisted of –
>
> (a) property derived from the deceased; or
> (b) consideration (not being property derived from the deceased) given by any person who was at any time entitled to, or amongst whose resources there was at any time included, any property derived from the deceased.

Where the will does not provide for the residue to be given to an interest in possession trust but rather to the surviving spouse absolutely and that surviving spouse made lifetime gifts to the deceased, perhaps made after the will was prepared, then this is a situation where s.103 is likely to present a problem. The argument from s.103 is that the making of the lifetime gift, which has swelled the deceased's estate, results in the deceased being able to give the same assets back to the surviving donor but only because the surviving spouse is willing to incur a debt in favour of the NRB discretionary trustees. So s.103 operates to disallow the debt as a deduction against the surviving spouse's own estate on death, thereby increasing the liability to IHT on the second death.

If the equitable charge route rather than the IOU route is adopted the circular problem of the surviving donor taking on the debt to the NRB discretionary trustees personally is removed, since it is the PRs who will charge the equitable interest in the property in favour of the discretionary trustees first; the PRs will then assign the equitable interest to the surviving spouse subject to that liability. The surviving spouse will not have created the debt personally and will not be personally liable to repay it.

Section 103 problems can arise again later if the property is sold. In such circumstances the debt would have to be repaid to the NRB discretionary trustees on any sale of the property. Where the will allows for the NRB discretionary trustees to make a new loan at this time to the surviving spouse, such a loan would inevitably then be a personal debt between the surviving spouse and the NRB discretionary trustees. It is the act of committing to a personal liability which reintroduces the s.103 problem at that stage.

Thus where it is possible that there might be a sale of the property during the survivor's lifetime with all the proceeds being used to buy a replacement, the gift of residue on the first death should preferably not be absolute, but left on interest in possession trusts for the surviving spouse. On the second death, the liability would be owed not by the survivor but by the trustees of the interest in possession trust. If the gift of the residue is absolute there is not much that can be done to avoid a s.103 problem, short of not making the fresh loan but rather encouraging the surviving spouse to simply buy a new property for less money and pay off the original loan.

It can be difficult to persuade clients to have two trusts in their wills (the NRB discretionary trust and the residuary interest in possession trust), so the trust administrator should not be surprised if a will has not set up this arrangement. The trust administrator should, if relevant, therefore mention the way in which s.103 might affect the situation when the NRB discretionary trust is being administered, so that the trustees and the beneficiaries appreciate the potential difficulties and make decisions with those issues in mind.

Repayable on demand

It is crucial to the success of the scheme that the debt or charge, whether or not carrying interest, is expressed to be repayable on demand. This means it is equivalent to cash and thus obviates any interest in possession argument from HMRC Capital Taxes.

The precedents provide the NRB discretionary trustees with the ability to impose conditions on the loan, such as making it subject to the payment of interest or index-linking the debt in line with the Retail Prices Index (RPI) or a property index such as the Halifax All Property index, so as to keep to a minimum the equity of the surviving spouse in the property (assuming that it is subject to capital appreciation between the dates of the two deaths).

Trustees

Particular care in the selection of trustees was hopefully taken. Trustees have a duty to act in the best interests of the trust and of *all* the beneficiaries. Their discretions cannot be fettered and therefore there can be no absolute guarantee that they will not call in the debt. Indeed, Peter Twiddy of HMRC Capital Taxes has said at several conferences that if HMRC can show that the testator arranged for the debt *not* to be called in during the lifetime of the surviving spouse – perhaps by letter of wishes or in correspondence with his solicitors – then this would have created a secret trust which was in effect giving the surviving spouse an interest in possession, which of course would enable HMRC to assess the value of the trust fund to IHT on the death of the surviving spouse.

In most cases the desire of the parties is to have the same people selected as PRs and NRB discretionary trustees, and often these people will include the surviving spouse. However, it is difficult to see how there will avoid being a conflict of interest if the spouse is both lender and borrower. There could easily come a point of difficulty if one of the NRB discretionary trustees believes it is in the interests of the beneficiaries of the discretionary trust for the debt to be repaid, but the surviving spouse, as borrower and possibly co-trustee, does not see the need for this and indeed refuses to cooperate.

With greater emphasis now on the equitable charge route (because of its treatment for SDLT) some commentators have raised a query as to whether the surviving spouse should ever be a PR or a trustee of the discretionary trust. So just who should be the PRs, discretionary trustees and possibly interest in possession trustees?

Where the surviving spouse is receiving the residuary estate absolutely and the debt scheme is to be used, the surviving spouse is going to be the debtor. It is therefore necessary to ensure that your wording requires that the discretionary trusts will not operate at any time when there are fewer than two trustees and to ensure that there is someone else appointed along with the surviving spouse at the outset to act as discretionary trustees. It is then possible for the surviving spouse to be a PR (and even a sole PR).

When you come to implement the arrangements, the surviving spouse as residuary beneficiary would be the debtor promising the discretionary trustees that the debt will be repaid. The discretionary trusts cannot operate without two trustees and you have appointed the surviving spouse and someone else to act as the trustees. The surviving spouse is therefore not contracting with only herself, but with a body of trustees of which the surviving spouse is one. It should be perfectly acceptable. In such a case, if there were trustees of the residue who were responsible for administering substitutionary trusts only if the surviving spouse had died, then there would be nothing wrong in having the same two people as PRs, discretionary trustees and residuary trust trustees.

Where the charge scheme is used there is an argument to say that the surviving spouse should be neither PR nor discretionary trustee. Why? The reasoning behind this is that because the equitable charge must be a non-recourse charge, and the concern is to ensure that there is no possible argument about whether acting in the representative role of PR or trustee would undermine the surviving spouse's position and imply that the surviving spouse was indeed responsible personally, in some way, for repayment of the loan.

It would be surprising if a surviving spouse were entirely happy with not having any role in the administration of the deceased spouse's estate. A distinction should be made between surviving spouses acting in their own individual capacity and a surviving spouse acting in a representative capacity. As long as there is someone else acting alongside the surviving spouse in the representative capacity of PRs and discretionary trustees, it seems unlikely that s.103 of the Finance Act 1986 could be argued against that spouse.

However, it is important to remember the need to avoid the same 'person' creating an interest in favour of himself. Would it not be better to have three PRs appointed and only two of those to act in the discretionary trust so that the PRs will not be contracting with themselves as discretionary trustees?

The same point arises where the residuary estate is not gifted to the surviving spouse absolutely but is put into an interest in possession trust. Now you have the prospect of the residuary trustees entering into a debt arrangement with the discretionary trustees so again with the debt scheme the two bodies of trustees would need to differ slightly – perhaps one person should be different in each case.

With the charge scheme there would have to be a difference between the bodies of PRs and discretionary trustees as they are contracting with each other. Section 82 of the Law of Property Act 1925 would make the contract unenforceable if the bodies were comprised of identical people.

It may be therefore that before proving the will or dealing with the debt or charge scheme, you should carefully consider whether you wish all the PRs to prove the will or, if they already have proved, if you want to have additional trustees appointed or whether you need one of them to retire either as trustee of the NRB discretionary trust or as trustee of any residuary trust.

14.4   SDLT – CURRENT POSITION AND OPTIONS

The long-awaited policy statement on the Stamp Duty Land Tax (SDLT) treatment of the NRB trust was posted on HMRC's website on 11 November 2004 (**www.hmrc.gov.uk/so/nilband.htm**). (Note that there were some earlier amendments and additions to the SDLT Manual added on 11 October 2004 but as at 16 November 2004 the relevant paragraphs which were at SDLTM00570 and the accompanying examples at SDLTM00570a have been removed.)

What has all the fuss been about?

Under stamp duty, when assets in an estate were transferred to the residuary beneficiary either subject to a debt of some kind or following a promise by the residuary beneficiary to pay a settled legatee their legacy, no stamp duty was payable.

SDLT commenced on 1 December 2003 and its provisions are contained in the Finance Act 2003 with further provisions added in the Finance Act 2004. It applies to a 'land transaction', which is the acquisition of a chargeable interest (s.43, Finance Act 2003). It is a 'chargeable transaction' if it is not exempt (s.49 and Sched.3). Under s.55, tax is charged as a percentage of the 'chargeable consideration' and that term is defined in s.50 and Sched.4.

A transaction for no consideration is exempt (para.1, Sched.3). Paragraph 2 of Sched.4 to the Finance Act 2003 defines consideration for SDLT purposes to include 'money or money's worth'. Paragraph 8 of Sched.4 deals with debt as consideration – debts satisfied or released or assumed (this is similar to the old s.57, Stamp Act 1891 concepts).

For many months practitioners were in the dark as to how the Inland Revenue were to treat the debt and charge schemes for SDLT purposes, with practitioners receiving conflicting decisions about the tax effectiveness of implementing either the debt or charge scheme or indeed creating the arrangements by deed of variation.

Where are we now?

The outcome of this long struggle for clarification is that in essence:

1. If you use the IOU and legal charge to secure the debt (debt scheme) in favour of the discretionary trustees, then SDLT will apply at the appropriate percentage (1 or 3 per cent) to the value of the debt to the extent that the PRs transfer to the residuary beneficiary an interest in land as a result of the IOU being given.
2. Where the legacy is secured by a non-recourse or equitable charge (charge scheme) entered into by the PRs before assignment of the estate's interest in the deceased's property to the residuary beneficiary, provided it is clear that no liability to pay this debt falls on the residuary beneficiary there will be *no* charge to SDLT.
3. Arrangements set up and implemented as a result of a deed of variation will not incur SDLT.

Note that the appropriate procedure for paying SDLT is normally to submit the SDLT1 within 30 days of the completion of the land transaction along with the appropriate sum in payment of the tax. If, therefore, the debt scheme is used, you will need to remember to arrange for the residuary beneficiary, as the provider of the IOU, to sign the SDLT1 form and pay the appropriate amount of SDLT (1 or 3 per cent) to HMRC. A failure to do this within 30 days of the trustees receiving the IOU and the equitable interests being transferred to the residuary beneficiary results in a late filing penalty of £100 and interest running on the tax paid late.

For all practical purposes it is likely that the charge scheme will be used in future implementations of the arrangements to remove the risk of having to pay SDLT. Remember that for the equitable charge to be properly deductible it must be for no more than the value of the equitable interests which are being charged. If, therefore, the deceased's interest in the property is worth less than the nil rate band and the settled legacy is intended to be for the full amount because other assets are being assigned to the residuary beneficiary, such as stocks and shares, then only an equitable charge for the value of the equities can be done and either an IOU will be required for the balance or actual assets to the value necessary to make up the nil rate band will have to be appropriated to the trustees instead.

14.5 IMPLEMENTATION SCHEDULE

1. The PRs decide whether to use the debt scheme or the charge scheme.
2. The trustees need to meet and minute what they have decided to choose as the return for the trust on the debt. They also need to consider whether it is prudent to require security for the IOU (if the PRs choose to use the debt method), in the form of a legal charge over the surviving spouse's property.
3. If the debt scheme is used the PRs arrange with the surviving spouse for the surviving spouse to provide an IOU in favour of the discretionary trustees on the basis of the terms required by the trustees.
4. If the charge scheme is used instead, the PRs will enter into an equitable charge with the discretionary trustees on the basis of the terms required by the trustees and expressly on the basis that there is no recourse to the residuary beneficiary for the repayment of this debt.
5. The PRs will then assign the deceased spouse's equitable interest to the surviving spouse as residuary beneficiary. In the case of the charge scheme this will be expressly subject to the equitable charge. The PRs will declare either in the assignment or separately that the surviving spouse as residuary beneficiary is the sole legal and equitable owner of the property. In the case of the equitable charge the PRs will state that the surviving spouse is not liable for repayment of the charge.
6. If the debt scheme is chosen the trustees will probably decide that it is prudent to have a legal charge over the property to back up the IOU securing the repayment of the debt against the property. This document will contain whichever arrangements the trustees prefer for achieving a

return on the loan – for example, the payment of interest or, more likely, the linking of the debt to an index.

7. If the debt scheme is used there is SDLT to pay, at the rate of 1 per cent if the settled legacy in question is no more than £250,000, and 3 per cent on the whole value if the settled legacy is over £250,000. The SDLT1 form will have to be signed by the residuary beneficiary and sent within 30 days to HMRC with the tax due. If the IOU is set up following a deed of variation where the ownership of the land does not change as a result of the deed there is no SDLT to pay and therefore an SDLT60 should be signed by the residuary beneficiary to this effect. Similarly, if the charge scheme is used there is no SDLT to pay and the SDLT60 should also be signed.

8. If the title to the property is unregistered an original copy of the deceased's death certificate should be placed with the deeds along with the assignment and declaration, since on the death of a joint proprietor the legal estate vests immediately and without further requirement on the sole survivor by virtue of the right of survivorship. Where the equitable interest is held as tenants in common and the deceased made a will, the equitable share falls to the estate under the will for distribution by the executors in accordance with the terms of the will and it is necessary to show that the restriction on the equities has been removed.

9. If the property is registered and the equitable share passes under the terms of a will, the executors will be able to enter into a deed of assignment of the equitable half share provided that they have the consent of any relevant beneficiaries who also need to join in to the deed in such circumstances. The Land Registry is not concerned with the issues as to how the share is assigned, unless that relates to the removal of the restriction mentioned below. In the event of a tenancy in common, it is likely that the register will have contained a Form A restriction in the following form:

> RESTRICTION: No disposition by a sole proprietor of the registered estate (except a trust corporation) under which capital money arises is to be registered unless authorised by an order of the court.

This means that if the trustees require a legal charge by the surviving spouse over the property the Land Registry may not register it unless it is satisfied that the entire equitable interest has passed to the survivor, in which case the restriction would be removed. The restriction is there to show that the survivor does not hold the entire beneficial interest and is not therefore capable of giving a good receipt for capital monies.

Accordingly, it would be necessary to produce to the Land Registry evidence that the equitable title in its entirety has passed to the survivor; this is done by submitting Form RX3 in confirmation that the entire legal and equitable interest has now vested in the survivor and is unencumbered in any way. The restriction could then be removed and the charge registered. The charge used can adapt Land Registry Form CH1.

Where the equitable charge is used then the Land Registry will *not* remove the Form A restriction. This is because what is effected is a charge over the beneficial interests and s.33(1)(a) of the Land Registration Act 2002 prohibits the entry of a notice in respect of an interest under a trust of land. Please refer to the Land Registry Practice Guide 24, *Private Trusts of Land.*

10. The creation of the discretionary trust may need to be notified to the relevant HMRC Trust Income Tax Office using Form 41G if income receipts are anticipated (e.g. your trust contains a mixture of debt and other income-producing assets or you have decided to charge interest on the loan rather than index-link the debt). If your firm is to act for the trustees in the administration of the trust, the agent's authorisation Form 64-8 should also be lodged. These are both available on HMRC website. It is strictly unnecessary to notify HMRC where the trust contains only an index-linked debt and no other investments, such as a sum of money, because a tax return will not be required until the debt is called in.

11. The trustees should decide who is to act as the trust administrator and they need to meet with him to discuss the following matters.

   (a) The contents of the trust deed, i.e. the will.
   (b) The contents of any letter of wishes and its effect upon the opera-tion of the trust.
   (c) Who are the eligible beneficiaries and any information about their status, needs and family or other connections.
   (d) The assets to be transferred to the trust fund and any documentation necessary to effect the transfers. In the case of the debt scheme the assets will be simply the IOU or charge.
   (e) The taxation provisions affecting the trust and the completion of the relevant notification forms mentioned above. In the event that the trustees later call in the debt, the question of who is to prepare the trust tax returns and deal with the requirements of self-assessment will need to be discussed.
   (f) The discretionary trustees will need to meet at least once per tax year to consider whether it is still appropriate not to call in the loan, bearing in mind their duties as trustees under the Trustee Act 2000. All decisions should be minuted.
   (g) If the discretionary trustees do call in the loan, there will inevitably be a tax return required (SA900) for that tax year. This must be requested from the Trust Income Tax Office no later than 5 October following the end of the tax year in which the repayment of the loan

takes place. There may be income tax or CGT to pay on the growth in the debt by virtue of the indexation provisions.

(h) If the discretionary trust continues, the trustees must invest the funds it receives by way of repayment of the loan appropriately and annual accounts and income tax returns will need to be prepared.

(i) The discretionary trust will be subject to IHT charges on every tenth anniversary (i.e. 10 years from the date of death and every 10 years thereafter until the trust ends) and when any capital is appointed out of the trust. It is therefore wise to make sure there are diary reminders for the 10-yearly charge dates in the usual way. The first date is important and as the trust may well be brought to an end within the first 10 years, it is a good idea to have a diary reminder to consider this in good time – say six months prior to the tenth anniversary date.

14.6 CALLING IN THE DEBT

The trust administrator may at some point have to advise the NRB discretionary trustees that the time has come to call in the debt. It might be because there is a 10-yearly anniversary charge for IHT and no funds otherwise to meet it; it might be that other beneficiaries have a need for funds from the trust rather than seeing all its money tied up in the investment of the debt; it might be that the surviving spouse has died and there is no longer the need to have the investments tied up in just the debt. Whatever the reason, the calling in of the debt will in all probability result in the house being sold.

If the debt has been index-linked the NRB discretionary trustees will probably receive a much greater sum than was originally loaned, by current growth in the indices. How is that 'profit' to be treated for tax purposes?

Whether or not there is an income tax charge or CGT charge on redemption of the loan depends on whether or not there is a debt on a security. Where there is an index-linked debt HMRC has been known to say that it is a 'relevant discounted security' (RDS) as defined in Sched.13 to the Finance Act 1996 and the 'profit' on the debt would be liable to income tax (representing rolled-up indexation) and not CGT.

Schedule 13 includes some difficult terminology, but in essence imposes a charge to income tax on the person who realises a profit from the discount in a relevant discounted security. However, a charge to income tax will only arise if there is a 'deep gain' and in the circumstances of the debt scheme arrangements it looks most unlikely that a 'deep gain' will arise on the redemption of the loan.

An index-linked debt will not be an RDS if the following apply.

1. The index-linked debt is an 'excluded indexed security' (para.3(2), Sched.13). To qualify, the loan must be index-linked to chargeable assets. If the loan has been linked to, for example, FTSE or the Retail Prices Index, it will apparently *not* qualify under the definition.
2. The debt is not a 'security'. If the debt does not carry interest and has no premium to pay on redemption then it will not be a debt on a security. In which case, CGT will apply to it instead of income tax and s.117(2AA) of the TCGA 1992 may possibly exempt the profit from any CGT charge.

For HMRC's view of the definition of 'security', see HMRC's *CGT Manual* at paras.53420–53436 (**www.hmrc.gov.uk/manuals/immanual/im1545.htm**). The question seems to be whether it would have been possible to sell the debt at a profit. In its manual, HMRC seems to consider that this will always be possible for indexed debts (presumably because of the guaranteed return) but if the rate of indexation is anticipated at the outset to be below commercial interest rates this may be a problem.

This leaves the trust administrator with something of a dilemma, as when the debt is called in the profit on it may be subject to income tax if it is an RDS but subject to CGT, or no tax even, if it is not. Clearly, the trust administrator must investigate the relevant approach in a particular case carefully and complete the relevant pages of the SA900.

CHAPTER 15

Managing an efficient and profitable practice

Robert Mowbray

15.1 PREPARING THE BUSINESS PLAN

Introduction

Many firms and departments within firms may say 'why do we need to bother with a business plan?' The main reason why this is necessary is because the world is changing and if we are going to cope effectively with a changing world then we have to plan for the changes rather than wait for the changes to affect us.

Good businesses should have short-term budgets, medium-term business plans and a long-term vision. If a firm only thinks over a certain timescale such as the short term then it may continue to do very well for a while, but in the medium and long term it will begin to struggle. Equally, if a firm only considered its long-term plan it might become insolvent in the shorter term. This section considers why and how a department should prepare its business plan.

The world of the trust lawyer is changing rapidly. Technology and communication have developed rapidly and continue to improve, meaning that clients can be serviced over a far wider geographical area. Some firms are beginning to move 'off shore' certain services to parts of the world with a lower cost base, which is simply a mimicking of other industries. The law affecting trusts continues to change, for example tax laws and the way legal services may be offered will soon change in the wake of Sir David Clementi's review (*Review of the Regulatory Framework for Legal Services in England and Wales*, Final Report, December 2004, **www.legal-services-review.org.uk/ content/report/index**). Changes to the law and lawyers clearly change the way in which services can be provided and also the range of services which clients are likely to require both now and into the future. In addition, the expectations of clients are developing rapidly. They have moved on from expecting a solicitor to react to their requests, to now having an expectation that the lawyer will proactively manage their affairs and keep them informed of developments. Failing to meet the expectations of clients will cause, over time, a serious problem for any trust department.

In putting a business plan together, whom does the department need to consider if the plan is going to be worth the paper it is written on? The first interested party is obviously the partners. They will only be willing to work hard within a department if they can have a realistic expectation of making a reasonable level of profit come the end of the year. Next come employees, who will not be attracted to work in a department unless they will be challenged, developed and rewarded properly for their endeavours. And most importantly, clients will not provide work to the department in the first place unless they anticipate that they will get the service they deserve at a price which is in line with market forces. Finally, some departments would now consider that other suppliers to the department are stakeholders in the plan, suppliers which the department needs if it is to operate efficiently. The department relies on not only its employees but also other suppliers of services, and therefore it is important to have good relationships with these other people. Probably the most common mistake made when generating a business plan together for the first time is that in generating the plan, only the needs of the owners are considered. It is not particularly difficult to develop a business plan that would theoretically create a high degree of profit, but whether or not this is achievable depends on whether or not the expectations of the other stakeholders are being met.

The required research and analysis

Figure 15.1 outlines the process that any department would need to go through in putting together a business plan for perhaps a 3–5 year period.

As can be seen, the first step is to analyse exactly where you currently stand. The next stage is to analyse exactly where the competition stands with regard to your position. Only once you know exactly where you are and where your competition is, is it possible to decide on a future course of action. The final thing that would need to be considered is the likely changes in the market place over the period which could impact on your route.

How will you start to do this analysis for yourself so that the plans you come up with are both realistic and achievable?

The most popular technique used by management consultants across the globe for this sort of analysis is SWOT analysis. As can be seen in Figure 15.2, SWOT stands for 'Strengths, Weaknesses, Opportunities and Threats'. Once you have analysed your department using this model, you can then analyse the information in a number of ways. For example, looking at the top half of the grid will give you a feel for the present position, while the bottom half of the grid gives an indication of what might happen in the future. Alternatively, looking at the left half of the grid you see the strengths of the organisation, while the right hand side reveals the weaknesses of the business.

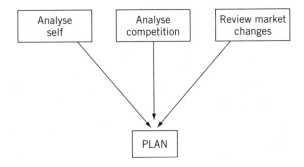

Figure 15.1 Research and analysis required for a business plan

Figure 15.2 SWOT analysis

The SWOT analyses will start with a discussion among the partners to see if some consensus can be reached. Then the discussion should be broadened to involve the rest of the team: other fee earners and, indeed, support staff in the discussion to gain their input. Once the self-analysis is complete, it is then appropriate to put a line through anything for which you do not have information to substantiate the item. In most cases this means most of the information is now removed! What becomes obvious at this stage is the need for better factual information coming out of more disciplined research. How can such research be undertaken? There are a number of sources of good information on yourself, including the following.

1. Look at your financial statements for previous years to see what has been happening to your financial performance; if possible, compare or benchmark your department against the financial performance of other similar sized departments.
2. Undertake a staff survey to see what employees within the department think about the department and the quality of service being offered to clients. This process has led to some major changes in some of the larger firms in the UK, as it took direct comments resulting from such a survey to make the partners realise the importance of certain changes.

3. Further information can be obtained from client surveys, which can be very large and grand and organised by external agencies or can be very informal and run by the department itself. Client surveys might include an annual questionnaire or more simply a questionnaire that clients are asked to complete at the end of each piece of work.

4. Exit and entry interviews of staff can give you still further information about the department and how it compares with other firms.

When it comes to analysing the competition the hardest step is to identify who your main competitors are. Do not forget to take into account potential competitors as well as those who already compete with you at the moment. Potential competitors could be based anywhere else in the UK, or indeed internationally, and would not necessarily be practising simply as solicitors.

Do a SWOT analysis of these competitors in the same way as you did for your own department and you will quickly appreciate that you know even less about your competitors than you do about yourselves. Further analysis and research is therefore required to get a greater understanding of competitors. Only if this is done thoroughly are you then in a position to identify action that your department should be taking.

The final step is to understand what is likely to happen over the timescale of your business plan to the market place in general. Issues likely to have an impact include:

1. developments in technology;
2. changes to client expectations;
3. changes to the law;
4. changes to employee expectations, e.g. home working or family-friendly policies;
5. economic changes both in the UK and internationally;
6. increased competition generally; and
7. reduced client loyalty.

Another useful tool to help in this review is the use of PESTEL analysis. A PESTEL analysis is a review of the external influences and factors operating on the department. It covers the following issues:

P – Political
E – Economic
S – Sociological
T – Technological
E – Environmental
L – Legal

Within a trust department, a PESTEL analysis might consider the following points.

Political

Structural reforms – this includes recent political decisions that have made an impact such as:

1. changes in regulation;
2. changes in how we may practise;
3. the permitting of authorised probate practitioners;
4. attacks on tax avoidance;
5. modernisation of the taxation system for trusts.

Economic

General economic forces impacting on:

1. property;
2. increasing wealth;
3. declining estate values.

Sociological

Social attitude influencing demand – for example, attitudes:

1. towards home ownership;
2. towards cohabitation, marriage, divorce and the family.

Consumer awareness affecting client expectations – for example:

1. price awareness;
2. heightened consumer awareness of legal rights;
3. increased expectations of the standard of service.

Demographic trends – for example:

1. population trends;
2. age structures, nationally and regionally.

Technological

Developments in the equipment available in the typical office – for example:

1. computers have revolutionised production and management techniques;
2. modern methods of doing business, e.g. online banking facilities, telegraphic transfers, e-mail, video links and others.

Environmental

The location of the office may offer specific advantages or challenges. The use of 'green' products such as recycled paper should be considered.

Legal

Compliance issues arising from:

1. changes in trust law, e.g. TLATA 1996 and the Trustee Act 2000;
2. the introduction of the Proceeds of Crime Act 2002 and the Money Laundering Directives.

Possible structure of the business plan

When it actually comes to putting pen to paper it is probably important to limit the number of headings so that the plan provides focus on just the key areas. Every department can decide on what these key issues are, but the following five headings are commonly used and are regularly core areas for development.

(a) Profitability

Given that the definition of a partnership is two or more people coming together to trade with a view to making a profit, this probably ought to be the starting point for all business plans. Increased profit is made through a combination of selling more and by selling at a higher margin.

This part of the business plan should therefore focus on the services that are to be offered by the department and the clients to whom the services are going to be sold to create fee income. This section of the plan will focus on how to increase the volumes of work being done but also how this work can be done more efficiently so as to maximise the margin on the work undertaken.

(b) Financing the department

While many professional firms make big profits, a recurring problem is always poor cashflow. Staff and most other overheads need to be paid almost immediately, while the delay between doing work and receiving cash from clients can be many, many months. This part of the plan should look in particular at how the financing of the firm is to be organised.

A starting point must always be to reduce the delay between doing work and receiving cash from clients. This may involve a number of things including re-educating clients, asking for money on account, a greater emphasis on interim billing and tighter credit control.

Trust administration work lends itself to interim billing. It is sensible to agree with each set of trustees a work plan and fee structure as part of your letter of engagement. It will then be clear what you are proposing to do for what fees, and this should make approval of the fees that much easier. For example, two different possible fee structures are illustrated below.

Trust One

1. To produce a set of quarterly accounts for the trustees' meetings.
2. To implement any agreed income distribution quarterly and supply information to the beneficiaries.
3. To prepare annual tax returns and tax certificates.
4. To maintain trust records.
5. To act as secretary for the trustees' meetings and take the minutes.
6. To manage the trust's investments.

For this you might agree to be paid quarterly based on a fixed fee for quarters 1–3 of, say, £500 each time and a variable fourth quarter fee based on the annual time records plus a value element.

Trust Two

1. To mandate all the income to the life tenant.
2. To produce annual accounts but no tax return, as the income is shown on the life tenant's return.
3. To review the investment performance of the agents annually.

For this you might agree to be paid a fixed fee of 1 per cent of the value of the fund under management, to be collected annually.

The financing of the firm could be dealt with by arranging additional bank finance as the firm grows, by asking partners to contribute more capital, or by asking partners to retain certain levels of profit each year to finance the increasing capital requirement of the firm. It is important to avoid a situation where a department finds that it has run out of money and crisis meetings have to be held. By thinking ahead in the business plan, you can address and resolve these issues.

(c) Fee growth

While it is possible to increase profitability on a steady level of fees through better margins, it is nearly always easier to seek to achieve larger levels of profit growth by increasing the volumes of fee income. This part of the business plan will look at how the growth in fees is to be achieved. Traditionally, when they were set up, most departments would take on any work from any client because they were desperate for fees. Only many years later would they begin to reject work that did not really fit the profile of the department. The result is that most departments undertake large amounts of work which, quite frankly, they should not be doing. Perhaps 50 per cent of the work done by the department is only creating 10 per cent of the fee income of that department and is not particularly profitable at all. This work could be defined as the 'dross' and a systematic process of dross dropping may be required so that fee earners have more time to concentrate on the higher value clients and to free up time to go out and market the department to higher value clients.

A file review will discover many historic trusts which are not profitable to the firm and, equally, not profitable for the beneficiaries. It is sensible to be proactive and approach trustees of those trusts which can be brought to an end economically and easily to recommend closure. A trust manager who is seen to act in a proactive manner rather than merely carry on as before is often hailed by families as a 'breath of fresh air' which, in itself, encourages future referrals to the firm.

The other issue which should be picked up in the business plan is that all of the marketing undertaken by the department needs to be focused on the work which the department would actually like for the future, rather than simply marketing to create work of any type.

(d) Staffing

Most recruitment decisions undertaken by professional firms are made as a reaction to short-term issues, such as the fact that a particular fee earner is now leaving or a new client has been taken on who requires a particular skill. Putting the business plan together may afford an opportunity to think about the overall structure of the department and whether or not this needs to be changed. With increasing competition for many services the price that can be charged is falling and it is therefore vitally important to make sure that the work is resourced with the appropriate level of staff.

The consequence of this change is that many traditional law firms are now beginning to employ unqualified staff to handle large amounts of the work being undertaken, rather than simply employing solicitors to do all the professional work. In the field of trust administration, basic training can be achieved through studying for the STEP Foundation Certificate, and for more advanced development the STEP Diploma would be appropriate. These qualifications offer recognition of competence which previously might only have been attainable as a solicitor or accountant.

(e) Productivity

As has been outlined above, there is pressure for all departments to reduce their cost base in order to provide legal services more efficiently. In addition to looking at staff structures, it is also important to make sure that firms are making best use of information technology and the use of standardised procedures and documents. There are quite a few practice areas which now make far more use of technology and require less use of legal time as a result of these competitive forces. (See **Chapter 16** for an examination of the ways IT can improve productivity in trust administration.) There are now signs that some law firms are beginning to relocate certain parts of their practice overseas in a further attempt to keep costs in line with the competition.

Implementation and follow through

The temptation when the business plan is complete is to put it in a desk drawer and not look at it again for several years. For the plan to be worthwhile, it has to be a living document that is used over the entire period of the plan.

If the plan is to be implemented, the first requirement is for everyone to know the objectives and how the team objectives translate into personal objectives. There will be different roles to be performed and these must be clearly allocated out amongst the partnership, fee earners and support staff. The plan must be followed up in routine office meetings and departmental meetings to ensure that momentum is maintained. There should be no need for additional meetings, as this should simply be an additional agenda item for existing meetings that take place within the department.

It is also important to remember that the business plan will almost certainly require the spending of money on certain things to achieve longer term goals, and it is therefore important that the short-term budgets reflect this expenditure, since otherwise it is simply unlikely to happen in the short term.

How often should the business plan be formally reviewed? Clearly it would be ridiculous to wait until the end of the three-year business plan before thinking about it again because the department would then be entering another period for which there was no plan. Realistically, perhaps the plan should be formally reviewed once a year so that there is always a three-year rolling business plan in place. At the end of a given year the changes necessary may be only minimal, but equally the market may have shifted quite dramatically over that period and it may be time to have a fundamental shift in the business plan.

15.2 MAKING MONEY IN TRUST DEPARTMENTS

Introduction

The historical norm for profitability, well known to experienced practitioners, is that good firms should make approximately one-third of their fee income as profit for the equity partners. The model can be broken down into more detail as follows:

	£
Fees	100
Less: professional staff costs	33
Gross profit	67
Less: overheads	34
Profit for the equity partners	33

To achieve a third of income as profit, the model was that a third of income would be spent on professional staff costs and the remaining third of income on overheads. In recent years this model has begun to alter in the more profitable firms, where increasingly the figure representing the professional staff costs becomes a smaller percentage of fees, perhaps down to about 20 per cent, leading to a growth in gross profit. At the same time, overheads have grown by as much as the professional staff costs have fallen, leaving a bottom line profit still of around 33 per cent. What has been happening in the more profitable firms is that a greater amount has been spent on the support of the fee earners through expenses such as IT, Professional Support Lawyers and training. As a result of this higher level of support, lawyers can now charge themselves out at a higher multiple of salary than was traditionally the case. The traditional model has shown a multiple of three times salary, while more recent figures are showing figures of five or even higher as a multiple of salaries.

While the best firms might achieve a third of income as profit, an average for firms has always been closer to 25 per cent of fee income. There is clearly a group of firms who underperform, going all the way down to underperforming firms which make losses.

The global model

The above model is UK specific, historic, and is not necessarily replicated in other countries. The following model is global and has always worked and will always work for every firm across the globe. The amount of profit earned per equity partner is equal to:

Gearing × Hours × Rate × Recovery × Margin

(a)   Gearing

'Gearing' is a number being 1 if an equity partner works on his own; the number then increases by 1 for every additional fee earner who works with that equity partner. So for example if an equity partner works with three other fee earners then the gearing figure is 4. If there are two equity partners working with eight other fee earners then gearing is 5.

(b)   Hours

This is the average number of recorded chargeable hours per annum per fee earner across the team.

(c)   Rate

This is the average chargeout rate for recording time across the team.

(d)   Recovery

This is also sometimes called 'realisation'. This is the percentage of work in progress created which is actually billed to the client. If there is a write-off of work in progress at the billing stage, the recovery is under 100 per cent.

(e)   Margin

This is the percentage of total billing which appears as profit. Another way of understanding margin is to say that the profit earned by the firm is equal to the fees billed less expenses incurred.

Is your department 'commercial' or 'sleeping'?

So what sort of results could be seen in a 'commercial' trust department and in a 'sleeping' trust department?

Table 15.1 Results in a 'commercial' and 'sleeping' trust department

	Commercial	Sleeping
Profit per equity partner	£270,000 p.a.	£64,800 p.a.
Gearing	4	3
Hours	1,250	900
Rate	£150	£120
Recovery	90	80
Margin	40	25

When one analyses the department in this way it may be possible to identify which variables can be changed most readily to improve profitability.

Gearing and staff structures

Gearing is the first of the five drivers which affect profitability. It is also sometimes referred to as 'leverage'. The theoretical level of gearing in a department will be determined by the complexity of the work being under-taken. If the work is extremely simple then it is possible to delegate most of the work to a large number of more junior fee earners who may or may not be legally qualified. If the work is extremely complex, it may be very difficult to delegate much of the work to more junior lawyers. Within a trust depart-ment it is possible to split the work being done into a number of different types, and for each of those types of work consideration should be given to the appropriate level of gearing, e.g. data entry and filing, tax advice and administration, managing case work.

In addition to thinking about the number of people who should be working in the department, it would also be appropriate to think about the analysis of those people in terms of their experience and qualifications. For particularly complex work, it would probably be appropriate to use qualified solicitors with a reasonable degree of seniority while for more routine work it may be possible to use trainees or unqualified staff such as paralegals, because they are supported by information technology.

Professional people are notoriously bad at delegating, as often they believe that only they can do the work properly. This lack of interest in delegation is one of the root causes of poor gearing in many firms. With proper thought it is definitely possible to gear up most trust departments over time to a level of at least four fee earners per equity partner. To achieve this level of gearing the partners have to be more focused on the generation of work in the first place and on the management of people. If a partner simply goes out and recruits staff but subsequently does not manage them properly, the gearing will not be maintained as people leave.

Maximising chargeable time

Time recording is perhaps the most important function undertaken in law firms. Unfortunately, most fee earners see it as an administrative chore and hence do not really give it the attention it deserves. The most important thing of all about time recording is consistency, since if time is not recorded in a consistent way it is impossible to bill clients fairly as the practitioner does not know what is in the work in progress figures. It is also impossible to manage a firm properly since most decisions are based on available information which is predominantly time-based information.

What are the main things that go wrong with time recording? The prob-lems can really be split into three areas: inconsistency, late submission of time sheets, and poor narratives.

Why do these problems appear so regularly in firms? The answer is prob-ably because of a combination of factors, such as the lack of a clear policy on time recording, little or no relevant training given to fee earners, and part-ners giving inconsistent feedback to fee earners about the way in which they are expected to record their time.

The firms that achieve the highest levels of time recording have made a clear distinction between the recording of time and billing. Time recording should be seen as the internal record of the time taken to undertake a task, while billing is the agreed fee with the client for a piece of work. It is clear that, just because a lawyer spends a great deal of time on a matter, a large fee will not necessarily be appropriate, and equally sometimes a large fee can be charged even if a small amount of time is spent. Unfortunately, many fee earners confuse the two processes and they discount time both at the time-recording stage and then again at the billing stage. This double discount leads to a lower level of fee than could otherwise be achieved and also means that firms do not have appropriate information to understand the real cost of doing work and of the efficiency or otherwise of their lawyers.

So what is currently seen as best practice to sort time-recording problems out once and for all? If a firm issues a detailed rule book, it is always possible that nobody other than the person who wrote the book will ever read it and apply it. A better approach is therefore to issue a short policy based on principles which are easily absorbed by fee earners and which fee earners can then apply to each and every situation. The three principles that need to be considered are as follows.

1. Record everything.
2. Record time as matter related or non-matter related.
3. Absorb short breaks.

It will be important to consider the definition of everything for the first policy statement. Best practice is probably to define everything as all time in the office apart from any personal lunch break, and all time spent on the firm's affairs while away from the office. In other words, if a fee earner attends a client meeting outside the office in the morning, this time should be recorded. The whole day spent in the office other than lunch should be recorded. In the evening when the lawyer returns home and watches television this time should not be recorded, but if that lawyer then took a shower, and while in the shower thought about a client matter, then strictly this time should be recorded.

The second principle requires all time to be recorded as matter related or non-matter related. This is a change from the terminology previously used, i.e. chargeable or non-chargeable time. The problem with the old definition is that it immediately confused the recording of time with the billing of time, so moving to matter related and non-matter related will help to resolve this problem.

The subtlety of the first two principles is that fee earners will no longer be able to 'not record' time. This undoubtedly occurred in the past, particularly for non-chargeable time which was seen as non-valuable time. The problem with the old mindset is that if you do not record all of your time, you cannot manage all of your time.

Applying the first two principles, if a lawyer now records all time and splits it between matter-related and non-matter-related time, this allows the lawyer to manage all of his time, and in particular he could manage down his non-matter-related time. Having achieved this, it is then possible to increase matter-related time in the same working day. Clearly the best long-term solution for increasing matter-related time is to do this without lengthening the working day.

The third principle deals with short breaks. The idea of this principle is that it becomes counter-productive for fee earners to record all of their time where the amounts of time spent on something are so small that the time taken to record the time would be greater than any benefit obtained from having that record. All of the day will still be recorded, but these short breaks will be absorbed within whatever was being done at the time. For example, if a lawyer spends two hours drafting a document, but during that two-hour period takes a one minute phone call from a colleague and takes two minutes going to get a cup of water from the water machine, this time could be included within the time taken for drafting. The policy would always say that a fee earner can do this, because if the fee earner is extremely good at recording his time electronically, he can record time down to the tiniest of amounts.

The next issue that needs to be considered is the way that narratives are written against time recorded. The principle that lawyers should always have followed in the past is that narratives should be accurate, honest and concise. In addition, when fee earners record narratives they should also make sure they are written in a 'client friendly' way, believing that the next person to read this narrative will be the client. If this is not the case then when the firm comes to bill it will be necessary to rewrite everything, which delays the process and increases the cost, which does not help anybody. An example of this might be when a lawyer travels from home in the morning directly to a client meeting and correctly records the time as matter-related time. If the narrative against the time is simply 'travelling to the meeting' then clients might question whether or not they should be paying for this time. However if the activity was described as 'travelling to and preparing for the meeting' then this probably puts a more favourable light on the time if it is to be communicated to the client.

The final thing that needs to be considered in the narrative is that the fee earner should be able to write down any comments about their perception of the value of the time. The fee earner should always record all of his time, but if he feels there has been some great efficiency or inefficiency this might be noted as an extra statement in the narrative. For example, if the fee earner feels that he has spent more time than maybe he should have done on researching an issue, supervising a junior member of the team or drafting a document, then he should still record all of his time but put an appropriate comment down against that time, so that when the bill is finalised a sensible judgement can be reached. Fee earners will probably only use the value description of their time in approximately 5 per cent of time entries, and 95 per cent of the time all that will be required is for the time to be recorded with a client friendly narrative against that time. It should be noted that even if it is decided not to charge the client for time, it is still important to record that time because when communicating with the client about fees, it would be possible to demonstrate the extra time that has been spent on the matter even if the firm is not attempting to charge for it. It goes without saying that this will obviously help to support the fee that is being rendered.

It should be recognised that fee earners record time subconsciously. To change their subconscious time-recording practice, it is necessary to work hard. In other words there probably needs to be some training followed by the issuance of a policy to reinforce what has been said. Over the following months, regular discussions should be held during departmental meetings to make sure that the change has sunk in and finally altered the fee earners' subconscious approach to time recording.

Setting chargeout rates

The chargeout rate of a fee earner is theoretically designed to cover the cost of employment of that person together with the associated overheads and an element of profit. Following on from the traditional profitability model that was described earlier, perhaps one-third of the chargeout rate covers the fee earner's salary, one-third covers overheads and one-third creates profit. Clearly, it is important to have differing rates at different levels to encourage delegation throughout the department. The traditional UK model for chargeout rates has always been that the rate of the most senior fee earner will be approximately three times the rate of the most junior fee earner. Occasionally the multiple becomes four times and in some firms it becomes as little as two times.

With a very low level of differential it is unlikely that senior fee earners will feel pressure to delegate work to more junior people. If delegation does not take place, the senior fee earner stagnates and the junior fee earner learns nothing new, which will obviously fuel inefficiency in the future. If the differential in the rates was to be widened, there would be more incentive for the more senior fee earner to delegate all or part of pieces of work. The fundamental problem is probably that the brand new trainee has been assigned too high a rate and this leads to inefficiency all the way up the spectrum. The solution is hopefully simple. If possible, reduce the rates of the most junior lawyers to a more appropriate level and at the same time increase the rates of the more senior lawyers to a higher level, without necessarily changing the overall amount that will be be charged to clients. Such a shift would increase efficiency, which is what all clients desire.

Departments have always found it difficult to implement this change because the partners in particular feel that they would not get any work if their rate is seen as being higher than that of competitors. Provided it is explained to clients up front as to why the changes are being made, there is no reason why clients will resist the change especially if it leads to an overall reduction in price for the work that is being done through greater delegation and efficiency.

Fee earners are normally given a rate which applies to all work that they do. Clearly some of the work undertaken should command a higher rate than other work undertaken. It is therefore important on instruction by a client that fee earners think about the appropriate rate for a matter irrespective of the rate that is being used to capture their time on the system. For larger and more complex items, a client is more likely to accept a rate that is above the standard hourly rate allocated to a particular fee earner. Another way of dealing with this is to tell clients that there is a standard rate for compliance work, e.g. preparation of tax returns, but a premium rate for consultancy work, e.g. tax planning. The sort of premium rate that might be appropriate is an uplift of 20–50 per cent on normal hourly rates.

A final point that is worth considering is what happens to the rate of a fee earner after becoming a partner. In most firms, the rate is subsequently held at a steady level with no further increases in the future. Given that most partners continue to learn after they are appointed partners, it would make sense for their rates to continue to rise over many years. If this were done, senior partners would be encouraged to delegate a great deal of their work to more junior partners, who in turn would delegate work to senior fee earners, etc., down the hierarchy. In most firms there is a culture which says that partners can only delegate to fee earners, and which does not encourage partners to delegate to other partners.

Recovery and effective client billing

A good recovery rate is achieved by good billing practice which also protects the goodwill that has been created with clients. Poor billing practice is perceived as 'ripping the client off' and this will lead to clients leaving the practice.

If there was an ideal recovery rate, this would probably be 90 per cent. If a firm ever recovers over 100 per cent, it is clearly overcharging and should certainly look again at its chargeout rates and time-recording policy. If, however, a department has high rates and is efficient at time recording and can still recover nearly all of its time, i.e. around 90 per cent, then it is probably very profitable.

What are the detailed considerations that need to be thought through if clients are to be billed effectively?

(a) Set a clear estimate at the beginning

It is very important to scope each and every piece of work so that the lawyer and the client have a clear understanding of the work to be performed and the price to be paid for that work. As well as communicating the price of the work, it is important to communicate the value of the service to the client in terms of the effort and skill to be used by the lawyer. If the work taken on is slightly open ended, caveats should be included in the original quote so that the client has an understanding at the outset that the fee may have to be revisited at a later date.

(b) Word the bill in line with the client's expectation

When work is taken on, it is useful to ask clients how they would like their bill to be worded. If the bill is in line with this expectation, there will be less chance of it being resisted.

(c) Keep the client informed on a regular basis

Even if invoices will not be generated at regular intervals, it is still advisable to keep clients informed as to how the work is progressing against the original estimate and let them know as soon as possible if any overrun which will lead into higher charges is anticipated. Many lawyers find it difficult to talk to clients about money. This is almost certainly because they wait too long before having the conversation.

(d) Bill more regularly

The perfect time to send clients a bill is as the 'tears of joy' roll down their cheeks. If a good service has been provided, there should be regular tears and hence regular bills. If billing is left until the end of a matter, some of the early joy will have been forgotten by the time the bill lands on the client's desk.

(e) Talk internally first

Fee earners should not discuss fees with clients until a proper conversation has taken place internally to consider the exact work done and the extras that have been undertaken so that these can then be discussed with the client to negotiate the maximum possible fee.

Most of the above items are not that difficult in principle, but the problem is that professional people do not always find time to deal with these things in a proactive way and they leave all issues to do with billing until far too late, when the client triggers the conversation.

A good trust practitioner will look at his work in progress at the start of each month and consider what needs to be done on each and every matter so that the client will see progress on each matter. By thinking in this way, work can be delegated to as low a level as possible which will ensure efficiency in the work undertaken. By planning ahead the month can be split into two halves and it can be determined which work will be done in the first fortnight and which work will be done in the second half of the month. On the back of this planning, it is then possible to bill clients in two stages for each month rather than leaving all of the billing for a mad panic at the month end.

Control of recovery is probably the main variable affecting profit on which partners are assessed. Because of the obsession in some partnerships to avoid write-offs this often has a negative impact on the initial recording of time. If a department is to achieve high chargeable hours, the partners must not concentrate too heavily on recovery.

Control of overheads

The expenses incurred within a department will be deducted from the fees to give the profit or margin for the period. It is clearly possible to both overspend and underspend on any one expense category, so the challenge for all departments is to work out the optimum level of expenditure for each and every overhead. How is this to be done? Possibly the best approach is to look at each overhead and calculate it as a percentage of fee income for the department for the previous five years. Most overheads will naturally increase in line with any growth in fees. For example, if I have one client and I send one letter, then if I have two clients I will probably send two letters. If over time a particular overhead is found to be growing faster than the growth in fees, this might suggest overspending and, equally, if an overhead is growing at a slower rate than fees, it may suggest underspending.

It is one thing to budget for overheads and it is another thing to manage them effectively. It is therefore important for somebody to take responsibility for the authorisation and management of the various overhead categories. It may be that just one partner will take responsibility for this, allowing all other partners and fee earners to concentrate on their main area of fee earning.

Putting a realistic departmental budget together

A good departmental budget will allocate responsibility to certain people for the control of overheads. It will embrace all of the fee earners and the control of the budgeted fee income.

The fee income budget should be split between fee earners, and in turn all individual fee earners should understand how they are going to achieve their fees through the chargeable hours which they need to record, the chargeout rate that will be applied to their time and the expectation of recovery rate.

Although many firms now put a great deal of effort into creating the budgets, the budgets are then often 'imposed' on the fee earners. If fee earners are to respond to the budgets they are given, they must 'buy in' to their budgets. It is important to discuss the budgets with fee earners at the start of the year so that they agree that the budgets they have been allocated are achievable and realistic. If this process is done properly, this greatly reduces the risk of not achieving the fee income budget for the year.

15.3 CREATING, DISTRIBUTING AND USING MANAGEMENT INFORMATION

Introduction

A well-run department should have budgets in place before the year starts, distribute appropriate management information to fee earners throughout the year and then reflect on performance for the year in total before finalising budgets for the following year.

Lawyers are very happy to use the term 'management information' but have perhaps not really worked out what they are talking about. A good definition of management information would be 'information on things on which the recipient can take action'. Management information does not therefore include items which the lawyer simply finds interesting. A common problem in many departments is that partners get information not only on their own performance but also on everybody else in the department, and indeed, everybody else in the firm. As an owner of the business, they should look at the firm in total perhaps once or twice a year, but what they need on a monthly basis in terms of management information will be just detailed information on the performance of their team.

If everybody within the firm concentrated their efforts on better management of their own part of the business, clearly the results of the firm in total would improve.

The necessary information for fee earners

Table 15.2 summarises a useful monthly management information sheet for all fee earners so that they get a 'big picture' overview of how they are performing.

Table 15.2 Summary of monthly management information for fee earners

	Actual	Agreed budget
Chargeable hours – month		
– YTD		
*WIP – £/Days		
Fees – Month		
– YTD		
Recovery – Month		
– YTD		
*Debtors – £/Days		

*also require detailed printout

The first thing that fee earners need feedback on is the amount of chargeable time that they have recorded for the month and year to date (YTD). This should be compared with their agreed budget for the period. Once chargeable time has been recorded, the fee earner is creating work in progress (WIP).

The next item on the sheet is therefore feedback on the total WIP currently carried by the fee earner. This is not a detailed listing, but just a figure in total to provide the big picture. If the figure is just provided as a monetary amount, it may not necessarily trigger the correct reaction from the fee earner and it is therefore important to also disclose the figure as a number of days' WIP. Fee earners may be horrified to see how long it is taking from recording time to billing it. When this information is conveyed, this will help them to appreciate that they need to get on with their billing.

If the billing is done promptly, in line with the client's expectation, appropriately worded and ensuring that the fee is discussed with other fee earners before talking to the client, then the fee earned should be high and the recovery rate should be good. The fee earner has now disposed of the WIP but has created in its place a debtor. The debtor figure is again in total for the fee earner and is shown both as a monetary amount and a number of days outstanding. If debts are shown as outstanding, this will encourage the fee earner to start chasing for cash. It would be possible to add an additional line on this sheet showing cash received, but this is not necessary since when the debtor's figure is zero all of the cash will have been received.

It will probably take a fee earner about five minutes each month to look at this information, but over a period of perhaps two years looking at this information on a regular basis will dramatically improve the fee earners' time recording, billing skills and ability to collect cash from clients. If this information is not provided, or fee earners pay no attention to it, then the best that can be hoped for over that time period is that the lawyer will become an even better lawyer! Clearly in this day and age it is important for lawyers to develop both technical skills and commercial fee earning skills.

Once the fee earners have looked at this summary sheet, they should also be provided with a detailed breakdown of their WIP and a detailed break-down of their debtors for them to work on in detail. A month later, when similar information is provided, they will see whether their endeavours have paid off in terms of better performance statistics. It is clearly impossible to ask fee earners to work at the margins if they receive no feedback on their performance.

Managing the distribution of information to partners and fee earners

Historically, most departments would produce a monthly report on a piece of paper which would be distributed through the departmental head to the relevant fee earners. Just because information is distributed does not automatically mean that the fee earner will look at it, understand it or accept any responsibility for the information provided.

It is clearly therefore important that fee earners are trained in what they should be doing with the information when it is distributed and the routine procedures that they should establish to control their financial performance.

With IT systems becoming more and more sophisticated, many fee earners can now access information on how they are performing on a daily basis. The danger is, of course, that they may choose not to look at the information and even less management will take place than in the days when paper-based information was the norm. Most firms will probably therefore benefit from continuing to distribute paper information on a monthly basis to fee earners, even if more up-to-date information is available on the system on a daily basis. An increasing number of fee earners complain that although there is much information available on the system, they are not really sure which items they should be looking at and with what frequency.

CHAPTER 16

Information technology

Charles Christian

16.1 INTRODUCTION

Thanks to the high profile that computer systems and information technology (IT) now enjoy (in most firms IT will be one of their top four areas of expenditure, with the average firm spending between 3 and 5 per cent of their total fee income every year on the stuff), there is a growing belief among solicitors' practices that computerisation is the universal panacea for all problems. However, while it might be nice to think that if not enough money is being generated out of a particular area of legal practice, installing a new case management system or similar form of technology will provide an easy solution, not only is this a far too simplistic approach, but it could prove commercially disastrous.

Leaving aside the cost and inevitable disruption (including the time taken up with administration matters that would otherwise be devoted to fee earning) associated with all computerisation projects, you risk running foul of the old computer industry adage: 'GIGO – garbage in, garbage out'. In other words, if your practice has problems, installing a computer will not fix those problems, it will merely computerise them.

For this reason, keep in mind the handy mnemonic 'PCPCT – People, Culture, Process, Change and then Technology'. The preliminary issues must be addressed first: what is the attitude of your fee earners towards technology and the delegation of work to support staff? For example, do all fee earners still dictate individual letters to every client or do they share precedents? Are there any obvious bottlenecks in the firm's working practices and can you get consensus on changing them? Once these business management issues have been resolved, you will be in a far better position to successfully implement your chosen IT solution.

That's the bad news. The good news is that a properly implemented law office computerisation project *will* yield positive benefits. In the case of trust practitioners, at the very least this should include reducing the time and overheads associated with trust work, so you can both increase the volume of work that you can handle and also increase the profitability of that work.

Topics covered

This chapter will therefore be looking at:

1. putting technology in its proper context in terms of practice development and return on investment;
2. the type of IT systems available;
3. how IT can help trusts practitioners;
4. how firms should approach the purchasing of IT systems (the principles of IT procurement); and
5. suppliers of trusts software systems.

16.2   TECHNOLOGY IN CONTEXT

The starting point for any discussion about legal technology must be the premise that technology is not an end in itself, but merely a tool to help implement a law firm's overall business and practice development plans. In other words the emphasis is upon the creation of a joined-up, rather than a semi-detached, strategy.

Unfortunately too many firms still approach computerisation projects from the wrong direction, putting the proverbial cart before the horse, and make the decision to invest in technology without fully thinking through its longer term implications. Just because the firm down the road has bought a new trusts system is not sufficient reason for your firm also to buy one, you must look at the bigger picture. For example, where is your firm planning to go over the next five years? Will you still be doing private client work? Do you plan to expand or contract your trusts practice? Could there be some major contracts out there that you could win if you invested in new IT systems to improve the way in which your services are delivered to your clients? Are there any obvious problems with the way you currently process trusts work that could benefit from technology? What benefits do you envisage technology delivering?

The answers to all these questions will help determine your priorities; however, particular emphasis should be paid to the issue of the anticipated benefits of technology, or the 'return on investment' (ROI). Solicitors' practices are notorious for fudging the answer to this question and despite the fact a firm can currently expect to spend between 3 and 5 per cent of its annual turnover on IT, the method of measuring the ROI is, to put it charitably, often naive and unscientific. It is unacceptable for a firm to justify a huge expenditure solely on the grounds that 'it will help us to provide a better service to our clients'.

It is obvious that you hope that it is going to help you to provide a better service, otherwise you would not be buying these systems. But warm, cosy, touchy-feely sentiments will not pay your bills – nor generate the fee income you need to keep the partnership happy. When assessing ROI, a firm should be asking questions such as 'How much money is this new system going to save us?' For example, will it be possible to reduce the number of staff in the trusts department – or at least improve fee-earner-to-secretarial staff ratios so you can take on more fee earners without a corresponding increase in support staff? Another relevant question will be 'How much in extra fees is this system going to help us earn?' For example, will the system enable the firm to handle more matters with the same staff resources?

Firms should also ensure that any ROI calculations focus upon profitability, as distinct from mere increases in turnover through the generation of more billable hours. The reason is that if this increased turnover has only been achieved at the expense of also increasing overheads, the slightest downturn in the economy or the loss of a major client will put pressure on your profit margins, which once again will not please the rest of the partnership.

16.3 TRUSTS SYSTEMS – SUPPLIERS AND CURRENT TRENDS

This is actually quite a frustrating area of legal technology, for although there is no shortage of software suppliers out there purporting to sell 'trusts and probate systems', they almost inevitably turn out to be merely case management systems for processing probate work that can also handle estate accounts and IHT returns. When it comes to a true trusts system (and in effect this is a trusts accounting system, i.e. a system that can cope with investment management, dividends, accounts, reporting and CGT on behalf of high net worth individuals, institutions and bodies such as charities), the emphasis is entirely different. In particular, probate-related work, even if there are trusts involved, tends to be a relatively short-term affair culminating in the winding up of the estate and the distribution of the assets. In contrast, trusts are longer running entities and, as a result, the CGT aspect is far more complex.

Software suppliers

Although to provide a comprehensive source of information, a listing of probate software suppliers is provided (see **para.16.16**), there are actually only five dedicated (or discrete) trusts systems currently available in this market. These are (in alphabetical order): Custodiens from Cognito Software, Isokon 2 from Isokon Systems, Probate and Trust Management from Timeslice, Troika from FinApps and Trust Accounts from MYOB. Some firms are still running other systems on older DOS and Unix hardware platforms, but as these are no longer being actively sold, they have not been included in this book.

System trends

The key consideration has to be that the system is compatible with the Trustee Act 2000 which introduced far more onerous obligations on trustees, including such things as the requirement to manage the risk profiles of investments. This is the type of task, i.e. monitoring a portfolio to ensure there has not been too much investment in a particular class of shares, such as high-tech stocks, at which computer systems excel. And, because the 2000 Act also introduced a greater emphasis upon 'know your client' and client reporting type issues, a modern trusts system will also give solicitors the tools they need for other regulatory tasks, such as compliance with the new anti-money laundering regulations.

Another feature you should expect to find in a modern trusts system is the ability to import data electronically from third party sources and information feeds rather than requiring it to be input manually, which always increases the risk of human error. For example, brokers may be providing you with information in transactions and portfolio values or there may be other systems running within your firm with which you need to exchange information. Either way, because much of this information already exists in an electronic format, you will need to be able to import and export it electronically.

The final consideration (which in recent years has become much less of a concern) is hardware. The trend today, and for the reasonably foreseeable future, is Microsoft with everything. That means you will almost certainly be looking at systems that run on PCs loaded with the latest versions of the Microsoft Windows operating system. Typically this will be Windows XP on the desktop (although you may also encounter Microsoft .NET, pronounced 'dot net'). Systems can also be expected to be compatible with Microsoft Office, in particular MS Word for wordprocessing and Excel for spreadsheets. It is important not to be tempted to scrimp on the PC hardware. To get the best performance, current specifications would be something along the lines of a Pentium 4 processor with a speed of 2.6GHz, a minimum of 512Mb of RAM memory and a 160Gb hard disk. Although in theory Windows XP can be run on older, slower PCs, performance will suffer. It is also worth noting that the newer the PC, the longer will be its life expectancy before it is, inevitably, rendered obsolete by further changes in technology.

16.4   HOW IT SYSTEMS CAN HELP PRACTITIONERS

This is a potentially contentious topic – it does not matter how good a computer system may be in theory because unless a firm is prepared to invest adequately in training, so its members really know how to operate the computers on their desks, the full benefits of the system will never be realised.

Whatever else you do, do not skimp on training. Leaving aside this important qualification, there are five potential areas of benefit.

Achieving immediate objectives

There are a number of situations that can arise where computerisation is successfully undertaken to achieve immediate, relatively limited, short-term objectives.

For example, suppose an experienced practitioner is heading for retirement and/or planning to work on a part-time consultancy basis. If the firm still has a healthy trusts practice that it wishes to continue, it may consider investing in IT that can provide a framework that will help a less experienced lawyer or any other member of staff working in a fee earning capacity, and for less than the cost of recruiting another trusts specialist. Similarly, if the firm were to win a major client, such as a financial institution, and with it the prospect of a substantial increase in the volume of its trusts work, then installing IT would be a cost-effective alternative to recruiting additional staff. This also meets one of the key measurements for ROI, namely how much will this system help us save?

Better information

In discussing computerisation, it is tempting to focus on the 'technology' aspect of 'information technology'. However, the 'information' angle should also be remembered.

Although computers have earned a poor reputation in the past for generating impenetrable reports of monumental length, modern systems are excellent tools for extracting valuable business information from large volumes of data – information that would be almost impossible, or at least time consuming, to obtain using manual methods.

For example, access to detailed information about clients and work types allows firms to be more precise in their marketing and cross-selling efforts. This aspect of legal practice is increasingly referred to as 'client relationship management' (or CRM) and might focus on the fact that the high net worth private clients, for whom you are managing trusts, may also be the directors or proprietors of businesses that could be a source of commercial, property, employment or other types of legal work for other departments within your firm.

Greater efficiency and productivity

One of the more obvious benefits of computerisation is that IT is very good at doing relatively dull repetitive tasks very quickly and accurately, such as adding up long columns of figures. In the trusts department this will typically mean error-free accounts and reports can be prepared within hours, or even minutes, whereas previously staff could be tied up for days. For example, many corporate events involve a transfer of cost from a parent security to one or more successors. These include mergers, demergers and takeovers. These events can be a nightmare to process manually or on a spreadsheet. The biggest problem arises on funds subject to CGT, because a proportion of the full capital history needs to be written up on each of the successors. If the client received scrip dividends in the parent company, or if they dealt actively in it, writing up the capital history can require dozens of calculations and entries for a single holding.

However, a trust accounts system can simplify the whole process. The terms of the corporate event are entered on the security. Once done, the system generates the necessary transactions on any client. If the event allowed the client to select between different options such as paper and cash, this is entered. The detailed transactions are automatically generated so that both the accounting treatment and the CGT treatment are correct. The process is simple, fast and accurate. Even better, it can be run by operators with no knowledge of CGT. This in turn means the firm now has the capacity to handle more work with the same or fewer resources so there is no need to recruit extra staff and/or existing staff may be allocated to other tasks. Once again this meets the ROI criteria for saving money and/or helping the firm make more money.

Better service

Having an IT system also opens up the possibility of offering services to clients which previously firms may have been reluctant to offer because of the additional workload involved. For example, producing reports and accounts becomes an automated click-of-a-button operation, even for previously daunting areas of work, such as multicurrency computations. Leaving aside the potential for generating extra fees – or taking less time to earn the same amount of fees – the ability to offer additional services is a plus point in terms of establishing a longer-term professional relationship with a client and helping to differentiate your firm from the competition.

Increased profitability

If an IT system can help increase productivity among secretarial, clerical and fee earning staff, so that they can get through more work in the same or less time, then this will clearly have an impact upon the firm's profitability in that it frees those staff to get on with additional fee earning activities. However, computerisation can also bring about an increase in profitability by its potential for reducing overheads.

271

For example, it is not uncommon to find that smaller firms have an administrative 'tail' with a ratio of 1 to 2. In other words, for every fee earner in the firm, there are two back office staff (including secretaries). But, if IT is introduced, fee earners can start doing jobs that would have previously involved dictating instructions to secretaries and waiting for them to effect them – it thus becomes possible to reduce the size of this tail. A 1 to 1 ratio is the minimum that firms will usually aim for (typically by sharing secretaries between fee earners, assigning some secretaries to quasi fee earning activities and reducing the reliance on 'temps') but many firms have already achieved 2 to 1 or greater.

Less reliance on support staff has, in turn, a number of other benefits. For example, it means it is possible to recruit more fee earners without also having to recruit a corresponding number of secretaries, which in turn delays the stage where an expanding firm has outgrown its existing office space. (It is also worth bearing in mind that employing a secretary involves more than just paying their wages – they will also need deskspace and IT systems plus all the other overheads associated with employment. At the time of writing it is estimated that the true cost of employing a legal secretary ranges from around £46,000 p.a. in central London to £20,000–£26,000 p.a. in the provinces.)

Clearly, employing proportionally fewer staff means less is being spent on overheads, which in turn means increased profits. However, bearing in mind the competitive market in which solicitors operate, carrying less overheads means firms can also afford to compete on price – for example against banks and other financial institutions – by cutting their margins while still managing to make some profit on a matter.

16.5 THE PRINCIPLES OF IT PROCUREMENT

Along with salaries, accommodation and professional indemnity insurance, for many solicitors' practices their investment in a new computer system, or some related form of IT, will be one of the single largest financial commitments they ever take on. Furthermore, unlike buying conventional office equipment, such as a new photocopier, an investment in IT will potentially alter the way in which the whole firm operates. Bookkeepers, secretaries, receptionists, fee earners, partners and clients will all find that the new technology has some impact upon them and the legal services they either supply or receive. It is, therefore, essential that the IT procurement process is as efficient and problem free as possible; for if you get it wrong, not only will a lot of time, money and effort have been wasted, but the firm's commercial viability and professional reputation may have been irreparably compromised.

Strategy

Most solicitors probably know of 'computing disasters' that have occurred within other firms. What is not always appreciated is that the bulk of these disasters stem not from choosing inappropriate hardware or software, but from attempts to implement fundamentally flawed IT strategies. The key element to bear in mind here (and with no apology for repeating part of the message that appeared at the outset of this Chapter) is that IT, even a stand-alone trust accounting system, is not some self-contained entity but is, instead, merely an enabling technology or tool that should be regarded as an integral part of the practice's overall business development plan. If you want your IT strategy to be right, your firm must first have (or devise) an appropriate general business strategy.

To give a simple example, there is no point wasting time choosing a supplier of trusts software, if the firm's only trusts practitioner is considering retirement. In addition, any strategy should also take into account the firm's medium-term requirements and longer-term aspirations, for example opening branch offices or diversifying into new areas of practice, such as trust and portfolio management. In other words, don't buy a system that meets your immediate needs – buy one that will also meet your anticipated needs.

The first stage in devising an IT strategy, therefore, has nothing to do with computers but instead actually involves drawing up a business or practice development plan. Only when this is in place should partners begin to consider how IT could be used to help implement that plan over the following years.

Next comes the process of drawing up more detailed specifications and requirements (in effect a computerisation shopping list) that will help realise the IT strategy. Whether or not you need to draw up a formal 'Invitation to Tender' (or ITT) document is a matter of policy but you certainly must have a clear understanding of your requirements if you are to be able to properly brief prospective suppliers and evaluate their responses on a like-for-like basis.

Budgets

It is essential at this stage to consider budgets and the availability of finance to support the proposed investment in IT (whether from cash reserves, leasing, bank loans, etc.). An important factor to bear in mind here is that calculating the overall IT spend is a lot more complicated than adding the cost of PC hardware and a single user software licence together and multiplying it by the total number of users.

Along with hardware (high-spec PC hardware currently retails from around £550–£600 per desktop) and software, there is the cost of installing the supporting network cabling, which in older premises may mean major rewiring and redecorating exercises. Software prices are always slightly academic as the cost will ultimately depend upon the number of users but, by way of an illustration, the price of typical Isokon systems being implemented by law firms falls into the £16,000–£72,000 bracket.

There is also the cost of training, and it cannot be stressed strongly enough that it is essential to properly train everyone who is intending to use computers. Then there are the ongoing costs, including insurance, annual maintenance contracts (usually 10–15 per cent of the initial software cost), renewable software licences, hardware and software upgrades, training for additional or replacement staff, and computer 'consumables' such as pre-printed 'continuous' stationery. As a rule of thumb, it is reasonable to assume that after your initial capital outlay, you will spend, on average, a further 30 per cent of this sum each and every year on ongoing running costs.

Finding a supplier

Having decided what you want to buy and how much you are prepared to pay for it, you are now in a position to look for a suitable supplier. This is actually not such a daunting task in this market as, once the probate systems suppliers have been excluded, there are really currently only four products to chose from.

Contact these suppliers to request further information, such as brochures and promotional literature containing details of their track records and installations. Also consider visiting their stands at exhibitions and attend any of the sales presentations they invite you to (often a useful way of getting to meet other users on an informal basis). Ask to visit or call their reference sites and talk to all your contacts within the profession and anyone else who has experience of dealing with these suppliers.

Send the suppliers under consideration copies of your tender document (if you have one) so you can evaluate their responses on a like-for-like basis and discuss how they would propose to handle the implementation of your project, including training. Incidentally, ensure that the staff who will actually be using the proposed new system attend these demonstrations.

Follow up any user references that are given and start exploring the contractual terms that are being offered, as this is frequently a protracted stage of the negotiations, not least because as lawyers you will inevitably find aspects of their contractual wording with which you will disagree!

Take notice of your own business instincts. Your relationship with the supplier does not end on the day the new computer goes 'live' – you will be dealing with them for at least the next three to five years, so be certain these are people you feel you can trust and work with on a longer-term basis.

Don't be blinded by science. A lot of suppliers are now claiming their respective products are better than their competitor's because they have been developed using 'better' software development tools. This is all 'under the bonnet' stuff. What really matters is the functionality of the software – does it do the job you want it to do, in the way you want it done?

Finally, do take into account that price should not be the key factor (even though in many firms it still appears to be the only factor) in the selection process. Along with the ROI issues mentioned earlier, for those firms that lack their own in-house IT resources (and most firms with up to 30 staff fall into this category) the availability of what is sometimes called a 'trusted supplier' (someone who can be relied on to help you out in a crisis) is essential. You rarely get this kind of service from suppliers who have been selected purely on the basis of price. It is also arguable that 'implementation' (see below), including installation, training (especially of lawyers) and ongoing support, is more important than selection.

Implementation

So you place the order – end of story? Well actually no, for you now enter the implementation phase, one of the most sensitive stages in the whole procurement process – and one where problems frequently arise because law firms do not devote sufficient management resources to this aspect of the project. At the very least, a partner should have responsibility for overseeing the project management side of system installation and implementation.

There is a co-ordination job to ensure that the installation of the network cabling, the delivery of the hardware, the loading of the software and, most importantly, the training of staff to use the new system is properly scheduled and takes place satisfactorily according to a mutually convenient and pre-agreed timetable. For example, you will probably want to avoid the holiday season, the end of your financial year and any other exceptionally busy times, when you will already be far too busy to cope with the installation of a new IT system.

16.6   SUPPLIERS OF TRUST SYSTEMS

As previously mentioned, the number of trusts accounts software suppliers is actually quite limited; however to provide a comprehensive listing, a separate category for suppliers of probate systems has also been provided.

Trusts systems

Cognito Software – Custodiens (tel: 01279 821400) **www.cognitosoftware.co.uk**
Isokon Systems – Isokon 2 (tel: 020 7482 6555) **www.isokon.com**
FinApps – Troika (tel: 01403 322900) **www.finapps.co.uk**
MYOB – Trust Accounts (tel: 020 8997 5500) **www.myob.com**

Timeslice – Probate and Trust Manager (tel: 020 7231 0073)
   www.timeslice.co.uk

Probate systems

AIM Professional (tel: 01482 326971) **www.aimlegal.com**
Axxia Systems (tel: 0118 960 2602) **www.axxia.com**
Civica Systems (tel: 0121 359 4861) **www.civica.co.uk**
Cognito Software (tel: 01279 821400) **www.cognitosoftware.co.uk**
DPS Software (tel: 020 8804 1022) **www.dpssoftware.co.uk**
Eclipse (tel: 01274 704100) **www.eclipselegal.co.uk**
Excelsior LawDesk (tel: 01273 494978)
Isokon Systems (tel: 020 7482 6555) **www.isokon.com**
Laserform (tel: 01925 750020) **www.laserform.co.uk**
Lawbase Legal Systems (tel: 0161 480 4420) **www.lawbase.co.uk**
Linetime (tel: 0113 250 0020) **www.linetime.co.uk**
Mountain Software (tel: 01476 573718) **www.mountainsoftware.co.uk**
Paula for Probate (tel: 01306 710041) **www.paula-accounts.co.uk**
Sweet & Maxwell Probate Plus (tel: 020 7449 1111)
   www.sweetandmaxwell.co.uk
Timeslice Systems (tel: 020 7231 0073) **www.timeslice.co.uk**
Videss (tel: 01274 851577) **www.videss.co.uk**
Visualfiles (tel: 0113 226 2000) **www.visualfiles.com**

The Legal Technology Insider website (**www.legaltechnology.com**) contains a regularly updated copy of this list.

Case Study: the Marion Fairweather 1995 Settlement

1. Outline
2. Fairweather family tree
3. Letter of engagement
4. Form 41G
5. Form 64-8
6. Trust and Estate Tax Returns for year ended 5 April 2005
7. Tax computation for year ended 5 April 2005
8. Capital gains computation for year ended 5 April 2005
9. R185 (Trust Income) – interest in possession beneficiary
10. R185 (Trust Income) – contingent beneficiary
11. Accounts for year ended 5 April 2005
12. Information for trust accounts for year ended 5 April 2007
13. Trust and Estate Capital Gains Tax Return for year ended 5 April 2007
14. Tax computation for year ended 5 April 2007
15. Capital gains computation for the year ended 5 April 2007

Outline

THE MARION FAIRWEATHER 1995 SETTLEMENT

Marion Jane Fairweather created an *inter vivos* A&M trust (the Marion Fairweather 1995 Settlement) on 5 July 1995 for such of her grandchildren who attained the age of 25; appointing as the trustees her daughter, Victoria Mint and her solicitor, Richard Murray. There are two grandchildren:

- Katrina Slade who was born in Fleetwood, Lancashire on 22 November 1981 and although studying at University in Loughborough still regards home as with her parents; and
- Paul Fairweather who was born in Bispham, Lancashire on 18 April 1990 and lives there with his parents.

The Trust includes provision for as yet unborn grandchildren who were born before death of the Settlor. It also allows for income accruing to be added to the whole fund and for powers of advancement and appointment to vary the shares in trust.

Mrs Fairweather died on 27 January 2005 by which time no additional grandchildren had been born so the class closed.

The Trust's assets comprise:

- 46–48 Main Road, Catmint Village, Kendal, Mintshire (a pair of semi-detached houses that are let on assured shorthold tenancies).
- A portfolio of quoted shares and unit trusts.
- £20,000 in National Savings Certificates.
- A savings account with the National & Provincial Building Society.
- A Trust bank account with HS TSB Bank plc.

INFORMATION FOR TRUST ACCOUNTS FOR YEAR ENDING 5 APRIL 2005

The Trustees sold 1,000 Marks & Spencer plc ordinary shares for £9,600 on 8 January 2005. These cost the Trust £1,826 and the relevant indexation allowance applicable is £1,152. They also sold 750 shares in Prudential plc on 3 April 2005 for £7,350. The shares were purchased on 1 April 1998 for £5,370.

The receipts and payments for the Trust for the year ending 5 April 2005 are as follows:

Receipts:	£
Rent (gross)	9,600
Dividends from UK companies (net)	2,700
UK dividends from unit trusts	900
Building society interest (net)	1,875
Bank interest (net)	13

Payments:

Professional fees and expenses:

- directly related to rental income — 1,175 (legal fees £940; insurance, etc. £184; repairs, etc. £51)
- on trust management — 2,250 of which £450 relates to income and the balance to capital.

Payments on account of the tax liability for 2003/04 (paid on 31 January 2004 and 31 July 2004)	1,100
To Paul Fairweather on his birthday	500
To Katrina Slade – income due	6,000

There is an unused tax pool brought forward of £615.00 as at 5 April 2004.

Fairweather family tree

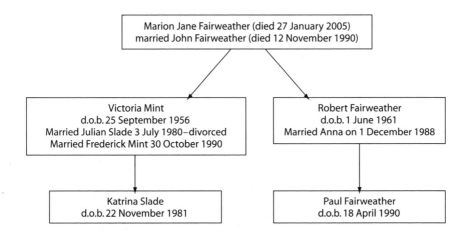

APPENDIX 1.3

Letter of engagement

Murray and Glacier
Imperial House
Fox Way
Kendal
Mintshire
KL1 1AC

Dear Victoria

The Marion Fairweather 1995 Settlement

As you know you act with me as a trustee in your mother's accumulation and maintenance settlement for her grandchildren. The trustees have instructed my firm to act on their behalf in the administration of the trusts.

I shall undertake the trust administration work personally, but in my absence please ask for Tim Sheriton (who is a Trust and Estates Practitioner) who will be pleased to assist you with your enquiry. My secretary, June Smith, will be able to take messages if either Tim or I are not available.

I will keep you informed of developments on a quarterly basis, but if you have any queries at any time please do not hesitate to contact me.

The firm's charges will be calculated by reference to the nature and complexity of the work and time spent by me and other members of the firm in dealing with the matter, in accordance with the attached Terms of Business, one copy of which please sign and return. I would estimate the likely annual charges for the trust administration work to be £2,500 plus VAT and disbursements per annum. I will issue interim bills on a three-monthly basis.

This letter provides some ideas which you might like to consider as to your responsibilities as trustee of the Marion Fairweather 1995 Settlement. It is not comprehensive, and if you would like further information I would be pleased to discuss the topic with you.

Payment of tax

Tax on all sources of income, and on capital gains, will be payable in a single sum on 31 January following the year of assessment. Some trusts have to pay interim payments on account of tax on 31 January in the year of assessment and 31 July following.

As the trust has rental income from 46–48 Main Road, Catmint, it is likely that such payments will be due, so that the trust will in future have two annual tax payment dates:

- 31 January – balancing payment for the year ending on the preceding 5 April, plus a first payment on account for the year in progress (estimated at 50 per cent of the tax for the preceding year)
- 31 July – second payment on account (estimated at 50 per cent of the tax for the preceding year)

It is possible to reduce the payments on account if the trustees believe that the income of the current year will be less than that for the preceding year. I can supply a copy of the appropriate Inland Revenue form for the purpose, but it remains the responsibility of the trustees to form their own view as to the likely tax liability of the year under review: there are potential penalties for negligently giving incorrect reasons in support of a claim to reduce these payments.

Although I will endeavour to inform you in good time as to the amount and timing of tax liabilities, it remains the responsibility of the trustees to make the necessary tax payments at the correct time. Interest is payable on all tax paid after the due date. Surcharges are payable in addition if tax is over 28 days overdue, with an additional surcharge if the tax is over six months late.

Making returns

Any return issued to any of the trustees must be submitted to the Inland Revenue by the due date. This is normally 30 September if the trustees wish the Inland Revenue to compute the tax bill, and 31 January if I am to compute the tax. In order for my firm to manage to meet this deadline I will need any information requested from you for this purpose by no later than 30 November.

The return has to be correct to the best of the trustees' knowledge and belief, and I recommend that the trustees consider carefully before signing each return. There are penalties for negligently submitting an incorrect tax return.

The trustees are jointly liable for completing the return accurately and timeously. Liabilities can be recovered at law from any of the 'relevant trustees', which in outline means any person who was a trustee at the relevant time or becomes a trustee later.

There are automatic penalties if the return is submitted late. The penalties vary, but the normal minimum is a £100 penalty for even the shortest delay.

Since I am to prepare the return, I undertake to send it to you in time for submission, but this depends on:

- Receiving all the necessary documents and information in good time so that I can prepare the return.
- Once I have sent the completed return to the trustees for signature, it being returned to me in time for the firm to send it on to the Inland Revenue.

The return has to be with the Inland Revenue by the specified date, and posting it on that date will not suffice.

Entries in the return

There can be legitimate differences of opinion as to the correct tax treatment of certain items, and some matters are a question of judgement. As required by our professional body, the firm operates a policy of full disclosure. Failure to include sufficient information in the return can also enable the Inland Revenue to reopen the trust's tax affairs for a longer period.

I will discuss with you any item where there may be a problem, so that you and I as the responsible trustees can make an informed decision as to the disclosure required. I will also need you to draw to my attention any matter which you think may be in doubt.

Inland Revenue practice on receipt of the return

On receipt the return will merely be checked by the Inland Revenue to make sure it is a valid return, for instance that it has been properly signed.

Over the 12 months following receipt of the return, it will be reviewed to decide whether the Inland Revenue wishes to make any enquiries. Such enquiries may vary from checking on a single item in the return to a full-scale investigation into the trust's tax affairs. The initial contact from the Inland Revenue will not specify which approach is being taken.

Before raising enquiries, the Inland Revenue has to issue a notice of its intention to do so, and it is most important that any such notice is forwarded to me immediately. The initial response is critical to the success of negotiations with the Inland Revenue.

Some returns will be selected for enquiries at random, but the Inland Revenue will not inform those chosen whether this applies in their case.

Keeping records

There is a legal obligation on trustees to keep and retain all the records necessary to make an accurate return As the trust has rental income, all the records (not just those relating to this source of income) have to be retained until five years from 31 January following the end of the tax year. If Inland Revenue enquiries are still in progress at that date, the records must be retained until those enquiries are completed.

As you might expect, there is a potential penalty for failing to keep the proper records. It is difficult to be prescriptive as to the correct records and if you are in any doubt I would be happy to discuss the issue with you.

Summary

The rules for self-assessment are complicated. If you are in any doubt about your responsibilities for either tax compliance or your other duties as a trustee please do not hesitate to contact me for further advice.

Murray and Glacier aims to provide a prompt and efficient service at reasonable cost. Please contact Ian Grabbit who is the partner with ultimate responsibility for trust/tax matters, if you have any problems.

Yours sincerely

Richard Murray
Solicitor, for and on behalf of
Murray and Glacier

APPENDIX 1.4

Form 41G

Inland Revenue

Trust details

Reference

1234 567890

Please use this reference if you write or call.
It will help to avoid delay.

Issued by

H M Inspector of Taxes
Nottingham Trust District
Huntingdon Court
90-94 Mansfield Road
Nottingham

NG1 3HG

Mr Richard Murray
Imperial House
Fox Way
Kendal
Mintshire

KL1 1AC

Please complete this form and return it to this office. If you pass the form to someone else to complete, please let me know the name and address of that person.

If you have already supplied this information to an Inland Revenue office you do not need to complete this form. Please let me know the name of that office and the reference number quoted.

If the trust is a bare trust - where the beneficiaries have immediate and absolute entitlement to all of the capital and income - and you are the trustee
- you do not need to complete this form but must let me have written confirmation that this is a bare trust
- you should complete this form if, exceptionally, you intend to submit returns of income as trustees.
Bare trust beneficiaries must show their own income and capital gains on their personal Tax Returns.

Part A   Complete in all cases

Trust

1   Full title of the trust

The Marion Fairweather 1995 Settlement

Trustees

2   Full name and address of each trustee
State first the trustee to whom return forms etc. should normally be sent. Continue on a separate sheet if necessary.

Name   Mr Richard Murray

Address   Imperial House

Fox Way

Kendal, Mintshire

Postcode   KL1 1AC

Name   Ms Victoria Mint

Address   Bendicks House

Fox Way

Kendal, Mintshire

Postcode   KL1 1AB

3   Contact details of any professional agent of acting

Name   Murray and Glacier

Address   Imperial House

Fox Way

Kendal, Mintshire

Postcode   KL1 1AC

Reference   023/FAIR04

Telephone number   01830 135790

✓ *as appropriate*

	Yes	No
4a. Is the trust governed by the laws of a country outside the UK?	☐	☑
4b. Is the trust's general administration carried on outsidey the UK?	☐	☑
4c. Is the trust established under Scots law, or administered from an address in Scotland?	☐	☑
4d. Has the trust been set up for the benefit of employees or is it otherwise employment related, whether set up by an employer or by someone else?	☐	☑

41G(Trust)

BS 3/02

286

| **Part B** | **Complete if trust established by a will or intestacy** |

The deceased

5 Full name and last address of the deceased

Name

Address

Postcode

6a. Date of death `/ /`

6b. Date trust commenced `/ /`

7a. Inland Revenue office which dealt with the deceased's last Tax Return (or received the probate, letters of administration etc.)

7b. Reference in that office or National Insurance number

√ as appropriate
Yes   No

Administration period

8 Has the administration period ended? ☐ ☐

If yes, tell me the date it ended `/ /`

Deed of variation or family arrangement

9a. Has a deed of variation or family arrangement altered the will or the intestacy provisions? ☐ ☐

If yes, give date `/ /`

If you answered 'yes' at question 9a complete Part C to give me details of each person that took less under the deed than they would have done under the will. Each such person is a settlor of the amount given up.

9b. Did the deed create a trust in addition to the one established under the will or intestacy provisions? ☐ ☐

If yes, refer to Part A and let me have the same information for the additional trust on a separate sheet.

| **Part C** | **Complete if trust established in settlor's lifetime** |

10 Date trust established `05 / July / 1995`

Details of settlor

11a. Full name and address of settlor
Where there is more than one settlor you should give details for each, using a separate sheet if necessary.

Name Marion Jane Fairweather

Address The Manor House

Lower Kend

Nr Kendal, Mintshire

Postcode KL29 5YZ

11b. Inland Revenue office which deals with the settlor's tax affairs

Kendal 1

11c. Reference in that office or National Insurance number

JS 49 67 28 C

Assets settled

12 Give details of the assets settled, including values. If land or buildings, state the address.

Please see attached schedule

| **Part D** | **Complete in all cases** |

Signature

Capacity in which signed Trustee

Full name in CAPITALS

Date `/ /`

287

**THE MARION FAIRWEATHER SETTLEMENT
REFERENCE: 1234 567890**

ADDITIONAL INFORMATION

12 Assets Settled

The assets settled in the trust are as follows:

	£
Property at 46–48 Main Road, Catmint Village, Kendal, Mintshire KL15 7YZ	100,000
Stocks and shares as per Stockbrokers schedule attached	
National Savings Certificates	20,000
National & Provincial Building Society	10,000
HS TSB Bank plc	2,500

Form 64-8

Inland Revenue

Authorising your agent

It is important that you complete these boxes so we can note our records.

Inland Revenue reference
1234 567890

National Insurance number (individuals only)

Company, Limited Liability Partnership or Limited Partnership registration number

Please read the notes on the back before completing this authority.

This authority overrides any earlier authority given to the Inland Revenue. We will hold the information you give us until you tell us that the details have changed.

I, (print your name) Victoria Mint, as Trustee of the Marion Fairweather 1995 Settlement

authorise (print your agent's business name) Murray and Glacier

to act on my behalf in connection with any matters within the responsibility of the Inland Revenue.

Signature _____ (please see note 1 on the back before signing) Date / /

• Please give your details here

Full address Bendicks House
Fox Way
Kendal, Mintshire
Postcode KL1 1AB
Telephone number 01830 246801
(If you are willing for us to contact you by phone)

• Please give your agent's details here

Full address Imperial House, Fox Way
Kendal
Mintshire
Postcode KL1 1AC
Telephone number 01830 135790
Fax number 01830 112233
E-mail address
Client reference RM/FA005

Only for Self Assessment customers (not including companies)

We will send your Statement of Account to you, but if you would like us to send it to your agent instead, please tick this box ☐

After you have completed this form, please send it to your Inland Revenue office.

For official use

• Customer's records noted - please complete the relevant boxes opposite

Please ✓

• Form(s) 64-6A issued ☐

/ /

Initials   Date

	Please ✓	Initials	Date		
Tax	☐			/	/
NICs	☐			/	/
Tax credits	☐			/	/
Others	☐			/	/

64-8

BS7/02

289

1 Who should sign the form

It depends who the authority is for. See the table below.

Who the authority is for	Who signs the form
You	You.
Company	The secretary or other responsible officer of the company.
Partnership	The partner responsible for the partnership's affairs. It applies only to the partnership. Individual partners need to sign a separate authority for their own affairs.
Trust	One or more of the trustees.

2 What else you should do

- If you have more than one agent acting with us on your behalf, please sign one of these forms for each one and send them to us with a letter telling us which agent deals with what for you. If you deal with more than one Inland Revenue office, please send it to just one office and we will pass on the information.

- If your agent doesn't deal with **all** your Inland Revenue affairs, please send a letter with this form giving us details of those that they do deal with.

3 What this authority means

- This authority allows us to exchange information about you with your agent, and to deal with them on any matters within the responsibility of the Inland Revenue.

- Once we have received your authority we will start sending letters and forms to your agent. But sometimes we need to send them to you as well as, or instead of, your agent. For the latest information on what forms we send automatically visit our website at **www/inlandrevenue.gov.uk/sa/agentlist.htm** or contact any Inland Revenue office.

- You won't receive your Self Assessment Statements of Account if you authorise your agent to receive them instead, but paying any amount due is your responsibility.

- Companies do **not** receive Statements of Account.

- We don't send National Insurance statements and requests for payment to your agent unless you have asked us if you can defer payment.

4 Data Protection Act

The Inland Revenue is a Data Controller under the Data Protection Act. We hold information for the purposes of taxes, social security contributions, tax credits and certain other statutory functions as assigned by Parliament. The information we hold may be used for any of the Inland Revenue's functions.

We may get information about you from others, or we may give information to them. If we do, it will only be as the law permits, to

- check accuracy of information
- prevent or detect crime
- protect public funds.

We may check information we receive about you with what is already in our records. This can include information provided by you as well as by others such as other government departments and agencies and overseas tax authorities. We will not give information about you to anyone outside the Inland Revenue unless the law permits us to do so.

Trust and Estate Tax Returns for year ended 5 April 2005

APPENDIX 1.6A: SA900

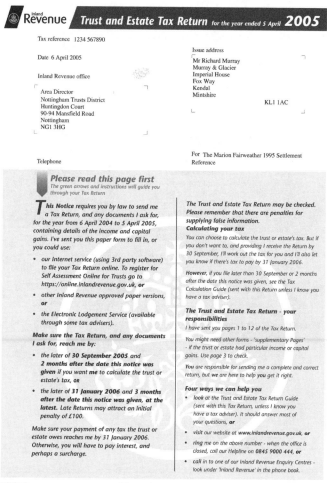

INCOME AND CAPITAL GAINS *for the year ended 5 April 2005*

Step 1

You may not have to answer all the questions in this Tax Return.

Tick if this applies ▼

- see notes on pages 4 and 6 of the Trust and Estate Tax Return Guide

1) **If you are the trustee of a bare trust** (except an unauthorised unit trust), that is, one in which the beneficiary(ies) has/have an immediate and absolute title to both capital and income you can go straight to Question 19 on page 11. ☐

2) **If you are the personal representative of a deceased person**, completing this Tax Return for a period of administration **and all** the points below apply:

- all the income arose in the UK
- you do not wish to claim reliefs
- no annual payments have been made out of capital
- all income has had tax deducted before you received it (or is UK dividends with tax credit)
- there are no accrued income charges or reliefs, no income from relevant discounted securities, gilt strips, offshore income gains, or gains on life insurance policies, life annuities or capital redemption policies where no tax is treated as having been paid on the gain.

Then, **if you have not made any chargeable disposals**, go straight to Question 19 on page 11 ☐

or, **if you have made chargeable disposals**, answer Questions 5 and 6 at Step 2, Question 8 and then Questions 17 to 22. ☐

3) **If you are the trustee of an interest in possession trust** (one which is exclusively an interest in possession trust), and:

- no income arose to the trust, **or** ☐
- you have mandated all the trust income to the beneficiary(ies), **or** ☐
- all the income arose in the UK and has had tax deducted before you receive it (or is UK dividends with tax credit), **or** ☐
- you have mandated part of the income to the beneficiary(ies) where the part you have not mandated comprises only income arising in the UK which has had tax deducted before you received it ☐

and all of the following points apply:

- the answer will be 'No' in boxes 8.11 and 8. * Question 8
- there are no accrued income charges or reliefs, no income from relevant discounted securities, gilt strips, company buy-backs, offshore income gains, or gains on life insurance policies, life annuities or capital redemption policies
- you do not wish to claim reliefs (Question 10)
- no annual payments have been made out of capital (Question 11)
- no further capital has been added to the settlement (Question 12)
- no capital payments have been made to or for the benefit of minor unmarried children of the settlor during his/her lifetime (Question 15A)
- the trust has never been non-resident and has never received any capital from another trust which is, or at any time has been, non-resident (Question 16).

Then, **if you have not made any chargeable disposals**, go straight to Question 19 on page 11 ☐

or, **if you have made chargeable disposals**, answer Questions 5 and 6 at Step 2, Question 8 and then Questions 17 to 22. ☐

4) **If you are the trustee of a charitable trust**, and:

- you are claiming exemption from tax on all your income and gains, you can go straight to Question 7, then Questions 10, 11 and 22, **or**
- you are claiming exemption from tax on only part of your income and gains, you must complete this Return for any income or gains for which you are not claiming exemption and answer Questions 10 and 11 as appropriate.

5) **In any other cases**, including if you are the trustee of an unauthorised unit trust, you should go to Step 2.

Step 2

Answer Questions 1 to 7 on page 3 to check if you need supplementary Pages to give details of particular income or gains. Pages 8 and 9 of the Trust and Estate Tax Return Guide will help. (Ask the Orderline for a Guide if I haven't sent you one with the Tax Return, and you want one.) If you answer '**Yes**', ask the Orderline for the appropriate supplementary Pages and Notes.

Ring the Orderline on **0845 9000 404** (textphone available) or fax on **0845 9000 604** for any you need (closed Christmas Day, Boxing Day and New Year's Day). Make sure you ask for the supplementary Pages for the Trust and Estate Tax Return.

Or you can go to our website www.inlandrevenue.gov.uk

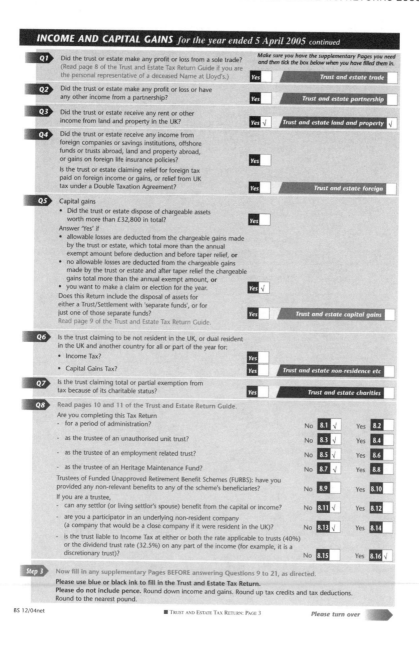

INCOME AND CAPITAL GAINS *for the year ended 5 April 2005* continued

Q1 Did the trust or estate make any profit or loss from a sole trade? (Read page 8 of the Trust and Estate Tax Return Guide if you are the personal representative of a deceased Name at Lloyd's.)

Make sure you have the supplementary Pages you need and then tick the box below when you have filled them in.

Yes ☐ | Trust and estate trade ☐

Q2 Did the trust or estate make any profit or loss or have any other income from a partnership?

Yes ☐ | Trust and estate partnership ☐

Q3 Did the trust or estate receive any rent or other income from land and property in the UK?

Yes ☑ | Trust and estate land and property ☑

Q4 Did the trust or estate receive any income from foreign companies or savings institutions, offshore funds or trusts abroad, land and property abroad, or gains on foreign life insurance policies?

Yes ☐

Is the trust or estate claiming relief for foreign tax paid on foreign income or gains, or relief from UK tax under a Double Taxation Agreement?

Yes ☐ | Trust and estate foreign ☐

Q5 Capital gains

- Did the trust or estate dispose of chargeable assets worth more than £32,800 in total?

Yes ☐

Answer 'Yes' if

- allowable losses are deducted from the chargeable gains made by the trust or estate, which total more than the annual exempt amount before deduction and before taper relief, **or**
- no allowable losses are deducted from the chargeable gains made by the trust or estate and after taper relief the chargeable gains total more than the annual exempt amount, **or**
- you want to make a claim or election for the year.

Yes ☑

Does this Return include the disposal of assets for either a Trust/Settlement with 'separate funds', or for just one of those separate funds?

Yes ☐ | Trust and estate capital gains ☐

Read page 9 of the Trust and Estate Tax Return Guide.

Q6 Is the trust claiming to be not resident in the UK, or dual resident in the UK and another country for all or part of the year for:

- Income Tax?

Yes ☐

- Capital Gains Tax?

Yes ☐ | Trust and estate non-residence etc ☐

Q7 Is the trust claiming total or partial exemption from tax because of its charitable status?

Yes ☐ | Trust and estate charities ☐

Q8 Read pages 10 and 11 of the Trust and Estate Return Guide.

Are you completing this Tax Return

- for a period of administration? | No 8.1 ☑ | Yes 8.2 ☐

- as the trustee of an unauthorised unit trust? | No 8.3 ☑ | Yes 8.4 ☐

- as the trustee of an employment related trust? | No 8.5 ☑ | Yes 8.6 ☐

- as the trustee of an Heritage Maintenance Fund? | No 8.7 ☑ | Yes 8.8 ☐

Trustees of Funded Unapproved Retirement Benefit Schemes (FURBS): have you provided any non-relevant benefits to any of the scheme's beneficiaries? | No 8.9 ☐ | Yes 8.10 ☐

If you are a trustee,

- can any settlor (or living settlor's spouse) benefit from the capital or income? | No 8.11 ☑ | Yes 8.12 ☐

- are you a participator in an underlying non-resident company (a company that would be a close company if it were resident in the UK)? | No 8.13 ☑ | Yes 8.14 ☐

- is the trust liable to Income Tax at either or both the rate applicable to trusts (40%) or the dividend trust rate (32.5%) on any part of the income (for example, it is a discretionary trust)? | No 8.15 ☐ | Yes 8.16 ☑

Step 3 Now fill in any supplementary Pages BEFORE answering Questions 9 to 21, as directed.

Please use blue or black ink to fill in the Trust and Estate Tax Return.
Please do not include pence. Round down income and gains. Round up tax credits and tax deductions. Round to the nearest pound.

BS 12/04net | ■ TRUST AND ESTATE TAX RETURN: PAGE 3 | *Please turn over* ➤

293

INCOME *for the year ended 5 April 2005*

Q9 Did the trust or estate receive any other income not already included on the supplementary Pages? **YES** √ — If yes, fill in boxes 9.1 to 9.40 as appropriate.

You may, **if you wish**, not complete some of the boxes in 9.1 to 9.40 in the following circumstances:

a) **If you are the trustee of an interest in possession trust (one which is exclusively an interest in possession trust)**, you may exclude income which has had tax deducted before you received it (or is UK dividends with tax credit) unless:

   (i) that income has not been mandated to the beneficiary and there is accrued income scheme relief to set against the interest or you are claiming losses against general income, **or**

   (ii) its exclusion would make you liable to make a payment on account which would not be due if you included it - see page 11 of the Trust and Estate Tax Calculation Guide concerning payments on account **before** following this guidance.

b) **If you are the trustee of a (non-interest in possession) trust where the income is treated as the settlor's for tax purposes** because the settlor has retained an interest (if in doubt ask the Orderline for *Help Sheet IR270: Trusts and settlements - income treated as the settlor's*) you may exclude income which has had tax deducted before you received it (or is UK dividends with tax credit) unless any of the following apply:

   - there is accrued income scheme relief to set against the interest, **or**

   - you are claiming reliefs (Question 10) which exceed the untaxed income, **or**

   - you are claiming losses against general income, **or**

   - the exclusion would make you liable to make payments on account which would not be due if you included it – see page 11 of the Trust and Estate Tax Calculation Guide concerning payments on account **before** following this guidance.

c) **If you are the personal representative of a deceased person** you may exclude income which has had tax deducted before you received it (or is UK dividends with tax credit) unless there is accrued income scheme relief to set against the interest. If the reliefs claimed at Question 10 on page 5 exceed untaxed income, you will need to include estate income that has had tax deducted to ensure a repayment can be calculated.

- Have you received any taxed income (or UK dividends with tax credit) which you have not included in this Trust and Estate Tax Return because (a), (b) or (c) above apply? **YES**

■ *Interest*

- Interest from UK banks and building societies (interest from UK Internet accounts must be included) – *if you have more than one bank or building society etc. account enter **totals** in the boxes.*

		Taxable amount
- where **no tax** has been taken off		**9.1** £

	Amount after tax taken off	Tax taken off	Gross amount before tax
- where **tax has** been taken off – *the Working Sheet on page 13 of the Guide will help you to fill in boxes 9.2 to 9.4.*	**9.2** £ 1,888	**9.3** £ 472	**9.4** £2,360

	Amount after tax taken off	Tax taken off	Gross amount before tax
• Interest distributions from UK authorised unit trusts and open-ended investment companies (dividend distributions go in boxes 9.18 to 9.20)	**9.5** £	**9.6** £	**9.7** £

		Taxable amount
• National Savings & Investments (other than First Option Bonds and Fixed Rate Savings Bonds)		**9.8** £

	Amount after tax taken off	Tax taken off	Gross amount before tax
• National Savings & Investments First Option Bonds and Fixed Rate Savings Bonds	**9.9** £	**9.10** £	**9.11** £

	Amount after tax taken off	Tax taken off	Gross amount before tax
• Other income from UK savings and investments (except dividends)	**9.12** £	**9.13** £	**9.14** £

INCOME *for the year ended 5 April 2005* continued

■ *Dividends*

● Dividends and other qualifying distributions from UK companies

Dividend/distribution	Tax credit	Dividend/distribution plus credit
9.15 £2,700	**9.16** £ 300	**9.17** £3,000

● Dividend distributions from UK authorised unit trusts and open-ended investment companies

Dividend/distribution	Tax credit	Dividend/distribution plus credit
9.18 £ 900	**9.19** £ 100	**9.20** £1,000

● Scrip dividends from UK companies

Dividend	Notional tax	Dividend plus notional tax
9.21 £	**9.22** £	**9.23** £

● Dividends and other qualifying distributions received by unauthorised unit trusts

Amount of dividend only
9.24 £

● Scrip dividends received by unauthorised unit trusts

Amount of dividend only
9.25 £

● Non-qualifying distributions and loans written off

	Notional tax	Taxable amount
9.26 £	**9.27** £	**9.28** £

■ *Gains on UK life insurance policies, life annuities and capital redemption policies*

● on which no tax is treated as paid

Amount of gain
9.29 £

● on which tax is treated as paid

Tax treated as paid	Amount of gain
9.30 £	**9.31** £

■ *Other income*

● Other income

Amount after tax taken off	Tax taken off	Gross amount before tax
9.32 £	**9.33** £	**9.34** £
	Losses brought forward	Losses used in 2004-05
	9.35 £	**9.36** £
	2004-05 losses carried forward	
	9.37 £	

● Deemed income etc. *(see pages 19 to 20 of the Trust and Estate Tax Return Guide)*

Taxable amount
9.38 £

● Company purchase of its own shares

Tax credit	Taxable amount
9.39 £	**9.40** £

OTHER INFORMATION *for the year ended 5 April 2005*

Q10 Do you want to claim any reliefs or have you made any annual payments? **YES**

If yes, fill in boxes 10.1 to 10.4 as appropriate. If not applicable go to question 11.

■ *Interest eligible for relief on qualifying loans*

Amount of payment

● Interest on loans to pay Inheritance Tax **10.1** £

■ *Other charges*

	Amount of payment	Tax taken off	Gross amount
● Annuities and other annual payments	**10.2** £	**10.3** £	**10.4** £

Q11 Were any annual payments made out of capital or out of income not brought into charge to Income Tax? **YES**

If yes, fill in boxes 11.1 to 11.3 as appropriate. If not applicable go to question 12.

	Amount of payment	Tax taken off	Gross amount
● Annual payments	**11.1** £	**11.2** £	**11.3** £

If you are a personal representative, go to Question 17. There is no need to fill in Questions 12 to 16.

Q12 Have any assets or funds been put into the trust? **YES**

If yes, fill in boxes 12.1 to 12.9 as appropriate. If not applicable go to question 13.

Settlor's name and address	Description of asset
12.1	**12.2**
Postcode	Value of asset **12.3** £

Settlor's name and address	Description of asset
12.4	**12.5**
Postcode	Value of asset **12.6** £

Settlor's name and address	Description of asset
12.7	**12.8**
Postcode	Value of asset **12.9** £

OTHER INFORMATION *for the year ended 5 April 2005*

If you ticked box 8.15 in Question 8, page 3, then you do **not** need to complete this page - please go to Question 16 on page 9 and carry on filling in the Tax Return.
If you have ticked box 8.16 in Question 8, page 3, complete Questions 13 to 15.

Q13 Is any part of the trust income not liable to tax at the rate applicable to trusts or the dividend trust rate?   **YES** √   If yes, fill in boxes 13.1 to 13.22 below. If not applicable, fill in boxes 13.13 to 13.22.

■ *Income treated as that of the settlor*

- Amount of income charged at the **10%** rate — **13.1** £
- Trust management expenses applicable to the income in box 13.1 — **13.2** £
- Amount of income chargeable at the **lower** rate — **13.3** £
- Trust management expenses applicable to the income in box 13.3 — **13.4** £
- Amount of income chargeable at the **basic** rate — **13.5** £
- Trust management expenses applicable to the income in box 13.5 — **13.6** £

■ *Income to beneficiaries whose entitlement is not subject to the trustees' (or any other person's) discretion*

- Amount of income charged at the **10%** rate — **13.7** £ 1,800
- Trust management expenses applicable to the income in box 13.7 — **13.8** £ 225
- Amount of income chargeable at the **lower** rate — **13.9** £ 944
- Trust management expenses applicable to the income in box 13.9 — **13.10** £
- Amount of income chargeable at the **basic** rate — **13.11** £ 3,285
- Trust management expenses applicable to the income in box 13.11 — **13.12** £

■ *Income allocated to specific purposes*

- Amount of income charged at the **10%** rate — **13.13** £
- Trust management expenses applicable to the income in box 13.13 — **13.14** £
- Amount of income chargeable at the **lower** rate — **13.15** £
- Trust management expenses applicable to the income in box 13.15 — **13.16** £
- Amount of income chargeable at the **basic** rate — **13.17** £
- Trust management expenses applicable to the income in box 13.17 — **13.18** £

- Total amount of deductible trust management expenses *(see notes on pages 21 to 24 of the Trust and Estate Tax Return Guide)* — **13.19** £ 450

- Expenses set against income not liable at the rate applicable to trusts — total of column above **13.20** £ 225

- Total income not liable to UK Income Tax and not included elsewhere on this Trust and Estate Tax Return (non-resident trusts only) — **13.21** £

- Exceptional deductions — **13.22** £

OTHER INFORMATION *for the year ended 5 April 2005*

If you ticked box 8.15 in Question 8, page 3, then you do **not** need to complete this page - please go to Question 16 on page 9 and carry on filling in the Tax Return.
If you have ticked box 8.16 in Question 8, page 3, complete Questions 13 to 15.

Q14 **Have discretionary payments of income been made to beneficiaries?** *Trustees of Heritage Maintenance Funds: do not complete these boxes for expenditure on heritage property. See notes on page 24 of the Trust and Estate Tax Return Guide before filling in these boxes.*

YES √

If yes, fill in boxes 14.1 to 14.15 as appropriate. If not applicable, fill in box 14.15 only.

Name of beneficiary		Net payment		Tick the box if the beneficiary was a minor and unmarried child of the settlor and the settlor was alive when payment was made.
14.1 Paul Fairweather		**14.2** £ 500		
14.3		**14.4** £		
14.5		**14.6** £		
14.7		**14.8** £		
14.9		**14.10** £		
14.11		**14.12** £		
14.13		**14.14** £		

- Amount, if any, of unused tax pool brought forward from last year (enter '0' if appropriate) **14.15** £ 615.00

Q15A **Have the trustees made any capital payments to, or for the benefit of, minor, unmarried children of the settlor during the settlor's lifetime?**

YES

If yes, fill in box 15.1. If not applicable go to question 15B.

- Total capital payments to minor unmarried children

Amount paid
15.1 £

Q15B **Were there capital transactions between the trustees and the settlors?**

YES

If yes, fill in boxes 15.2 to 15.13 as appropriate. If not applicable go to question 16.

■ *Capital transactions between the trustees and settlors (Read page 24 of the Trust and Estate Tax Return Guide)*

Date	Amount	Name of company (if appropriate)
15.2 / /	**15.3** £	**15.4**

15.5 Registered office

Postcode

Date	Amount	Name of company (if appropriate)
15.6 / /	**15.7** £	**15.8**

15.9 Registered office

Postcode

Date	Amount	Name of company (if appropriate)
15.10 / /	**15.11** £	**15.12**

15.13 Registered office

Postcode

OTHER INFORMATION *for the year ended 5 April 2005*

Q16 Has the trust at any time been non-resident or received any capital from another trust which is, or at any time has been, non-resident?

YES ☐

If YES, have the trustees made any capital payments to, or provided any benefits for, the beneficiaries?

YES ☐

If yes, read pages 24 and 25 of the Trust and Estate Tax Return Guide and if appropriate fill in box 16.1. If not applicable go to question 17.

- Total capital payments or value of benefits provided

16.1 £ ☐

Please give details of the payments in box 16.1 in the boxes below. If there are insufficient boxes please provide the additional details on a separate sheet.

Name of beneficiary
16.2 ☐

Name of beneficiary
16.3 ☐

Address of beneficiary
16.4 ☐
Postcode

Address of beneficiary
16.5 ☐
Postcode

Amount/value of payment/benefit
16.6 £ ☐

Amount/value of payment/benefit
16.7 £ ☐

Name of beneficiary
16.8 ☐

Name of beneficiary
16.9 ☐

Address of beneficiary
16.10 ☐
Postcode

Address of beneficiary
16.11 ☐
Postcode

Amount/value of payment/benefit
16.12 £ ☐

Amount/value of payment/benefit
16.13 £ ☐

Name of beneficiary
16.14 ☐

Name of beneficiary
16.15 ☐

Address of beneficiary
16.16 ☐
Postcode

Address of beneficiary
16.17 ☐
Postcode

Amount/value of payment/benefit
16.18 £ ☐

Amount/value of payment/benefit
16.19 £ ☐

If you have received capital from any other trust which is, or at any time has been, non-resident please provide the following details:

Name of trust
16.20 ☐

Date trust set up
16.21 / /

Address of trustee
16.22 ☐
Postcode

Amount of value received
16.23 £ ☐

OTHER INFORMATION *for the year ended 5 April 2005*

Q17 Do you want to calculate the tax? `YES √`

If yes, do it now and then fill in boxes 17.1 to 17.9 below. The Trust and Estate Tax Calculation Guide will help you.

- Total tax due for 2004-05 **before** you made any payments on account *(put the amount in brackets if an overpayment)* `17.1 £ 4,221.93`

- Tax due for earlier years `17.2 £`

- Tick box 17.3 if you have calculated tax overpaid for earlier years and enter the amount in box 17.4 `17.3` `17.4 £`

- Tick box 17.5 if you are making a claim to reduce your payments on account, enter your **reduced** payment in box 17.7 and say why in the 'Additional information' box, box 21.9, on page 12 `17.5`   Tick box 17.6 if you do not need to make payments on account `17.6`

- Your first payment on account for 2005-06 *(include the pence)* `17.7 £1,620.77`

- Tick box 17.8 if you are claiming a repayment of 2005-06 tax now and enter the amount in box 17.9 `17.8` `17.9 £`

Q18 Do you want to claim a repayment if the trust or estate has paid too much tax? `YES`

(If you do not tick 'Yes', or the tax overpaid is below £10, I will use the amount you are owed to reduce the next tax bill.)

If yes, fill in boxes 18.1 to 18.12 as appropriate. If not applicable go to question 19.

Repayments will be sent direct to your bank or building society account. This is the safest and quickest method of payment. If you do not have an account, tick box 18.8A. If you would like repayment to your nominee, tick box 18.2 or 18.8B.

Should the repayment (or payment) be sent:

- to your bank or building society account? Tick box 18.1 and fill in boxes 18.3 to 18.7 `18.1`

- If you do not have a bank or building society account, read the notes on page 25, *tick box 18.8A* `18.8A`

or

- to your nominee's bank or building society account? *Tick box 18.2 and fill in boxes 18.3 to 18.12* `18.2`

- If you would like a cheque to be sent to your nominee, *tick box 18.8B and fill in boxes 18.9 to 18.12* `18.8B`

- If your nominee is your agent, *tick box 18.9A* `18.9A`

Name of bank or building society `18.3`	Agent's reference for you (if your nominee is your agent) `18.9`
Name of account holder `18.4`	I authorise Name of your nominee/agent `18.10`
Branch sort code `18.5`	Nominee/agent address `18.11`
Account number `18.6`	Postcode to receive on my behalf the amount due
Building society reference `18.7`	`18.12` *This authority must be signed by you. A photocopy of your signature will not do.* Signature

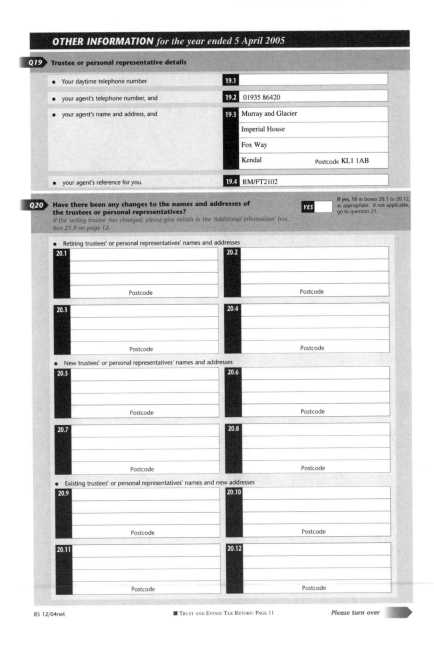

OTHER INFORMATION *for the year ended 5 April 2005*

Q19 Trustee or personal representative details

- Your daytime telephone number
  19.1

- your agent's telephone number, and
  19.2 01935 86420

- your agent's name and address, and
  19.3 Murray and Glacier

  Imperial House

  Fox Way

  Kendal   Postcode KL1 1AB

- your agent's reference for you.
  19.4 RM/FT2102

Q20 Have there been any changes to the names and addresses of the trustees or personal representatives?
If the 'acting trustee' has changed, please give details in the 'Additional information' box, box 21.9 on page 12.

YES

If yes, fill in boxes 20.1 to 20.12, as appropriate. If not applicable, go to question 21.

- Retiring trustees' or personal representatives' names and addresses

  20.1
  Postcode

  20.2
  Postcode

  20.3
  Postcode

  20.4
  Postcode

- New trustees' or personal representatives' names and addresses

  20.5
  Postcode

  20.6
  Postcode

  20.7
  Postcode

  20.8
  Postcode

- Existing trustees' or personal representatives' names and new addresses

  20.9
  Postcode

  20.10
  Postcode

  20.11
  Postcode

  20.12
  Postcode

OTHER INFORMATION for the year ended 5 April 2005

Q21 Other Information

- If you are completing this Trust and Estate Tax Return as a personal representative, please enter in box 21.1 the date of death of the deceased.

  21.1   Date   /   /

- If the administration period ceased in the year to 5 April 2005, please enter in box 21.2 the date of cessation.

  21.2   Date   /   /

- Tick box 21.3 if the administration period ceased in the year to 5 April 2005 and there is a continuing trust.

  21.3

- If you are a trustee and the trust was terminated in the year to 5 April 2005 please enter in box 21.4 the date of termination and, in the 'Additional information' box, box 21.9 below, the reason for termination.

  21.4   Date   /   /

- If this Trust and Estate Tax Return contains any figures that are provisional because you do not yet have final figures, please tick box 21.5. Pages 25 to 26 of the Trust and Estate Tax Return Guide explains the circumstances in which provisional figures may be used and asks for some additional information to be provided in box 21.9 below.

  21.5

- If any 2004-05 tax was refunded directly by the Inland Revenue office, or (personal representatives only) by the Benefits Agency (in Northern Ireland, the Social Security Agency), please enter the amount in box 21.6. Do **not** include any refunds of excessive payments on account or any Gift Aid repayments claimed on form R68(2000).

  21.6   Amount   £

- **Disclosure of tax avoidance schemes** – if the trust or estate is a party to one or more disclosable tax avoidance schemes you must complete boxes 21.7 and 21.8. Give details of each scheme (up to 3) on a separate line. If the trust or estate is a party to more than 3 schemes give further details in the 'Additional information' box, box 21.9.

Scheme reference number

Tax year in which the expected advantage arises - year ended 5 April

21.7

21.8

21.9   *Additional information*

Q22 Declaration

I have filled in and am sending back to you the following Trust and Estate Tax Return Pages:

	Tick		Tick
1 to 12 of this form	√	**Trust and estate land and property**	√

					Tick
Trust and estate trade		**Trust and estate foreign**		**Trust and estate non-residence etc**	

Trust and estate partnership		**Trust and estate capital gains**	√	**Trust and estate charities**	

Before you send the completed Tax Return back to the Inland Revenue office, you must sign the statement below.

If you give false information or conceal any part of trust or estate income or chargeable gains, you may be liable to financial penalties and/or you may be prosecuted.

22.1   The information I have given in this Tax Return is correct and complete to the best of my knowledge and belief.

Signature   Date

- Please PRINT your name in box 22.2

  22.2   Richard Murray

- Enter the capacity in which you are signing

  22.3   Trustee

APPENDIX 1.6B: SA903

Income for the year ended 5 April 2005

Inland Revenue

TRUST AND ESTATE LAND AND PROPERTY

Name of trust or estate

Fill in these boxes first

The Marion Fairweather 1995 Settlement

Tax reference

1234 567890

If you want help, look up the box numbers in the Notes on Trust and Estate Land and Property.

Answer this question to help you decide which parts of Pages TL1 and TL2 to fill in.

Is the income from furnished holiday lettings?

If not applicable, turn over and fill in Page TL2 to give details of the property income

YES

If 'Yes', fill in boxes 3.1 to 3.18 before completing Page TL2

Furnished holiday lettings in the UK

- Income from furnished holiday lettings — **3.1** £

■ *Expenses* (furnished holiday lettings only)

- Rent, rates, insurance, ground rents etc. — **3.2** £
- Repairs, maintenance and renewals — **3.3** £
- Finance charges, including interest — **3.4** £
- Legal and professional costs — **3.5** £
- Cost of services provided, including wages — **3.6** £
- Other expenses — **3.7** £

total of boxes 3.2 to 3.7

3.8 £

Net profit (put figures in brackets if a loss)

box 3.1 *minus* box 3.8

3.9 £

■ *Tax adjustments*

- Private use — **3.10** £
- Balancing charges — **3.11** £

box 3.10 + box 3.11

3.12 £

- Capital allowances — **3.13** £
- Tick box 3.13A if box 3.13 includes enhanced capital allowances for environmentally friendly expenditure — **3.13A**

boxes 3.9 + 3.12 *minus* box 3.13

Profit for the year (copy to box 3.19). If loss enter '0' in box 3.14 and put the loss in box 3.15 — **3.14** £

boxes 3.9 + 3.12 *minus* box 3.13

Loss for the year (if you have entered '0' in box 3.14) — **3.15** £

- Loss offset against 2004-05 total income — **3.16** £

see Notes, page TLN4

- Loss - relief to be calculated by reference to earlier years — **3.17** £

see Notes, page TLN4

- Loss offset against other income from property (copy to box 3.37) — **3.18** £

SA903

BS 12/04net   TRUST AND ESTATE TAX RETURN ■ LAND AND PROPERTY: PAGE TL1   *Please turn over*

Other property income

■ Income

• Furnished holiday lettings profits	**3.19** £	*copy from box 3.14*
• Rents and other income from land and property	**3.20** £9,600	**3.21** £ *Tax taken off*
• Chargeable premiums	**3.22** £	
• Reverse premiums	**3.22A** £	*boxes 3.19 + 3.20 + 3.22 + 3.22A* **3.23** £9,600

■ Expenses (do not include figures you have already put in boxes 3.2 to 3.7 on Page TL1)

• Rent, rates, insurance, ground rents etc.	**3.24** £ 184
• Repairs, maintenance and renewals	**3.25** £ 51
• Finance charges, including interest	**3.26** £
• Legal and professional costs	**3.27** £ 940
• Costs of services provided, including wages	**3.28** £
• Other expenses	**3.29** £

total of boxes 3.24 to 3.29 **3.30** £ 1,175

Net profit (put figures in brackets if a loss)   *box 3.23 minus box 3.30* **3.31** £ 8,425

■ Tax adjustments

• Private use	**3.32** £
• Balancing charges	**3.33** £

box 3.32 + box 3.33 **3.34** £

• Capital allowances	**3.35** £
• Tick box 3.35A if box 3.35 includes a claim for 100% capital allowances for flats over shops	**3.35A**
• Tick box 3.35B if box 3.35 includes enhanced capital allowances for environmentally friendly expenditure	**3.35B**
• Landlord's energy saving allowance	**3.35C** £
• 10% wear and tear	**3.36** £
• Furnished holiday lettings losses (from box 3.18)	**3.37** £

total of boxes 3.35 to 3.37 **3.38** £

Adjusted profit (if loss enter '0' in box 3.39 and put the loss in box 3.40)   *boxes 3.31 + 3.34 minus box 3.38* **3.39** £ 8,425

Adjusted loss (if you have entered '0' in box 3.39)   *boxes 3.31 + 3.34 minus box 3.38* **3.40** £

• Loss brought forward from previous year   **3.41** £

Profit for the year   *box 3.39 minus box 3.41* **3.42** £ 8,425

• Loss offset against total income (read the note on page TLN8)	**3.43** £
• Loss to carry forward to following year	**3.44** £

Tick box 3.45 if these Pages include details of property let jointly   **3.45**

Now go back to page 3 of the Trust and Estate Tax Return and finish filling it in. ➤

APPENDIX 1.6C: SA905

For the year ended 5 April 2005

Inland Revenue

TRUST AND ESTATE CAPITAL GAINS

Fill in these boxes first

Name of trust or estate	Tax reference
The Marion Fairweather 1995 Settlement	1234 567890

If you want help, look up the box numbers in the Notes on Trust and Estate Capital Gains.

Chargeable gains and allowable losses

Once you have completed Pages TC2 to TC7 fill in this Page.

Have you ticked any row in Column B 'Tick box if estimate or valuation used' on Page TC2? **YES**

Have you given details in Column G on Pages TC2 and TC3 of any capital gains reliefs claimed or due? **YES**

Are you claiming and/or using any 'clogged losses' (see Notes, page TCN10)? **YES**

Enter the number of transactions from column AA on Page TC2, as follows:

- transactions in quoted shares or other securities box Q 2
- transactions in other shares or securities box U
- transactions in land and property box L
- transactions in other assets box 0

Total taxable gains from Page TC3 **5.7** £6,551

Only Trustees need consider boxes 5.8 and 5.9

If the trust was made after 6 June 1978 how many trusts that were made after 6 June 1978 by the settlor of this trust still existed during the year to 5 April 2005? **5.8** 1

Is this trust for a disabled person? If yes, tick box 5.9 **5.9**

minus Annual exempt amount (see Notes, page TCN6) **5.10** £4,100

box 5.7 minus box 5.10

- Taxable gains for 2004-05 (leave box 5.11 blank if '0' or negative) **5.11** £2,451

Capital losses

(Remember, if your loss arose on a transaction with a connected person, see page TCN13, you can only set that loss against gains you make on disposals to that same connected person. See the Notes on clogged losses on page TCN10.)

■ *This year's losses* from box 5.2

- total from Page TC3 **5.12** £
- used against gains **5.13** £
- 2004-05 losses transferred to beneficiaries during the year and 2004-05 losses carried back (see Notes, page TCN10) **5.14** £

box 5.12 minus (boxes 5.13 + 5.14)

- carried forward losses of 2004-05 **5.15** £

■ *Summary of earlier years' losses*

- unused losses of 1996-97 and later years **5.16** £
- used this year (losses from box 5.16 are used in priority to losses from box 5.17A) **5.16A** £

box 5.16 minus box 5.16A

- remaining unused losses of 1996-97 and later years **5.17** £
- unused losses of 1995-96 and earlier years **5.17A** £

from box 5.6 minus box 5.16A

- used this year (losses from box 5.16 are used in priority to losses from box 5.17A) **5.17B** £

■ *Total of unused losses to carry forward* box 5.15 + box 5.17

- Carried forward losses of 1996-97 and later years **5.18** £

box 5.17A minus box 5.17B

- Carried forward losses of 1995-96 and earlier years **5.18A** £

SA905

BS 12/04net

TRUST AND ESTATE TAX RETURN ■ CAPITAL GAINS: PAGE TC1

Please turn over

Your 2004-05 Capital Gains Tax liability

A Brief description of asset	AA* Type of disposal. Enter Q, U, L or O	B Tick box if estimate or valuation used	C Tick box if asset held at 31 March 1982	D Enter the later of date of acquisition and 16 March 1998	E Enter the date of disposal	F Disposal proceeds	G Enter details of any elections made, reliefs claimed or due and state amounts (£)
Gains on assets which are either wholly business or wholly non-business							
1 Marks & Spencer - 1,000 Ordinary 25p shares	Q			16/03/98	08 01/05	£9,600	
2 Prudential - 750 Ordinary 25p shares	Q			16/03/98	03/04/05	£7,350	
3				/ /	/ /	£	
4				/ /	/ /	£	
5				/ /	/ /	£	
6				/ /	/ /	£	
7				/ /	/ /	£	
8				/ /	/ /	£	
Gains on assets which are partly business and partly non-business (see the notes on pages TCN17)							
9				/ /	/ /	£	
10				/ /	/ /	£	

* For transactions in
- quoted shares or other securities (the definition is on page TCN2), enter **Q**
- other shares or securities, enter **U**
- land and property, enter **L**
- other assets (for example, goodwill or valuable antiques), enter **O**

Complete Pages TCS to TC7 for all transactions identified as U, L or O

Losses

Description of asset	Type of * disposal. Enter Q, U, L or O	Tick box if estimate or valuation used	Tick box if asset held at 31 March 1982	Enter the later of date of acquisition and 16 March 1998	Enter the date of disposal	Disposal proceeds	Enter details of any elections made, reliefs claimed or due and state amounts (£)
13				/ /	/ /	£	
14				/ /	/ /	£	
15				/ /	/ /	£	
16				/ /	/ /	£	

Total losses of

H Chargeable Gains after reliefs but before losses and taper	I Enter 'Bus' if business asset	J Taper rate	K Losses deducted			L Gains after losses	M Tapered gains (gains from column L x % in column J)
			K1 Allowable losses of the year	K2 Income losses set against gains	K3 Unused losses b/f from earlier years		
£ 6,622		75 %	£	£	£	£	£ 4,967
£ 1,980		80 %	£	£	£	£	£ 1,584
£		%	£	£	£	£	£
£		%	£	£	£	£	£
£		%	£	£	£	£	£
£		%	£	£	£	£	£
£		%	£	£	£	£	£
£		%	£	£	£	£	£
£	Bus	%	£	£	£	£	£
£		%	£	£	£	£	£
£	Bus	%	£	£	£	£	£
£		%	£	£	£	£	£

Total **5.1** £ _____ *Total column H*

5.5 £ _____ *Total column K2* **5.6** £ _____ *Total column K3*

5.6B £ 6,551 *Total column M*

	Losses arising	

Boxes 5.3 and 5.4 are not used on these Pages

Amount chargeable on the settlor **5.6A** £ _____

| £ |
| £ |
| £ |
| £ |

box 5.6B minus box 5.6A

Total taxable gains (after allowable losses and taper relief) £ 6,551

Copy to box 5.7 on Page TC1

year **5.2** £ _____

Copy to box 5.12 on Page TC1 and unless you need only complete the totals boxes (see page TCN4), complete column K1

Other events in the year

Ignore this Page if you are a personal representative

Please tick the boxes which apply and provide the information requested.

Has any person holding an interest in possession in settled property died during the year?
If yes, tick the box and give details below — **5.19**

Name and address of life tenant or liferenter, etc.	Date of death
	/ /

Has any person become absolutely entitled to any part of the property during the year?
If yes, tick the box and give details below — **5.20**

Name and address of beneficiary	Date beneficiary became absolutely entitled
	/ /

Nature of asset	Value of asset vesting	Amount of loss transferred to beneficiary
	£	**5.20A** £

Have the trustees ceased being resident in the UK, or did they become dual resident?
If yes, tick the box and give details below — **5.21**

Description of assets held	Date of change	Amount of chargeable gains
	/ /	£

Were any chargeable gains chargeable on the settlor?
If yes, tick the box and give details below — **5.22**

Name and address of settlor	Amount of chargeable gains
	£
	Enter this amount in box 5.6A on Page TC3

If you have used an extra sheet, tick this box — **5.23**

Now go back to page 3 of the Trust and Estate Tax Return and finish filling it in.

Other shares or securities (U) - further information

If you have more than two transactions of this type of asset to return, please photocopy this Page **before** completion and send all completed Pages with your Tax Return.

1st transaction

Description of shares or securities - including name of company, company registration number (if known), number, class and nominal value of shares. Also, if possible, give a history of the shares disposed of, for instance, if there has been a reorganisation or takeover (give details of the original company and shares held in that company).

Tick box if you have already submitted form CG34 ☐

State any connection between you and the person from whom you acquired the asset or to whom you disposed of the asset (see Notes, page TCN13)

If you have used an estimate or valuation in your capital gains computation but have not submitted form CG34, please enter the date to which the valuation relates, the amount (£) and the reason for the estimate or valuation. Please also attach a copy of any valuation obtained.

2nd transaction

Description of shares or securities - including name of company, company registration number (if known), number, class and nominal value of shares. Also, if possible, give a history of the shares disposed of, for instance, if there has been a reorganisation or takeover (give details of the original company and shares held in that company).

Tick box if you have already submitted form CG34 ☐

State any connection between you and the person from whom you acquired the asset or to whom you disposed of the asset (see Notes, page TCN13)

If you have used an estimate or valuation in your capital gains computation but have not submitted form CG34, please enter the date to which the valuation relates, the amount (£) and the reason for the estimate or valuation. Please also attach a copy of any valuation obtained.

Land and property (L) - further information

If you have more than two transactions of this type of asset to return, please photocopy this Page **before** completion and send all completed Pages with your Tax Return.

1st transaction

Full address of land/property affected (attach a copy of any plan if this helps identification)

Description of land/property disposed of, including details of your ownership, for example freehold/leasehold and any tenancies affecting your ownership at the date of disposal and any other date for which a valuation has been made, and except in the case of an outright disposal of all of your interests, the interest which you have disposed of, or granted.

Tick box if you have already submitted form CG34

State any connection between you and the person from whom you acquired the asset or to whom you disposed of the asset (see Notes, page TCN13)

If you have used an estimate or valuation in your capital gains computation but have not submitted form CG34, please enter the date to which the valuation relates, the amount (£) and the reason for the estimate or valuation. Please also attach a copy of any valuation obtained.

2nd transaction

Full address of land/property affected (attach a copy of any plan if this helps identification)

Description of land/property disposed of, including details of your ownership, for example freehold/leasehold and any tenancies affecting your ownership at the date of disposal and any other date for which a valuation has been made, and except in the case of an outright disposal of all of your interests, the interest which you have disposed of, or granted.

Tick box if you have already submitted form CG34

State any connection between you and the person from whom you acquired the asset or to whom you disposed of the asset (see Notes, page TCN13)

If you have used an estimate or valuation in your capital gains computation but have not submitted form CG34, please enter the date to which the valuation relates, the amount (£) and the reason for the estimate or valuation. Please also attach a copy of any valuation obtained.

Other assets (O) - further information

If you have more than two transactions involving any other type of asset to return, please photocopy this Page **before** completion and send all completed Pages with your Tax Return.

1st transaction

Full description of the asset (other than shares or land/property) affected and any other information which helps identify the asset

Tick box if you have already submitted form CG34 ☐

State any connection between you and the person from whom you acquired the asset or to whom you disposed of the asset (see Notes, page TCN13)

If you have used an estimate or valuation in your capital gains computation but have not submitted form CG34, please enter the date to which the valuation relates, the amount (£) and the reason for the estimate or valuation. Please also attach a copy of any valuation obtained.

2nd transaction

Full description of the asset (other than shares or land/property) affected and any other information which helps identify the asset

Tick box if you have already submitted form CG34 ☐

State any connection between you and the person from whom you acquired the asset or to whom you disposed of the asset (see Notes, page TCN13)

If you have used an estimate or valuation in your capital gains computation but have not submitted form CG34, please enter the date to which the valuation relates, the amount (£) and the reason for the estimate or valuation. Please also attach a copy of any valuation obtained.

5.24 *Additional information*

Tax computation for year ended 5 April 2005

THE MARION FAIRWEATHER 1995 SETTLEMENT
TAX COMPUTATION
YEAR ENDED 5 APRIL 2005

	£	Total income £	Tax deducted at source £	Basic rate £	Lower rate £	Dividend rate £
Rental income	9,600					
Less: Expenses	1,175	8,425		8,425		
Building society interest		2,344	468.80		2,344	
Bank interest		16	3.25		16	
Dividends from UK companies		3,000	300.00			3,000
Dividends from UK unit trusts and OEICs		1,000	100.00			1,000
		14,785	872.05	8,425	2,360	4,000
Less: Allowable management expenses	450					
Grossed up at 10%	50	500				500
		14,285		8,425	2,360	3,500
Tax at basic rate or equivalent		2,725.55		1,853.50	472.05	400.00
Tax at rate applicable to trusts (half income only)		1,388.03		758.25	236.03	393.75
		4,113.58		2,611.75	708.08	793.75
Less: Tax deducted at source and tax credits		872.05				
Income tax due for 2004/05		3,241.53				

Capital gains tax		
£4,091 at 40%		980.40
Total tax due for 2004/05		4,221.93
Less: Payments on		
account made		
31 January		
2005	1,100.00	
31 July		
2005	1,100.00	
		2,200.00
Tax due on 31 January		£2,021.93
2006		
First payment on account		
for 2005/06		
Due 31 January 2006		£1,620.77
Second payment on		
account for 2005/06		
Due 31 July 2006		£1,620.76

APPENDIX 1.8

Capital gains computation for year ended 5 April 2005

**THE MARION FAIRWEATHER 1995 SETTLEMENT
CAPITAL GAINS COMPUTATION
YEAR ENDED 5 APRIL 2005**

	Indexation factor	Date	Nominal	Cost	Indexation	Indexed pool £	Proceeds	Gains before before taper or loss relief £	Loss relief £	Gains after loss relief £	Complete years for taper relief	Taper relief %	Gains after taper and loss relief £
Marks & Spencer plc													
Ordinary 25p shares		7 Jul 95	1,000	1,826		1,826							
Indexation	0.631				1,152	1,152							
				1,826	1,152	2,978							
Sold		8 Jan 05	(1,000)	(1,826)	(1,152)	(2,978)	9,600	6,622		6,622	7	75	4,967
Prudential plc													
Ordinary 25p shares		1 Apr 98	1,250	8,950									
Sold		3 Apr 05	(750)	(5,370)			7,350	1,980		1,980	6	80	1,584
Carried forward			500	3,580					0				
												6,551
Less: Annual exemption													(4,100)
Net gains chargeable to tax													2,451
Potential capital gains tax liability													980.40

315

R185 (Trust Income) – interest in possession beneficiary

Statement of income from trusts

Inland Revenue

Trustees: use this form to advise beneficiaries about income payments made under discretion, and income entitlement from trusts. For annuities and other annual payments, use form R185.

Beneficiaries: keep this form and refer to it if making a Tax Return or claiming a tax repayment. The box numbers 7.1 to 7.12 below refer to the box numbers on the *Trusts* page of the Tax Return.

Trustee's declaration

I certify that
(Name and address of beneficiary)

Full name	Miss Katrina Slade
Address	The Old House
	Fleetwood
	Lancashire
Postcode	LA32 7FW

is a beneficiary of
(name of trust)

The Marion Fairweather 1995 Settlement

Tax reference of trust	1234 567890	Agent's/Solicitor's reference	FAI005/VM

The information below is correct

Signature of trustee

Date   /   /

Discretionary income payment from a trust

I paid income to the beneficiary as follows:

	Net amount	Tax credit at the rate applicable to trusts	Taxable amount	Year ended 5 April
Total payments in tax year *(see Notes 1 and 2 overleaf)*	**7.1** £	**7.2** £	**7.3** £	

Non discretionary Income entitlement under a trust

The beneficiary's income entitlement for year ended 5 April 2005 was:

Income taxed at:	Net amount	UK tax or tax credit	Taxable amount	Type of income for a non-resident beneficiary *(see Note 6 overleaf)*
basic rate *(see Note 3 overleaf)*	**7.4** £ 3,285 75	**7.5** £ 926 75	**7.6** £ 4,212 50	
lower rate *(see Note 4 overleaf)*	**7.7** £ 944 00	**7.8** £ 236 00	**7.9** £ 1,180 00	
non-payable dividend rate *(see Note 5 or 11 overleaf)*	**7.10** £ 1,575 00	**7.11** £ 175 00	**7.12** £ 1,750 00	

		Taxable amount	Type of income
Untaxed income *(see Note 8 or 12 overleaf)*		£	

	Net amount	UK tax paid	Taxable amount
Foreign income *(see Note 6 or 13 overleaf)*	£	£	£
		Foreign tax paid	
		£	

	Dividend	Notional tax	Dividend + notional tax
Stock/scrip dividends *(see Note 14 overleaf)*	£	£	£

R185(Trust Income)   BS6/04

316

R185 (TRUST INCOME) – INTEREST IN POSSESSION BENEFICIARY

Trustees should read only Notes 1 - 8. Beneficiaries should read only Notes 9 - 14.

Notes for Trustees

1 Boxes 7.1 to 7.3 should be used to record discretionary income payments only. Boxes 7.4 to 7.12 should be used to record non-discretionary income entitlement only.

2 Enter in box 7.1 the actual amount paid, in box 7.2 the amount of tax treated as deducted at the rate applicable to trusts, and in box 7.3 the total of the amounts in boxes 7.1 and 7.2. The rate applicable to trusts is 34% for payments up to 5 April 04, and 40% for payments after that date.

Examples:

Discretionary income payment in tax year 2003-2004:

If the discretionary payment to the beneficiary is £660, enter 660 in box 7.1, 340 in box 7.2, and 1000 in box 7.3.

Discretionary income payment in tax year 2004-2005:

If the discretionary payment to the beneficiary is £600, enter 600 in box 7.1, 400 in box 7.2, and 1000 in box 7.3.

3 Income taxed at the basic rate includes rental income. It does not include interest or dividend income.

4 Income taxed at the lower rate includes savings income such as interest.

5 Income taxed at the dividend rate includes dividends from UK companies.

6 'Foreign tax' is the lower of
  • the foreign tax actually withheld
  • the amount of tax to which the trust was liable under the terms of a Double Taxation Agreement.

7 If the beneficiary is not resident in the UK, please use the boxes provided to specify the type of income, for example, rent.

8 Use the box on the right to specify the type of income, for example, rent.

Notes for Beneficiaries

9 If you are making a Tax Return, transfer the information from this form to the corresponding boxes on the Tax Return.

10 If you are making a claim for tax repayment, use the information on this form to complete section 6 of form R40.

11 The 10% tax credit on UK dividends is non-payable from tax year 1999-2000. This means that you will be given credit for the 10% against your income, but we will not repay any excess. If you are making a claim on form R40, mark the entry at section 6 for this income 'non-payable'.

12 If you are making a Tax Return, include this income in the pages of your Tax Return dealing with that particular type of income, not the *Trusts* page. For example, if the income is rent, include it in the *Land and Property* pages.

13 If you are making a Tax Return, include this information in the *Foreign* pages of your Tax Return if you are resident in the UK, not the *Trusts* page.

14 If you are making a Tax Return, include this in the scrip dividends boxes of the main Tax Return, not the *Trusts* page.

R185 (Trust Income) – contingent beneficiary

Statement of income from trusts

Inland Revenue

Trustees: use this form to advise beneficiaries about income payments made under discretion, and income entitlement from trusts. For annuities and other annual payments, use form R185.

Beneficiaries: keep this form and refer to it if making a Tax Return or claiming a tax repayment. The box numbers 7.1 to 7.12 below refer to the box numbers on the *Trusts* page of the Tax Return.

Trustee's declaration

I certify that
(Name and address of beneficiary)

Full name Paul Fairweather

Address 2 Main Road

Bispham

Lancashire

Postcode BM3 2MR

is a beneficiary of
(name of trust)

The Marion Fairweather 1995 Settlement

Tax reference of trust 1234 567890

Agent's/Solicitor's reference FAI005/VM

The information below is correct

Signature of trustee

Date / /

Discretionary income payment from a trust

I paid income to the beneficiary as follows:

	Net amount	Tax credit at the rate applicable to trusts	Taxable amount	Year ended 5 April
Total payments in tax year *(see Notes 1 and 2 overleaf)*	7.1 £ 500 00	7.2 £ 333 33	7.3 £ 833 33	2005

Non discretionary Income entitlement under a trust

The beneficiary's income entitlement for year ended 5 April _____ was:

Income taxed at:	Net amount	UK tax or tax credit	Taxable amount	Type of income for a non-resident beneficiary *(see Note 6 overleaf)*
basic rate *(see Note 3 overleaf)*	7.4 £	7.5 £	7.6 £	
lower rate *(see Note 4 overleaf)*	7.7 £	7.8 £	7.9 £	
non-payable dividend rate *(see Note 5 or 11 overleaf)*	7.10 £	7.11 £	7.12 £	

			Taxable amount	Type of income
Untaxed income *(see Note 8 or 12 overleaf)*			£	

	Net amount	UK tax paid	Taxable amount	
Foreign income *(see Note 6 or 13 overleaf)*	£	£	£	
		Foreign tax paid £		

	Dividend	Notional tax	Dividend + notional tax	
Stock/scrip dividends *(see Note 14 overleaf)*	£	£	£	

R185(Trust Income)

BS6/04

Trustees should read only Notes 1 - 8. Beneficiaries should read only Notes 9 - 14.

Notes for Trustees

1 Boxes 7.1 to 7.3 should be used to record discretionary income payments only. Boxes 7.4 to 7.12 should be used to record non-discretionary income entitlement only.

2 Enter in box 7.1 the actual amount paid, in box 7.2 the amount of tax treated as deducted at the rate applicable to trusts, and in box 7.3 the total of the amounts in boxes 7.1 and 7.2. The rate applicable to trusts is 34% for payments up to 5 April 04, and 40% for payments after that date.

Examples:

Discretionary income payment in tax year 2003-2004:

If the discretionary payment to the beneficiary is £660, enter 660 in box 7.1, 340 in box 7.2, and 1000 in box 7.3.

Discretionary income payment in tax year 2004-2005:

If the discretionary payment to the beneficiary is £600, enter 600 in box 7.1, 400 in box 7.2, and 1000 in box 7.3.

3 Income taxed at the basic rate includes rental income. It does not include interest or dividend income.

4 Income taxed at the lower rate includes savings income such as interest.

5 Income taxed at the dividend rate includes dividends from UK companies.

6 'Foreign tax' is the lower of
   • the foreign tax actually withheld
   • the amount of tax to which the trust was liable under the terms of a Double Taxation Agreement.

7 If the beneficiary is not resident in the UK, please use the boxes provided to specify the type of income, for example, rent.

8 Use the box on the right to specify the type of income, for example, rent.

Notes for Beneficiaries

9 If you are making a Tax Return, transfer the information from this form to the corresponding boxes on the Tax Return.

10 If you are making a claim for tax repayment, use the information on this form to complete section 6 of form R40.

11 The 10% tax credit on UK dividends is non-payable from tax year 1999-2000. This means that you will be given credit for the 10% against your income, but we will not repay any excess. If you are making a claim on form R40, mark the entry at section 6 for this income 'non-payable'.

12 If you are making a Tax Return, include this income in the pages of your Tax Return dealing with that particular type of income, not the *Trusts* page. For example, if the income is rent, include it in the *Land and Property* pages.

13 If you are making a Tax Return, include this information in the *Foreign* pages of your Tax Return if you are resident in the UK, not the *Trusts* page.

14 If you are making a Tax Return, include this in the scrip dividends boxes of the main Tax Return, not the *Trusts* page.

Accounts for year ended 5 April 2005

THE MARION FAIRWEATHER 1995 SETTLEMENT

ACCOUNTS

FOR THE YEAR ENDED 5 APRIL 2005

THE MARION FAIRWEATHER 1995 SETTLEMENT
ACCOUNTS FOR THE YEAR ENDED
5 APRIL 2005
SOLICITORS REPORT

We have prepared the accounts from the information and explanations supplied to us by the trustees. We have not carried out an audit.

The bank balances have been checked with the bank statements and are correct.

Mr Murray, one of the trustees, is a partner in this firm.

Murray and Glacier

Date

Imperial House
Fox Way
Kendal
Mintshire
KL1 1AC

THE MARION FAIRWEATHER 1995 SETTLEMENT
ACCOUNTS FOR THE YEAR ENDED
5 APRIL 2005
TRUST INFORMATION

Settlor	Marion Fairweather (Date of Death 27 January 2005)
Date of Creation	5 July 1995
Trustees	Richard Murray Victoria Mint
Accumulation Period	21 Years (ends 4 July 2016)
Beneficiaries	The grandchildren of the Settlor:
	Miss Katrina Slade (date of birth 22 November 1981) Paul Fairweather (date of birth 18 April 1990)
Trust Terms	The trust fund is held for the grandchildren of the Settlor, who reach the age of 25 and if more than one in equal shares. The class of beneficiaries closed on the death of the Settlor.
	The grandchildren are entitled to the income of their expected share of the trust fund on reaching the age of 18.

This summary is an aide memoire to the terms of the trust. The Trust Deed and any subsequent Deeds or relevant documents should be considered when necessary.

Solicitors	Murray and Glacier Imperial House Fox Way Kendal Mintshire KL1 1AC
Bankers	HS TSB plc 20 High Street Kendal Mintshire KL1 3AB
Stockbrokers	Made Millions 43 London High Street London EC1A 1AA

THE MARION FAIRWEATHER 1995 SETTLEMENT
ACCOUNTS FOR THE YEAR ENDED
5 APRIL 2005
BALANCE SHEET AT 5 APRIL 2005

	Capital £	2005 Income £	Total £	2004 £
FIXED ASSETS				
Properties 46–48 Main Road, Catmint Village, Kendal, Mintshire KL15 7YZ	100,000.00	0.00	100,000.00	100.000
National Savings Certificates	20,000.00	0.00	20,000.00	20,000
Investments	99,305.00	0.00	99,305.00	106,501
	219,305.00	0.00	219,305.00	226,501
CURRENT ASSETS				
Stockbroker's account	14,764.43	451.00	15,215.43	0
National & Provincial Building Society	7,476.52	21,453.48	28,930.00	28,120
Bank current account	516.00	421.61	937.61	1,869
Other debtors	0.00	253.00	253.00	0
	22,756.95	22,579.09	45,336.04	29,989
CURRENT LIABILITIES				
Inland Revenue	980.40	2,141.53	3,121.93	1,021
Professional fees	1,175.00	1,292.50	2,467.50	2,350
Other creditors	0.00	0.00	0.00	1,437
	2,155.40	3,434.03	5,589.43	4,808
NET ASSETS	£239,906.55	£19,145.06	£259,051.61	£251,682
REPRESENTED BY				
CAPITAL ACCOUNT	239,906.55	0.00	239,906.55	236,458
INCOME ACCOUNT	0.00	19,145.06	19,145.06	15,224
	£239,906.55	£19,145.06	£259,051.61	£251,682

Agreed by the trustees on . . . .

. . . .

Richard Murray   Victoria Mint

THE MARION FAIRWEATHER 1995 SETTLEMENT
ACCOUNTS FOR THE YEAR ENDED
5 APRIL 2005
CAPITAL ACCOUNT

		2005		2004
		£		£
Balance brought forward at 6 April 2004		236,457.95		240,619
Add: Profit/(loss) on investment disposals	9,754.00		6,482	
Less: Provision for capital gains tax	(980.40)		(872)	
		8,773.60		5,610
		245,231.55		246,229
Less: Expenses				
Legal fees	1,800.00		1,431	
Investment management fees	3,525.00		3,290	
Other capital expenses	0.00		50	
		5,325.00		4,771
		239,906.55		241,458
Less: Capital distributions		0.00		5,000
Balance carried forward at 5 April 2005		£239,906.55		£236,458

THE MARION FAIRWEATHER 1995 SETTLEMENT
ACCOUNTS FOR THE YEAR ENDED
5 APRIL 2005
INCOME ACCOUNT

	£	2005 £	£	£	2004 £	£
INVESTMENT INCOME						
Dividends from UK companies			2,700.00			3,420
Dividends from UK unit trusts			900.00			855
Building society interest			1,875.00			1,800
Bank interest			13.00			16
			5,488.00			6,091
PROPERTY INCOME						
Rents from properties		9,600.00			9,000	
Less: Expenses	1,175.00			1,034		
		1,175.00			1,034	
		8,425.00			7,966	
Less: Provision for basic rate tax		(1,853.50)			(1,753)	
			6,571.50			6,213
			12,059.50			12,304
Less: Expenses						
Professional fees		450.00			2,000	
Trustees fees		0.00			130	
Other expenses		0.00			25	
			450.00			2,155
			11,609.50			10,149
Less: Provision for trust rate tax			(1,388.03)			(348)
			10,221.47			9,801
Add: Balance brought forward at 6 April 2004			15,223.59			5,423
			25,445.06			15,224
Less: Income distributions			6,300.00			0
Balance carried forward at 5 April 2005			£19,145.06			£15,224

**THE MARION FAIRWEATHER 1995 SETTLEMENT
ACCOUNTS FOR THE YEAR ENDED
5 APRIL 2005
BENEFICIARY'S ACCOUNT**

CAPITAL ACCOUNTS

	Katrina Slade £	Paul Fairweather £	Total £
Balance at 6 April 2004	121,323.45	115,134.50	236,457.95
Add: Net profits on investment disposals	4,386.80	4,386.80	8,773.60
	125,710.25	119,521.30	245,231.55
Less: Expenses	(2,662.50)	(2,662.50)	(5,325.00)
	123,047.75	116,858.80	239,906.55
Less: Capital distributions	0.00	0.00	0.00
	£123,047.75	£116,858.80	£239,906.55

INCOME ACCOUNTS

	Katrina Slade £	Paul Fairweather £	Total £
Balance due at 6 April 2004	268.42	14,955.17	15,223.59
Income received in the year	6,029.75	6,029.75	12,059.50
Less: Expenses	225.00	225.00	450.00
Provision for tax at rate applicable to trusts	–	1,388.03	1,388.03
	5,804.75	4,416.72	10,221.47
	6,073.17	19,371.89	25,445.06
Less: Distributions	(5,800.00)	(500.00)	(6,300.00)
Balance due at 5 April 2005	£273.17	£18,871.89	£19,145.06

THE MARION FAIRWEATHER 1995 SETTLEMENT
ACCOUNTS FOR THE YEAR ENDED 5 APRIL 2005
INVESTMENT SCHEDULE

	At 6 April 2004		Additions		Disposals			At 5 April 2005		
	Nominal	Cost £	Nominal	Cost £	Nominal	Proceeds £	Profit/(loss) £	Nominal	Cost £	Market value £
UK Companies										
City of London Investment Trust plc										
Ordinary shares	3,500	8,750						3,500	8,750	15,481
GlaxoSmithKline plc										
Ordinary shares	500	10,000						500	10,000	15,943
Granada plc										
Ordinary shares	1,000	7,500						1,000	7,500	8,243
Henderson Electric & General Investment Trust plc										
Ordinary shares	800	16,000						800	16,000	8,986
Lloyds TSB plc										
Ordinary shares	1,000	7,143						1,000	7,143	1,574
Marks & Spencer plc										
Ordinary shares	1,000	1,826			1,000	9,600	7,774	0	0	
Prudential plc										
Ordinary shares	1,250	8,950			750	7,350	1,980	500	3,580	11,804

THE MARION FAIRWEATHER 1995 SETTLEMENT
ACCOUNTS FOR THE YEAR ENDED
5 APRIL 2005
INVESTMENTS (continued)

	At 6 April 2004		Additions		Disposals		At 5 April 2005		
	Nominal	Cost £	Nominal	Cost £	Proceeds £	Profit/(loss) £	Nominal	Cost £	Market value £
Scottish Power Ordinary shares	900	2,550					900	2,550	7,527
Shell (Transport & Trading) plc Ordinary shares	1,570	10,000					1,570	10,000	18,861
Temple Bar Investment Trust plc Ordinary shares	2,450	16,870					2,450	16,870	8,265
Witan Investment Trust plc Ordinary shares	1,500	6,912					1,500	6,912	8,437
		96,501		0	16,950	9,754		89,305	105,121
UK Unit Trusts									
M & G High Income Fund Income Units	3,530.500	5,000					3,530.500	5,000	4,428

THE MARION FAIRWEATHER 1995 SETTLEMENT
ACCOUNTS FOR THE YEAR ENDED
5 APRIL 2005
INVESTMENTS (continued)

	At 6 April 2004		Additions		Disposals Proceeds	Profit/(loss)	At 5 April 2005		Market value
	Nominal	Cost £	Nominal	Cost £	£	£	Nominal	Cost £	value £
Merrill Lynch UK General Fund Accumulation units	2,415.655	5,000					2,415.655	5,000	5,481
		10,000		0	0	0		10,000	9,909
Total		£106,501		£0	£16,950	£9,754		£99,305	£115,030

329

THE MARION FAIRWEATHER 1995 SETTLEMENT
ACCOUNTS FOR THE YEAR ENDED
5 APRIL 2005
NOTES TO THE ACCOUNTS

1. FIXED ASSETS

The fixed assets are shown in the accounts at their historical cost. The current market value is included in the investment schedule for information only.

2. BENEFICIARIES ACCOUNTS

The balances brought forward are not shared equally between the beneficiaries as the accumulated income held for Miss Katrina Slade when she reached the age of 18 was capitalised. The capital attributable to Miss Katrina Slade is apportioned as follows:

	£
Capital share	115,134.50
Accumulated income	6,188.95
	121,323.45

The provision for tax at the rate applicable to trusts is not allocated to Miss Katrina Slade as she is entitled to her share of the income and tax at the rate applicable to trusts is not charged on the income due to her.

Information for trust accounts for year ended 5 April 2007

The receipts and payments for the Trust for the year ending 5 April 2007 are as follows:

Receipts:	£
Rent (gross)	8,550
Dividends from UK companies (net)	3,600
UK dividends from unit trusts	1,350
Building society interest (net)	1,752
Bank interest (net)	20
Stockbroker's interest (paid gross)	316

Payments:

Professional fees and expenses:

• directly related to rental income	1,645 (Professional fees £411.25; insurance, etc. £243; repairs, etc. £990.75)
• on trust management	2,250 (Income related £450, balance to capital)

Payments on account of the tax liability for 2003/04 (paid on 31 January 2004 and 31 July 2004)	1,350 (each)
To Paul Fairweather on his birthday	1,000
To Katrina Slade	8,000

The income takes into account the fact that Katrina Slade reached the age of 25 on 22 November 2006 and became entitled to her share of the capital. Income arising after that date was paid to Miss Slade and is not included as Trust income.

The Trustees decided that they would advance one of the two properties to Miss Slade. The two properties are identical semi-detached houses of equal value. The property was valued and the market value was £175,000. Total expenses of £750.00 were incurred in valuing the property, and dealing with the conveyancing and registration of the property in Miss Slade's name

Surplus funds were reinvested after the payments out to Miss Slade. One disposal was made before Miss Slade's birthday in November.

Trust and Estate Capital Gains Tax Return for year ended 5 April 2007

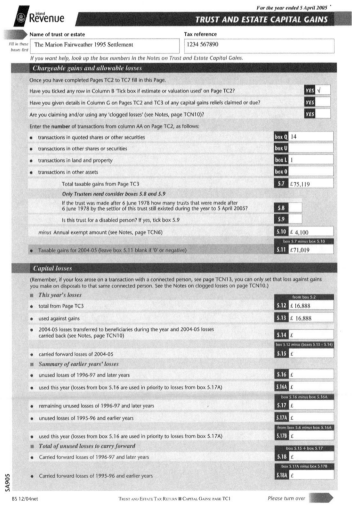

*Of necessity we have used the 2005 form for illustration but the information included is as is likely to be required of the form that is current in 2007.

Your 2004-05 Capital Gains Tax liability

Page 1 of 3

A Brief description of asset	AA* Type of disposal. Enter Q, U, L or O	B Tick box if estimate or valuation used	C Tick box if asset held at 31 March 1982	D Enter the later of date of acquisition and 16 March 1998	E Enter the date of disposal	F Disposal proceeds	G Enter details of any elections made, reliefs claimed or due and state amounts (£)
Gains on assets which are either wholly business or wholly non-business							
1 Henderson Electric & General - 800 Ord shares	Q			26/08/05	25/07/06	£ 27,056	
2 P&O Princess Cruises	Q			15/03/06	22/11/06	£ 3,564	
3 Scottish Power - 450 Ordinary shares	Q			30/11/05	22/11/06	£ 2,018	
4 Temple Bar Inv Trust - 900 Ordinary shares	Q			16/03/98	22/11/06	£ 6,348	
5 48 Main Rd, Catmint Village, Kendal	P	√		16/03/98	22/11/06	£ 175,000	
6 HSBC - 500 Ordinary shares	Q			26/08/05	22/11/06	£ 4,457	
7				/ /	/ /	£	
8				/ /	/ /	£	
Gains on assets which are partly business and partly non-business (see the notes on pages TCN17)							
9				/ /	/ /	£	
10				/ /	/ /	£	

* For transactions in
- quoted shares or other securities (the definition is on page TCN2), enter **Q**
- other shares or securities, enter **U**
- land and property, enter **L**
- other assets (for example, goodwill or valuable antiques), enter **O**

Complete Pages TC5 to TC7 for all transactions identified as U, L or O

Losses

Description of asset	Type of * disposal. Enter Q, U, L or O	Tick box if estimate or valuation used	Tick box if asset held at 31 March 1982	Enter the later of date of acquisition and 16 March 1998	Enter the date of disposal	Disposal proceeds	Enter details of any elections made, reliefs claimed or due and state amounts (£)
13 City of London Inv Trust - 1,750 Ordinary shares	Q			16/03/98	22/11/06	£ 3,895	
14				/ /	/ /	£	
15 Prudential - 1,750 Ordinary shares	Q			15/03/06	22/11/06	£ 1,394	
16 ICI - 1,250 Ordinary shares	Q			26/08/05	22/11/06	£ 3,271	

Total losses of

334

Page 1 of 3

H Chargeable Gains after reliefs but before losses and taper	I Enter 'Bus' if business asset	J Taper rate	K Losses deducted			L Gains after losses	M Tapered gains (gains from column L x % in column J)
			K1 Allowable losses of the year	K2 Income losses set against gains	K3 Unused losses b/f from earlier years		
£ 10,894		100%	£ 10,894	£	£	£	£
£ 518		100%	£ 518	£	£	£	£
£ 622		85 %	£ 622	£	£	£	£
£ 0		65 %	£	£	£	£	£
£119,700		65 %	£ 4,133	£	£	£ 115,567	£75,119
£ 721		100 %	£ 721	£	£	£	£
£		%	£	£	£	£	£
£		%	£	£	£	£	£
£	Bus	%	£	£	£	£	£
£		%	£	£	£	£	£
£	Bus	%	£	£	£	£	£
£		%	£	£	£	£	£

Total **5.1** £ _____
Total column H

5.5 £ _____   Total column K2
5.6 £ _____   Total column K3

5.6B £ 75,119
Total column M

Losses arising			Boxes 5.3 and 5.4 are not used on these Pages

Amount chargeable on the settlor **5.6A** £ _____

| £ 564 |
| £ |
| £ 1,795 |
| £ 3,338 |

Total taxable gains (after allowable losses and taper relief)

box 5.6B minus box 5.6A
£75,119
Copy to box 5.7 on Page TC1

year **5.2** £ 16,888

Copy to box 5.12 on Page TC1 and unless you need only complete the totals boxes (see page TCN4), complete column K1

Your 2004-05 Capital Gains Tax liability

Ref: 1234 567890
Page 2 of 3

A Brief description of asset	AA* Type of disposal. Enter Q, U, L or O	B Tick box if estimate or valuation used	C Tick box if asset held at 31 March 1982	D Enter the later of date of acquisition and 16 March 1998	E Enter the date of disposal	F Disposal proceeds	G Enter details of any elections made, reliefs claimed or due and state amounts (£)
Gains on assets which are either wholly business or wholly non-business							
1				/ /	/ /	£	
2				/ /	/ /	£	
3				/ /	/ /	£	
4				/ /	/ /	£	
5				/ /	/ /	£	
6				/ /	/ /	£	
7				/ /	/ /	£	
8				/ /	/ /	£	
Gains on assets which are partly business and partly non-business (see the notes on pages TCN17)							
9				/ /	/ /	£	
10				/ /	/ /	£	

* For transactions in
  * quoted shares or other securities (the definition is on page TCN2), enter **Q**
  * other shares or securities, enter **U**
  * land and property, enter **L**
  * other assets (for example, goodwill or valuable antiques), enter **O**

Complete Pages TCS to TC7 for all transactions identified as U, L or O

Losses

Description of asset	Type of * disposal. Enter Q, U, L or O	Tick box if estimate or valuation used	Tick box if asset held at 31 March 1982	Enter the later of date of acquisition and 16 March 1998	Enter the date of disposal	Disposal proceeds	Enter details of any elections made, reliefs claimed or due and state amounts (£)
13 Shell - 785 Ordinary shares	Q			16/03/98	22/11/06	£ 3,851	
14 Temple Bar Inv Trust - 900 Ordinary shares	Q			09/05/06	22/11/06	£ 4,638	
15 Vodafone - 500 Ordinary shares	Q			15/03/06	22/11/06	£ 806	
16 Witan Inv Trust - 750 Ordinary shares	Q			30/11/00	22/11/06	£ 2,657	

Total losses of

336

TRUST AND ESTATE CAPITAL GAINS TAX RETURN YEAR ENDED 5 APRIL 2007

Ref: 1234 567890
Page 2 of 3

H Chargeable Gains after reliefs but before losses and taper	I Enter 'Bus' if business asset	J Taper rate	K Losses deducted			L Gains after losses	M Tapered gains (gains from column L x % in column J)
			K1 Allowable losses of the year	K2 Income losses set against gains	K3 Unused losses b/f from earlier years		
£		%	£	£	£	£	£
£		%	£	£	£	£	£
£		%	£	£	£	£	£
£		%	£	£	£	£	£
£		%	£	£	£	£	£
£		%	£	£	£	£	£
£		%	£	£	£	£	£
£		%	£	£	£	£	£
£	Bus	%	£	£	£	£	£
£		%	£	£	£	£	£
£	Bus	%	£	£	£	£	£
£		%	£	£	£	£	£

Total 5.1 £ _____ Total column H

5.5 £ Total column K2 **5.6** £ Total column K3

5.6B £ Total column M

Losses arising

Boxes 5.3 and 5.4 are not used on these Pages

Amount chargeable on the settlor **5.6A** £ _____

£ 1,240

£ 5,518

Total taxable gains (after allowable losses and taper relief)

box 5.6B minus box 5.6A

£ _____

£ 599

Copy to box 5.7 on Page TC1

£ 921

year 5.2 £ _____ *Copy to box 5.12 on Page TC1 and unless you need only complete the totals boxes (see page TCN4), complete column K1*

BS 12/04net

TRUST AND ESTATE TAX RETURN ■ CAPITAL GAINS: PAGE TC3

337

Your 2004-05 Capital Gains Tax liability

Ref: 1234 567890
Page 3 of 3

A Brief description of asset	AA* Type of disposal. Enter Q, U, L or O	B Tick box if estimate or valuation used	C Tick box if asset held at 31March 1982	D Enter the later of date of acquisition and 16 March 1998	E Enter the date of disposal	F Disposal proceeds	G Enter details of any elections made, reliefs claimed or due and state amounts (£)
Gains on assets which are either wholly business or wholly non-business							
1				/ /	/ /	£	
2				/ /	/ /	£	
3				/ /	/ /	£	
4				/ /	/ /	£	
5				/ /	/ /	£	
6				/ /	/ /	£	
7				/ /	/ /	£	
8				/ /	/ /	£	
Gains on assets which are partly business and partly non-business (see the notes on pages TCN17)							
9				/ ./	/ /	£	
10				/ /	/ /	£	

* For transactions in
  - quoted shares or other securities (the definition is on page TCN2), enter **Q**
  - other shares or securities, enter **U**
  - land and property, enter **L**
  - other assets (for example, goodwill or valuable antiques), enter **O**

➤ *Complete Pages TC5 to TC7 for all transactions identified as U, L or O*

Losses

Description of asset	Type of * disposal. Enter Q, U, L or O	Tick box if estimate or valuation used	Tick box if asset held at 31March 1982	Enter the later of date of acquisition and 16 March 1998	Enter the date of disposal	Disposal proceeds	Enter details of any elections made, reliefs claimed or due and state amounts (£)
13 M&G High IncomeFund - 1,765.25 Income units	Q			24/07/02	22/11/06	£ 1,716	
14 Merrill Lynch UK Gen Fund - 1,207.828 Acc unit	Q			24/07/02	22/11/06	£ 625	
15				/ /	/ /	£	
16				/ /	/ /	£	
						Total losses of	

338

Ref:1234 567890
Page 3 of 3

	H Chargeable Gains after reliefs but before losses and taper	I Enter 'Bus' if business asset	J Taper rate	K Losses deducted			L Gains after losses	M Tapered gains (gains from column L x % in column J)
				K1 Allowable losses of the year	K2 Income losses set against gains	K3 Unused losses b/f from earlier years		
	£		%	£	£	£	£	£
	£		%	£	£	£	£	£
	£		%	£	£	£	£	£
	£		%	£	£	£	£	£
	£		%	£	£	£	£	£
	£		%	£	£	£	£	£
	£		%	£	£	£	£	£
	£		%	£	£	£	£	£
	£	Bus	%	£	£	£	£	£
	£		%	£	£	£	£	£
	£	Bus	%	£	£	£	£	£
	£		%	£	£	£	£	£

Total **5.1** £ _____ Total column H

5.5 £ _____ Total column K2   **5.6** £ _____ Total column K3

5.6B £ _____ Total column M

Losses arising

Boxes 5.3 and 5.4 are not used on these Pages

Amount chargeable on the settlor **5.6A** £ _____

	Losses arising
	£ 922
	£ 1,991
	£
	£

box 5.6B *minus* box 5.6A
£ _____

Total taxable gains (after allowable losses and taper relief)

Copy to box 5.7 on Page TC1

year **5.2** £ _____   ➤ *Copy to box 5.12 on Page TC1 and unless you need only complete the totals boxes (see page TCN4), complete column K1*

Other events in the year

Ignore this Page if you are a personal representative

Please tick the boxes which apply and provide the information requested.

Has any person holding an interest in possession in settled property died during the year?
If yes, tick the box and give details below **5.19** ☐

Name and address of life tenant or liferenter, etc.

Date of death
/   /

Has any person become absolutely entitled to any part of the property during the year?
If yes, tick the box and give details below **5.20** ☐

Name and address of beneficiary

Miss Katrina Slade
The Old House
Fleetwood
Lancashire
LA32 7FW

Date beneficiary became absolutely entitled
22 / 11 / 2006

Nature of asset

Property at 48 Main Road, Catmint Village, Kendal, Mintshire, KL15 7YZ
Proceeds from disposal of investments held in trust
(see pages TCN2 and 3)

Value of asset vesting
£ 212, 270

Amount of loss transferred to beneficiary
5.20A £ 0

Have the trustees ceased being resident in the UK, or did they become dual resident?
If yes, tick the box and give details below **5.21** ☐

Description of assets held

Date of change
/   /

Amount of chargeable gains
£

Were any chargeable gains chargeable on the settlor?
If yes, tick the box and give details below **5.22** ☐

Name and address of settlor

Amount of chargeable gains
£

Enter this amount in box 5.6A on Page TC3

If you have used an extra sheet, tick this box **5.23** ☐

Now go back to page 3 of the Trust and Estate Tax Return and finish filling it in.

Other shares or securities (U) - further information

If you have more than two transactions of this type of asset to return, please photocopy this Page **before** completion and send all completed Pages with your Tax Return.

1st transaction

Description of shares or securities - including name of company, company registration number (if known), number, class and nominal value of shares. Also, if possible, give a history of the shares disposed of, for instance, if there has been a reorganisation or takeover (give details of the original company and shares held in that company).

Tick box if you have already submitted form CG34

State any connection between you and the person from whom you acquired the asset or to whom you disposed of the asset (see Notes, page TCN13)

If you have used an estimate or valuation in your capital gains computation but have not submitted form CG34, please enter the date to which the valuation relates, the amount (£) and the reason for the estimate or valuation. Please also attach a copy of any valuation obtained.

2nd transaction

Description of shares or securities - including name of company, company registration number (if known), number, class and nominal value of shares. Also, if possible, give a history of the shares disposed of, for instance, if there has been a reorganisation or takeover (give details of the original company and shares held in that company).

Tick box if you have already submitted form CG34

State any connection between you and the person from whom you acquired the asset or to whom you disposed of the asset (see Notes, page TCN13)

If you have used an estimate or valuation in your capital gains computation but have not submitted form CG34, please enter the date to which the valuation relates, the amount (£) and the reason for the estimate or valuation. Please also attach a copy of any valuation obtained.

Land and property (L) - further information

If you have more than two transactions of this type of asset to return, please photocopy this Page **before** completion and send all completed Pages with your Tax Return.

1st transaction

Full address of land/property affected (attach a copy of any plan if this helps identification)

48 Main Road, Catmint Village, Kendal, Mintshire, KL15 7YZ

Description of land/property disposed of, including details of your ownership, for example freehold/leasehold and any tenancies affecting your ownership at the date of disposal and any other date for which a valuation has been made, and except in the case of an outright disposal of all of your interests, the interest which you have disposed of, or granted.

Tick box if you have already submitted form CG34 ☐

The trust held the freehold of the property, which is let on an assured shorthold tenancy (copy enclosed). The property is a semi-detached house and the trustees also own 46 Main Road, the other half of the building.

State any connection between you and the person from whom you acquired the asset or to whom you disposed of the asset (see Notes, page TCN13)

The property was transferred to Miss Katrina Slade, a beneficiary of the Trust, as part of the capital due to her.

If you have used an estimate or valuation in your capital gains computation but have not submitted form CG34, please enter the date to which the valuation relates, the amount (£) and the reason for the estimate or valuation. Please also attach a copy of any valuation obtained.

The market value of the property at 22 November 2006 is estimated at £180,000. Miss Slade became absolutely entitled to her share of the trust capital at that date. We enclose a copy of the valuation obtained from Mr I Survey, FRICS.

2nd transaction

Full address of land/property affected (attach a copy of any plan if this helps identification)

Description of land/property disposed of, including details of your ownership, for example freehold/leasehold and any tenancies affecting your ownership at the date of disposal and any other date for which a valuation has been made, and except in the case of an outright disposal of all of your interests, the interest which you have disposed of, or granted.

Tick box if you have already submitted form CG34 ☐

State any connection between you and the person from whom you acquired the asset or to whom you disposed of the asset (see Notes, page TCN13)

If you have used an estimate or valuation in your capital gains computation but have not submitted form CG34, please enter the date to which the valuation relates, the amount (£) and the reason for the estimate or valuation. Please also attach a copy of any valuation obtained.

Other assets (O) - further information

If you have more than two transactions involving any other type of asset to return, please photocopy this Page **before** completion and send all completed Pages with your Tax Return.

1st transaction

Full description of the asset (other than shares or land/property) affected and any other information which helps identify the asset

Tick box if you have already submitted form CG34 ☐

State any connection between you and the
person from whom you acquired the asset
or to whom you disposed of the asset
(see Notes, page TCN13)

If you have used an estimate or valuation in your capital gains computation but have not submitted form CG34, please enter the date to which the valuation relates, the amount (£) and the reason for the estimate or valuation. Please also attach a copy of any valuation obtained.

2nd transaction

Full description of the asset (other than shares or land/property) affected and any other information which helps identify the asset

Tick box if you have already submitted form CG34 ☐

State any connection between you and the
person from whom you acquired the asset
or to whom you disposed of the asset
(see Notes, page TCN13)

If you have used an estimate or valuation in your capital gains computation but have not submitted form CG34, please enter the date to which the valuation relates, the amount (£) and the reason for the estimate or valuation. Please also attach a copy of any valuation obtained.

5.24 *Additional information*

344

Tax computation for year ended 5 April 2007

THE MARION FAIRWEATHER 1995 SETTLEMENT
TAX COMPUTATION
YEAR ENDED 5 APRIL 2007

	£	Total income £	Tax deducted at source £	Basic rate £	Lower rate £	Dividend rate £
					Applicable tax rate	
Rental income	8,550					
Less: Expenses	1,645	6,905		6,905		
Building society interest		2,190	438.00		2,190	
Bank interest		20	4.00		20	
Stockbroker account interest		316			316	
Dividends from UK companies		4,000	400.00			4,000
Dividends from UK unit trusts and OEICs		1,500	150.00			1,500
		14,931	992.00	6,905	2,526	5,500
Less: Allowable management expenses	450					
Grossed up at 10%	50	500				500
		14,431		6,905	2,526	5,000

THE MARION FAIRWEATHER 1995 SETTLEMENT
TAX COMPUTATION
YEAR ENDED 5 APRIL 2007 (continued)

	£	Total income £	Tax deducted at source £	Basic rate £	Lower rate £	Dividend rate £
				Applicable tax rate		
Tax at basic rate or equivalent		2,574.30		1,519.10	505.20	550.00
Tax at rate applicable to trusts (part income only)		1,917.35		756.00	317.60	843.75
		4,491.65		2,275.10	822.80	1,393.75
Less: Tax deducted at source and tax credits		992.00				
Income tax due for 2006/07		3,499.65				
Capital gains tax		28,407.60				
Total tax due for 2006/07		31,907.25				
Less: Payments on account made		2,700.00				
Tax due on 31 January 2008		£29,207.25				
First payment on account for 2007/08 Due 31 January 2008		£1,749.83				
Second payment on account for 2007/08 Due 31 July 2008		£1,749.82				

Capital gains computation for year ended 5 April 2007

THE MARION FAIRWEATHER 1995 SETTLEMENT
CAPITAL GAINS COMPUTATION
YEAR ENDED 5 APRIL 2007

	Indexation factor	Date	Nominal	Cost	Indexation	Indexed pool £	Proceeds	Gains before taper or loss relief £	Loss relief £	Gains after loss relief £	Complete years for taper relief	Taper relief %	Gains after taper and loss relief £
City of London Investment Trust plc													
Ordinary shares													
Sold		15 Sep 99	3,500	8,750									
		22 Nov 06	(1,750)	(4,375)			3,811	(564)	564	0	7	75	0
Carried forward			1,750	(4,375)									
Henderson Electric & General Investment Trust plc													
Ordinary shares													
Sold		26 Aug 05	800	16,000									
		25 Jul 06	(800)	(16,000)			26,894	10,894	(10,894)	0	0	100	0
Carried forward			0	0									
HSBC plc													
Ordinary shares													
Sold		26 Aug 05	1,000	7,143									
		22 Nov 06	(500)	(3,572)			4,293	721	(721)	0	0	100	0
Carried forward			500	3,571									

THE MARION FAIRWEATHER 1995 SETTLEMENT
CAPITAL GAINS COMPUTATION
YEAR ENDED 5 APRIL 2007 (continued)

	Indexation factor	Date	Nominal	Cost	Indexation	Indexed pool £	Proceeds	Gains before taper or loss relief £	Loss relief £	Gains after loss relief £	Complete years for taper relief	Taper relief %	Gains after taper and loss relief £
Imperial Chemical Industries													
Ordinary shares		26 Aug 05	2,500	12,843									
Sold		22 Nov 06	(1,250)	(6,422)			3,084	(3,338)	3,338	0	0	100	0
Carried forward			1,250	6,421									
P & O Princess Cruises													
Ordinary shares		15 Mar 06	2,000	5,873									
Sold		22 Nov 06	(1,000)	(2,937)			3,455	518	(518)	0	0	100	0
Carried forward			1,000	2,936									
Prudential													
Ordinary shares		15 Mar 06	3,000	5,170									
Sold		22 Nov 06	(1,750)	(3,016)			1,221	(1,795)	1,795	0	5	85	0
Carried forward			1,250	2,154									
Scottish Power													
Ordinary shares		30 Nov 00	900	2,550									
Sold		22 Nov 06	(450)	(1,275)			1,897	622	(622)	0	5	85	0
Carried forward			450	1,275									
Shell (Transport & Trading) plc													
Ordinary shares		20 Aug 95	1,570	10,000		10,000							
Indexation	0.085				850	850							
						10,850							
Sold		22 Nov 06	(785)	(5,000)	(425)	(5,425)	3,760	(1,240)	1,240	0	9	65	0
Carried forward			785	5,000	425	5,425							

THE MARION FAIRWEATHER 1995 SETTLEMENT
CAPITAL GAINS COMPUTATION
YEAR ENDED 5 APRIL 2007 (continued)

	Indexation factor	Date	Nominal	Cost	Indexation	Indexed pool £	Proceeds	Gains before taper or loss relief £	Loss relief £	Gains after loss relief £	Complete years for taper relief	Taper relief %	Gains after taper and loss relief £
Temple Bar Investment Trust plc													
Ordinary shares		9 May 96	2,450	16,870		16,870							
Indexation	0.063				1,063	1,063							
				16,870	1,063	17,933							
Sold		22 Nov 06	(900)	(6,197)	(390)	(6,587)	6,205	0		0	9	65	0
Carried forward			1,550	4,375	275	4,650							
Temple Bar Investment Trust plc													
Ordinary shares		15 Mar 06	650	10,000									
Sold		22 Nov 06	(650)	(10,000)			4,482	(5,518)	5,518	0	0	100	0
Carried forward			0	0									
Vodafone plc													
Ordinary shares		15 Mar 06	1,000	2,594									
Sold		22 Nov 06	(500)	(1,297)			698	(599)	599	0	0	100	0
Carried forward			500	1,297									
Witan													
Ordinary shares		30 Nov 00	1,500	6,912									
Sold		22 Nov 06	(750)	(3,456)			2,535	(921)	921	0	5	65	0
Carried forward			750	3,456									

349

THE MARION FAIRWEATHER 1995 SETTLEMENT
CAPITAL GAINS COMPUTATION
YEAR ENDED 5 APRIL 2007 (continued)

	Indexation factor	Date	Nominal	Cost	Indexation	Indexed pool £	Proceeds	Gains before taper or loss relief £	Loss relief £	Gains after loss relief £	Complete years for taper relief	Taper relief %	Gains after taper and loss relief £
M & G High Income Fund													
Income units													
Sold		24 Jul 02	3,530.500	5,000									0
		22 Nov 06	(1,765.250)	(2,500)			1,578	(922)	922	0	4	90	
Carried forward			1,765.250	2,500									
Merrill Lynch UK General Fund													
Accumulation units													
Sold		24 Jul 02	2415.655	5,000									0
		22 Nov 06	(1207.828)	(2,500)			509	(1,991)	1,991	0	4	90	
Carried forward			1,207.827	2,500									
Property at 48 Main Road, Catmint Village, Kendal, Mintshire KL15 7YZ													
Market value at 5 July 1995 (agreed with District Valuer)				50,000									
Indexation July 1995 to April 1998	0.091			4,550									
Total of acquisition cost plus indexation				54,550			174,250	119,700	(4,133)	115,567	9	65	75,119
									0				
													75,119
Less: Annual exemption													(4,100)
Net gains chargeable to tax													71,019
Potential capital gains tax liability													£28,407.60

Forms and Checklists

Form IHT100 – with IHT100b, IHT100c and IHT100d

Inland Revenue Account for Inheritance Tax

Inland Revenue Capital Taxes

Fill in this account to tell us about any of the events listed below. You should read the related guidance notes before filling in any particular box on this or the accompanying forms. Complete all names and addresses in CAPITALS.

A · About the Chargeable event

Tick one of the following boxes.

		Tick box	Event form
A1	Gifts and other transfers of value including failed potentially exempt transfers.		IHT100a
A2	Ending of an interest in possession in settled property.		IHT100b
A3	Assets in a discretionary trust ceasing to be relevant property (proportionate charge).		IHT100c
A4	Discretionary trust ten-year anniversary (principal charge).		IHT100d
A5	Assets ceasing to be held on special trusts (flat rate charge). *See page 9 of the notes "How to fill in form IHT100".*		IHT100e
A6	Cessation of conditional exemption and disposal of trees or underwood (recapture charge).		IHT100f

This account must be accompanied by the event form shown against the box you have ticked.

B · About the transferor/settlement

Title of transferor/settlor
B1

Surname of the transferor/settlor
B2

Forename(s) of the transferor/settlor
B3

Address, or last usual address of the transferor/settlor
B4

Post Code

Date of birth of the transferor/settlor
B5

Date of death of the transferor/settlor (where appropriate)
B6

IHT reference for the transferor/settlor (where appropriate)
B7

Tax District of the transferor/settlor
B8

Income tax or self assessment reference of the transferor/settlor
B9

National Insurance number of the transferor/settlor
B10

Domicile of the
• settlor when the settlement was made, or
• testator at the date of death, or
• transferor at the date of transfer
B11

Name of the settlement (where appropriate)
B12

IHT reference for the settlement (if known)
B13

Income tax reference for the settlement
B14

IHT100   093120022003DTP

C *Person we should contact*

Name and address of the person to whom
communications should be sent

C1

DX number and exchange

C3

Telephone number

C4

Reference

C5

Post code

Contact name C2

Capacity C6

Important. Read the following notes and the more detailed instructions in IHT110 "How to fill in form IHT100" before filling in the rest of this form. One of the event forms IHT100a, IHT100b, IHT100c, IHT100d, IHT100e or IHT100f must be filled in and returned with this form.

Fill in **D** **E** and **F** to tell us about *the assets included in the chargeable event you are telling us about as follows:*

If you have ticked box
- *A1 tell us about the assets that were given or transferred.*
- *A2 tell us about the assets in respect of which this interest in possession ceased.*
- *A3 tell us about the assets that ceased to be relevant property. (Proportionate charge).*
- *A4 tell us about the relevent property in the settlement. (Principal charge).*
- *A5 tell us about the assets which ceased to be held on special trusts. (Flat rate charge).*
- *A6 tell us about the assets on which a charge to inheritance tax arises. (Recapture charge).*

D *Supplementary pages*

You must answer all the questions in this section. You should read the notes starting at page 12 of form IHT110 before answering the questions. If you answer *yes* to a question you will need to fill in the supplementary pages shown. If you do not have all of the supplementary pages you should telephone our Orderline on 0845 234 1000.

		Yes	No	
• *Domicile outside the United Kingdom*	Was the transferor domiciled outside the UK at the date of the transfer or the date of the settlement?			D31
• *Stocks and shares*	Do the assets about which you are telling us include stocks and shares?			D32
• *Debts due to the settlement*	Was there any money on loan from the settlement either on mortgage or by personal loan, that had not been repaid at the date of the chargeable event?			D33
• *Insurance*	Were any insurance policies included in the transfer?			D34
• *Household and personal goods*	Do the assets being reported include household and personal goods?			D35
• *Land and buildings: Interests in land: Trees or underwood*	Do the assets being reported include any land, buildings, trees or underwood in the UK?			D36
• *Agricultural relief*	Are you deducting agricultural relief?			D37
• *Business relief*	Are you claiming business relief?			D38
• *Foreign assets*	Do the assets being reported include any assets outside the UK?			D39
• *Other information*	Use this form to provide any additional information.			D40

2

353

E Assets in the UK where tax may not be paid by instalments

Quoted stocks, shares and investments *(box SS1 form D32)*	E1	£0.00
UK Government and municipal securities *(box SS2 form D32)*	E2	£0.00
Unquoted stocks and shares *(details from form D32)*	E3	£0.00
Traded unquoted stocks and shares *(details from form D32)*	E4	£0.00
Dividends or interest *(details from form D32)*	E5	£0.00
National Savings Investments *(show details on form D40)*	E6	£0.00
Bank and building society accounts *(show details on form D40)*	E7	£0.00
Cash	E8	£0.00
Debts due to the settlement or trust and secured on mortgage *(box DD1 form D33)*	E9	£0.00
Other debts due to the settlement *(box DD1 form D33)*	E10	£0.00
Life assurance policies *(box IP1 form D34)*	E11	£0.00
Capital gains tax repayment	E12	£0.00
Household and personal goods *(box HG1 form D35)*	E13	£0.00
Other assets *(show details on form D40)*	E14	£0.00
Total assets *(sum of boxes E1 to E14)*	E15	£0.00

- **Liabilities**

Name of creditor	Description of liability	Amount £
		£0.00
		£0.00
		£0.00
Total liabilities	E16	£0.00
Net total of assets less liabilities *(box E15 less box E16)*	E17	£0.00

- *Exemption and reliefs (Do not include any annual exemption)*

Total Exemptions and reliefs	E18	£0.00
Chargeable value of assets in the UK where tax may *not* be paid by instalments *(box E17 less box E18)*	E19	£0.00

3

354

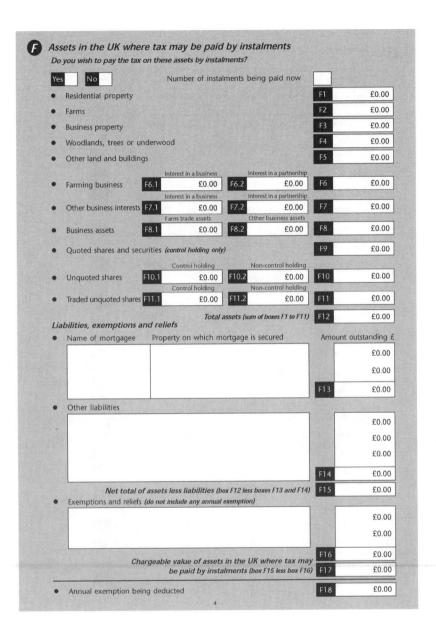

F **Assets in the UK where tax may be paid by instalments**

Do you wish to pay the tax on these assets by instalments?

Yes ☐ No ☐   Number of instalments being paid now ☐

● Residential property	F1	£0.00
● Farms	F2	£0.00
● Business property	F3	£0.00
● Woodlands, trees or underwood	F4	£0.00
● Other land and buildings	F5	£0.00

	Interest in a business		Interest in a partnership			
● Farming business	F6.1	£0.00	F6.2	£0.00	F6	£0.00

	Interest in a business		Interest in a partnership			
● Other business interests	F7.1	£0.00	F7.2	£0.00	F7	£0.00

	Farm trade assets		Other business assets			
● Business assets	F8.1	£0.00	F8.2	£0.00	F8	£0.00

● Quoted shares and securities *(control holding only)*	F9	£0.00

	Control holding		Non-control holding			
● Unquoted shares	F10.1	£0.00	F10.2	£0.00	F10	£0.00

	Control holding		Non-control holding			
● Traded unquoted shares	F11.1	£0.00	F11.2	£0.00	F11	£0.00

Total assets (sum of boxes F1 to F11)	F12	£0.00

Liabilities, exemptions and reliefs

● Name of mortgagee   Property on which mortgage is secured   Amount outstanding £

	£0.00
	£0.00
F13	£0.00

● Other liabilities

	£0.00
	£0.00
	£0.00
F14	£0.00

Net total of assets less liabilities (box F12 less boxes F13 and F14)	F15	£0.00

● Exemptions and reliefs *(do not include any annual exemption)*

	£0.00
	£0.00
F16	£0.00

Chargeable value of assets in the UK where tax may be paid by instalments (box F15 less box F16)	F17	£0.00

● Annual exemption being deducted	F18	£0.00

4

355

G **Summary of the chargeable event**

If you wish to work out the tax yourself you should fill in form IHT100WS so that you can copy the figures to this section and to section H. You do not have to work out the tax. If you do not wish to do so, leave this section and section H blank and go straight to section I.
Guidance on how to fill in parts G and H are given on page 25 of the guide - "How to fill in form IHT100". The box number WSA1 etc, refer to the boxes in the worksheet from which the figures come.

Lifetime transfers (event forms IHT100a and IHT100b)

Previous transfers made by the transferor which need to be taken into account *(box WSA1)*	G1	£0.00
Threshold at date of transfer *(box TX2)*	G2	£0.00
Balance of threshold available *(box TX3)*	G3	£0.00

Assets where the tax may not be paid by instalments

• Assets in the UK *(box WSA2)*	G4	£0.00
• Foreign assets *(box WSA3)*	G5	£0.00
Value of assets where tax may not be paid by instalments *(box WSA4)*	G6	£0.00

Assets where the tax may be paid by instalments

• Assets in the UK *(box WSA5)*	G7	£0.00
• Foreign assets *(box WSA6)*	G8	£0.00
Total assets where tax may be paid by instalments *(box WSA7)*	G9	£0.00
Total value of transfer *(box WSA8)*	G10	£0.00
Annual exemption *(box WSA9)*	G11	£0.00
Chargeable transfer (box WSA10)	G12	£0.00

Go to box H1 on page 6 to work out the tax.

Non-interest in possession settlements (event forms IHT100c and IHT100d)

Assets where the tax may not be paid by instalments

• Assets in the UK *(box WSB1)*	G13	£0.00
• Foreign assets *(box WSB2)*	G14	£0.00
Value of assets where tax may not be paid by instalments *(box WSB3)*	G15	£0.00

Assets where the tax may be paid by instalments

• Assets in the UK *(box WSB4)*	G16	£0.00
• Foreign assets *(box WSB5)*	G17	£0.00
• Value of assets where tax may be paid by instalments *(box WSB6)*	G18	£0.00
• *Total value on which tax is chargeable (box WSB7)*	G19	£0.00

Go to box H7 on page 6 to work out the tax

5

Flat rate charge and Recapture charge (event forms IHT100e and IHT100f)

- Value of assets where tax may not be paid by instalments
  (flat rate charge box WSC3: recapture charge box WSD3) | **G20** | £0.00 |

- Value of assets where tax may be paid by instalments
  (flat rate charge box WSC6: recapture charge box WSD4) | **G21** | £0.00 |

- Total value of assets on which tax arises
  (flat rate charge box WSC7: recapture charge box WSD5) | **G22** | £0.00 |

ⓗ *Working out the tax*

Lifetime transfers (event forms IHT100a and IHT100b)

- Value chargeable to tax *(box WSA10)* | **H1** | £0.00 |
- *Tax (box TX9)* | **H2** | £0.00 |
- Relief on successive charges *(box TX10)* | **H3** | £0.00 |
- Double taxation relief *(box TX11)* | **H4** | £0.00 |
- Tax previously paid on this transfer, if any *(box TX12)* | **H5** | £0.00 |
- *Tax due on this transfer (box TX13) Go to box H13* | **H6** | £0.00 |

Principal and proportionate charges (event forms IHT100c and IHT100d)

Value on which tax is chargeable *(box WSB7)* | **H7** | £0.00 |

Rate *(box R24)* | **H8** | £0.00 |

Tax *(principal charge box TX39 plus box TX46: proportionate charge box TX59 plus box TX67)* | **H9** | £0.00 |

Reduction against tax *(principal charge only box TX40 plus box TX47)* | **H10** | £0.00 |

Double taxation relief *(principal charge box TX42 plus box TX49: proportionate charge box TX60 plus box TX68)* | **H11** | £0.00 |

Tax payable on this transfer
(principal charge box TX43 plus box TX50: proportionate charge box TX61 plus box TX69) | **H12** | £0.00 |

Working out the tax that is payable on this account

• *Lifetime transfers*	• *Principal charge*	• *Proportionate charge*

- Tax which may not be paid by instalments
  (lifetime: box TX18, principal: box TX41, proportionate: box TX59) | **H13** | £0.00 |

- Successive charges relief *(lifetime: box TX19)* | **H14** | £0.00 |

- Double taxation relief
  (lifetime: box TX20, principal: box TX42, proportionate: box TX60) | **H15** | £0.00 |

- Tax previously paid, if any *(box TX21)* | **H16** | £0.00 |

- Interest *(lifetime: box TX23, principal: box TX44, proportionate: box TX62)* | **H17** | £0.00 |

Tax and interest which may not be paid by instalments
(lifetime: box TX24, principal: box TX45, proportionate: box TX63) | **H18** | £0.00 |

6

357

- Tax which may be paid by instalments
  (lifetime box TX29: principal box TX48: proportionate box TX67) **H19** £0.00

- Successive charges relief *(lifetime box TX30)* **H20** £0.00

- Double taxation relief
  (lifetime box TX31: principal box TX49: proportionate box TX68) **H21** £0.00

- Tax previously paid *(lifetime box TX32)* **H22** £0.00

- Number of instalments being paid now
  (lifetime box TX34: principal box TX51: proportionate box TX70) **H23** / 10

- Tax now payable
  (lifetime box TX35: principal box TX52: proportionate box TX71) **H24** £0.00

- Interest on instalments to be added
  (lifetime box TX36: principal box TX53: proportionate box TX72) **H25** £0.00

- *Tax and interest being paid now which may be paid by instalments*
  (lifetime box TX37: principal box TX54: proportionate box TX73) **H26** £0.00

- *Total tax and interest payable on this account*
  (lifetime box TX38: principal box TX55: proportionate box TX74) **H27** £0.00

Working out the tax. Flat rate charge (event form IHT100e)
Recapture charge (event form IHT100f)

- Tax which may not be paid by instalments
  (flat rate charge box TX75: recapture charge box TX104 or box TX117) **H28** £0.00

- Double taxation relief on the tax which may not be paid by
  instalments *(flat rate charge box TX76)* **H29** £0.00

- Tax not payable by instalments *(flat rate charge box TX77)* **H30** £0.00

- Interest *(flat rate charge box TX78: recapture charge box TX105 or box TX118)* **H31** £0.00

- *Tax which may not be paid by instalments and interest now*
  payable (flat rate charge box TX79: recapture charge box TX106 or box TX119) **H32** £0.00

- Tax which may be paid by instalments
  (flat rate charge box TX80: recapture charge box TX110 or box TX120) **H33** £0.00

- Double taxation relief on the tax which may be paid by instalments
  (flat rate charge box TX81) **H34** £0.00

- Tax which may be paid by instalments
  (flat rate charge box TX82) **H35** £0.00

- Number of instalments due *(flat rate charge box TX83: recapture charge*
  box TX111 or box TX121) **H36** / 10

- Tax now payable *(flat rate charge box TX84: recapture charge box TX112 or*
  box TX122) **H37** £0.00

- Interest *(flat rate charge box TX85: recapture charge box TX113 or box TX123)* **H38** £0.00

- *Tax which may be paid by instalments and interest now payable*
  (flat rate charge box TX86: recapture charge box TX114 or box TX124) **H39** £0.00

- *Tax and interest now payable on this account*
  (flat rate charge box TX87: recapture charge box TX115 or box TX125) **H40** £0.00

7

358

J Authority for repayment of inheritance tax

In the event of any inheritance tax being overpaid the payable order for the overpaid tax and interest in connection with this chargeable event estate should be made out to:

K Declaration

To the best of my/our knowledge and belief, the information I/we have given and the statements I/we have made in this account and in the event form

K1

and the supplementary pages

K2

attached (together called "this account") are correct and complete.

I/We understand that I/we may be liable to prosecution if I/we deliberately conceal any information that affects the liability to inheritance tax arising on the chargeable event OR if I/we deliberately include information in this account which I/we know to be false.

I/We understand that I/we may have to pay financial penalties if this account is incorrect by reason of my/our fraud or negligence OR if I/we fail to remedy anything in this account which is incorrect in any material respect within a reasonable time of it coming to my/our notice.

I/We understand that where we have elected to pay tax by instalments that I/we may have to pay interest on any unpaid tax according to the law.

Each person delivering this account whether as transferor, transferee or trustee, must sign below to indicate that they have read and agreed the statements above.

Full name and address	Full name and address
Signature Date	Signature Date
Capacity:	Capacity:
Full name and address	Full name and address
Signature Date	Signature Date
Capacity:	Capacity:

See notes

8

359

Inland Revenue
Capital Taxes

Termination of an interest in possession

Note: If you are telling us about the ending of an interest in possession in settled property on the death of a life tenant do not work out the tax. We will do that for you.

Name of transferor

Date of transfer

1 About the transfer

1.1

Names and addresses of transferees	Relationship with transferor	Share and/or interest taken

1.2 Name and address of the person who will pay any tax due on this transfer.

Name	Address

1.3 Did the interest in possession come to an end on the death of the life tenant?

Yes ☐ Go to section 5   No ☐ Answer question 1.4

1.4 Did the transferor receive any assets in return for the assets transferred?

Yes ☐ Answer question 1.5   No ☐ Go to question 1.6

1.5 Describe the assets received

	Value at date of transfer
	£0.00
	£0.00
	£0.00
Total	£0.00

1.6 Was the transfer part of a wider series of transactions or arrangements?

Yes ☐ Answer question 1.7   No ☐ Go to question 1.8

IHT100b

1

093921022003DTP

360

1.7 Describe the position below

1.8 Was the transfer connected in any way with the purchase of or other dealing with an assurance policy or an annuity?

Yes ☐ *Answer question 1.9*   No ☐ *Go to question 2.1*

1.9 Describe the situation below

2 *Earlier transfers*

2.1 Is the transferor alive or did they survive the transfer by more than seven years?

Yes ☐ *Answer question 2.2*   No ☐ *Go to question 2.3*

2.2 Did the transferor make any gifts or other transfers of value that were chargeable to tax at the time they were made during the period of seven years ending on the date of this transfer?

Yes ☐ *Answer questions 2.4 and 2.5*

No ☐ N/A ☐ *Go to question 2.6*

2.3 Did the transferor make any gifts or other transfers of value (including potentially exempt transfers) during the seven years ending on the date of death and before the date of this transfer *or* any gifts or other transfers of value that were chargeable at the time they were made during the seven years ending on the date of this transfer.

Yes ☐ *Answer questions 2.4 and 2.5*

No ☐ *Go to question 2.6*

2.4 State the chargeable value of the previous transfers.   £0.00

2.5 State the IHT file reference for the previous transfers (if known)

2.6 Tax threshold   £0.00

The tax threshold to be used is normally the threshold applicable at the date of the gift you are telling us about. If this gift occurred within seven years of the date of the transferor's death and the threshold at that date is higher enter the tax threshold applicable at the date of death.

2

361

3   *Gift with reservation*

Answer only if the transferor has died

3.1 Did the transferee take full possession of the assets transferred?

> **Yes**   *Go to section 4*
>
> **No**   *Go to section 3.2*

3.2 If the gift was land, did the transferor or their spouse continue to enjoy any right or interest or were they party to any arrangement in relation to the land?

> **Yes**   **No**

3.3 If the gift was of any other asset(s) did the deceased continue to have any right from all or any part of the asset(s)?

> **Yes**   **No**

3.4 If you have answered **yes** to questions 3.2 or 3.3 state the value of the assets at the date of death or the time the rights, benefits or interest came to an end (if earlier) and describe the position below.

> £0.00

If you have answered 'No' to question 3.1 do not work out the tax yourself. We will work it out for you.

4   *Reliefs against tax*

Taper relief

Fill in this section if you wish to claim taper relief

4.1 Date of the transferor's death

4.2 Rate of relief   %

5   *Relief on successive charges*

Fill in this section if you wish to claim relief on successive charges

5.1 Date of transfer under which the assets which are comprised in this transfer became settled property in which the transferor had an interest in possession *(this is the first transfer)*

5.2 Net value of the first transfer   £0.00

5.3 Inheritance tax paid on the first transfer   £0.00

3

362

5.4	Assets from first transfer included in this transfer on which tax may *not* be paid by instalments	£0.00
5.5	Assets from first transfer included in this transfer on which tax may be paid by instalments	£0.00
5.6	Rate of relief	%

6	**Double taxation relief**	
	Fill in this section if you wish to claim double taxation relief	
6.1	Foreign tax paid on assets on which IHT may *not* be paid by instalments	£0.00
6.2	Foreign tax paid on assets on which IHT may be paid by instalments	£0.00
6.3	Total foreign tax paid *(box 6.1 plus box 6.2)*	£0.00

7	**Tax previously paid on this transfer (if any)**	
7.1	Tax which may *not* be paid by instalments	£0.00
7.2	Tax which may be paid by instalments	£0.00
7.3	Total *(box 7.1 plus box 7.2)*	£0.00

4

363

Inland Revenue Capital Taxes

Assets ceasing to be held on discretionary trusts. Proportionate charge

Note: if the settlement commenced before 27 March 1974 and the event you are telling us about took place before the first ten-year anniversary of the settlement contact our Helpline for advice. See page 2 of the guide 'How to fill in form IHT100' (IHT110).

Name of settlement

Date of commencement

1 About the chargeable event

1.1 Date of the chargeable event

1.2 Describe the chargeable event

1.3 Have the discretionary trusts come to an end? Yes ☐ No ☐

About the transferees

1.4 Names and addresses of the transferees

1.5 Share and interest taken

About the payment of tax

1.6 Tick this box if the tax is *not* being paid out of the assets ceasing to be held on discretionary trusts ☐

1.7 Inheritance tax threshold at the date of this transfer £0.00

2 Answer the questions in this section only if the chargeable event you are telling us about occurred within ten years of the commencement of the discretionary trust. (If the chargeable event you are telling us about took place more than ten years after the settlement commenced go to section 3).

2.1 Value of the assets comprised in the settlement immediately after it commenced. £0.00

2.2 Have any assets been added to the settlement since it commenced?

Yes ☐ Answer questions 2.3 and 2.4   No ☐ Go to question 2.5

2.3 Value of any assets added to the settlement after the date on which it commenced at the date they were added. £0.00

2.4 IHT file reference under which the additions were dealt with (if known).

IHT100c

1

094321022003DTP

2.5 Did the settlor set up any other settlements on the same day as this settlement?

Yes   Answer question 2.6   No   Go to question 2.7

2.6 State the total value of all the settlements made by the settlor on the same date as this settlement at the date on which the settlements were set up.   £0.00

2.7 Did the settlor make any other *chargeable* transfers during the seven years prior to the date of this settlement?

Yes   Answer question 2.8 and 2.9   No   Go to question 2.10

2.8 State the total value of chargeable transfers made by the settlor during the seven years immediately before this settlement was set up.   £0.00

2.9 State IHT file reference under which the previous transfers have been dealt with (if known).

2.10 Did any of the relevant property on which tax is now being charged become relevant property since the settlement commenced?

Yes   Answer question 2.11   No   Go to section 4

2.11

Description of asset(s)	Date on which the asset(s) last became relevant property	Value at the date the asset(s) last became relevant property
Assets on which the tax may *not* be paid by instalments		
		£0.00
		£0.00
		£0.00
		£0.00
		£0.00
	Total	£0.00
Assets on which the tax may be paid by instalments		
		£0.00
		£0.00
		£0.00
		£0.00
		£0.00
	Total	£0.00

3 *Answer the following questions if the chargeable event you are telling us about occurred more than ten years after the settlement commenced.*

3.1 Date of the last ten-year anniversary.

3.2 What was the value on which the rate of tax was calculated on the last ten-year anniversary of this settlement?   £0.00

3.3 State the total value on which proportionate charges arose in the ten years preceding the last ten-year anniversary.   £0.00

3.4 State the total value of previous chargeable transfers taken into account in calculating the tax at the last ten-year anniversary.   £0.00

3.5 Value of the Settlement at the date of the last ten-year anniversary to be taken into account *(box 3.2 minus 3.3 minus box 3.4)*.

£0.00

3.6 Have there been any additions to this settlement since the last ten-year anniversary?

Yes   *Answer question 3.7*   **No**   *Go to question 3.8*

3.7 Provide the following details about the additions to this settlement since the last ten-year anniversary.

Description of the asset(s)	Date on which the asset(s) was added to the settlement or if later the date on which it last became relevant property	Value of the asset(s) at the date it was added or if later the date it became relevant property
		£0.00
		£0.00
		£0.00
		£0.00
		£0.00
		£0.00
	Total	£0.00

3.8 Did any assets in the settlement at the date of the last ten-year anniversary which were not relevant property at that time, become relevant property between the date of the last ten-year anniversary and this chargeable event?

Yes   *Answer question 3.9*   **No**   *Go to question 3.10*

3.9 Provide the following information about the assets in the settlement at the date of the last ten-year anniversary which were not relevant property at that time, which have become relevant property between the date of the last ten-year anniversary and this chargeable event.

Date on which the asset(s) last became relevant property	Description of the asset(s)	Value at the last ten-year anniversary	Value at this chargeable event	Column D minus Column C
A	B	C £0.00	D £0.00	E £0.00
		£0.00	£0.00	£0.00
		£0.00	£0.00	£0.00
		£0.00	£0.00	£0.00
		£0.00	£0.00	£0.00
		£0.00	£0.00	£0.00
		£0.00	£0.00	£0.00
	Totals	£0.00	£0.00	£0.00

3

366

3.10 Are any assets which became relevant property since the date of the last ten-year anniversary comprised in this chargeable event?

| Yes | Answer question 3.11 | No | Go to section 4 |

3.11 Provide the following information about the assets comprised in the chargeable event which became relevant property since the last ten-year anniversary.

Assets on which the tax may **not** be paid by instalments		
Asset	Date on which the asset last became relevant property, or, if later the date of the last TYA	Value at this chargeable event
		£0.00
		£0.00
		£0.00
		£0.00
		£0.00
		£0.00

Assets on which the tax may be paid by instalments		
Asset	Date on which the asset last became relevant property, or, if later the date of the last TYA	Value at this chargeable event
		£0.00
		£0.00
		£0.00
		£0.00
		£0.00
		£0.00

4 Double taxation relief

Fill in this section if you wish to claim double taxation relief

4.1 Foreign tax paid on assets on which IHT may **not** be paid by instalments — £0.00

4.2 Foreign tax paid on assets on which IHT may be paid by instalments — £0.00

4.3 Total foreign tax paid *(box 4.1 plus box 4.2)* — £0.00

4

367

Non Interest in possession Settlements Principal charge (ten-year anniversary)

Inland Revenue Capital Taxes

Name of settlement

Date of Settlement

1.1 Date of ten-year anniversary

1.2 Did any of the relevant property in the settlement at the date of the ten-year anniversary become relevant property (1) after the settlement started and (2) during the ten-year period immediately before the ten-year anniversary?

Yes [ ] *Answer question 1.3*   No [ ] *Go to question 1.4*

1.3 Provide the following information about the relevant property in the settlement which became relevant property after the settlement started and during the ten-year period immediately before the ten-year anniversary.

Description of the asset	Date on which the asset last became relevant property	Value at the date of the ten-year anniversary
Assets on which tax may *not* be paid by instalments		
		£0.00
		£0.00
		£0.00
		£0.00
		£0.00
	Total	£0.00

Assets on which tax may be paid by instalments		
		£0.00
		£0.00
		£0.00
		£0.00
		£0.00
	Total	£0.00

1.4 Have any proportionate charges arisen in the period of ten years ending on the anniversary date?

Yes [ ] *Answer question 1.5*   No [ ] *Go to question 1.6*

1.5 State the total value on which proportionate charges arose in the ten years ending on the day before the present ten-year anniversary *(only include the amount taxable)*.   £0.00

1.6 Did the settlor make any other *chargeable* transfers during the seven years prior to the date of the settlement? *(Answer no if the settlement commenced before 27 March 1974)*.

Yes [ ] *Answer question 1.7*   No [ ] *Go to question 1.8*

IHT100d   1   095021022003DTP

1.7 State the total of chargeable transfers made by the settlor during the seven years ending immediately before the settlement was set up. *(Disregard any transfers made on or before 27th March 1974)·*   £0.00

1.8 Did the settlor make any chargeable transfer :

- after the settlement commenced and
- after 8th March 1982 and
- before the present ten-year anniversary

which increased the value of the settlement?

Yes *Answer question 1.9*   **No** *Go to question 1.10*

1.9 State the total value of the chargeable transfers made by the settlor during the seven years ending on the date of the transfer referred to in question 1.8. Ignore any transfers made on the date of the transfer referred to in question 1.8 and any transfers made into this settlement. *(If there was more than one such transfer answer the question by reference to the transfer that gives the highest amount. See notes in IHT110).*   £0.00

1.10 Enter the higher of 1.7 and 1.9.   £0.00

1.11 Have any assets been put into the settlement which are not and never have been relevant property? *(Answer no if the settlement commenced before 27 March 1974).*

Yes *Answer question 1.12*   **No** *Go to question 1.13*

1.12 Provide the following information in respect of the assets in the settlement which are not and never have been relevant property. *(Ignore if this settlement commenced before 27th March 1974).*

Description of the asset	Date on which the asset was placed in the settlement	Value at the date it was put into the settlement
Assets on which the tax may *not* be paid by instalments		
		£0.00
		£0.00
		£0.00
		£0.00
		£0.00
	Sub Total	£0.00
Assets on which the tax may be paid by instalments		
		£0.00
		£0.00
		£0.00
		£0.00
		£0.00
	Sub Total	£0.00

Total of all assets that are not and never have been relevant property   £0.00

2

369

1.13 Did the settlor make any other settlements on the same day as this settlement?
(Answer no if the settlement commenced before 27 March 1974).

| Yes | Answer questions 1.14 and 1.15 | No | Go to question 1.16 |

1.14 State the total value of all the settlements made by the settlor on the same date as this settlement at the date on which they were set up.

£0.00

1.15 State the IHT file reference for the other settlements

1.16 Threshold at the date of the chargeable event

£0.00

2 **Double taxation relief**

Are you claiming double taxation relief?

| Yes | Answer questions 2.1 to 2.3 | No | That completes this form |

2.1 Foreign tax paid on assets on which IHT may *not* be paid by instalments

£0.00

2.2 Foreign tax paid on assets on which IHT may be paid by instalments

£0.00

2.3 Total foreign tax paid *(box 2.1 plus box 2.2)*

£0.00

3

Trust creation – taxation checklist

1. Will there be a chargeable gain on creating the trust?

   (a) CGT holdover relief?

	Business property	Other property
• Interest in possession	Yes	No
• A&M	Yes	No
• Discretionary	Yes	Yes

   (b) s.260 holdover?
   (c) Any indexation allowance?
   (d) Taper relief:

	Business property	Non-business property
• Asset		
• No. of years		
• Percentage		

2. (a) Will the gift be a PET for IHT?

   - Interest in possession
   - A&M
   - Discretionary

   (b) If not, what is settlor's cumulative total?

3. (a) Will IHT business or agricultural property relief be available?
   (b) Is there any likelihood of clawback of relief?

4. Will settlor, spouse or civil partner be interested in the trust? (NB Risk of reservation of benefit for IHT)
5. What are the domicile, nationality and habitual residence of the settlor, trustees and beneficiaries?
6. What is the Settlor's state of health and insurability?
7. What is the effect of settlement likely to be on the settlor's future income, on his will and subsequent IHT position?

Trust instruction sheet

Instructing firm:		Contact person	
Contact telephone no:		Your ref:	
E-mail:			

Our ref:		Date instructions received:	
Cost estimate given:			

1. Settlor

Full name and title:	
Status:	
Date of birth:	
Age:	
Address:	
Domicile:	
Nationality	
Usual place of residence:	

2. Type of trust required: (delete as appropriate)

Interest in possession   Accumulation &   Discretionary   Bare
                             maintenance

3. Name to be given to trust:

4. Whom does the settlor wish to benefit?

Full name	Address	Date of birth and age	Relationship to settlor	Domicile	Nationality	Residence

5. In what way does the settlor wish the beneficiary to benefit

	✓ or x	Specification
Limited by time e.g. Life		
Only when attained a specified age e.g. 25		
Only when need is greatest		
Some other specified contingency		
On a discretionary basis		

6. Trustees

Full name	Address	Occupation	Relationship to settlor

7. Protector(s)

To be appointed	Yes	No

(especially relevant for non-resident discretionary trusts – have a veto for crucial powers of the trustees e.g. advancement, appointment, investment; adding/excluding beneficiaries; moving jurisdiction of trust, etc. In non-resident situation they should be non-resident)

Full name	Address	Occupation	Relationship to settlor

8. Trust fund – what property is to be settled?

Real property	Address	Nature of interest

Personal property	Description	Amount
(i) Chattels		
(ii) Cash		
(iii) Shares		
Is there to be a provision to add more in future?		

9. Ultimate/default beneficiary

(Note: Ultimate gifts should be unconditional/absolute e.g. to children, charity, etc. to avoid tax problems on reverter to settlor)

Full name	Address	Date of birth	Relationship to settlor

10. Position of trustees

	Settlor	Spouse	Exors	Trustees
Who will have the power to appoint/discharge trustees?				

	Unanimous?	By majority?
Is voting to be . . .		

	Yes	No
Exercise of powers – is settlor's consent to be required?		

11. If assets other than cash are going into trust there may be a chargeable gain on creating the trust. Who is to advise on tax consequences of creation?

Name	Address	Contact no.

12. Depending on the type of trust created there maybe an immediate charge to IHT. Who is to advise on tax consequences of creation?

Name	Address	Contact no.

13. What other lifetime gifts have been made? Please list all.

Assset	Value	Recipient

14. Transfer documents required. Who is to prepare these?
(For example share transfers, conveyances, etc. NOTE: for unquoted shares, review Memorandum & Articles of company to check pre-emption rights and obtaining waivers thereof)

Name	Address	Contact no.

15. Will settlor/spouse be interested?
(Risk of gift with reservation)

16. Settlor's state of health and insurability?

17. Effect of settlement on settlor's future income/will and subsequent IHT position

18. Timing – when required?

19. Notices? Who is to prepare?
(s.218 IHTA 1984 – where professionals, other than barristers, are concerned with the making of a non-resident settlement and the settlor is UK domiciled, notification must be given to the Revenue)

Name	Address	Contact no.

20. Settlor's wishes. Who is to prepare any memorandum/letter of wishes recording non-binding wishes of settlor to his trustees?

21. Motives. Please outline the settlor's main reasons for wanting to create a trust

22. Who will administer the trust? Please indicate if advice is needed upon what is required.

Name & address/Contact tel./E-mail		
Advice required? (✓ or x)	Yes	No

23. **List of settlor's other assets**

Asset	Value (£)	Liabilities

24. Any other relevant information

APPENDIX 2.4

Trust information form

Name of trust					
Client matter no.					
Document storage ref. no.		**Date created**			
Contact person in firm					
Creation document					
Other documents					
Associated trusts?					
Deed of variation?					
Appointments of new trustees?					
Appointments of capital?					

Trustees: Name				
Address				
Phone				
Fax				

Beneficiaries: Name	Address	Interest	Vesting date	UK resident?
1.				
2.				
3.				
4.				
5.				
6.				

Beneficiaries' special requirements or contingencies						
Income policy		Monthly ❏	Quarterly ❏	Half Yearly ❏	Yearly ❏	Accumulate ❏
Income beneficiaries						

Bank details	Current Ac. No.		Deposit Ac. No.		Sort Code	

Type of trust				
Controlled trust	Yes	❏	No	❏
Trust period				
Accumulation period				

Trustees' powers					
1. (a) Do the functions under Trusts of Land & Appointment of Trustees Act 1996 apply?					
(b) Are there any restrictions of extensions?					
2. Investment	STEP ❑	Trustee Act 2000 ❑	Other (specify)		
3. Appropriation	STEP ❑	s.41 Admin. Estates Act 1925 ❑	Other (specify		
4. Advancement/Benefit					
– Income	STEP ❑	s.31 Trustee Act 1925 ❑	Other (specify)		
– Capital	STEP ❑	s.32 Trustee Act 1925 ❑	Other (specify)		
5. Appointment of capital					
6. Insurance	STEP	s.19 Trustee Act 1925	Other (specify)		
7. Nominee company	STEP	❑	Other (specify)		Trustee Act 2000
8. Delegation	STEP	❑	Other (specify)		Trustee Act 2000
9. Right of occupation	s.12 TLATA 1996 ❑		Other (specify)		
10. Power to permit occupation					
Appointment of new trustees	Settlor ❑	Continuing trustees ❑	TLATA ❑	Other (specify)	
Special diary events					
Bank accounts	A/c No.	Institution (name, address, Tel. No.)			
– Income					
– Capital					
Building society a/cs	A/c No.	Institution (name, address, Tel. No.)			
– Income					
– Capital					
Taxation					
Income tax rate	Basic		Rate applicable to trusts		

CGT	Blanket election	Yes ❑ No ❑
	Indexation allowance details	
	Taper relief details	
	Holdover elections – details	
	Rollover details	
IHT	(a) Tax payable on settlor's death?	
	(b) Conditional exemption – heritage property?	
	(c) Relevant business/agricultural property	
	(d) 10-year anniversary dates	
	(e) Exit charges?	
Who is to prepare tax return?		
If accountants:	Name	
	Address	
	Tel. No.	
	Their ref.	
	Tax Office ref.	
	Name Tax Office	
	Address Tax Office	
	Tel. No. Tax Office	
	Contact person (if known)	

Investments	
Up-to-date portfolio listing	
Share histories & location of certificates (if any)	
Stockbroker/investment manager Name	
Address	
Tel. No.	
Contact person	
Authorisation under FSA	
Nominee company?	
Investment strategy	
Discretionary management ❑	Execution only ❑	Advisory ❑
FSA reminder date	

Land/Property		Property 1	Property 2
	Agent		
	Name		
	Address		
	Tel. No.		
	Contact person		
Who pays:	• Maintenance		
	• Insurance premium		
	• Council tax		
	• Any other outgoings		
Insurance details		**Real property**	**Chattels**
Insurance company			
	Name		
	Address		
	Tel. No.		
	Contact person		
Policy number			
Renewal date			
Amount of cover			

Property information form

Name of trust			
Client ref.		Deed packet No.	
Property			
Who is in occupation?		Interest in trust?	
Location of keys		Remarks	
Powers over property			
Freehold		Date built	
Leasehold		Date built	
Date of lease		Term of lease	
Annual rent		Annual service charge	
Payment dates			
Rent review date		Lease/Tenancy renewal date	
Name and address of lessor			

Name and address of managing agents or person to whom notice should be sent		Date notice sent	
Mortgage (if any)			
Lender's name			
Account No.			
Amount required to redeem as at date of death			
Outcome			
Assent			
Assignment			
Sale			
Insurance			
Postcode			

Number of bedrooms		Normal contruction	Yes ❑	No ❑

Detached ❑	Semi ❑	Terraced ❑	Bungalow ❑	Semi Bungalow ❑	Flat ❑

When property built	1919 or earlier	1920– 1945	1946– 1979	1980 onwards
Building value				

APPENDIX 2.6

Trust review form

Name of trust/settlement		Partner/Manager	
Client matter number		Administrator	
Document storage ref. No.		Date	

Type of trust/settlement – brief terms			
Date created		Date due to come to an end	
Date end of accumulation period		Is this a controlled trust?	Yes ❑ No ❑

Settlor	Name	
	Address	
	Tel. No.	
Current Trustees	Name 1.	
	Address	
	Tel. No.	
	Name 2.	
	Address	
	Tel. No.	
	Name 3.	
	Address	
	Tel. No.	
	Name 4.	
	Address	
	Tel. No.	

Beneficiaries	Name 1.			
	Address			
	Tel. No.		Date of birth	
	Name 2.			
	Address			
	Tel. No.		Date of birth	
	Name 3.			
	Address			
	Tel. No.		Date of birth	
	Name 4.			
	Address			
	Tel. No.		Date of birth	
Income policy	Monthly ❑	Quarterly ❑	Half Yearly ❑	Yearly ❑	Accumulate ❑

Review	Action
1. Do we have terms and conditions of business on file?	
2. Do we have a copy of the trust deeds on the copy documents file?	
3. If we are one of the trustees, have we reviewed our obligations on such matters as rent reviews, investment policy, etc.?	
4. Are all documents of title in correct form and up-to-date copies of minutes, etc., on file?	
5. Have we submitted a tax return for the last fiscal year? If not, what is the current position? Are any sanctions likely?	
6. Do we prepare accounts? If so, have these been done?	
7. Have we prepared and distributed R185 certificates/passed details of income and gains to beneficiaries' tax agent?	
8. Where appropriate, have we completed and submitted children's repayment claims?	
9. Have any necessary holdover elections been made for capital gains tax purposes? If not, when does the 6-year time limit expire?	
10. Have any assets been sold which are previously subject to a holdover claim?	

Review	Action
11. Has a 1982 rebasing election been made? If not, was there any relevant disposal in the previous 2 years?	
12 Have all FSA requirements been met?	
13. If controlled trust, have accounts been notified?	
14. Should the share portfolio be transferred to a nominee?	
15. Compare nominal amounts and values, descriptions, etc., to investment valuation and safe custody certificates and update records.	
16. Are we satisfied with investment performance? Does strategy neeed review in light of current tax/beneficiary changes?	
17. Is any real property adequately insured?	
18. If property is rented out, has all rent been received, bad debts provided for and any relevant legal action considered?	
19. Have any rent review provisions been dealt with?	
20. Deeds audit – are we holding correct title deeds?	
21. Is all personal property adequately insured?	

Administrator .... **Signed**

Partner .... **Signed**

Dated ....

Relevant legislation as amended at July 2005

1. Inheritance Tax Act 1984, s.71
2. Trustee Act 1925, s.31
3. Trustee Act 1925, s.32
4. Income and Corporation Taxes Act 1988, s.686
5. Income and Corporation Taxes 1988, s.687

Inheritance Tax Act 1984, s.71

71 ACCUMULATION AND MAINTENANCE TRUSTS

(1) Subject to subsection (2) below, this section applies to settled property if–

(a) one or more persons (in this section referred to as beneficiaries) will, on or before attaining a specified age not exceeding twenty-five, become beneficially entitled to it or to an interest in possession in it, and
(b) no interest in possession subsists in it and the income from it is to be accumulated so far as not applied for the maintenance, education or benefit of a beneficiary.

(2) This section does not apply to settled property unless either–

(a) not more than twenty-five years have elapsed since the commencement of the settlement or, if it was later, since the time (or latest time) when the conditions stated in paragraphs (a) and (b) of subsection (1) above became satisfied with respect to the property, or
(b) all the persons who are or have been beneficiaries are or were either–

(i) grandchildren of a common grandparent, or
(ii) children, widows or widowers of such grandchildren who were them-selves beneficiaries but died before the time when, had they survived, they would have become entitled as mentioned in subsection (1)(a) above.

(3) Subject to subsections (4) and (5) below, there shall be a charge to tax under this section–

(a) where settled property ceases to be property to which this section applies, and
(b) in a case in which paragraph (a) above does not apply, where the trustees make a disposition as a result of which the value of settled property to which this section applies is less than it would be but for the disposition.

(4) Tax shall not be charged under this section–

(a) on a beneficiary's becoming beneficially entitled to, or to an interest in possession in, settled property on or before attaining the specified age.
(b) on the death of a beneficiary before attaining the specified age.

(5) Subsections (3) to (8) and (10) of section 70 above shall apply for the purposes of this section as they apply for the purposes of that section (with the substitution of a reference to subsection (3)(b) above for the reference in section 70(4) to section 2(2)(b)).

(6) Where the conditions stated in paragraphs (a) and (b) of subsection (1) above were satisfied on 15th April 1976 with respect to property comprised in a settlement which commenced before that day, subsection (2)(a) above shall have effect with the substitution of a reference to that day for the reference to the commencement of the settlement, and the condition stated in subsection (2)(b) above shall be treated as satisfied if–

(a)   it is satisfied in respect of the period beginning with 15th April 1976, or
(b)   it is satisfied in respect of the period beginning with 1st April 1977 and either there was no beneficiary living on 15th April 1976 or the beneficiaries on 1st April 1977 included a living beneficiary, or
(c)   there is no power under the terms of the settlement whereby it could have become satisfied in respect of the period beginning with 1st April 1977, and the trusts of the settlement have not been varied at any time after 15th April 1976.

(7) In subsection (1) above 'persons' includes unborn persons; but the conditions stated in that subsection shall be treated as not satisfied unless there is or has been a living beneficiary.
(8) For the purposes of this section a person's children shall be taken to include his illegitimate children, his adopted children and his stepchildren.

Trustee Act 1925, s.31

31 POWER TO APPLY INCOME FOR MAINTENANCE AND TO ACCUMULATE SURPLUS INCOME DURING A MINORITY

(1) Where any property is held by trustees in trust for any person for any interest whatsoever, whether vested or contingent, then, subject to any prior interests or charges affecting that property–

(i) during the infancy of any such person, if his interest so long continues, the trustees may, at their sole discretion, pay to his parent or guardian, if any, or otherwise apply for or towards his maintenance, education, or benefit, the whole or such part, if any, of the income of that property as may, in all the circumstances, be reasonable, whether or not there is–

(a) any other fund applicable to the same purpose; or
(b) any person bound by law to provide for his maintenance or education; and

(ii) if such person on attaining the age of [eighteen years] has not a vested interest in such income, the trustees shall thenceforth pay the income of that property and of any accretion thereto under subsection (2) of this section to him, until he either attains a vested interest therein or dies, or until failure of his interest:

Provided that, in deciding whether the whole or any part of the income of the property is during a minority to be paid or applied for the purposes aforesaid, the trustees shall have regard to the age of the infant and his requirements and generally to the circumstances of the case, and in particular to what other income, if any, is applicable for the same purposes; and where trustees have notice that the income of more than one fund is applicable for those purposes, then, so far as practicable, unless the entire income of the funds is paid or applied as aforesaid or the court otherwise directs, a proportionate part only of the income of each fund shall be so paid or applied.

(2) During the infancy of any such person, if his interest so long continues, the trustees shall accumulate all the residue of that income [by investing it, and any profits from so investing it] from time to time in authorised investments, and shall hold those accumulations as follows–

(i) If any such person–

(a) attains the age of [eighteen years], or marries under that age, and his interest in such income during his infancy or until his marriage is a vested interest; or

(b) on attaining the age of [eighteen years] or on marriage under that age becomes entitled to the property from which such income arose in fee simple, absolute or determinable, or absolutely, or for an entailed interest;

the trustees shall hold the accumulations in trust for such person absolutely, but without prejudice to any provision with respect thereto contained in any settlement by him made under any statutory powers during his infancy, and so that the receipt of such person after marriage, and though still an infant, shall be a good discharge; and

(ii) In any other case the trustees shall, notwithstanding that such person had a vested interest in such income, hold the accumulations as an accretion to the capital of the property from which such accumulations arose, and as one fund with such capital for all purposes, and so that, if such property is settled land, such accumulations shall be held upon the same trusts as if the same were capital money arising therefrom;

but the trustees may, at any time during the infancy of such person if his interest so long continues, apply those accumulations, or any part thereof, as if they were income arising in the then current year.

(3) This section applies in the case of a contingent interest only if the limitation or trust carries the intermediate income of the property, but it applies to a future or contingent legacy by the parent of, or a person standing in loco parentis to, the legatee, if and for such period as, under the general law, the legacy carries interest for the maintenance of the legatee, and in any such case as last aforesaid the rate of interest shall (if the income available is sufficient, and subject to any rules of court to the contrary) be five pounds per centum per annum.

(4) This section applies to a vested annuity in like manner as if the annuity were the income of property held by trustees in trust to pay the income thereof to the annuitant for the same period for which the annuity is payable, save that in any case accumulations made during the infancy of the annuitant shall be held in trust for the annuitant or his personal representatives absolutely.

(5) This section does not apply where the instrument, if any, under which the interest arises came into operation before the commencement of this Act.

Trustee Act 1925, s.32

32 POWER OF ADVANCEMENT

(1) Trustees may at any time or times pay or apply any capital money subject to a trust, for the advancement or benefit, in such manner as they may, in their absolute discretion, think fit, of any person entitled to the capital of the trust property or of any share thereof, whether absolutely or contingently on his attaining any specified age or on the occurrence of any other event, or subject to a gift over on his death under any specified age or on the occurrence of any other event, and whether in possession or in remainder or reversion, and such payment or application may be made notwithstanding that the interest of such person is liable to be defeated by the exercise of a power of appointment or revocation, or to be diminished by the increase of the class to which he belongs:

Provided that–

(a)   the money so paid or applied for the advancement or benefit of any person shall not exceed altogether in amount one-half of the presumptive or vested share or interest of that person in the trust property; and
(b)   if that person is or becomes absolutely and indefeasibly entitled to a share in the trust property the money so paid or applied shall be brought into account as part of such share; and
(c)   no such payment or application shall be made so as to prejudice any person entitled to any prior life or other interest, whether vested or contingent, in the money paid or applied unless such person is in existence and of full age and consents in writing to such payment or application.

(2) This section does not apply to capital money arising under the Settled Land Act 1925.
(3) This section does not apply to trusts constituted or created before the commencement of this Act.

Income and Corporation Taxes Act 1988, ss.686

686 ACCUMULATION AND DISCRETIONARY TRUSTS: SPECIAL RATES OF TAX

(1)   So far as income arising to trustees is income to which this section applies it shall (subject to section 686D) be chargeable to income tax at the rate applicable in accordance with subsection (1AA) below, instead of at the basic rate or, in accordance with section 1A, at the lower rate or the dividend ordinary rate.

(1AA)   The rate applicable in accordance with this subsection is–

(a) in the case of so much of any income to which this section applies as is distribution type income, the dividend trust rate; and
(b) in the case of any other income to which this section applies, the rate applicable to trusts.

(1A)   In relation to any year of assessment for which income tax is charged–

(a) the dividend trust rate shall be 25 per cent, and
(b) the rate applicable to trusts shall be 34 per cent,

or, in either case, such other rate as Parliament may determine.
For the purposes of assessments for the year 1993–94 and in relation to years of assessment for which tax at the basic rate and the additional rate was separately chargeable, references to the charging of income with tax at the rate applicable to trusts shall be taken to include references to the charging of income with tax both at the basic rate and at the additional rate.

(2)   This section applies to income arising to trustees in any year of assessment so far as it–

(a) is income which is to be accumulated or which is payable at the discretion of the trustees or any other person (whether or not the trustees have power to accumulate it); and
(b) is not, before being distributed, either–

(i) the income of any person other than the trustees, or
(ii) treated for any of the purposes of the Income Tax Acts as the income of a settlor; and

(c) is not income arising under a trust established for charitable purposes only or, subject to subsection (6A) below, income from investments, deposits or other property held–

(i) for the purposes of a fund or scheme established for the sole purpose of providing relevant benefits within the meaning of section 612; or

(ii) for the purposes of a personal pension scheme (within the meaning of section 630) which makes provision only for benefits such as are mentioned in section 633; [and]

(d) [repealed]

(2AA)   The rate at which income tax is chargeable on so much of any income arising to trustees in any year of assessment as–

(a)   is income to which this section applies, and
(b)   is treated in accordance with section 689B as applied in defraying the expenses of the trustees in that year which are properly chargeable to income (or would be so chargeable but for any express provisions of the trust),

shall be the rate at which it would be chargeable on that income apart from this section, instead of the rate applicable to trusts or the dividend trust rate (as the case may be).

(2A)   For the purposes of this section where–

(a)   any trustees have expenses in any year of assessment ('management expenses') which are properly chargeable to income or would be so chargeable but for any express provisions of the trust, and
(b)   there is income arising to them in that year ('the untaxed income') which does not bear income tax for that year by reason wholly or partly of the trustees not having been resident in the United Kingdom or being deemed under any arrangements under section 788, or any arrangements having effect by virtue of that section, to have been resident in a territory outside the United Kingdom,

there shall be disregarded for the purposes of subsection (2AA) above such part of the management expenses as bears the same proportion to all those expenses as the untaxed income bears to all the income arising to the trustees in that year.

(2B)   For the purposes of subsection (2A) above where the income tax borne by any income arising to trustees is limited in accordance with section 128 of the Finance Act 1995 (limit on income chargeable on non-residents), the income arising to the trustees which shall be taken not to bear tax by reason wholly or partly of their not having been resident in the United Kingdom shall include so much of any income arising to them as–

(a)   is excluded income within the meaning of that section; and
(b)   is not income which is treated for the purposes of subsection (1)(b) of that section as income the tax on which is deducted at source.

(5A)   In this section 'distribution type income', in relation to trustees, means–

(a)   income chargeable under Chapter 3 of Part 4 of ITTOIA 2005 (dividends etc. from UK resident companies etc.);
(b)   income chargeable under Chapter 4 of that Part (dividends from non-UK resident companies);
(c)   income treated as arising to the trustees under Chapter 5 of that Part (stock dividends from UK resident companies);
(d)   income chargeable under Chapter 6 of that Part (release of loan to participator in close company);
(e)   a relevant foreign distribution chargeable under Chapter 8 of Part 5 of that Act (income not otherwise charged); or

(f) any amount which, by virtue of section 686A of this Act, is treated for the purposes of the Tax Acts as if it were income to which this section applies.

(5B) [Not reproduced here]

(6) In this section 'trustees' does not include personal representatives; but where personal representatives, on or before the completion of the administration of the estate, pay to trustees any sum representing income which, if personal representatives were trustees within the meaning of this section, would be income to which this section applies, that sum shall be deemed to be paid to the trustees as income and to have borne income tax at the applicable rate.

This subsection shall be construed as if it were contained in Chapter 6 of Part 5 of ITTOIA 2005.

(6A) The exemptions provided for by subsection (2)(c) above in relation to income from investments, deposits or other property held as mentioned in sub-paragraph (i) or (ii) of that paragraph do not apply to income derived from investments, deposits or other property held as a member of a property investment LLP.

686A CERTAIN DISTRIBUTIONS TO BE TREATED AS INCOME TO WHICH SECTION 686 APPLIES

(1) This section applies where–

(a) a qualifying distribution is made to trustees;

(b) the trustees are not the trustees of a unit trust scheme; and

(c) the qualifying distribution falls within subsection (2) below.

(2) A qualifying distribution falls within this subsection if it is a payment made by a company–

(a) on the redemption, repayment or purchase of its own shares; or

(b) on the purchase of rights to acquire its own shares.

(3) The relevant part of the distribution shall be treated for the purposes of the Tax Acts as if it were income to which section 686 applies.

(4) In subsection (3) above the reference to the relevant part of the distribution is a reference to so much (if any) of the distribution as–

(a) is not income falling within paragraph (a) of section 686(2);

(b) does not fall to be treated for the purposes of the Income Tax Acts as income of a Settlor;

(c) is not income arising under a trust established for charitable purposes; and

(d) is not income from investments, deposits or other property held for any such purposes as are mentioned in sub-paragraph (i) or (ii) of section 686(2)(c).

(5) Subsection (6) of section 686 shall apply for the purposes of this section as it applies for the purposes of that section.

Income and Corporation Taxes Act 1988, s.687

687 PAYMENTS UNDER DISCRETIONARY TRUSTS

(1) Where in any year of assessment trustees make a payment to any person in the exercise of a discretion, whether a discretion exercisable by them or by any other person, then if the payment–

(a) is for all the purposes of the Income Tax Acts income of the person to whom it is made (but would not be his income if it were not made to him), or

(b) is treated for those purposes as the income of the Settlor by virtue of section 629 of ITTOIA 2005 (income paid to unmarried minor children of settlor),

the following provisions of this section apply with respect to the payment in lieu of section 348 or 349(1).

(2) The payment shall be treated as a net amount corresponding to a gross amount from which tax has been deducted at the rate applicable to trusts for the year in which the payment is made; and the sum treated as so deducted shall be treated–

(a) as income tax paid by the person to whom the payment is made or, as the case may be, the Settlor; and

(b) so far as not set off under the following provisions of this section, as income tax assessable on the trustees.

(3) The following amounts, so far as not previously allowed, shall be set against the amount assessable (apart from this subsection) on the trustees in pursuance of subsection (2)(b) above–

(a) the amount of any tax on income arising to trustees which (not being income the tax on which falls within paragraphs (a1) to (bc) below) is charged in pursuance of section 686 at the rate applicable to trusts or the dividend trust rate;

(a1) the amount of tax at a rate equal to the difference between the dividend ordinary rate and the dividend trust rate on any income of the trustees chargeable under Chapter 3 of Part 4 of ITTOIA 2005 (dividends etc. from UK resident companies etc.);

(a2) the amount of tax which, by virtue of section 399 of ITTOIA 2005 (non-UK residents other than eligible non-UK residents receiving qualifying distributions), is charged, at a rate equal to the difference between the dividend ordinary rate and the dividend trust rate, on the amount or value of the whole or any part of any qualifying distribution included in the income arising to the trustees;

(aa) the amount of tax which, by virtue of section 400 of that Act (non-qualifying distributions), is charged, at a rate equal to the difference between the dividend ordinary rate and the dividend trust rate, on the amount or value of the whole or any part of any non-qualifying distribution included in the income arising to the trustees;

(b) the amount of tax at a rate equal to the difference between the dividend ordinary rate and the dividend trust rate on any sum treated, under section 410(3) of ITTOIA 2005 (when stock dividend income arises), as income of the trustees;

(bb) the amount of tax at a rate equal to the difference between the dividend ordinary rate and the dividend trust rate on any sum treated under section 416(3) of ITTOIA 2005 (income charged on release of loan to participator in close company) as income of the trustees;

(bc) the amount of tax at a rate equal to the difference between the dividend ordinary rate and the dividend trust rate on any sum treated under section 686A as income of the trustees;

(c) [Repealed]

(d) an amount of tax in respect of income found on a claim made by the trustees to have been available to them for distribution at the end of the year 1972–73, which shall be taken to be two-thirds of the net amount of that income;

(e) the amount of any tax on income arising to the trustees by virtue of section 761(1) and charged at the rate applicable to trusts by virtue of section 764; and

(f) the amount of any tax on annual profits or gains treated as received by trustees by virtue of section 714(2) or 716(3) of this Act or paragraph 2(2) or (3) of Schedule 22 to the Finance Act 1985 and charged at the rate applicable to trusts by virtue of section 720(5) of this Act or paragraph 8(1) of Schedule 23 to that Act;

(g) the amount of any tax on income which arose to the trustees by virtue of section 38(2) of the Finance Act 1974 (development gains) and charged at a rate equal to the basic rate and the additional rate in pursuance of section 43(1) of that Act;

(h) the amount of any tax on an amount which is treated as income of the trustees by virtue of paragraph 4 of Schedule 4 and is charged to tax at the rate applicable to trusts by virtue of paragraph 17 of that Schedule;

(i) the amount of any tax on an amount which is treated as income of the trustees by virtue of paragraph 5 of Schedule 11 to the Finance Act 1989 and is charged to tax at the rate applicable to trusts by virtue of paragraph 11 of that Schedule;

(j) the amount of any tax on an amount which is treated as income of the trustees by virtue of paragraph 12 of Schedule 10 to the Finance Act 1990 and is charged to tax at the rate applicable to trusts by virtue of paragraph 19 of that Schedule;

(k) the amount of any tax on an amount which is treated as income of the trustees by virtue of paragraph 1 of Schedule 13 to the Finance Act 1996 and is charged to tax at the rate applicable to trusts by virtue of paragraph 6 of that Schedule.

(l) the amount of any tax on an amount which is treated as income of the trustees by virtue of Chapter 8 of Part 4 of ITTOIA 2005 (profits from deeply discounted securities) and is charged to tax at the rate applicable to trusts by virtue of section 457 of that Act.

(4) In this section 'trustees' does not include personal representatives within the meaning of section 701(4).

(5) References in this section to payments include payments in money or money's worth.

Index

Trusts
    advantages and disadvantages 18–19
    appropriateness of 14–20
    case study 279–350
    choice of types 20–1
    motives for creation 3–9
    types 10–14
    see also individual topics

Unanimity 51
Unmarried couples 17

Vulnerable beneficiaries 201
    capital gains tax (CGT) 206–7

    claim for special tax treatment
        203–4
    income tax 204–6
    Inland Revenue enquiries 207–8
    penalties for failure to supply information
        208
    qualifying trusts 202–3
    who is vulnerable 201–2

Wills
    trust gifts under a will 28
Words
    certainty of 22–3
Working documents file 83

Elderly Client Handbook

3rd edition

General Editors:
Caroline Bielanska & Martin Terrell
Consultant Editor:
Gordon R. Ashton

Published in association with
Solicitors for the Elderly

Advising elderly clients requires an
up-to-date knowledge of many varied
areas of law and practice. This book
provides a succinct guide to all the relevant law, together with practical
advice on the running and marketing of an elderly client practice.

It provides clear and up-to-date analysis of:
• British Banking Association's guidelines
• Mental Incapacity Bill
• Financial Services Act 2000
• Reforms to health and social care
• Care Standards Act 2000
• Changes to the Court of Protection and Public Guardianship Office
• Benefits including Pension Credit.

The third edition has been fully revised by a team of new
contributors drawn from the membership of Solicitors for the Elderly
and experts in the fields of mental capacity, mental health law and
employment law.

Available from Marston Book Services:
Tel. 01235 465 656

1 85328 872 1
520 pages
March 2004
£44.95

The Law Society

Probate Practitioner's Handbook

4th edition
General Editor: *Lesley King*

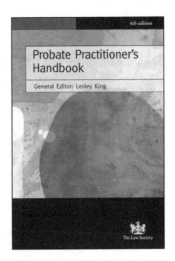

Written by a carefully chosen team
of leading experts, this practical work
covers all aspects of probate – the
regulatory framework, law and
practice, marketing, practice
management, and information
technology. The book also includes
authoritative commentary on Law
Society best practice guidance.

New features include:
- brand new chapters on Managing an Effective Practice, and Wills
- support for offering legal services via the internet
- the latest best practice guidance from the Law Society
- analysis of the changes resulting from the Trustee Act 2000 and
  the Financial Services and Markets Act 2000
- guidance on dealing with deaths abroad and requests for
  unusual funerals
- advice on tracing beneficiaries and dealing with estates that
  appear to be bona vacantia.

The practical nature of the book is enhanced by the use of sample
letters, case histories, checklists and worked examples.

The *Probate Practitioner's Handbook* should be the first choice for any
practitioner seeking authoritative guidance on probate practice.

Available from Marston Book Services:
Tel. 01235 465 656.

1 85328 831 4
408 pages
£44.95
2002

The Law Society

Will Draftsman's Handbook

8th Edition

Robin Riddett

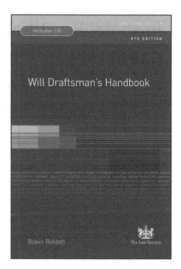

This authoritative reference book provides the will draftsman with the tools needed to prepare wills for the more commonly encountered situations. The text is split into three parts:

- commentary – provides an analysis of the underlying law
- precedent clauses which can be readily assembled to make up wills for most circumstances
- statutory material – extracts from the legislation which informs the law.

Written in plain English, the book takes a practical and up-to-date approach to will drafting which helps make wills comprehensible to clients. As well as commonly used draft wills, over 75 individual clauses are appended on an accompanying CD-ROM for easy word-processing.

Available from Marston Book Services:
Tel. 01235 465 656.

1 85328 826 8
224 pages with CD-ROM
£49.95
Sept. 2004

The Law Society